Language and Ecology
in Southern and Eastern Arabia

Bloomsbury Advances in Ecolinguistics

Series Editors:
Arran Stibbe and Mariana Roccia

Advisory Board:

Nadine Andrews (Lancaster University, UK)
Maria Bortoluzzi (University of Udine, Italy)
Martin Döring (University of Hamburg, Germany)
Sue Edney (University of Bristol, UK)
Alwin Fill (University of Graz, Austria)
Diego Forte (University of Buenos Aires, Argentina)
Amir Ghorbanpour (Tarbiat Modares University, Iran)
Nataliia Goshylyk (Vasyl Stefanyk Precarpathian National University, Ukraine)
Huang Guowen (South China Agricultural University, China)
George Jacobs (Independent Scholar)
Kyoohoon Kim (Daegu University, South Korea)
Katerina Kosta (Oxford Brookes University, UK)
Mira Lieberman-Boyd (University of Sheffield, UK)
Keith Moser (Mississippi State University, USA)
Douglas Ponton (University of Catania, Italy)
Robert Poole (University of Alabama, USA)
Alison Sealey (University of Lancaster, UK)
Nina Venkataraman (National University of Singapore, Singapore)
Daniela Francesca Virdis (University of Cagliari, Italy)
Sune Vork Steffensen (University of Southern Denmark, Denmark)

Bloomsbury Advances in Ecolinguistics emerges at a time when businesses, universities, national governments and many other organisations are declaring an ecological emergency. With climate change and biodiversity loss diminishing the ability of the Earth to support life, business leaders, politicians and academics are asking how their work can contribute to efforts to preserve the ecosystems that life depends on.

Language and Ecology
in Southern and Eastern Arabia

Edited by Janet C.E. Watson, Jon C. Lovett and
Roberta Morano

BLOOMSBURY ACADEMIC
LONDON • NEW YORK • OXFORD • NEW DELHI • SYDNEY

BLOOMSBURY ACADEMIC
Bloomsbury Publishing Plc
50 Bedford Square, London, WC1B 3DP, UK
1385 Broadway, New York, NY 10018, USA
29 Earlsfort Terrace, Dublin 2, Ireland

BLOOMSBURY, BLOOMSBURY ACADEMIC and the Diana logo
are trademarks of Bloomsbury Publishing Plc

First published in Great Britain 2023
This paperback edition published 2024

Copyright © Janet C.E. Watson, Jon C. Lovett and Roberta Morano, 2023

Janet C.E. Watson, Jon C. Lovett and Roberta Morano have asserted their right under the
Copyright, Designs and Patents Act, 1988, to be identified as Editors of this work.

For legal purposes the Acknowledgements on p. xvi constitute
an extension of this copyright page.

Cover design: Ben Anslow

All rights reserved. No part of this publication may be reproduced or transmitted
in any form or by any means, electronic or mechanical, including photocopying,
recording, or any information storage or retrieval system, without prior
permission in writing from the publishers.

Bloomsbury Publishing Plc does not have any control over, or responsibility for,
any third-party websites referred to or in this book. All internet addresses given
in this book were correct at the time of going to press. The author and publisher
regret any inconvenience caused if addresses have changed or sites have ceased
to exist, but can accept no responsibility for any such changes.

A catalogue record for this book is available from the British Library.

A catalog record for this book is available from the Library of Congress.

ISBN:	HB:	978-1-3501-8447-3
	PB:	978-1-3503-4696-3
	ePDF:	978-1-3501-8448-0
	eBook:	978-1-3501-8449-7

Series: Bloomsbury Advances in Ecolinguistics

Typeset by Integra Software Services Pvt. Ltd.

To find out more about our authors and books visit www.bloomsbury.com
and sign up for our newsletters.

Contents

List of Figures	vii
List of Maps	ix
List of Tables	x
List of Contributors	xi
Acknowledgements	xvi
Introduction *Janet C. E. Watson, Jon C. Lovett and Roberta Morano*	1
1 Language, Gesture and Ecology in Modern South Arabian Languages *Jack Wilson, Janet C.E. Watson, Andrea Boom and Saeed al-Qumairi*	15

Part 1 Arabia: The Significance of Names and Words

2 What's in a Name? *Miranda Morris*	47
3 When Water Shapes Words: Musandam's Kumzari People and the Language of the Sea *Erik Anonby, AbdulQader Qasim Ali Al Kamzari and Yousuf Ali Mohammed Al Kamzari*	81
4 Water and Culture among the Modern South Arabian-Speaking People *Fabio Gasparini and Saeed al-Mahri*	105
5 A Botanical and Etymological Approach to Plant Names in Southern Arabia *Shahina A. Ghazanfar and Leonid Kogan*	119
6 Traditional Knowledge and Vocabulary around Weather and Astronomy in Qatar *Kaltham Al-Ghanim*	149
7 Plant and Animal Terms in Ḥaḍramī Arabic Idiomatic Expressions, Proverbs and Chants *Abdullah Hassan al-Saqqaf*	167

Part 2 Arabia: Narratives and Ecology

8 The Language of Kumzari Folklore *Christina van der Wal Anonby*	189
9 Orature and Nature in Southern Arabia *Kamela al-Barami, Ahmed al-Mashikhi and Sam Liebhaber*	199
10 Climatic Disasters and Stories of Resilience in Southern and Northern Oman *Suad Al-Manji and Janet C.E. Watson*	213

Part 3 Arabia: Conservation and Revitalization

11 Peoples' (non-)participation in Conservation: A Case from
   Oman *Dawn Chatty*   241

Conclusions *Jon C. Lovett, Janet C.E. Watson and Roberta Morano*   261

List of Geographic Place Names   267
Index   272

List of Figures

1.1	M001 producing "hooked point" gesture	22
1.2	M068 gesturing while describing route	29
1.3	M017 gesturing while describing different times in the morning	33
1.4	M017 gesturing upward while referring to midday	33
1.5	YMGh004 gesturing while describing how to remove hair from animal hide	34
1.6	J046 gesturing while describing how to remove the skin from a fish	35
1.7	YMGh004 depicting plant in gesture	36
1.8	YMGh005 producing first-person gestures while describing a camel's bridle	37
1.9	M001 depicting path in gesture	38
1.10	M001 depicting placement of a bus stop in gesture	39
1.11	M001 depicting path while reduplicating the word *ghōm*	39
3.1	Entering Kumzar on a *lanj* 'motorized dhow' with guests and supplies for a wedding	82
3.2	The lower and upper ends of Kumzar	84
3.3	Kumzar Inlet in windy weather	85
3.4	The waters around Musandam Island in calm weather	85
3.5	*Ūmat* 'sardines' drying on the shore by Kumzar	86
3.6	Mending nets on the shore by Kumzar	87
3.7	Sirg shelters, Kumzari quarter, Khasab	87
3.8	Kumzar divided into east and west sides by the wadi	88
3.9	A *lanj* 'motorized dhow' moored in a fishing cove on Ġōban Inlet	88
3.10	Seashells in a ceremonial mound in the abandoned mountain settlement of Sabt Rāshid	89
3.11	Clouds gathering against the mountains above Kumzar	89
3.12	The stones of Kumzar's well worn into grooves by centuries of ropes drawing water	90
3.13	Plastic waste floating in Kumzar's well	90
3.14	A morning's catch from the nets of fishermen from Kumzar	91
3.15	Aerial view of the three sister islands of *Mōmur*, *Dīdamur* and *Pānakō* in the strait to the north of Kumzar	92

3.16	Kumzar Inlet in the direction of the open sea, as seen from the surrounding mountains	92
3.17	Kōkba fishing cove on the west shore of Kumzar Inlet	93
3.18	The pierced rock, šāratē, after its partial collapse in recent years	93
3.19	A traditional *battil* fishing dhow, built from natural materials, brought onto Kumzar's beach for annual maintenance	94
3.20	The fisherman Ḥama Šēx (Muhammad Sheikh) describes the parts of the *battil* fishing dhow using a model that he constructed	95
3.21	An inventory of boat parts in the Kumzari lexicon	96
3.22	Goats in Kumzar survive dry periods of months or years by eating dried sardines	97
3.23	A Kumzari *ṭarrādē* 'motorboat' full of barracuda for sale to fish markets in Dubai	98
3.24	A catch of small fish for sale to fish markets in Dubai	98
3.25	A news article announcing a 'dead zone' in the Arabian Sea	99
3.26	*Xumba* 'clay commodity jars' left in the abandoned mountain settlement of Xwēr	101
3.27	A beach made of shells washed ashore on Musandam Peninsula	102
3.28	Fishermen depart from Kumzar at dawn in the direction of their fishing grounds	103
5.1	'Lawsonia inermis – Arb. *ḥennā. ḥinnāʔ*'	127
5.2	'Ziziphus spina-christi – Arb. *sidr*'	135

List of Maps

0.1	Southern and Eastern Arabian Peninsula with main settlements	4
0.2	Languages spoken in the Arabian Peninsula	7
3.1	Kumzar in the context of Musandam Peninsula and the surrounding waters	81
11.1	The Arabian Peninsula	242
11.2	Jiddat il-Ḥarāsīs	249

List of Tables

0.1	Ḥaḍrami and Qatari Arabic Consonantal System and Transcription	10
0.2	MSAL Consonantal System and Transcription	11
0.3	Soqoṭri Consonantal System and Transcription	12
0.4	Kumzari Consonantal System and Transcription	13
1.1	Table of Pointing Types in Mehri and Śḥerēt	21
1.2	Expression of Direction in Mehri and Śḥerēt	27
1.3	Temporal Terms in Mehri	32
2.1	Plant Names in Eastern and Western Soqoṭra	50
2.2	Soqoṭri Names Describing Herd or Flock Size	64
5.1	Fifteen Common South Arabian plants with Names in Arabic and Other Semitic Languages	121
6.1	Spring Phases	155
6.2	Summer Phases	155
6.3	Autumn Phases	156
6.4	Winter Phases	156
8.1	Abstract Plurals and Natural States	190
8.2	Geography of the Sea in *Sōntyō*	192
8.3	The Sensory Evidential *tamna*	195
10.1	Most Critical Cyclones, 1890–2018	219

List of Contributors

Kamela al-Barami is a PhD candidate in the School of Languages, Cultures and Societies at the University of Leeds. Her current research is multidisciplinary exploring the role of media in the revitalisation of endangered languages and their cultures. Particularly, the Modern Southern Arabian languages (MSAL) in the Sultanate of Oman. Kamela is a member of the Centre for Endangered Languages, Cultures and Ecosystems (CELCE) and the Centre for World Cinemas and Digital Cultures (WCDC) at the University of Leeds. She has participated in various workshops on culture, poetry, language and nature.

Kaltham Al-Ghanim is Director of the Social & Economic Survey Research Institute (SESRI) at Qatar University and of the Centre for Humanities and Social Sciences in the College of Arts and Sciences at Qatar University. Professor Kaltham conducted and published several researches related to social issues, culture, heritage and human development. She led several interdisciplinary research projects funded by various national and international institutions. She maintains relationships with many national, regional and international institutions as an expert in socio-cultural studies and human development. She also contributed to the preparation of many national strategies plans.

Yousuf Ali Mohammed Al Kamzari is Nursing Coordinator at the Ministry of Health in Musandam Governorate, Sultanate of Oman. He is interested in local history, especially that of the Musandam region, and specializes in the Kumzari language and the influences it has encountered during various time periods. Al Kamzari has attended many courses and seminars on history and language and has participated in the local digital publication of articles on the history of the village of Kumzar. He often travels in order to obtain various sources that enrich his knowledge of the region and its inhabitants.

AbdulQader Qasim Ali Al Kamzari is English Language Educational Supervisor at the General Directorate of Education in Musandam Governorate, Sultanate of Oman. Passionate about teaching foreign languages and teaching methods, he completed a Master's degree at the University of Exeter, UK, in 2016. His research focuses on educational issues including educational technology, foreign language acquisition and educational methodology. Al Kamzari has participated in many educational and linguistics conferences in the Sultanate of Oman and abroad, and has published on the use of technology in teaching English (2016) and difficulties facing students in learning Arabic (2017).

Saeed al-Mahri holds a BA in English Literature from Dhofar University, Oman. He completed his MA in Translation at the University of Salford, UK. He joined a documentary project funded by the Leverhulme Trust for three years as Research Assistant and Administrative Assistant. The project was led by Prof Janet C.E. Watson and Dr Miranda Morris. He has worked on transcribing both Mehri and Shehri and translated a number of audio texts into Arabic and English. He has been involved in training local participants in translation and transcription. He has attended several conferences virtually and in person on topics related to Modern South Arabian and nature.

Suad Al-Manji heads the risk management department at the Ministry of Education in Oman. She gained her PhD in Geography on Disaster Management and Community Resilience from the University of Leeds. She works as a part-time researcher and lecturer at Sultan Qaboos University (Oman) in the Department of Geography. Dr Al-Manji has published various papers in disaster management. Her most recent publication, *The Role of Omani Women in Disaster Management in Oman*, is published in Arabic.

Ahmed al-Mashikhi is a retired academic from the Department of Communication, College of Arts & Social Sciences at Sultan Qaboos University, Oman. His professional career started with the Ministry of Information in 1987. Between 2011 and 2019, he was a member of State Council, and from 2015 to 2019 he was Chairman of the Culture, Information and Tourism Committee. He retired in 2021. Al-Mashikhi's research interests focus on broadcasting media, culture and society, media and crises, media policies, and new media. He has published *Internet as a New Media Tool* (1989), *Culture and Globalization* (1999), *Communication Revolution and Societies in the GCC* (2008). His most recent book is *Effective Communication* (2014).

Saeed al-Qumairi is Deputy Dean of the College of Applied & Human Sciences, Hadhramawt University (HU), Yemen. His research interests focus on generative linguistics, syntax, morphology and semitics. He has published *Minimalist Analysis of the Animal Coding System in Mehri* (2015), *Verbal Agreement in Mehri*

Word Order (2018), *Language in Educational System Yemen* (2018) and *Syntax of Applicative Constructions in Sudanese Arabic* (2018). In 2018, he conducted a project entitled 'Community Documentation of Biocultural Diversity of Al-Mahrah'. His most recent paper is 'Syntax of Possessive ḏa- in Mehri' (2020).

Abdullah H. al-Saqqaf is an independent researcher in linguistics. He has been Associate Professor in Linguistics at Dhofar University, Oman. He has lectured in several universities in the Middle East and holds a Diploma in Phonetics from Edinburgh and a PhD from Exeter universities, UK. He has contributed to the *Encyclopedia of Arabic Language and Linguistics* and the four volumes *Word Atlas of Arabic Dialects*. Currently, he is working on the linguistics of South Arabian dialects of Arabic. He is an occasional reviewer for the *Journal of International Phonetic Association* (*JIPA*) and some other international journals in linguistics.

Erik Anonby is Professor of Linguistics and French at Carleton University in Ottawa, Canada. His interdisciplinary research focuses on the importance of linguistic diversity in individual human experience and collective heritage. He studies ways in which language mapping can involve end users in language documentation, accommodate contrasting perspectives on language identity and language distribution, and refine visualizations of these perspectives using linguistic data corpuses. Anonby contributes to several language atlas projects, has written seven books including *Adaptive Multilinguals: Language on Larak Island* (2011), and has published extensively in journals such as *Linguistics*, *Journal of Semitic Studies* and *Journal of Ethnobiology*.

Andrea Boom is Commonwealth Scholar and PhD Candidate at the University of Leeds. She studies the link between endangered languages, cultures and ecosystems (LC&E) in Southern Arabia. She is specifically interested in the human connection with the natural world and how LC&E adapt to their local environment. This research is particularly important today as people become disconnected from their immediate dependence on the natural world and knowledge of the symbiotic relationship between humans and their environment is disappearing.

Dawn Chatty is Emeritus Professor in Anthropology and Forced Migration and former Director of the Refugee Studies Centre, University of Oxford, UK. She was elected Fellow of the British Academy in 2015. Her research interests include refugee youth in protracted refugee crises, conservation and development, pastoral society and forced settlement. She is the author of *Displacement and Dispossession in the Modern Middle East* (2010), *From Camel to Truck* (2013) and *Syria: The Making and Unmaking of a Refuge State* (2018).

Fabio Gasparini received his PhD in African, Asian and Mediterranean Studies from the University of Naples 'L'Orientale', Italy. He currently holds a Postdoc position funded by Thyssen Stiftung at the Department of Semitic Studies of Freie Universität Berlin, Germany. His research focuses on the Modern South Arabian languages and Semitic in general from a comparative and typological perspective.

Shahina A. Ghazanfar is Senior Botanist at the Royal Botanic Gardens, Kew, in Science. Her research focuses on the floras, vegetation, biogeography and conservation of the plants of the Middle East. Her interests include plants used in traditional medicine in the Middle East, their etymology and history of use. She is author of the *Flora of Oman* (4 volumes: 2003–18), co-editor of the *Flora of Tropical East Africa* and author and editor of *Flora of Iraq*. Shahina A. Ghazanfar is Fellow of the Linnean Society and is recipient of the Linnean Medal (Botany) 2021.

Leonid Kogan is Professor of Akkadian Language at the Higher School of Economics, National Research University in Moscow, Russia. His research interests are Semitic languages and he has published widely on Akkadian, Hebrew and Soqoṭri. His latest publication includes the article *The Soqoṭri Lexical Archive: The 2013 Fieldwork Season* (2022).

Sam Liebhaber is Professor of Arabic in the Department of Arabic at Middlebury College in Vermont, USA. His research interests are oral poetry in Southern Arabia, transitional texts in the Arab world and literary modernism in Yemen. He is author of *When Melodies Gather* (2018), a digital exhibit of oral poetry in the Mehri language of Yemen and Oman.

Jon C. Lovett holds the Leadership Chair in Global Challenges in the School of Geography at the University of Leeds, UK. With Janet C.E. Watson he is Co-Director of the Centre for Endangered Languages, Cultures and Ecosystems (CELCE). A botanist by training, his work has taken him to many countries, including those in southern Arabia, Africa, India, Nepal and Indonesia. He has co-authored several hundred journal articles and his books include *Biogeography* *and Ecology of the Forests of Eastern Africa*, *A Field Guide to the Moist Forest Trees of Tanzania* and *A Handbook of Environmental Management*.

Roberta Morano is Visiting Oman Research Fellow at Leibniz-Zentrum Moderner Orient (ZMO) in Berlin, Germany. She completed a PhD in linguistics at the University of Leeds, UK, in 2019, working on the Arabic varieties spoken in northern Oman. Her research interests focus on language documentation and ecolinguistics, especially the relationship between the environment and its representation in language. She has published several articles on the morphosyntax and sociolinguistics of Omani dialects.

Miranda Morris is an independent researcher who has published widely on the languages and cultures of the MSAL-speaking communities of southern Arabia. Her most recent publication is *The Oral Art of Soqotra: A Collection of Island Voices* (2021).

Christina van der Wal Anonby is Research Professor at Carleton University in Ottawa, Canada. She was a co-founder of the Alberta environmental club Rare Earth that led her to endangered language research at the University of Alberta, Canada, and Leiden University in the Netherlands. Dr van der Wal Anonby has carried out linguistic and anthropological field work on indigenous languages in Iran and Oman. Her publications include works on morphology, syntax, discourse, poetics, education and oral literature.

Janet C. E. Watson holds the Leadership Chair for Language@Leeds at the University of Leeds. She is Co-Director of the Centre for Endangered Languages, Cultures and Ecosystems (CELCE) and Fellow of the British Academy. Her research interests lie in Modern South Arabian and Yemeni Arabic dialects, with particular focus on theoretical phonological and morphological approaches. Her key works include *Phonology and Morphology of Arabic*, *The Structure of Mehri*, *A Comparative Cultural Glossary of Modern South Arabian* (with Miranda Morris et al.) and *Təghamk Āfyət: A Course in Mehri of Dhofar* (with Abdullah al-Mahri et al.).

Jack Wilson is Lecturer in English Language at the University of Salford, UK. His research interests focus on linguistic semantics, pragmatics and gesture studies. He has published on the relationship between language and gesture in MSAL as well as a range of topics related to pragmatics.

Acknowledgements

We want to thank the AHRC for an International Network Grant (2017–19), Qatar University for hosting the first network workshop in February 2018, the University of Leeds for hosting the second network workshop in April 2019 and, finally, all the participants for reading and editing the various chapters.

The editors and publisher gratefully acknowledge the permission granted to reproduce the copyright material in this book.

Every effort has been made to trace copyright holders and to obtain their permission for the use of copyrighted material. However, if any have been inadvertently overlooked, the publishers will be pleased, if notified of any omissions, to make the necessary arrangements at the first opportunity.

Introduction

Janet C.E. Watson, Jon C. Lovett and Roberta Morano

This edited volume emerged from an AHRC-funded network on Language and Nature in Southern and Eastern Arabia, which ran from 2017 to 2019. The network included three-day, face-to-face workshops at Qatar University in February 2017 and the University of Leeds in April 2019, and a video conference in October 2018.

The volume takes a multidisciplinary view of the relationship between Language and Ecology, examining expressions of, and threats and challenges to, the Language–Ecology relationship in southern and eastern Arabia. Regions of the world with greatest biodiversity are shown to exhibit greatest linguistic diversity, strongly suggesting that the relationship between Language and Ecology is both symbiotic and spatially and temporally determined. Indigenous languages reflect the close relationship between people and their natural environment, embodying the complex relationship humans enjoy with landscape and seasons. These connections can be broken when indigenous languages are severed from the ecosystems in which they arose, a situation that can arise through replacement of indigenous languages by alien lingua franca, through degradation of the ecosystem, through depopulation, or through forced or voluntary removal of the indigenous language community from the local ecosystem. The volume provides a case study within a region of the world that has not traditionally been considered in the discourse around the relationship between endangered languages and ecosystems.

Geographical region

Our geographical region of Southern and Eastern Arabia focusses on Eastern Yemen, Soqoṭra, Oman and Qatar: in economic terms, we discuss the richest state per capita in the world (Qatar), and one of the poorest (Yemen). However, in geographical terms the region has much in common: a hot, arid climate in the summer months. The north has milder winter months, while the south of the region, which from June to early September receives the monsoon rains on the mainland, and strong monsoon winds on Soqoṭra, has four distinct seasons. The whole region is rich in coastline, which runs to over 3,500km, resulting in significant maritime activities and climatic events, to which we refer.

Eastern Yemen and Soqoṭra

Eastern Yemen has two principal governorates: Ḥaḍramawt and al-Mahrah, the largest and second-largest Yemeni governorates, respectively. Ḥaḍrami Arabic is spoken in Ḥaḍramawt, with two main varieties, as al-Saqqaf explains; in addition to Arabic, two of the endangered Modern South Arabian languages (MSAL), Mehri and Hobyōt, are spoken in al-Mahrah. In this volume, Abdullah al-Saqqaf examines plant and animal terms in sayings, proverbs and poetry in Ḥaḍrami Arabic; al-Barami, al-Mashikhi and Liebhaber look at Mehri poetry produced in al-Mahrah and Dhofar; and Wilson, Watson, Boom and al-Qumairi look at the role of communicative gesture among MSAL speakers in Dhofar and al-Mahrah.

The Soqoṭra Archipelago lies between the Guardafui Channel and the Arabian Sea, about 340km southeast of Yemen.[1] The archipelago comprises four islands: Soqoṭra, ʿAbd al-Kūri, Samḥa and Darsah. It was designated a UNESCO World Heritage Site in 2008, and is described as the fourth most biodiverse archipelago on the planet. It was attached politically to the governorate of Ḥaḍramawt in 2004, becoming its own governorate in 2013. Soqoṭra island, the largest island of the archipelago, has an area of 3,600km^2, and a population of around 60,000.[2] The indigenous language of Soqoṭra is the MSAL Soqoṭri. Two chapters address Soqoṭra island in this volume: Ghazanfar and Kogan examine terms relating to Soqoṭran flora; Morris examines the importance of nomenclature in Soqoṭri and the other MSAL.

Oman

The Sultanate of Oman is located in the south-eastern part of the Arabian Peninsula, sharing land borders with the United Arab Emirates to the northwest, Saudi Arabia to the west and the Republic of Yemen to the southwest. Oman has two offshore territories, Masirah Island to the east and the Ḥallāniyyāh Islands off the southern coast.[3] Oman has an area of approximately 309,500km², much of which is covered by a vast gravel desert plain, with a coastal plain and mountain ranges along the north and to the south (Dhofar). The 2,810km-long shoreline of Oman[4] includes the northern exclave of the Musandam Peninsula by the Strait of Hormuz, and then runs south of al-Fujayrah in the north to the Republic of Yemen in the south. The population figure in Oman for 2019 was 4.95m, of whom approximately half are expatriate workers. Oman is arguably the most linguistically diverse state in the Arabian Peninsula: alongside the official language, Arabic, languages include Kumzari, Shiḥḥi, Swahili, Baluchi and five of the endangered MSAL: Mehri, Śḥerēt, Ḥarsūsi, Hobyōt and Baṭḥari. Within this volume, chapters discuss Dhofar, the southern governorate of Oman, Jiddat il-Ḥarāsīs, centred around Haima within the central plain, the Al-Ḥajar mountain area in northern Oman, and the Musandam Peninsula in the far north of Oman. Five chapters address the language–ecology relationship in Dhofar: Wilson, Watson, Boom and al-Qumairi look at the role of communicative gesture among Mehri and Śḥerēt speakers in Dhofar and al-Mahrah; al-Manji and Watson examine the role of historical narratives within Dhofar as well as the Al-Ḥajar mountains in bolstering resilience in the face of climatic events; al-Barami, al-Mashikhi and Liebhaber discuss Mehri and Śḥerēt poetry of Dhofar and al-Mahrah; Gasparini and al-Mahri discuss water terminology among MSAL speakers in Dhofar; and Morris examines nomenclature among MSAL speakers in Dhofar and Soqoṭra. The chapter by Chatty focusses on Jiddat il-Ḥarāsīs, examining community participation. Two chapters focus on the Musandam Peninsula: Anonby, Al Kamzari and Al Kamzari present a poetic account of water among the Kumzari community; and van der Wal Anonby examines nature in Kumzari folklore.

Qatar

The peninsula of Qatar is situated on the north-eastern coast of the Arabian Peninsula, occupying 11,437 sq km and extending approximately 160km into the Arabian Gulf.[5] It shares a land border with the Kingdom of Saudi Arabia, is separated from the Peninsula of Bahrain by the Gulf of Bahrain, and its remaining territory is surrounded by the Arabian Gulf, giving over 560km of coastline. In 2019, it had a population of 2.832 million, of whom under 400,000 were Qatari nationals. With proven oil reserves of 15 billion barrels and gas fields that exceed 13 per cent of the global resource, Qatar is the richest state per capita in the world. According to the Emissions Database for Global Atmospheric Research, Qatar has one of the highest carbon dioxide emissions in the world, averaging 30 tonnes per person.[6] The language spoken in Qatar is Qatari Arabic. Al-Ghanim focuses on Qatar in her discussion of terminology around weather and astronomy.

A map of the geographical area of study with main settlements noted is presented below. Note that in contrast to the chapters, place names on the map are presented without diacritics to facilitate reading:

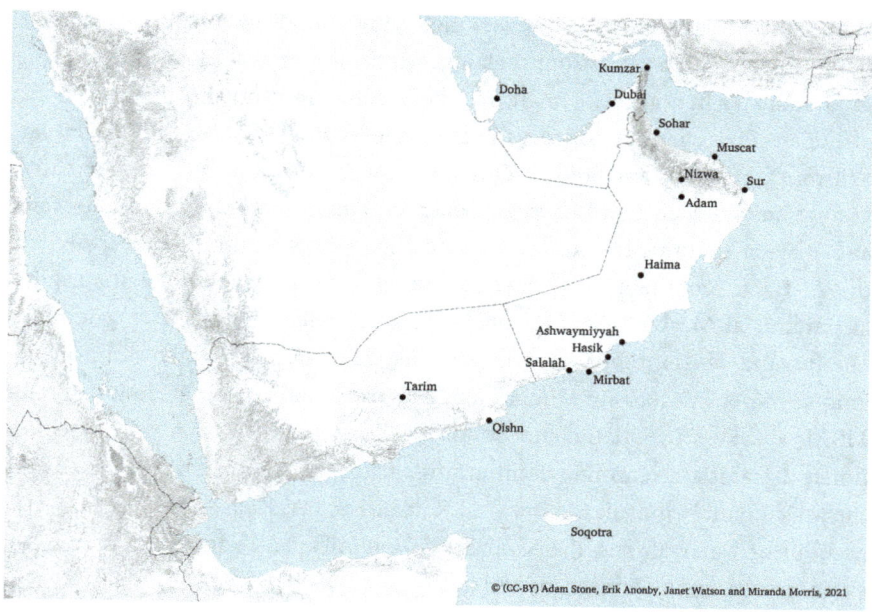

Map 0.1 Southern and Eastern Arabian Peninsula with main settlements.

Languages

We examine material from three groups of languages: Arabic dialects of Ḥaḍramawt in Yemen, of Qatar, and of the al-Ḥajar mountains in Oman; the MSAL – Mehri, Śḥerēt, Soqoṭri, Hobyōt, Ḥarsūsi and Baṭḥari; and the mixed language, Kumzari, spoken on the Musandam peninsula.

Arabic

In terms of Arabic, the chapter by al-Saqqaf examines dialects of Ḥaḍramawt, the chapter by Al-Ghanim examines dialects of Qatar, and the chapter by al-Manji and Watson describes interviews conducted in the Arabic dialects of the al-Ḥajar mountains in northern Oman.

Modern South Arabian

The MSAL, Mehri, Soqoṭri, Śḥerēt (also known as Jibbāli or Shaḥri), Ḥarsūsi, Hobyōt and Baṭḥari are unwritten Semitic languages spoken by minority populations in south-east Yemen, the island of Soqoṭra, southern Oman and the fringes of southern and eastern Saudi Arabia. The name 'Modern South Arabian' is somewhat confusing, as these unwritten languages are neither 'modern' nor comprehensible to an Arabic speaker. They are called 'Modern South Arabian' languages to differentiate them from 'Old South Arabian', which refers to the four related languages which were written in the Ancient South Arabian script and are now extinct. The MSAL belong to the South Semitic branch of the Semitic language family, which also includes Ethiopian Semitic. This is distinguished from the Central Semitic branch, which includes the more widely known Arabic, Aramaic and Hebrew. The MSAL are believed to be the remnants of a pre-Arabic substratum that once stretched over the whole of southern Arabia, and across the Red Sea, into the highlands and littoral of East Africa.

Due to rapid economic and socio-political change in recent decades, the spread of Arabic among MSAL speakers has resulted in the MSAL increasingly falling into disuse. In both Oman and Yemen today, the official language is Arabic: of education, government, the media and commerce. Being in competition with another more widely spoken, scripted language is a common problem for purely oral languages across the globe. However, in the case of the MSAL, where the official language in question is Arabic, the problem is more than simply one of competing with an official, nation-state language: as Arabic is also the language of the Quran, and one which Muslims (nearly a quarter of the world's population) work hard to learn and understand, these six minority languages are in competition with an extremely high-prestige, globally recognized language.

The six languages of this group are in varying stages of endangerment. With the exception of speaker numbers for Soqoṭri and Baṭḥari, however, the figures given below are best estimates; speaker numbers for all MSAL are rapidly declining, with the majority of MSAL speakers also speaking Arabic:

i. Mehri is the most widespread MSAL, spoken by people of the Mahrah tribes in Oman, Yemen and parts of southern and eastern Saudi Arabia. The Mahrah are estimated to be some 200,000 people, though the actual number of Mahrah who now speak Mehri is difficult to estimate since the language is spoken across three state boundaries, and many Mahrah no longer speak Mehri;
ii. Soqoṭri, spoken exclusively in the islands of the Soqoṭra Archipelago, has some 100,000 speakers (Kogan and Bulakh 2019);
iii. Śḥerēt, spoken by a variety of tribes within the Dhofar region of Oman, has some 30,000 speakers;
iv. Ḥarsūsi, formerly spoken by members of the Ḥarsūsi tribe across the Jiddat al-Ḥarāsīs in central Oman, has under 1,000 speakers;
v. Hobyōt, spoken by a variety of tribes on both sides of the Yemeni / Omani border, likewise has under 1,000 speakers;
vi. Baṭḥari, spoken by members of the Baṭḥari tribe who live along the shore opposite the Al-Ḥallāniyyāt islands and in the desert plateau above, has fewer than thirty speakers.

The areas in which the MSAL are still spoken are the only regions within the Arabian Peninsula to have retained the Semitic languages spoken prior to the spread of Islam and subsequent Arabization of the Peninsula. In all other communities, Arabic appears to have superseded the original languages. As such, the documentation and description of the MSAL is of crucial importance to understanding the historical development of the Semitic language family as a whole.

Kumzari

Kumzari (autoglottonym: *kumẓārī*) is spoken by about 4,000 people on the Musandam Peninsula in the town of Kumzar and in parts of the cities of Khasab and Diba. The closely related variety Lāraki, is spoken by about 500 people on Lārak Island, some 40km to the north of Kumzar (Anonby and Yousefian 2011). Kumzari has been described as a mixed language with well-developed Arabian and Persian components at all levels of the language, as well as significant internal innovations (van der Wal Anonby 2014). Van der Wal Anonby (2015)

Introduction

has written a grammatical description of the language, along with a historical overview and analysed oral texts. The rich oral traditions of the Kumzari-language community and their detailed knowledge of the sea are evident in the contributions in this volume by Anonby, Al Kamzari and Al Kamzari (Chapter 3) and van der Wal Anonby (Chapter 8).

A map of the area studied with position of languages spoken is given below. As for the map with place names, in contrast to the chapters, no diacritics are provided for place names on the map:

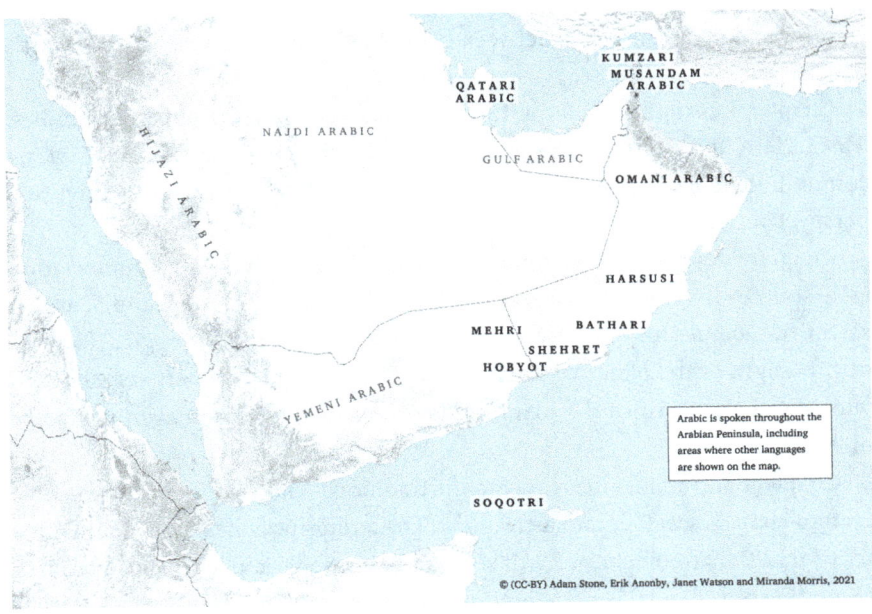

Map 0.2 Languages spoken in the Arabian Peninsula.

Themes and genres

With the aim of studying the relationship between language and ecology in the Arabian Peninsula with a multidisciplinary approach, this edited volume explores the ecological themes of water, flora, fauna, conservation, weather and climate, and natural resource management. The genres examined are poetry, folklore and historical narratives, and communicative gesture. In doing so, the book is divided into three main parts: 'Arabia: the significance of names', 'Arabia: narratives and ecology' and 'Arabia: conservation and revitalisation'.

Prior to these parts, Chapter 1 investigates the semiotic role of gestures in the context of endangered MSAL-speaking communities of South Arabia. Gestures are a means to express the relationship between nature and local knowledge, outlining the interrelationship between language and ecology.

The part on 'Arabia: the significance of names' is opened by Chapter 2 on the importance of naming not only in expressing the links between language and environment, but also for preserving cultural practices. Specifically, this chapter sheds a light on plant, lifestyle, livestock, people, place names and how MSAL-speaking communities mark time.

Chapter 3 is a photo essay that guides the reader through the landscape of Kumzar and the relationship between it and the Kumzari people through words and images.

Chapter 4 examines a central topic in landscape and environmental studies: water. Here, the authors investigate the relationship between MSAL-speaking communities in South Arabia and water in an anthropological and linguistic perspective.

Chapter 5 reports on the importance of plant names and flora nomenclature as a source of regional history and culture. If, on the one hand, Latin – scientific – names for flora usually allude to diagnostic morphological features or the origin of the plant, vernacular names, by contrast, are often associated with the characteristics the plant holds or the uses local communities make of it.

Chapter 6 introduces the reader to the traditional knowledge of Qatari people around climate, weather and astronomy. The author provides the reader with a set of traditional nomenclature of stars and atmospheric phenomena in Qatar, reiterating how pivotal is nomenclature for indigenous cultures.

Finally, Chapter 7 investigates the use of plant and animal names in the figurative speech of Ḥaḍramī Arabic (Yemen), including local proverbs, songs and idiomatic expressions, demonstrating, once again, the crucial relationship between local languages and their environment.

The second part on 'Arabia: narratives and ecology' includes three chapters dealing with the traditional narrative of climatic events and environmental issues in various communities of Southern and Eastern Arabia.

Chapter 8 follows the Kumzari people of northern Oman and their lifestyle based on a close relationship with nature: as nomadic fishers and date cultivators, their livelihoods often depend on the environment and climate. The indigenous Kumzari knowledge shared in the lexicon of weather, plants and boats is crucial to their survival in a changing and challenging environment.

Chapter 9 presents classical and vernacular poetry from the Arabian Peninsula encapsulating the close relationship that people from this region entertain with the natural environment. The chapter presents the narration of climatic events and relationship with the environment through the lens of poetry.

Finally, Chapter 10 offers a detailed analysis of resilience to climatic events through the voices of community members. Here, the authors consider instances of local resilience during climatic events that affected northern and southern Oman.

The last section on 'Arabia: conservation and revitalization' includes one chapter – Chapter 11 – that engages with the conceptual debates emerged in the nineteenth and twentieth centuries on the role that individuals and communities should play in conservation and environmental protection. This chapter explores the lived experiences of the Ḥarāsīs tribe in the Jiddat il-Ḥarāsīs (Oman) and the reintroduction of the Arabian oryx into their traditional territory.

Transcription

The systems used to transcribe Arabic dialects, MSAL and Kumzari are based on that of the Journal of Semitic Studies. We present below the transcription symbols for Arabic, MSAL and Kumzari.

Vowels

Short vowels are represented by simple symbols. For the Arabic dialects examined here and for Kumzari, these are: /a, i, u/. The MSAL vary between two short vowels, as in Mehri, /a, ə/ (with marginal /e, ɛ, i, o, u/), and seven, as in Soqoṭri and Śḥerēt, /a, e, ɛ, ə, i, o, u/. Long vowels are represented by a macron over the plain symbol, as in: /ā, ī, ē, ō, ɔ̄, ū/. In addition to long counterparts /ā, ī, ū/ to its three short vowels, Kumzari and the Arabic dialects examined have the long mid vowels, /ē, ō/.

Consonants

Here, we present the symbols used for transcription of consonants according to language groupings: Arabic, MSAL and Kumzari. Emphatic consonants and the pharyngeal aspirate, characteristic of all three groups, are transcribed with a subscript dot below the character; interdental fricatives are transcribed with a subscript underline; the unbreathed (voiced) uvular fricative is transcribed with a superscript dot; and the palato-alveolar sibilant is transcribed with a caron (ˇ) (also referred to as a hachek or wedge).

Arabic

The consonantal systems for the Arabic varieties referred to in the book are given in Table 0.1 below. Alternative transcriptions are placed after '/', as in: x/kh/ḫ.

Table 0.1 Ḥaḍrami, Qatari and Northern Omani Arabic Consonantal System and Transcription

	Phonation		*labial*	*dental*	*alveolar*	*pal-alveolar*	*palatal*	*velar*	*uvular*	*pharyngeal*	*glottal*
PLOSIVE	+br				t			k			
	-br	vd	b		d			g			ʔ/ʾ/ʔ
	emph.				ṭ				q		
FRICATIVE	+br		f	ṯ	s	š		x/kh/ḫ		ḥ	h
	-br	vd		ḏ	z	j/ž			ġ	ʕ/ʿ/ʕ	
	emph.			ḏ̣	ṣ						
LATERAL	+br										
	-br	vd			l						
	emph.										
nasal			m		n						
rhotic					r						
glide			w				y				

Modern South Arabian

For the continental MSAL – Mehri, Śḥerēt, Baṭḥari, Hobyōt and Ḥarsūsi – the consonantal inventory is provided in Table 0.2 below. Where languages differ in the articulation of certain consonants – for example, while Mehri, Baṭḥari, Hobyōt and

Ḥarsūsi have a palato-alveolar emphatic /ṧ/, Śḥerɛ̄t has a labialized alveo-palatal /ṧ/ – the articulation most common across the language family is provided first, followed by ' / ' and the less common articulation. As for other consonantal tables, alternative transcriptions are also placed after '/'. Phonemes with minor phonological load are provided in round brackets, as for (ṛ), the emphatic rhotic. Note that in addition to alveolar /s/ and palato-alveolar /š/, Śḥerɛ̄t has an alveo-palatal /š̃/ with lip-pouting (Bellem and Watson 2017), placed in parentheses in the palato-alveolar column:

Table 0.2 MSAL Consonantal System and Transcription

	phonation		labial	dental	alveolar	pal-alveolar	palatal	velar	uvular	pharyngeal	glottal
PLOSIVE	+br				t			k			
	-br	vd	b		d	ǧ/j		g			ʔ/'/ʔ
		emph.			ṭ			ḳ			
FRICATIVE	+br		f	ṯ	s	š/ṧ			x/kh/ḫ	ḥ	h
	-br	vd		ḏ	z	ž/z̃			ġ	ʕ/'/ʕ	
		emph.		ṯ/ḏ̣	ṣ	ṣ̌/ṣ̌̇					
LATERAL	+br					ś					
	-br	vd			l	(ź)					
		emph.				ṣ́/ẓ́/ẓ					
nasal			m		n						
rhotic					r(ṛ)						
glide			w				y				

In contrast to most research on Arabic and Modern South Arabian, the consonants are organized into 'breathed' and 'unbreathed' consonants (Heselwood and Maghrabi 2015; Watson and Heselwood 2016), due to the way in which these consonants pattern in the languages. 'Breathed' consonants include what in English are termed 'voiceless', such as /t, ṯ, k, s, š/. These involve aspiration or the release of audible breath on their release.

'Unbreathed' consonants involve no aspiration on their release. In the Arabic dialects considered here and Modern South Arabian, these are consonants that are voiced – i.e. they involve vibration of the vocal folds – and the emphatics, which typically do not involve vibration of the vocal folds.

Soqoṭri

Soqoṭri lacks a number of consonants attested in the continental MSAL, and has a few consonants not found in the sister languages. The consonantal table for Soqoṭri is given in Table 0.3 below[7]: note that Kogan and Ghazanfar adopt symbols used in Kogan's earlier work.

Table 0.3 Soqoṭri Consonantal System and Transcription

		phonation	*labial*	*alveolar*	*pal-*	*palatal*	*velar*	*uvular*	*pharyngeal*	*glottal*
PLOSIVES		+br		t			k			
	-br	vd	b	d			g			ʔ
		emph.		ṭ			ḳ			
FRICATIVES		+br	f	s	š			x/kh/ḫ	ḥ	h
	-br	vd		z	ž			ġ	ʕ	
		emph.		ṣ	ṣ̌					
LATERALS		+br			ś					
	-br	vd	l							
		emph.	ḷ	ṣ́/ẓ̂						
nasal			m	n						
rhotic				r						
GLIDES		+br				yʰ				
	-br		w			y				

Kumzari

The Kumzari consonantal system resembles those of nearby Arabic dialects of the Gulf, as well as languages from other families represented in the region.

Noteworthy regional characteristics include absence of an interdental series, presence of the voiceless pharyngeal /ḥ/ but absence of its voiced counterpart /ʕ/, a robust emphatic series with secondary uvular-pharyngeal articulation (Anonby 2020), and presence of the additional phonemic obstruents /p, č, g/. The emphatic sibilant /ẓ/ has no plain counterpart. A chart of Kumzari consonants, adapted from Anonby (2011) and van der Wal Anonby (2015), is given in Table 0.4 below

Table 0.4 Kumzari Consonantal System and Transcription

	labial bial	alveolar	emphatic alv.	palato-alv.	palatal	velar	uvular	pharyngeal	glottal
plosive (vl.)	p	t	ṭ	č		k	q		ʔ/ʼ
(vd.)	b	d	ḍ	j		g			
fricative (vl.)	f	s	ṣ	š			x	ḥ	h
(vd.)			ẓ				ġ		
nasal	m	n							
rhotic		r							
lateral		l	ḷ						
glide	w				y				

Notes

1 Socotra | History, Population, & Facts | Britannica Retrieved 25 November 2020.
2 Can Socotra, Yemen's 'Dragon's Blood Island,' be saved? (nationalgeographic.com) Retrieved 26 November 2020.
3 Oman | History, Map, Flag, Capital, Population, & Facts | Britannica Retrieved 25 November 2020.
4 List of countries by length of coastline – Wikipedia Retrieved 25 November 2020.
5 NOAA | National Center for Environmental Information Retrieved 25 November 2020.
6 Fossil CO_2 and GHG emissions of all world countries – Publications Office of the EU (europa.eu) Retrieved 25 November 2020.
7 With thanks to Leonid Kogan for sharing the Soqoṭri symbols.

References

Anonby, Erik (2011), 'Illustrations of the IPA: Kumzari', *Journal of the International Phonetic Association*, 41 (3): 375–80.

Anonby, Erik (2020), 'Emphatic Consonants beyond Arabic: The Emergence and Proliferation of Uvular-pharyngeal Emphasis in Kumzari', *Linguistics*, 58 (1): 275–328.

Anonby, Erik and Pakzad Yousefian (2011), *Adaptive Multilinguals: A Survey of Language on Larak Island*, Uppsala: Acta Universitatis Upsaliensis.

Bellem, Alex and Janet C. E. Watson (2017), 'South Arabian Sibilants and the Śḥerēt ś̃ ~ š contrast', in Laïla Nehmé and Ahmad Al-Jallad (eds), *To the Madbar and Back Again: Studies in the Languages, Archaeology, and Cultures of Arabia Dedicated to Michael C.A. Macdonald*, 622–43, Leiden: Brill.

Heselwood, Barry and Reem Maghribi (2015), 'An Instrumental-Phonetic Justification for Sībawayh's Classification of ṭā, qāf and hamza as majhūr consonants', *Journal of Semitic Studies*, 60: 131–75.

Kogan, Leonid and Maria Bulakh (2019), 'Soqoṭri', in John Huhnergard and Na'ama Pat-El (eds), *The Semitic Languages*, 280–320, London & New York: Routledge.

van der Wal Anonby, Christina (2015), *A Grammar of Kumzari: A Mixed Perso-Arabian Language of Oman*, Leiden: Leiden University.

van der Wal Anonby, Christina (2014), 'Traces of Arabian in Kumzari', in Orhan Elmaz and Janet C.E. Watson (eds.), *Languages of Southern Arabia: Special Session of the Seminar for Arabian Studies*, Oxford: Archaeopress: 137–46.

Watson, Janet C. E. and Barry Heselwood (2016), 'Phonation and Glottal States in Modern South Arabian and San'ani Arabic', in Youssef Haddad (ed.), *Perspectives on Arabic Linguistics*, 28: 3–37.

1

Language, Gesture and Ecology in Modern South Arabian Languages

Jack Wilson, Janet C.E. Watson, Andrea Boom and Saeed al-Qumairi

Introduction

Kockelman (2005) uses the notion of *semiotic community* as an extension of *speech community* (Bloomfield 1933; Gumperz 2001 [1968]) to capture commonalities in semiotic practice amongst individuals. *Semiotic practice* can be used to refer to anything that indexes a particular community. Such practices may contrast one community from another, or, in the right circumstances, a practice can be used by a community member to reflect their membership. In this chapter, we are using the concept of semiotic community to develop a notion of *gesture community* by examining the shared practices across speakers of various Modern South Arabian languages (henceforth MSAL).

MSAL are spoken in parts of Oman, Yemen, Saudi Arabia and the Gulf (see Introduction, this volume). They comprise Mehri, Ḥarsūsi, Baṭḥari, Hobyōt, Śḥerēt (aka Jibbāli) and Soqoṭri, and form part of the Semitic language family (Simeone-Senelle 1997; 2011). Historically, documentation of the MSAL has mainly been in text, without video or audio. The distribution of MSAL speech communities is typically considered on two dimensions: language and region. However, by considering MSAL semiotic communities the analyst is then able to incorporate multiple dimensions. Unlike language and region, such dimensions may not stack neatly on top of one another. What may be shared or not shared at one level (e.g. language use) may not entail sharedness at another level (e.g. gesture use). This creates a multidimensional conceptualization of

---

Thanks are due to the Leverhulme Trust for the project grant RPG-2012-599 awarded to Janet Watson (2013–2016) and to the ELDP for a small project grant 2017–19 awarded to Janet Watson and Saeed al-Qumairi. We also thank our consultants, who for reasons of anonymity are not named here.

community where each dimension (e.g. the incidence of a particular pointing gesture) might represent a unique characteristic for a community. The analyst, then, can frame a community depending on the particular semiotic dimension of interest. Our ability to frame a community depending on a particular semiotic frame is of critical importance when considering users of MSAL, because language users are far from homogeneous in a range of respects. For example, a Mehri speaker may have grown up in a particular environment; they may have children for whom Mehri is not a dominant language; they may be from a particular agricultural background (with traditions dating back thousands of years).

Gesture can be a somewhat vague term. Here we are using the term 'gesture' to refer to a non-linguistic contribution to communication (see Abner et al. 2015 for a detailed introduction to gesture). Gestures are chiefly visible behaviours and most commonly realized with the hands or head. The human propensity to accompany speech with gesture is thought to be universal, but historical investigations into the universal nature of gesture have led to confusion. Here, we will adopt Cooperrider's (2019) distinction between *gestural conventions*, *gestural practices* and *gestural kinds*. *Gestural conventions* are specific form-meaning mappings, such as the 'thumbs up' or 'ok' gesture in British English. Such gestures convey a particular meaning within a community but may mean something different to members of different communities. *Gestural practices* may be specific to particular communities, but they do not involve specific form-meaning mappings. For example, it has been observed that many communities typically point to the location of the sun at a particular time when referring to that time (Brown 2012). There is no fixed requirement of handshape, but the practice itself is conventional. *Gestural kinds* refer to the methods of signalling (Clark 1996) rather than the relationship between meaning and form. For example, a gesture may depict an action (in the form of pantomime), it may depict a referent representationally, or it may be used to point to a referent. When we think in terms of gestural kinds, we are focusing on the semiotic method of communication more broadly, where speech (or language more broadly) and gesture may favour the deployment of distinct semiotic methods (e.g. symbolic for speech and iconic/indexical for gesture).

When we consider the relationship between a semiotic community and gesture or we attempt to document gesture diversity, it is often easier or more obvious to focus on gestural conventions. However, this may miss commonalities in gestural practices or gestural kinds adopted within a particular community, which are often connected to culture-specific instrumental actions. In this chapter, we will show how knowledge relating to culture-specific practices (such as animal hide preparation) or region-specific understanding (such as what local flora look like) may be realized using gesture rather than speech. This is not because the gesture form / gestural practice used is conventionalized but because the particular individual recorded produced a gesture which depicts the behaviour. However, such gestures often reveal the deep level of knowledge and understanding of the practice described, which is itself a defining characteristic of a semiotic community.

The video data for this chapter comes from the ELAR Mehri archive (Watson and Morris 2016a), the ELAR Śḥerēt archive (Watson and Morris 2016b) and the Community Documentation of Biocultural Diversity in the Eastern Yemeni Province of al-Mahrah archive (al-Qumairi and Watson 2020). The data from the first two archives was recorded by Janet Watson with native-speaker interviewers using a Canon HDXA20 video recorder with an external Audio-Technica microphone and saved as either MOV or MTS files. Data from the Mehri and Śḥerēt archives was collected as part of a four-year Leverhulme Trust-funded project on the Documentation and Ethnolinguistic Analysis of Modern South Arabian (DEAMSA), which recorded in total over 200 hours of audio material and fifteen hours of audio-visual material from the five mainland MSAL, Mehri, Śḥerēt, Ḥarsūsi, Hobyōt and Baṭḥari relating to traditional cultural activities and exploitation of traditional ecosystems. All the data from these archives that we describe in this chapter was recorded in Dhofar: in Sadḥ, eastern Dhofar, in and around the desert village of Rabkūt, and in Ṣaḥalnōt, a new settlement close to Salalah. The Community Documentation of Biocultural Diversity in the Eastern Yemeni Province of al-Mahrah project data we refer to in this chapter was recorded in Wādi Hanwōf and Wādi Shawmīt respectively, both tributary wadis to Wādi Gēzaʕ and around 30km to the north of al-Ghaydhah, provincial capital of al-Mahrah, towards the Najd. This data was recorded by Saeed al-Qumairi on a Sony HDR-PJ410 Handycam and saved in MTS format.

Our seven speakers come from four different types of settlement and practise four different lifestyles: one Śḥerēt speaker, J047, is a well-respected fisherman in his 70s from the coastal town of Sadḥ, in eastern Dhofar. A member of the ʕAmri sub-tribe of al-Mahrah, J047 was born and brought up in the mountains between Ḥadbīn and Ḥāsik, moving to the fishing town of Sadḥ as a young adult. He spent the majority of his life fishing off the coast of Sadḥ. In common with many men from this region in the period prior to Sultan Qaboos coming to power in 1970, he spent some time as a young adult working in Kuwait. It was during this time that he learnt the Arabic he occasionally uses in his recordings.

Note that Arabic loans are represented in the transcriptions with superscript [A]. His recordings were produced in his house in Sadḥ. The other Śḥerēt speaker we refer to, J108, was in his early 30s at the time of recording. He is from the ʿĀmər Gīd sub-tribe of al-Mahrah, educated to secondary level and works in an office in Sadḥ. He was recorded by Wilson and Watson in the phonetics laboratory at the University of Leeds in 2015.

We take data from five Mehri speakers: three from Dhofar, the southern province of Oman, and two from al-Mahrah in Yemen. M068 was born in 1997 and educated to college level. A member of the Bit Iḵḥōr sub-tribe of Bit Thuwār, a major sub-tribe of al-Mahrah, he was brought up in the gravel desert village of Rabkūt, which he frequently visits, and moved four years ago to Salalah, the provincial capital of Dhofar. He is bilingual in Mehri and Arabic. Despite his young age, M068 has significant competence both in Mehri and in the ecosystems of the gravel desert due to his upbringing. His mother is a monolingual Mehri speaker from the Bit Blēḥ sub-tribe of Bit Thuwār, and is well known within the community as a source for Mehri. M001 was born in 1993, and is educated to college level. He is the elder brother of M068. He was brought up speaking Mehri and learnt Arabic from school level; due to his upbringing, he has significant competence in Mehri. M017 was born around 1960, and is literate but did not undergo any formal education. A member of the Bit Amoush sub-tribe of Bit Thuwār, he lives in the gravel desert village of Dhahbūn to the east of Rabkūt. A prominent member of his tribe, M017 raises camels and has a date palm plantation in Bishʕīthān, north-east of Marmūl. M017 is bilingual in Mehri and Arabic, but has significantly more competence in Mehri.

Both YMGh004 and YMGh005 are camel herding pastoralists from the Bit Kalšāt sub-tribe of al-Mahrah: YMGh004 is in his mid-50s and from Wādi Hanwōf; YMGh005 is in his late 60s and from Wādi Shawmīt. Both YMGh004 and YMGh005 lack formal education beyond that of the Qurʾān. In our videos, they are being interviewed by Saʿd Kalšāt from Bit Kalšāt, who is in his early 40s and educated to primary level. The interviewer currently works for the Mehri Center for Studies and Research in al-Ghaydhah.

In this chapter, we demonstrate how recording gesture use accompanying MSAL can complement linguistics fieldwork and develop understandings of culture-specific practices. One of the main reasons for the importance of gesture when exploring endangered rural languages is because as languages experience attrition, features lost linguistically may remain gesturally. If we assume that a semiotic community may involve commonalities in language, gesture, belief systems, etc., then attrition in one does not necessarily lead to attrition in another. Understanding how to interpret gesture is key to developing a fuller picture of endangered languages now and historically. This work is not a comprehensive survey but a current snapshot of what we know. Our aim is to provide further evidence for the importance of collecting gesture data of MSAL and to suggest avenues for future research.

The following section will focus on pointing, representations of space, descriptions of manual action, expert understanding of flora, representations of time, acoustic paths and personification of animals. These are cases where distinct gestures illuminate links between communicative practice, cultural practice and ecological knowledge in ways that cross language boundaries and that also may persist past language attrition.

Pointing

Background

Pointing gestures are typically characterized by the fact that the producer creates a vector directing the recipient to a space within which the referent is 'located' (Clark 2003). However, pointing gestures tend to have a culturally determined conventional form.

Conventional pointing behaviours can be placed into two large groups: manual pointing and non-manual pointing. Within studies on manual pointing, handshape or the movement of the hand can differentiate the meaning of the gesture. For example, in the 'Neapolitan' gestures observed by Kendon and Versante (2003) there is a contrast between pointing with the index finger when the palm of the hand is down and pointing when the palm vertical. The palm down pointing gesture is used to specifically individuate a referent whereas the palm vertical pointing gesture can be used to refer to some quality of the referent. Similarly, Wilkins's (2003) analysis of the Australian language, Arrente, distinguishes one-finger pointing gestures which identify a single object or place; wide hand pointing that is used to identify groups of objects or expanses; and flat hand pointing that is used to identify linear orientations or project paths. Ola Orie's (2009) study of Yoruba pointing also reveals further characteristics of pointing behaviours not typically conventionalized in an English-speaking context. Most notably there is a 'secret' pointing gesture in which the thumb and index finger are extended, which is typically used when the Yoruba are among non-Yoruba. It is secret because to someone who is not familiar with the gesture it seems to be directing the recipient with the index finger. However, the producer's true intention is to direct with the thumb, pointing in a direction perpendicular to the index.

Within Western Educated Industrialized Rich Democratic (WEIRD) contexts (Henrich et al. 2010), it is often believed that pointing with the index finger is the prototypical form of pointing. While there is some evidence for a phylogenetic origin for index-finger pointing (Povinelli and Davis 1994) and it seems that index finger pointing is a universal communicative practice (Liszkowski et al. 2012), there is great diversity in pointing gestures around the world and many communities adopt non-manual pointing more often than other forms (Cooperrider et al. 2018). Lip pointing (Enfield 2001), for example, has been demonstrated in a range of speech communities, including examples from Africa, the Americas, Asia, Australia, Papua New Guinea (see Cooperrider et al. 2018, for further details). However, there is evidence that preferred pointing behaviours are not solely the result of regional variation. Li and Cao (2019) explored whether occupation had an effect on the preference for manual vs non-manual pointing within a Chinese community. In an experimental study, half the participants were farmers (a job which requires a high degree of manual labour) and the other half were herders (a job that does not require the hands to be occupied for long periods of time). Li and Cao demonstrate that the farmers were significantly more likely to use non-manual pointing, suggesting that a lifestyle where manual pointing may not be possible might promote alternative pointing methods.

Studying the conventional aspects of gesture is critical for understanding the environmental niche (Lupyan and Dale 2010) in which a community exists. While the focus on the effect of an environment niche has historically focused on linguistic structures, Cooperrider, Slotta, and Nunez (2018) argue that *communicative practice* more generally is affected. McNeill (1992: 61) observes that a 'head toss' gesture with the meaning of negation is used in Italy south of the Volturno River near Naples. However, those living north of the Volturno River use the head shake gesture that is common in England and North America. Interestingly, the same head toss gesture also appears in Greece and nowhere else. McNeill believes that the reason for the presence of this gesture south of the Volturno River is because the southern region of Italy was colonized by the Greeks in the seventh or eighth century BCE. If McNeill is correct this would mean that this gesture has not changed its meaning in roughly 2,700 years in both southern Italy and Greece. This provides evidence for the idea that conventional gestures differ across geographical regions rather than across languages and therefore could be evidence for historical cultural contact. This evidence could be used to reinforce existing accounts of contact based on linguistic evidence or in situations where linguistic evidence of contact has disappeared.

Pointing in MSAL

Wayfinding

Wayfinding is the description of how to traverse through space. It has been of topic of interest to both linguists and anthropologists (see Kataoka 2013 for a review). Wayfinding is important to MSAL users and many narratives include detailed descriptions of how to get from one place to another or descriptions of historically significant journeys.

Although we do not have publishable video data which can be presented in this chapter, researchers working in Oman have observed distinct uses of pointing gestures during wayfinding and route descriptions. Such gestures have been documented for speakers of both Mehri and Śḥerēt. From these observations, we believe that single-finger pointing, two-finger pointing and flat hand pointing can all be used for directing an audience's attention to a referent. It is also possible that such gestures are used contrastively in a manner similar to that reported in Wilkins (2003). Based on discussions with Omanis and researchers, we believe the contrast shown in Table 1.1 exists for speakers of Mehri and Śḥerēt:

Table 1.1 Table of Pointing Types in Mehri and Śḥerēt

Pointing type	
Index finger / one finger	*Single referent*
Index + middle finger / two finger	*Route or path*
Whole hand (splayed)	*Region*

Following this typology, a single-finger point during wayfinding appears to be used to refer to a place, person or thing. A pointing gesture including two fingers can be used to refer to a route and may trace the route on the landscape. A pointing gesture in which the whole hand is splayed can be used to refer to a region. Additional video data is needed to verify these findings, but it is in line with findings in the literature.

Hooked point

One pointing gesture that has been documented in Oman appears to be unique to users of Mehri and has not been reported as being used by other speakers of other languages in Dhofar. In example 1, Figure 1.1, we have included the utterance that accompanies the use of the gesture and then the entire explanation of the pointing behaviour.

(1)

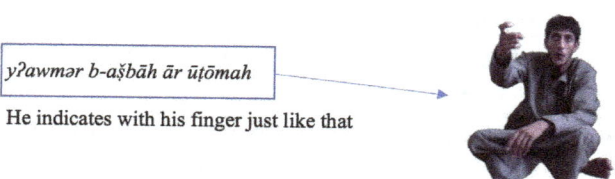

yʔawmər b-aṣ̌bāh ār ūṭōmah

He indicates with his finger just like that

Figure 1.1 M001 producing "hooked point" gesture.

(2)

In the transcription below and elsewhere, pauses in speech are marked by /.

M001: ṣarōm əmnēdəm wət ḥābū ḏ-ixxyīlən ərḥəmēt yʔamrəm / ḏ-ixxyīlən / yax hōba yəś́ayn əl-ḥō̃h thakbəl walā mən ḥōō̃h tənkē̄ wə-śīni əmənwōt mən thakbūl mənṣāwən / walā mən lḥak walā mən mārīb walā mən maśkayṣ / wa-śīni mənwōt thakbūl ūdih / yʔawmər lā / yəmġōṭ b-aṣ̌bāh ūṭōmah lā / hōbah ūṭōmah twōli mənwōt lā / **yʔawmər b-aṣ̌bāh ār ūṭōmah** / ḥāwəlōy yʔamrəm / hām amərk ūṭōmah / l-ād tnakak lā / āmēr ār ūṭōmah / ūṭōmah lagrē tənkēk /

English translation

M001: Now when someone, when people are scouting for rain, they say, he is scouting for rain (ḏ-ixxyīlən). That means they look to see where it is going or where it is coming from. When they see a rain cloud coming from the direction the flood waters flow, or from where they come from, or from the west or from the east. When he sees the rain cloud coming towards him, he doesn't point with his finger like that, I mean like that towards the rain cloud. **He indicates with his finger just like that [hooked].** Our forefathers used to say, if you indicated like that it wouldn't come, just indicate like that so that it comes to you.

It is clear from the image of M001 together with the larger stretch of discourse that the hooked pointing gesture is being contrasted with the index finger pointing with a straightened finger. According to M001, the condition in which this gesture is used is when a cloud is already coming towards the gesture producer and that historically, it was believed that pointing directly at the cloud would result in the cloud not coming.

The origin of the hooked pointing gesture is unclear. However, it is possible to postulate at least three potential origins. The first is that it is the combination of two pointing gestures into a single handshape. One pointing gesture is aimed at the cloud (directing the recipient to the cloud) and the other is pointing in the direction of the speaker (referring to the direction the speaker wants the cloud to come). A second is that it is an indexical use of an iconic gesture which depicts a hook. The producer is metaphorically hooking the cloud so that it comes in their direction. The third, and the one potentially favoured by M001, is that it is a blunted pointing gesture, due to superstition surrounding the critical importance of clouds (or more precisely rain) for the maintenance of livestock. If there is a general belief that a pointed finger might lead to a cloud's dispersal, then blunting the point may stop this from happening. Saeed al-Qumairi, one of the authors of this chapter, has provided further evidence for this third interpretation, stating that 'one should not point at the sky because there is God there' and reported that his mother told him not to do so as a child. Regardless of its origin, this third understanding of the point results in the idea that not pointing at clouds and the handshape is the result of taboo. This would be very similar to the blunted point used by many politicians so as not to perform the culturally rude gesture of pointing directly at someone.

Environmental factors on lip and tongue pointing

Lip pointing involves the lips protruding together with eye gaze and a quick head tilt (Enfield 2001). It has been reported as a conventional pointing gesture in many diverse cultures around the world. However, there are no published reports of lip pointing accompanying Semitic languages (Cooperider et al. 2018). Unfortunately, we do not have recorded video data of naturally occurring lip pointing accompanying MSAL. However, researchers have observed lip and tongue pointing produced by Śḥerēt speakers living in the mountains and by Mehri speakers by the coast and mountains. There are fewer reported incidences of lip pointing among Mehri speakers, but it is not clear whether there is a regional element to this. One Mehri speaker said that the difference between when to use lip pointing versus finger pointing is based on proximity of referent and addressee. If the referent is close, then pointing with the lips is permissible. Since it has been reported that lip pointing is used more frequently by those living in the mountains and less by those living on the plains, this might imply an areal distinction based on geography. Those living in the mountains are more likely to be in close proximity and may not have to communicate over large distances. If this is the case, then such an environment might promote lip pointing while living in a wide-open space may promote finger pointing. This could be compared to the lip pointing vs finger pointing preference found in the Chinese farmers vs herders in Li and Coa's (2019) study discussed above.

Representations of space

Background

Gesture is a spatial behaviour and it is often used to depict spatial representations and spatial concepts. There is a lot of evidence for variation in spatial conceptualization cross-culturally (see Levinson 2003) and a fruitful research enterprise has been established exploring the relationship between how people think, speak and gesture about space.

One of the dominant ways in which space is discussed in the literature (see Talmy 2000) is in terms of *frame of reference* (FOR). When describing space, people will often separate a focal entity (the *figure*) from the background (or *ground*). Around the world, communities often differ depending on whether they primarily use an egocentric or geocentric frame of reference when describing space. An egocentric FOR refers to a representation where the arrangement of figure and ground are relative to someone's perspective (e.g., 'the fork is to the right of the spoon'). A geocentric FOR refers to a representation where the arrangement of figure and ground relative to the world (e.g. 'the fork is to the north of the spoon'). It has been demonstrated (Levinson 2003; Majid et al. 2004) that languages which have a preference for a geocentric FOR not only produce utterances (speech and gesture) that reflect this, but that speakers of such languages behave geocentrically in non-communicative tasks. Furthermore, users of languages that are socialized into geocentric frames of reference also have incredible dead-reckoning abilities (Levinson 2003: 244–71). Speakers of such languages have been shown to point to something non-visible (up to 100km away) with a very small degree of error. Speakers of egocentric systems are particularly bad at this (see Levinson 2003: 228).

In contrast, Kita and Özyürek (2003) present evidence that speakers of American English who, after watching video depicting a character swinging across the screen from left to right, would produce gestures that depicted the character swinging from left to right regardless of whether or not this was expressed linguistically. This suggests that in the same way speakers of languages that encode space geocentrically are always monitoring their position relative to some encompassing ground, speakers whose language adopts an egocentric frame of reference conceptualize space on a relative lateral axis. Further evidence for this can be found in the difference between gestures representing the lateral axis (left/right) for two Mayan cultures in Central America (Kita 2009). For the Yucatec (in Mexico) the lateral axis is contrastive, whereas for the Mopan (in Belize) it is not. The Mopan language does not have any words equivalent to the English 'left' and 'right', but the Yucatec language does. Mopan speakers will give the same description to two lateral mirror images, leaving the orientation of the figure and ground on the lateral axis underspecified. This difference in underlying linguistic organization is also reflected in the use of gestures. When gesturing, speakers of the Mopan language do not use gestures for left and right contrastively, whereas speakers of the Yucatec language do.

However, there is growing disagreement about the close relationship between a preference for a particular FOR in speech and gesture. There is evidence of speakers who consistently gesture using one FOR that is not regularly found in speech (Calderon et al. 2019; Le Guen 2011). There is also evidence of gender differences with communities that manifest themselves linguistically but not gesturally (Le Guen 2011).

Le Guen (2011) observes that studies exploring FOR within Yucatan Maya communities have not been able to agree on a preferred FOR. Le Guen argues gesture, rather than knowledge of spatial terms, is a better indicator of preferred FOR. In a corpus study, Le Guen found that there was no use of 'left'/'right' terms and limited use of cardinal terms. Speakers were more likely to use intrinsic terms (e.g. 'front', 'back', etc.) and deictic expressions (e.g. 'here'/ 'there'). Regardless of this, the Yucatan Maya speakers studied have a strong preference for a geocentric FOR in a non-linguistic rotation task. Furthermore, in a task where participants are required to describe the location of an object relevant to a ground (both of which were 30 miles away from the speaker) it was observed that speakers tend to be linguistically underspecific by using deictic terms, for example (this was also observed by Meakins 2011 for Gurindji Kriol) but use a geocentric FOR in gesture.

Meakins (2011) found that the Gurindji people in Australia performed in a way expected of a geocentric speaker regardless of whether they spoke Gurindji or an English-lexified creole, Gurindji Kriol, in which the cardinal terms are not present. This suggests that geocentric conceptualization is present regardless of the language a person uses, and that cultural transmission of geocentricism might not necessarily be linguistic (a similar point is made by Le Guen 2011). Similarly, a monolingual Spanish-speaking community in Mexico who would have historically spoken Ixcatec but no longer do still retain geocentric conceptualizations even though Ixcatec has not been used for three generations (Adamou and Shen 2017).

Calderon, De Pascale and Adamou (2019) investigated the severely endangered language Ngigua spoken in Mexico. In the study, they explored the linguistic and non-linguistic practices of seventeen Ngigua-Spanish bilinguals and seventeen Spanish monolinguals from the same community. They found that in a localization task, all speakers used more geocentric and direct pointing gestures than egocentric gestures. Interestingly, it was the Spanish speakers who used more geocentric gestures and language, which Calderon, De Pascale and Adamou (2019) argue is the result of cardinal terms in Spanish strengthening pre-existing geocentric cognitive representations.

These findings lead to two suggestions. One is that for some languages spatial descriptions are distributed over language and gesture, such that neither modality can specify spatial arrangement on its own. The second is that as some endangered rural languages experience attrition they move from a geocentric to intrinsic, egocentric, or an underspecified linguistic system. With the move away from a geocentric system, gesture becomes the main output for an underlying geocentric conceptualization of space.

Spatial representations in MSAL

Focusing on Mehri and Śḥerēt as spoken in Dhofar, Watson and Wilson (2017) explored the coupling of speech and gesture in face-to-face interaction exposing linguistic, cultural and cognitive practices related to the structure of each language. Watson and Wilson (2017) used lab-based recordings produced during interactional tasks to demonstrate that previously undocumented semantic and syntactic features of MSAL are observable in gesture. One of the tasks in Watson and Wilson (2017) required participants to describe the route depicted on a two-dimensional 'treasure' map for a confederate. From this task, Watson and Wilson (2017) report a finding relating to the use of 'right' and 'left' terms, which for Śḥerēt and Mehri are traditionally documented as adjectival modifiers of the lexeme hand (i.e. 'on your right hand'). Table 1.2 shows the typical usage in both Śḥerēt and Mehri. All examples are second person feminine singular because the same confederate was used in all recordings.

Table 1.2 Expression of Direction in Mehri and Śḥerēt

Śḥerēt		
Left:	l-īd-ɛš̃ to-hand-2fs	šemǝl-ēt left-fs
Right:	l-īd-ɛš̃ to-hand-2fs	ɛmǝl-ēt right-fs
Down:	hērit go.down.2fs	aġaʰl down
Mehri		
Left:	ǝl-ḥayd-ǝš to-hand-2fs	śaymǝl left-fs
Right:	ǝl-ḥayd-ǝš to-hand-2fs	ḥaymǝl right-fs
Down:	kfēdi go.down.2fs	xōṭǝr down

Table 1.2 shows that Śḥerēt and Mehri pattern very similarly. A directional or positional verb (e.g. Śḥerēt: ǝrdid [return.2fs]) can be modified by the complex phrase l-īd-ɛš̃ šemǝl-ēt. So ǝrdid l-īd-ɛš̃ šemǝl-ēt can be translated as 'return right'. However, in both languages this can be compared to other directions, such as 'down', where it is obligatory that the verb is modified for direction. In other words, hērit literally means 'go down', but still requires the obligatory modification with the preposition aġaʰl. Syntactically, this means that the spatial phrase and the verb are produced separately in descriptions of left/right but not in descriptions of up/down. Since Watson and Wilson (2017), it has been confirmed by local researchers that the use of 'left/right' for speakers of Mehri and Śḥerēt is most acceptable in the paradigm reflected in Table 1.2.

A further observation of Watson and Wilson (2017) was that when speakers are describing orientation on a horizontal axis (but not a vertical one), they tend to break up gestural depictions used during the map task into two gestures, one depicting the path going in a particular direction and one depicting the orientation of the two objects being described (we refer interested readers to the examples analysed in Watson and Wilson (2017: 65–70)). It was also observed that gestures depicting the direction of the route were less likely to co-occur with the part of the descriptions including the terms for 'left hand/right hand'. For example (speaker J108):

(3) ẓḥamš b-ōrəm min sɛr haram / nāṣanun ərdid l ... l-īdɛš śeməlēt
come.PERF-2fs with-DEF.path from behind pyramid / now return.2fs to- to-hand-2fs left-fs
'You've taken a path behind the pyramid. Now go back to your left hand'

The gesture which accompanied (3) stopped before the word śeməlēt. These findings can be compared to the findings of Kita and Özyürek (2003) who demonstrated that speakers of languages which package information in particular ways are more likely to package gesture in this way (see Fritz et al. 2019 for a recent review). What is interesting about this finding is that it is not about egocentric vs geocentric spatial descriptions, but about the syntactic structure. In other words, because Śḥerēt and Mehri require terms for 'left' and 'right' to modify hand, they cannot directly modify the verb or an object that is not a hand. Further evidence for this comes from our observations of code-switching from Śḥerēt to Arabic in order to use left as an adverb (e.g. 'going left'), as in example (2), also from J108, where the Arabic adverb yimīn 'right' is being used to describe direction:

(4) lā hit hit nāṣanun ḥa-tġid ᴬmaṯalan yimīnᴬ xērɛn / trif ᴬyimīnᴬ / ṭanuh / īd-ɛš ɛməl-ēt
no you.fs you.fs now FUT-go.2fs for.example right [Arabic] a.little / go.forward.2fs right / like.that / hand-2fs right-fs
No, you, you now will go, for example, right a little, turn right, like that, to your right hand

In other words, it appears that the separation of direction and orientation on the horizontal axis in language is reflected in a separation in gesture. Interestingly, M001 (one of the Mehri speakers in Watson and Wilson 2017) has no problem using śayməl or ḥayməl in a range of syntactic contexts. For example, M001 uses śayməl as an adjective modifying a noun that is not 'hand' when describing the orientation to the left of the birds:

(5) kəfēdī xōṭər hāl / mən śərūḵ ḏ-āḵāb l-śərūḵəsən śayməl
where from side of-bird.PL to-side-3fpl left
'in relation to the birds to their left'

M001 can also describe orientation using ḥayməl as a noun:

(6) wə-ḵfēdi mən śərūḵəh / ḏə-ḥḥayməl
and-go.down.2fs from side.3ms of-right
'and come down on the right side of it'

While these two examples show that this speaker is able to refer to 'left/right' in a way that does not reflect the syntactic convention of Mehri, it is still the case that a separate gesture is produced with each direction and orientation element of the descriptions. However, this speaker also uses *ḥaymǝl* as an adverb, where it is realized without *ǝl-ḥayd-ǝš*:

(7) wǝ-ghēmi ḥaymǝl
 and-go.2fs right
 'and go right'

For (7), a single gesture is produced depicting the rightward direction of the path. This data points to the fact that for M001, 'left' and 'right' are being used in a way distinct from other speakers of Mehri or Śḥerēt. We argue that this relates to the fact that the direction and orientation of the paths are conceptualized as two distinct units and thus realized as two distinct gestures. One objection to this[1] was that the map task, which forces speakers to describe a two-dimensional space, is atypical and that the separation of orientation and direction in gesture may be an artefact of the task. To address this, in this section we will show an example of a Mehri speaker describing a route description, recorded in Oman by another Mehri speaker.

(8)

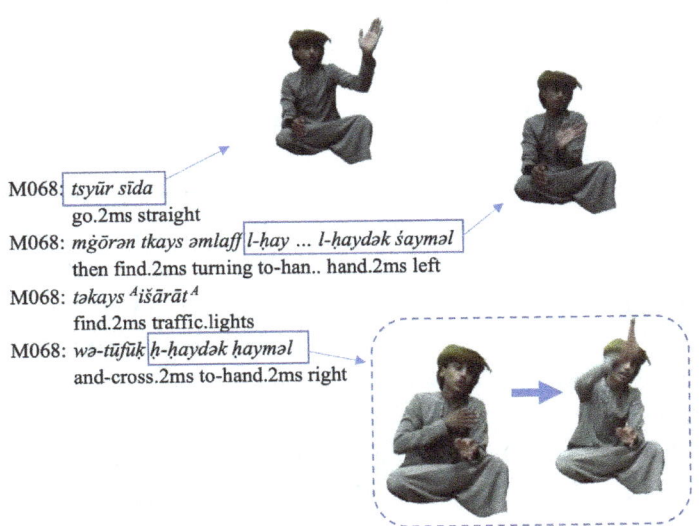

M068: *tsyūr sīda*
  go.2ms straight
M068: *mġōrǝn tkays ǝmlaff l-ḥay ... l-ḥaydǝk śaymǝl*
  then find.2ms turning to-han.. hand.2ms left
M068: *tǝkays ⁴išārāt⁴*
  find.2ms traffic.lights
M068: *wǝ-tūfūk h-ḥaydǝk ḥaymǝl*
  and-cross.2ms to-hand.2ms right

Figure 1.2 M068 gesturing while describing route.

In (8), Figure 1.2, M068 is describing the route he would take from the Old Market to his house, both in Dhofar. In the section presented here, M068 describes approaching some traffic lights and crossing the road. It is possible to break his description into four units:

I. Go straight
II. Turn to left
III. Find traffic lights
IV. Cross to right

Units (I), (II), and (IV) are all descriptions of moving along a path towards a destination. The boxes around the text represent the stroke phases (the moving part) of the gestures that accompany the speech. There is one stroke per path description. The first description *tsyūr sīda* (go straight) is accompanied by a gesture in which the left hand depicts an upward trajectory. Following this, M068 brings his left hand towards his body, holding it while he says *mġōrən tkays əmlaff* releasing his hand to create the gesture alongside *l-ḥay ... l-ḥaydək śayməl*. Interestingly, the movement of the hand is timed so as to co-occur with the false start *l-ḥay*. Importantly, the speaker has not produced a gesture which co-occurs with the noun *əmlaff*, 'the turning'. The same thing happens with the next path description. M068 moves his hands into position while he says *təkays ᴬišārāt ᴬ*, holds them during *wə-tūfuḵ* and releases them so that the movement co-occurs with *ḥ-ḥaydək ḥayməl*. This example demonstrates that even outside of the maptask context we see the same separation of terms of 'left/right' and other direction/orientational terms.

These observations point to a conceptual, linguistic and gesture separation of 'left/right' from other spatial terms. Why this is the case should be the subject of future investigation. However, one possible argument is that the obligatory use of 'left/right' as an adjectival modifier of 'hand' preferences what is referred to as a character viewpoint (see McNeill 2015: 51). Character viewpoint gestures are gestures produced co-expressively with speech but represent something from the perspective of the actor being described. They are contrasted with observer viewpoint, where the gesture depicts a scene from a third person perspective. Since the use of the word 'hand' privileges a character viewpoint, this is what is depicted in the gesture. This is interesting because it suggests that the gesture is linked not to the underlying conceptualization of space (as suggested by theories focusing on FOR) nor to a conventional gesture practice, but to the linguistic packaging of what a speaker is trying to communicate. In other words, a constraining factor at the level of syntax is having an effect on the realization of gesture.

Going back to the map task, it could be argued that a two-dimensional map privileges an observer viewpoint. This clash between the task-based representation (which promotes an observer viewpoint) and the syntactic structure of the language (which promotes a character viewpoint when describing 'left/right') pushes language users to separate the gestures depicting the route and those depicting the direction/orientation. Why this still persists in the route description which is describing three-dimension space as seen in example (8) should be the subject of future work.

Representations of time

Background

Conceptualizations of time are intimately related to conceptualization of space. English speakers tend to talk about time using metaphors of the future being in front and the past behind and any timeline of events would be expected to run from left to right (Núñez and Sweetser 2006). There are two distinct ways to talk about time: *deictic time* and *sequence time* (Nunez and Cooperrider 2013). For deictic time the present time acts as origo (e.g. 'now') and the past and future are represented as relative to this origo (e.g. 'tomorrow'). The origo associated with deictic time can be considered internal to the speaker (through the use of 'in front') or external to the speaker (through the use of 'left' or 'right'). Sequence time is where time is considered to be in a sequence (e.g. 'earlier' comes before 'later' but there is no need to specify 'now').

It has been observed that for some cultures these spatial metaphors behave in different ways to English. For example, Núñez and Sweetser (2006) observed that in Aymara, an Amerindian language spoken in Bolivia, Peru and Chile, the future is 'behind' and the past is 'in front' whereas for the Yupno an indigenous group from Papua New Guinea, the past is 'downhill' and the future 'uphill' (Nunez et al. 2012). It has also been observed that sequence time is described as being on an 'east/west' axis in Pormpuraaw (Boroditsky and Gaby 2010). These findings are not limited to rural languages. Mandarin speakers describe the past as 'above' and the 'future' below (Fuhrman et al. 2011). In the studies reported by Nunez and Cooperrider (2013), there is a relationship between whether languages have a preference for an egocentric or geocentric FOR and whether they use non-deictic or non-egocentric temporal descriptions.

It has been shown that there is a clear relationship between the way that people conceptualize time and the way they gesture when discussing it. Languages that conceptualize the past as 'in front' produce gestures that reflect this (Núñez and Sweetser 2006) and languages that describe time on a vertical axis use this axis in gesture (Fuhrman et al. 2011). For example, Gu et al. (2017) show gestures accompanying temporal descriptions in Chinese suggest that the conceptualization of time as appearing on a vertical pane affects direction of the gestures' path.

Brown (2012) argues that speakers of Tzeltal, who encode spatial descriptions geocentrically, do not necessarily encode time this way. Although it was not the focus of the study, Brown also does not report on a particular preference for FOR in gesture. However, speakers of Tzeltal are reported to use gesture in a particular way when describing time. They will point to the location the sun is likely to be in the sky at the time they are discussing. This has also been demonstrated for the Brazilian indigenous language, Nheengatu (Floyd 2016). In their discussion of representations of time in Yeli Dnye, Levinson and Majid (2013) suggest that because languages that represent space geocentrically produce gestures that are 'inspected for direction veracity' (Levinson and Majid 2013: 4), temporal gestures are constrained. It is for this reason, they argue, that gestures relating to time are literally spatial in that they point to celestial bodies (e.g. the location of the moon or sun).

Representations of time in MSAL

Mehri has a rich temporal lexis. Morphologically, the words for 'come' and 'go' are unique depending on the time of day. Like many languages discussed above, Mehri has conventionalized lexical descriptions for time that refer to the position of the sun (during the day) and the depth of darkness during the night.

Table 1.3 Temporal Terms in Mehri

ḏuwēlēbən	'early mid-morning'
ḏʔawbən	'late morning'

We do not have video data reflecting the conversational usages of temporal terms, nor do we have video data including descriptions of terms relating to the night. However, in one video M017 is describing how Mehri speakers refer to different times in the day. Accompanying this description, he produces the following:

(9)

Figure 1.3 M017 gesturing while describing different times in the morning.

Here, M017 is contrasting *ḍuwēlēbən* ('early mid-morning') with *ḏʔawbən*, see Table 1.3. Temporally concurrent with *ḍuwēlēbən* the speaker produces the first gesture and then produces the second gesture with *ḏʔawbən*. If we assume that the speaker is conceptualizing the position of the sun as being on an arch starting to his left and ending on his right so that at mid-day the sun would be in a position in line with his head, these gestures make perfect sense. The sun is located lower at *ḍuwēlēbən* than at *ḏʔawbən* and this is clearly reflected in gesture.

Further evidence for this comes from multiple sources. M017 uses right-handed beat gestures throughout his monologue; it is only when he is talking times before midday that he produces left-handed gestures. Once he begins to talk about times after midday, he switches to right-handed gestures (see 10, Figure 1.4).

(10)

Figure 1.4 M017 gesturing upward while referring to midday.

Also, even though the speaker is sitting indoors, we believe that his gestures are geographically accurate. The east would be to his left and the west to his right based on where he is sitting.

Gestures displaying environmental expertise

Descriptions of manual action

A constituting factor of any semiotic community is the material artefacts that it produces. These may include the production of certain food stuffs, clothing or other material goods. A very common object produced in Yemen and Oman is the *nīd* or 'waterskin', which is made from goat leather. The production of artefacts such as *nīd* involves a complex series of actions, which individuals memorize and are able to retell. One theory of gesture takes gesture to be the result of simulated action (Hostetter and Alibali 2008, 2019). With this in mind, gesture has the potential to reveal aspects of the action sequences involved in the creation of culture-specific artefacts.

In one of our recordings, YMGh004 is describing the process of producing a waterskin. Once the animal is killed and the skin removed, the next step is to remove the hair. To do this, the hide is submerged in a liquid solution, made of water and the seeds from a local plant, which softens the hair so it can be scraped off. When YMGh004 is describing this process, he says the following, (11), Figure 1.5:

(11)

gēd ḏakmah yəḳalbəm tah bərk ḥəmoh wa-yəxrīg mənəh aśśaff
that hide they put into water and they remove the hair from it

Figure 1.5 YMGh004 gesturing while describing how to remove hair from animal hide.

While producing this utterance in (11), YMGh004 slides the fingers on his right hand over his left hand. His two hands are perpendicular to each other, giving the impression that his right hand is a blade sliding over his left hand, which is depicting the hide. Notice that his utterance is not determinate in regard to how this process works. This demonstration provides information not present in the speech. This example provides evidence of two important aspects of gesture data. First, since the production of the *nīd* involves culture-specific knowledge, this example demonstrates information that would not be present in the speech alone. Second, this gesture demonstrates that not only does this speaker know how to describe the preparation of *nīd*, he also knows which actions are involved in such preparation and would likely be able to do it himself. In other words, while the gesture form is not particularly unique from a typological perspective, what it depicts is culture-specific knowledge/expertise.

Similarly, consider the following example in (12), Figure 1.6:

(12)

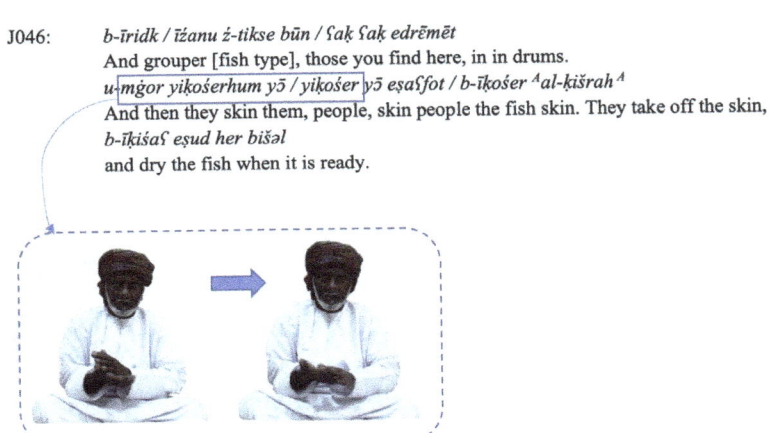

J046:   b-īridk / īźanu ź-tikse būn / ʕaḳ ʕaḳ edrēmēt
And grouper [fish type], those you find here, in in drums.
u-mġor yiḳośerhum yɔ̄ / yiḳośer yɔ̄ eṣaʕfot / b-īḳośer ᴬal-ḳiśrahᴬ
And then they skin them, people, skin people the fish skin. They take off the skin,
b-īḳiśaʕ eṣud her biśəl
and dry the fish when it is ready.

Figure 1.6 J046 gesturing while describing how to remove the skin from a fish.

In (12) J046 is producing an almost identical gesture to YMGh004 (although the hands are reversed). However, what this speaker is describing is the process of taking the skin off a fish. Like (11), (12) is a display of expert knowledge indexing the community of the speaker. Like (11), the linguistic description of the process of skinning the fish is left underspecified.

These two examples, which relate the preparation of *nīd* and dried fish respectively, are important because the speakers come from different regions, speak different languages and are describing different cultural practices. However, in both instances the linguistic contribution to their description underdetermines the process they are describing and in both cases the gesture provides additional information. This information not only helps preserve the underlying knowledge associated with such activities but also demonstrates the speaker-specific expertise involved in such processes.

Expert understanding of flora

Continuing the idea of gesture revealing speaker-specific expertise, when YMGh004 describes the process of producing waterskins he also describes several local florae which are used in the process. One plant which is used in this process is referred to as *xūrṭərāṭ*. When the speaker mentions *xūrṭərāṭ* he produces the first gesture in the gesture sequence, where the fingers on his right are splayed and pointing upwards. He then goes on to direct his recipient to his gesture and produces a more elaborate two-handed gesture. This two-handed gesture appears to depict the same thing.

(13)

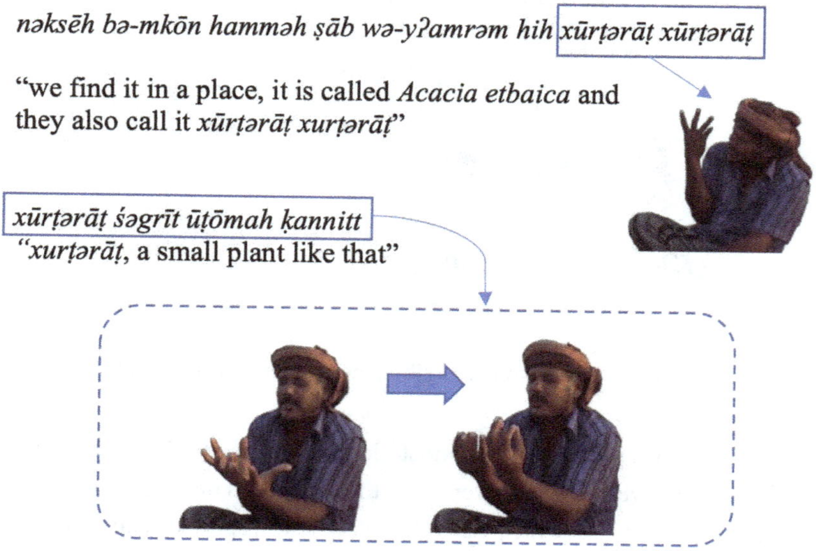

nəksēh bə-mkōn hammǝh ṣāb wǝ-yʔamrǝm hih *xūrṭərāṭ xūrṭərāṭ*

"we find it in a place, it is called *Acacia etbaica* and they also call it *xūrṭərāṭ xurṭərāṭ*"

xūrṭərāṭ ṣ̌əgrīt ūṭōmah kannitt
"*xurṭərāṭ*, a small plant like that"

Figure 1.7 YMGh004 depicting plant in gesture.

In (13), Figure 1.7, the speaker, who does not describe what the plant looks like linguistically, is nonetheless able to represent what the plant looks like using representational gesture. The speaker produces the first gesture represented in (13) two times to coincide with the emphatic /ṭ/ at the end of the word *xūrṭərāṭ*. This gesture appears to depict the opening of a flower with the fingers representing the petals. He then produces a similar handshape, this time incorporating both hands, explicitly directing his interlocutor to his gesture *ūṭōmah ḳannitt* ('like that, small').

Personification of animals

In this section, we outline a practice frequently found within the data that include the description of animals. This is where the speaker produces character viewpoint gestures in which they take the place of the animal described. As mentioned above character viewpoint gestures involve producing gestures from a first-person perspective. In the recordings, we regularly see gestures where the perspective of an animal (specifically livestock) is adopted in gesture.

In the description shown in (14), Figure 1.8, YMGh005 is describing how a bridle is fitted to a camel's head. However, when he is describing the placement of the bridle, he uses his own body as a locus of the different locations the bridle needs to be attached.

(14)

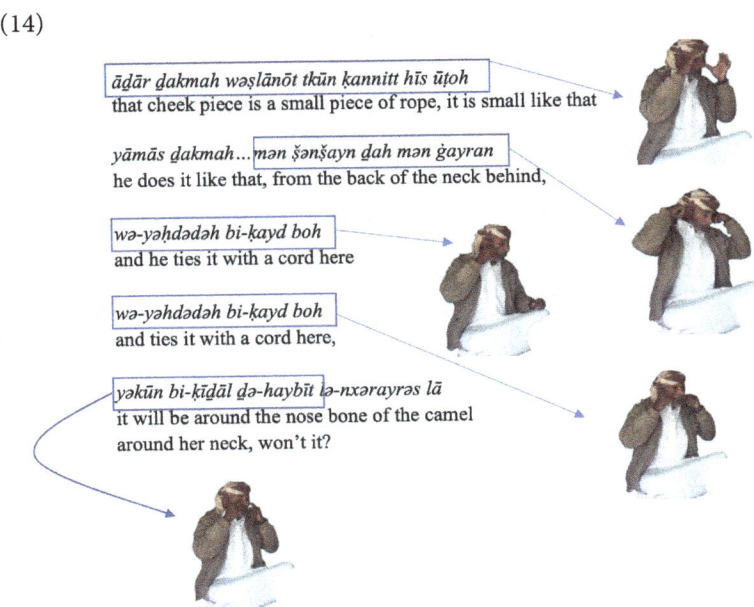

āḏār ḏakmah waṣlānōt tkūn ḳannitt hīs ūṭoh
that cheek piece is a small piece of rope, it is small like that

yāmās ḏakmah... mən šənšayn ḏah mən ġayran
he does it like that, from the back of the neck behind,

wə-yəḥdədəh bi-ḳayd boh
and he ties it with a cord here

wə-yəḥdədəh bi-ḳayd boh
and ties it with a cord here,

yəkūn bi-ḳīḏāl ḏə-haybīt lə-nxərayrəs lā
it will be around the nose bone of the camel around her neck, won't it?

Figure 1.8 YMGh005 producing first-person gestures while describing a camel's bridle.

Character viewpoint gestures are a regular gestural practice seen around the world. However, we think character viewpoint gestures used in Mehri demonstrate the close relationship that individuals have with their livestock.

Acoustic paths

In speech, it is possible to elongate or reduplicate when placing emphasis on something being described. For example, when given someone directions the description of a particularly long stretch could be present as 'you go::::: down the road' or 'you go and go and go and go down the road'. The first, which involves elongation, might be accompanied by a long, slow gesture depicting the length of the path, whereas the second might be accompanied by several repeated gestures. While some people might not consider such vocalizations to be gestures, they have been analysed within the ideophone literature as involving relative iconicity, often appearing in pairs (see Dingemanse et al. 2015). In the lab-based Śḥerēt and Mehri data, both of these patterns have been found (Watson and Wilson 2017). There also seems to be a language-specific dimension, with Śḥerēt speakers reduplicating and Mehri speakers elongating (however more data is needed to confirm this). Here, we focus on the usage of elongation and reduplication with accompanying gesture as produced by Mehri speaker M001. Our main point is that these practices are not simply about emphasis. The speaker appears to be vocally depicting either the length of some event (in space or time) or the intensity of an action. This data was recorded in the UK and the speaker was asked to describe the route from the university (where he was sitting) to the researcher's house which is about 2 miles away.

In (15–16), Figures 1.9–1.10, the speaker is describing walking to a bus stop. The vowel of the second syllable /ō/ of the word *təghōm* is elongated. Accompanying this elongated word is a gesture depicting the traversed path. As the speaker describes the end point of this path (the bus stop) he produces a placing gesture, depicting the bus stop at the end of the path he has just gestured.

(15)

tighō::::m tā tūṣōl
"You go until you reach"

Figure 1.9 M001 depicting path in gesture.

Language, Gesture and Ecology in Modern South Arabian Languages 39

(16)

ɛ: ḥanit / maḥaṭṭah ḏ-abāṣāt kiḏa / lin əghōm li-ʃʃimya lā
"er, such-and-such the bus stop because I don't go by foot"

Figure 1.10 M001 depicting placement of a bus stop in gesture.

In (17), Figure 1.11, the same speaker is describing a similar event where a path is being traversed until a salient point is reached. In this example, the end point is an alley. However, this time there is no vowel elongation. Instead, the verb *ghōm* 'go m.s.' is reduplicated and each reduplication is accompanied by a downward gesture.

(17)

wə-ghōm ghōm ghōm attā təksē məġṣayṣ
"and keep going until you find an alley"

Figure 1.11 M001 depicting path while reduplicating the word *ghōm*.

What is the difference between these two vocal gestures: elongation and reduplication? We believe that elongation is about time/space whereas reduplication is about repeated action. Although more data is required, further evidence for this can be found in the same narrative. There is no visible gesture accompanying (18), but the meaning of the verb is elongated, which is interesting.

(18) ḏayk ḏ-agarəs / dfiṣəs / wa-slō::::b / wət / attā yūḵōf wət ūḵawf kfēd /
'that for the bell. Press it. And wait. When it stops, when it stops get out'

In this example, the verb *slōb* 'wait' is elongated. Since waiting does not contain an obvious repeatable behaviour, it makes sense that it can be described using elongation if elongation relates to the time of an event.[2] However, when a speaker says *ghōm*, they may be referring to the path travelled or the act of travelling. In which case, there are obvious repeated behaviours that make up travelling (e.g. the repeated movement of the legs). We believe the difference between elongation and reduplication relates to what the speaker wants to focus on, either the length (in space or time) or the repeated activity. Notice also that this is not determined by the particular vowel used since examples (15–17) include the same vowel.

Conclusions

In this chapter we have shown only a snapshot of the gestural practices used by speakers of MSAL. This is primarily because gestural practices have not been the focus of past work on the MSAL. Our aim was to demonstrate that such practices are a crucial constituent part of a semiotic community and worthy of documentation. We have shown that gesture can reflect conventional visual practice (in the form of pointing handshapes). Such practices are instantly recognizable to community members, who may share an explicit understanding of their use and origin. We have highlighted how gesture can be linked to conceptualizations of space and time, potentially revealing phenomena that may not be observable otherwise. In doing so, we have also shown that gesture can interact with syntax in ways that help refine understandings of the grammatical structure of languages. Gesture also reveals culture-specific knowledge in relation to manual practice, expertise of local flora and the relationship between community members and livestock. Finally, we have also shown that gesture is not simply visual but may be realized vocally.

Notes

1. This objection comes from Stephen Levinson who questioned the data when it was presented as part of an invited talk.
2. A local Mehri researcher has said it is possible to reduplicate the verb '*slōb*' in the sense of 'wait quickly' or 'when it is urgent that someone waits'. This seems to match the pattern suggested here where reduplication relates to manner of the action rather than the length of time it takes.

References

Abner, N., K. Cooperrider and S. Goldin-Meadow (2015), 'Gesture for Linguists: A Handy Primer', *Language and Linguistics Compass*, 9 (11): 437–49.

Al-Qumairi, S. and J. C. E. Watson (2020), *Community Documentation of Biocultural Diversity in the Eastern Yemeni Province of al-Mahrah*, London: SOAS. Endangered Languages Archive, ELAR: ELAR Collections (elararchive.org)

Bloomfield, L. (1933), *Language*, London: Unwin University Books.

Boroditsky, L., O. Fuhrman and K. McCormick (2011), 'Do English and Mandarin Speakers Think about Time Differently?', *Cognition*, 118 (1): 123–9.

Brown, P. (2012), 'Time and Space in Tzeltal: Is the Future Uphill?', *Frontiers in Psychology*, 3 (212).

Calderon, E., S. De Pascale and E. Adamou (2019), 'How to Speak "Geocentric" in an "Egocentric" Language: A Multimodal Study among Ngigua-Spanish Bilinguals and Spanish Monolinguals in a Rural Community of Mexico', *Language Science*, 74: 24–46.

Clark, H. H. (1996), *Using Language*, Cambridge: Cambridge University Press.

Clark, H. H. (2003), 'Pointing and Placing', in S. Kita (ed.), *Pointing: Where Language, Culture, and Cognition Meet*, 243–68, London: Lawrence Erlbaum Associates Publishers.

Cooperrider, K. (2019), 'Universals and Diversity in Gesture: Research Past, Present and Future', *Gesture*, 18 (2–3): 209–38.

Cooperrider, K., J. Slotta and R. Nunez (2018), 'The Preference for Pointing with the Hand Is Not Universal', *Cognitive Science*, 42 (4): 1375–90.

Dingemanse, M., D. E. Blasi, G. Lupyan, M. H. Christiansen and P. Monaghan (2015), 'Arbitrariness, Iconicity, and Systematicity in Language', *Trends in Cognitive Sciences*, 19 (10): 603–15.

Enfield, N. J. (2001), 'Lip-Pointing: A Discussion of Form and Function with Reference to Data from Laos', *Gesture*, 1 (2): 185–211.

Floyd, S. (2016), 'Modally Hybrid Grammar? Celestial Pointing for Time-of-Day Reference in Nheengatu', *Language*, 92 (1): 31–64.

Fritz, I., S. Kita, J. Littlemore and A. Krott (2019), 'Information Packaging in Speech Shapes Information Packaging in Gesture: The Role of Speech Planning Units in the Coordination of Speech-Gesture Production', *Journal of Memory and Language*, 104: 56–69.

Fuhrman, O., K. McCormick, E. Chen, H. Jiang, D. Shu, S. Mao and L. Boroditsky (2011), 'How Linguistic and Cultural Forces Shape Conceptions of Time: English and Mandarin time in 3D', *Cognitive Science*, 35 (7): 1305–28.

Gu, Y., L. Mol, M. Hoetjes and M. Swerts (2017), 'Conceptual and Lexical Effects on Gestures: The Case of Vertical Spatial Metaphors for Time in Chinese', *Language, Cognition and Neuroscience*, 32 (8): 1048–63.

Gumperz, J. (2001 [1968]), 'The Speech Community', in A. Duranti (ed.), *Linguistic Anthropology: A Reader*, 43–52, Malden, MA: Blackwell.

Henrich, J., S. J. Heine and A. Norenzayan (2010), 'The Weirdest People in the World?' *Behavioral and Brain Sciences*, 33 (2–3): 61–83.

Hostetter, A. B. and M. W. Alibali (2008), 'Visible Embodiment: Gestures as Simulated Action', *Psychonomic Bulletin & Review*, 15 (3): 495–514.

Hostetter, A. B. and M. W. Alibali (2019), 'Gesture as Simulated Action: Revisiting the Framework', *Psychonomic Bulletin & Review*, 26 (3): 721–52.

Kataoka, K. (2013), '"We Just Don't Get It Right!" – Multimodal Competence for Resolving Spatial Conflict in Wayfinding Discourse', *Language & Communication*, 33 (4, Part A): 404–19.

Kendon, A. and L. Versante (2003), 'Pointing by Hand in "Neapolitan"', in S. Kita (ed.), *Pointing: Where Language, Culture, and Cognition Meet*, 117–46, London: Lawrence Erlbaum Associates Publishers.

Kita, S. (2009), 'Cross-Cultural Variation of Speech-Accompanying Gesture: A Review', *Language and Cognitive Processes*, 24 (2): 145–67.

Kita, S. and A. Özyürek (2003), 'What Does Cross-Linguistic Variation in Semantic Coordination of Speech and Gesture Reveal? Evidence for an Interface Representation of Spatial Thinking and Speaking', *Journal of Memory and language*, 48 (1): 16–32.

Kockelman, P. (2005), 'The Semiotic Stance', *Semiotica*, 157 (1/4): 233–304.

Le Guen, O. (2011), 'Modes of Pointing to Existing Spaces and the Use of Frames of Reference', *Gesture*, 11 (3): 271–307.

Levinson, S. C. (2003), *Space in Language and Cognition: Explorations in Cognitive Diversity*, Cambridge: Cambridge University Press.

Levinson, S. C. and A. Majid (2013), 'The Island of Time: Yelî Dnye, The Language of Rossel Island', *Frontiers in Psychology*, 4 (61): 1–11.

Li, Heng and Yu Cao (2019), 'Hands Occupied: Chinese Farmers Use More Non-Manual Pointing Than Herders', *Lingua*, 222 (April): 1–9.

Lupyan, G. and R. Dale (2010), 'Language Structure Is Partly Determined by Social Structure', *PLoS One*, 5 (1): e8559.

Liszkowski, U., P. Brown, T. Callaghan, A. Takada and C. de Vos (2012), 'A Prelinguistic Gestural Universal of Human Communication', *Cognitive Science*, 36 (4): 698–713.

Majid, A., M. Bowerman, S. Kita, D. Haun and S. C. Levinson (2004), 'Can Language Restructure Cognition? The Case for Space', *Trends in Cognitive Sciences*, 8 (3): 108–14.

McNeill, D. (1992), *Hand and Mind: What Gestures Reveal about Thought*. Chicago: University of Chicago Press.

McNeill, D. (2015), *Why We Gesture: The Surprising Role of Hand Movements in Communication*. Cambridge: Cambridge University Press.

Meakins, F. (2011), 'Spaced Out: Intergenerational Changes in the Expression of Spatial Relations by Gurindji People', *Australian Journal of Linguistics*, 31 (1): 43–77

Nunez, R. and K. Cooperrider (2013), 'The Tangle of Space and Time in Human Cognition', *Trends in Cognitive Science*, 17 (5): 220–9.

Nunez, R., K. Cooperrider, D. Doan and J. Wassmann (2012), 'Contours of Time: Topographic Construals of Past, Present, and Future in the Yupno Valley of Papua New Guinea', *Cognition*, 124 (1): 25–35.

Núñez, R. E. and E. Sweetser (2006), 'With the Future behind Them: Convergent Evidence from Aymara Language and Gesture in the Crosslinguistic Comparison of Spatial Construals of Time', *Cognitive Science*, 30 (3): 401–50.

Ola Orie, O. (2009), 'Pointing the Yoruba Way', *Gesture*, 9 (2): 237–61.

Povinelli, D. J. and D. R. Davis (1994), 'Differences between Chimpanzees (Pan Troglodytes) and Humans (Homo Sapiens) in the Resting State of the Index Finger: Implications for Pointing', *Journal of Comparative Psychology*, 108 (2): 1–34.

Simeone-Senelle, M-Cl. (1997), 'Modern South Arabian', in R. Hetzron (ed.), *The Semitic Languages*, 378–423, London: Routledge.

Simeone-Senelle, M-Cl. (2011), 'Modern South Arabian', in S. Weniger, G. Khan, M. Streck and J. C. E. Watson (eds), *The Semitic Languages: An International Handbook*, 1073–113, Berlin: Walter de Gruyter.

Talmy, L. (2000), *Toward a Cognitive Semantics, Vol. II: Typology and Process in Concept Structuring*, Cambridge, MA: MIT Press.

Watson, J. C. E. and M. J. Morris (2016a), *Documentation of the Modern South Arabian Languages: Mehri*. ID: Mehri (0307), London: SOAS. Endangered Languages Archive, ELAR: ELAR Collections (elararchive.org).

Watson, J. C. E. and M. J. Morris (2016b), *Documentation of the Modern South Arabian Languages: Shehret*. ID: Shehret (0308), London: SOAS. Endangered Languages Archive, ELAR: ELAR Collections (elararchive.org).

Watson, J. C. E. and J. Wilson (2017), 'Gesture in Modern South Arabian Languages: Variation in Multimodal Constructions during Task-Based Interaction', *Brill's Journal of Afroasiatic Languages and Linguistics*, 9: 49–72.

Wilkins, D. (2003), 'Why Pointing with the Index Finger Is Not a Universal (in Sociocultural and Semiotic Terms)', in S. Kita (ed.), *Pointing: Where Language, Culture, and Cognition Meet*, 179–224, London: Lawrence Erlbaum Associates Publishers.

Part One

Arabia: The Significance of Names and Words

2

What's in a Name?

Miranda Morris

I wish to acknowledge here my immense debt to all the people in Dhofar and Soqoṭra who offered me hospitality. They gave so generously of their time to help me, and displayed such patience and forbearance under a constant barrage of requests for information and elucidation. Apart from some material on plant names (in Miller A.G. and Morris M.J. 1988 and 2004) and the odd reference in various articles, the information presented here has not previously appeared in print.

Introduction

The Roman playwright, Plautus, (c. 254–184 BCE), wrote: *Nomen est omen*, 'The name is a sign', a statement I want to look into as regards the Modern South Arabian Languages (MSAL[1]) and the culture of the communities who speak them. Naming is one of the most basic elements of language, one of the first acquired by infants (Boysson-Bardies 2001) and both defining and defined by our cultures (Evans 2010).

> The material discussed here was collected over many years. I lived in Dhofar from 1975–80, first working for the Civil Aid Department, Office of the Minister of Dhofar, and then helping to establish the Dhofar Rural Health Service for the Ministry of Health. Thereafter (1982–95), sponsored by the Diwan of Royal Court and at the request of the late Sultan Qaboos (whose mother was from Dhofar), I made two two-month-long fieldtrips to Dhofar a year, living with families from the different language communities to work on the non-Arabic languages of the region and the culture and traditions of their speakers. Much of the material below, in Hobyōt, Śḥerēt, Mehri and Baṭḥari, is from this period. I made my first visit to the island of Soqoṭra in 1989 and went on to work there on a variety of projects until 2011. During this period, I continued to make sporadic visits to Dhofar, and then from 2012–16 worked with Janet Watson on the project Documentation and ethnolinguistic analysis of the Modern South Arabian languages, funded by the Leverhulme Trust. This involved some four months of fieldwork a year in Dhofar, during which I was able to develop and expand my earlier research.

Languages are closely linked to their environment (Dunn 2017; Loh and Harmon 2014; Prance 1991; WWF 2018) and here I discuss the naming practices that demonstrate the links the MSAL and their related cultures have to their environment. It is immediately clear that many names give useful clues about the thing named, a matter of key importance for a child starting to learn about the natural environment. In this chapter I discuss the various ideas around naming in the MSAL-speaking communities, and the ways a name can in itself help identify the entity named. I illustrate this with multiple examples in the various languages.

In the first section I talk about the way a name can teach children something about a plant, suggest habit or lifestyle of the thing named, point to a specific characteristic or evoke some cultural significance. Examples of evocative and colourful names are given, and of names which amuse or entertain, all helpful to recognition. I then look at how matters of great communal consequence are described in exhaustive detail.

In the second section I review naming as it concerns the appearance of the thing named, how names can be shared and how they are often linked in pairs, either by one name being a diminutive form of the other, or by one marking a positive aspect of an entity and the other a negative one. I then look at naming as it concerns livestock husbandry, people (individually and as part of a group), places and the marking of time. Next, I give examples of names which have short ditties or rhymes attached to them, before looking briefly at how names can change over time.

In the third section, I look at the way some names are avoided, suppressed, deliberately obfuscated or concealed.

The importance of names

Names can be important for indicating crucial distinctions, for signalling cultural significance, and especially for educating the next generation. This has been shown to be true in cultures around the world when investigating the systems of categorization in other cultures as well (Leonti 2011).

Vegetation and livestock

All languages divide the natural environment around them into a variety of categories (Evans 2010). Where the MSAL are notable is in the level of detail each name has. Whereas in English we often modify generic words such as 'tree' with a type – 'apple tree', 'palm tree', 'maple tree', etc. – the MSAL have unique names for many plant species found in their environment. These names can help children learn which plants benefit which animals. For example, an annual Cyperaceae which produces tiny underground bulbils is called (H) *rġod ḏə-ṣāʿar*, 'grazing for gazelle'; on Soqoṭra, *Pulicaria diversifolia* and *Heliotropium riebeckii* are *ḥáṣ̌keḳ di-ilhítin*, '*ḥáṣ̌keḳ* for cows', while *Scrophularia arguta* is *ṣafáḳa di-ílǝhe*, 'the *ṣafáḳa* for cattle' (*ṣafáḳa* referring to a group of plants with irritating or stinging hairs, as *Urtica* [Urticaceae] and *Tragia* [Euphorbiaceae]). Tough, cushion-forming plants like *Indigofera marmorata*, much liked by camels, are *zeydiro di-bəʿeyr*, '*zeydiro* for camels'; another favoured by donkeys *zeydiro di-ḥə́mār*, 'donkey's *zeydiro*', while a prostrate *Convolvulus* of the high plateau sheep-walks is *ḳaʾ di-tētin*, 'threads for sheep'. Bird names too can be helpful in identification, as (H) *ʿakəbít maġəlíf*, 'bird of the *məġalíf* "*Ruttya fruticosa*" plant', the name for the sunbird which loves these nectar-filled flowers.

Names can also teach children what is good about a plant. On Soqoṭra we find many small plants with names from the root √ḥlb, 'to milk an animal' and √ḥlbb, '(female) to leak milk', such as *di-ḥálbeb, di-ḥalbíbihon* (pl.), *ḥalébleb ~ ḥalebéboh* (dim.). Browsing such plants is believed to improve milk yield. Other plants regarded as especially rich fodder have names like *di-məḥáḥōn*, pl. *il-məḥáhon*, from *maḥḥ*, 'bone marrow', regarded as the richest part of a carcass. In Dhofar, various small but excellent fodder plants such as *Kickxia qaraica* are (Ś) *tūr érún*, 'dates for she-goats', and plants like *Ruttya fruticosa* which offer the most succulent rains-grazing for camels are *tūr iyyél*, 'dates for she-camels'. In Mehri, *Omania* or *Lindenbergia* plants are often called *tōmər ḏə-bʿayr*, 'dates for the camel', and on Soqoṭra, a group of delicate plants with sweet-smelling flowers are called *tímihor* or *támerhən*, 'little dates' (dim. forms of *támer*, 'dates'). Before sugar became widely available in southern Arabia, dates were the principal source of sweetness, so it is perhaps not surprising that names involving dates should appear for plants valued for their 'sweetness'.

A name can also advise when a plant is not a good fodder for livestock, as on Soqoṭra, where various small and unpalatable ferns and Cyperaceae species of no nutritional value are called *ḥámẓ̌ig*, 'milk-less' or 'lacking in generosity'.

A name can suggest where and when a plant is likely to be found. On Soqoṭra, it is not uncommon to find the same plant bearing a different name in eastern and western parts of the island, as shown in Table 2.1.

Table 2.1 Plant Names in Eastern and Western Soqoṭra

Plant	Name in Eastern Soqoṭra	Name in Western Soqoṭra
Leucas virgata	harítreṭ	nówḥul or nōmḥul
Gnidea socotrana	ḳíṭaher	laʔēyəf
Adenium obesum	tərīmo	ásfəd
Punica protopunica	rihīni	míśəṭ

Many plant names helpfully describe where a plant is likely to grow: nówḥel ḥégirhi, 'nówḥel of the central highlands', distinguishing *Leucas penduliflora* from other *Leucas* species; faʔ ḥagərhīyo, 'Aerva of the central mountains', differentiating *Aerva lanata* from the more widespread *A. javanica*, and kerṯīb adáʕan, 'kerṯīb of the stony plain', distinguishing the poisonous *Euphorbia hadramautica* from the harmless *Dorstenia foetida* 'kerṯīb' of other regions. *Anogeissus dhofarica* is called (H) míśeṭ in western Dhofar and (Ś) ṣgót in the centre and east. The name (S) məṣírbihon for a group of leafy herbs that come up after the winter rains (ṣerb) on Soqoṭra indicates when these plants are likely to be found.

Names indicating habit or lifestyle

A name can suggest something about the habit or lifestyle of the entity named. In the insect world, for example, the fearsome-looking water scorpion is called (H) ḥéjər də-ḥəmóh, 'the water guardian'; the antlion (Myrmeleontidae), digging its traps in sandy ground to catch other insects, (H) ṭebərīn əboṯḥ, 'the hyena of soft ground', and a very venomous snake məḳérreb əl-kfen, 'the one that brings the shroud close'. Ants are believed to be aware of impending rainfall: on Soqoṭra, black ants scurrying across the ground carrying their eggs are thought to be moving their young out of reach of forthcoming rain and are called sébəha (< √sby, 'to pack up and move one's family elsewhere'), while in Dhofar, people seeing the same thing say (Ś) iniśún iṭīréd īnōhum, 'the ants are taking their children to a place of shelter (from rain)'.

Among plants, the sweetly scented lavender is known rather charmingly as (Ś) heryên ɛ-kulún, 'the little plant of the bridal bed'; the wild olive, a vital timber tree, is called (Ś) mōṭīn, while the smaller shrub, *Rhamnus staddo*, is either called (Ś) jifərít mōṭīn (jifərít is a dried cucumber kept back for seed, or a worn-out leather milk-skin) or (H) ḥojirít də-mīṭīn, 'the female slave of the wild olive', signalling its inferiority.

It was extremely important that children learn to recognize certain key plants, and not only to distinguish between edible ones and those that are poisonous or harmful. For example, in earlier times in Dhofar, there was a tradition that the camels and goats of the dry areas behind and in front of the monsoon mountains would not come into the mountains to feed on the lush greenery (Ś *śéfe*, 'grazing as yet untouched') brought up by the monsoon drizzle and mists until the leaves of the deciduous *śɔ́kof* '*Commiphora gileadensis*' and the *zəbrót* '*Jatropha dhofarica*' had begun to turn colour and fall. It was vital that children of herding families knew from an early age which these trees were and what they signified.

Among the Baṭāḥira, both the rainbow runner and the black-banded trevally are named *ḥagərít lə-ṣəṭráx* 'female slave of the greater amberjack'. Both these fish are indeed related to the highly prized *ṣəṭráx* 'greater amberjack', but their name clearly indicates their lesser value. A brightly coloured wrasse that follows parrotfish around, picking up invertebrates disturbed by their passage or feeding on any debris they let fall, is (Ś) *ʿáṣər ɛ-xēṭ* 'the close friend of the parrotfish', which teaches that a sighting of this wrasse suggests a parrotfish in the vicinity.

A name can point to a specific characteristic of the entity named. For example, a weed which spreads rapidly across the ground after rains is (Ś) *īdərór* 'seeded' (< √bdr, 'to sow seed'), while a species of *Cocculus* is (Ś) *herúm īdərí* 'strange plant', and this plant is indeed rare in Dhofar. The Baṭāḥira call the suckerfish (remora) *ləṣāk̲*, 'sticks on', and certain stingrays, *mənāk̲iś* (< √nk̲ś, 'to prick, penetrate the skin'), while on Soqotra we find *ṣəṭīʿo* (< *esṭīʿo*, pl. *ésṭaʿ*, 'cinder, red ember') as a name for stingrays. Striped species of Moray eel with their fearsome teeth and skulking manner are (Ś) *k̲éṣer ɛ-rébrem ~ ɛ-rémnem*, (M) *k̲ayṣer d̲ə-rōnəm*, (B) *k̲ēṣər l-ərawnə*, 'leopard of the sea'. Some names have onomatopoeic elements as well: grunters (Haemulidae, 'grunt' deriving from the noise made by the grinding of their pharyngeal teeth) are (B) *gəmgēm* (< √gmgm, 'to make muffled sounds; to mutter beneath the breath'), and the whirligig beetle (Gyrinidae) is (S) *gəligɔ́lo*, pl. *gəlōgəhil* (< √glgl, 'to move this way and that').

A name can describe a specific aspect of the thing named. In plants, the tough *Campylanthus spinosus* is (S) *mírigo*, 'causing gaps in the teeth'; the painfully spiny *Campylanthus spinosus* (S) *zímgilo*, 'swarm of bees'; spiked plants (S) *ṣáʿiyud* or *məṣūʾidān* (√ṣʾd, 'to prick or pierce'); crisp plants such as *Lachnocapsa* are (S) *śáhyīm* (< √śhm, 'to crunch sth. hard'), and many *Launaeas* with their milky exudate are called either (S) *dúwrir* 'exuding a little blood' or (S) *śíberhən* 'with caustic latex'. A very tough grass of Dhofar is known as (Ś) *fḏolót ɛ-ġóṣeb*, (H) *fḏilót eġóṣeb*, 'yanks out the teeth of the breeding bull' (the same name was also given to a type of very hard sorghum which was imported in a year when local harvests failed). In the animal world, the porcupine is (Ś) *enṭelít* (< √nṭl, 'to fire a projectile'), while (H) has *ber ḥaśwēk*, 'the one with spines'. The taste of a plant can appear in its name: in all the MSAL, various acidic-tasting herbs are given names based on the term *ḥamṣ*, 'fermented milk', while aloes are called variants of *ṭuf* or *ṭayf*, 'bitter', accurately describing the taste of the medicinal gel extracted from them. For plants with sour-tasting leaves we find on Soqoṭra *ṣəbérhon*, *ṣábəher* and the diminutive form *ṣabérbəher* 'sour', and for plants such as *Dyerophytum* with their salty leaves and stems *ómlaḥ* (< *mílḥo*, 'salt'). *Ruttya fruticosa* shrubs whose bright red, nectar-filled flowers are sucked for their sweetness are called (Ś and M) *mṣīṣí* 'good to suck' and (H) *débəh ḏə-ḥaybīt*, 'honey for the she-camel', while on Soqoṭra, *mīṣeṣ* (from the same root with the same meaning), is the name given to *Ballochia* and *Trichocalyx* species whose flowers are similarly nectar-rich.

Some creatures have informative and colourful names that make it easier for children to learn them. Examples among insects are: (S) *ṣhárihin*, pl. *ṣhérəhan*, 'cauterises itself', for moths, from their attraction to flame; (S) *ʔídbihir d-ikādaḥ*, 'buzzing insect that drills' (< √kdḥ, 'to rub sticks to make a fire; to dig in with the point of sth.'), for a sawfly, in reference to the saw-like ovipositor of the female; (S) *miẑōbihin di-ġob / di-ʕub*, 'roller of faecal matter', for a dung beetle (< √gbn, 'to squeeze and roll into a sausage or ball shape'). In Hobyōt a dung beetle is *yḵalʕōd b-kerdót*, 'it rolls a lump of human excrement'.[2] Among MSA-speaking communities, the praying mantis is associated with the supernatural: (Ś) *gūl ɛ-ṣáḥer*, 'riding camel of the sorcerer'; (B) *ḥaybīt lə-ġínniy*, 'female riding camel of a jinn'; (H) *rēkeb eswāḥer*, 'mount of the sorcerers'; (M) variously *ḥaybīt ḏə-gehəlét*, 'female camel of a male demon', *erkīb ḏə-ginní*, 'mount of a jinn', or *rēkəb ḏ-iblīs*, 'mount of the devil'. The anteater spider (?Oecobiidae), hiding in its burrow, is (S) *ḵeṣer ɛ-ḏibbót*, (B) *ḵéṣer lə-ḏəbīb*, (M) *ḵayṣer ḏə-ḏəbēb*, 'leopard of the flies', or (H) *tebərīn əbóṯḥ* 'hyena of soft ground'.

Many birds have memorable names: (H) *ḏə-ḵəbərót ʕōms*, (Ś) *eḵērót ʕōs*, 'she buried her grandfather', for the pheasant-tailed Jacana,[3] because 'it is always poking away in lagoons'; (S) *məkídoʰ* 'startling' (< √wkd, 'to startle') for the sandgrouse, from the way it whirrs up from the ground at the last moment. (It has an alternative descriptive name: *girgíro*, pl. *girōgihir*, 'chuckling, gurgling'.) On Soqoṭra, an owl is *šigídəhān* (< *šígəhid*, 'to stare fixedly at sth., so.'), but it has other names illustrating other aspects of the bird: *di-ḵəwrēni*, 'two horned', *d-iṣályən mágərib*, 'it performs the sunset prayers', or *d-iṣályən tarāwiḥ*, 'it performs the night-time prayers of Ramadan'.

Naming and cultural significance

A name can suggest the cultural significance of the thing named. On Soqotra, *Heliotropium odorata* is called *ḳəṭmámhiyon*, a diminutive form of *ḳáṭəmhim*, 'lump of fresh butter', and this plant was used to tan leather, especially the leather bags in which butter was churned, in the belief that this would encourage the butter to form. The living plant was also gathered and fed to livestock to increase their milk yield. In Dhofar, a common plant of the coastal plains, *Blepharis linariaefolia*, is called (Ś) *śebbīn*, 'young men', as its seed heads were charred and pulverized to dress the wounds of circumcision, an operation traditionally carried out on adolescents. On Soqotra, the small carpal bone, the *os pisiformis*, of a goat or sheep carcass is *di-ʿarāyis*, 'of the bride': is said that a nervous and distracted young bride would sometimes eat this by mistake and choke on it. The Baṭāḥira say of the bat: *əmaḥwəṭāt el ḥad yəḳśébəh wələ ḥad yaʿwéḏən teh la mən sāʿat, mən hes xalákan: ḥawṭət*, 'The bat: no-one harms or cuts it, from ages past, from the day we were created: this would bring on a *ḥawṭət* curse'. *maḥwəṭāt* is from the same root as *ḥawṭət*, 'a (divine) curse placed on a person as a result of unacceptable behaviour.' One name for the solitary hoopoe with its striking crest feathers is (Ś) *ʿeśyít ɛ-sebəró(r)*, (H) *ʿakəbít esebəró(r)*, 'bird of the spirits of the dead', or (Ś) *ṣaʿnín ɛ-sebəró(r)*, 'cockscomb of the spirits of the dead', voicing the misgivings speakers have about this bird (though both languages have a more prosaic name for it as well: Ś *ēśerék*, H *meśerék*, 'comb' in reference to its crest). In the days before wrist watches, children were taught to tell the time by observing plants. For example, the flowers of *Luffa acutangula* (H *jénijend*, Ś *iśi*) turn to face the sun in the afternoon, even when there is cloud, and those of *Hermannia paniculata* (H and Ś *xarṭerít*) do the same at midday: the first gives the time of the afternoon prayer and the second the time for the midday prayer. Among the Baṭāḥira, specific terms describe when fish have been netted: *ḥōbēb*, 'netted at dusk'; *ġadf*, 'netted late at night', and *ġamśét*, 'netted in the earliest dawn'.

Naming to amuse

Names can be amusing or ribald, which no doubt makes them easier to recall. Some examples in plants are (Ś): *ʿagəréz ɛ-śáxər*, 'old man's testicles' for the brown, wrinkled bulbs of a *Pancratium* species of no value to humans or livestock; ōsɔ́t ɛ-šaxərít, 'old woman's pubic hair' for small *Portulaca* species which form grey, wispy cushions. A low-growing, spiky plant that grows amongst the *Gladiolus* whose delicious corms are dug up and eaten is called (H) *xumḵ beḏəḥōtən*, 'pokes the bottoms of the women gathering *Gladiolus* corms', or *yənīk ḥaynəṯ* 'fornicates with the women'. *Sarcostemma viminale* is (H) *ṣ́áxəm jēber* (< √ṣ́xm, 'to chew on sth. hard' or 'to eat sth. not quite respectable', *jēber* 'vagina'), and *Antichariss glandulosa*, a figwort in the Scrophulariaceae, is (M) *gēbər ḳāṣəm*, 'cold vagina'. Soqoṭra's 'rudest' plant name seems to be *ṣ́erṭhanítin*, 'many farts', a name given to all the foul-smelling *Neogaillona* spp., and even this is usually toned down to *di-ṣīnem*, 'the stinker'.

Naming in minute detail

A striking feature of naming is the way elements of great cultural significance to a community are described in particular detail.

Flora

In plants, this is true of *Acacia tortilis*, the key plant of the drier and desert areas of Dhofar, or the famous *Boswellia* frankincense tree.[4] On Soqoṭra, similar attention to detail is given to the Dragon's Blood tree, *Dracaena cinnabari*, once commercially important, and to the vital date palm. Each part of the plant has a specific name, and any member of the community hearing one of these would know immediately which plant was being discussed.

Examples of terms for *Acacia tortilis* are (Ś): *maʕśíś*, 'new green shoots'[5] > *ʔekóś*, 'unfurled new leaves' > *axəlít́*, 'fallen mature leaves' or 'desiccated young leaves' > *ḥarér*, 'buds' > *sōr*, 'flowers' > *forṣ́*, 'immature pods' > *ḥīźít*, 'mature pods' > *enḳíśít*, 'dry pods fallen to the ground'. Or (B): *ewḳāś*, 'new green foliage' > *ḥebəlīt*, 'full-sized green pods' > *ḥebéb*, 'seeds now forming inside pods' > *ʕanəṣāt*, 'fully grown pods, changing colour and seeds hardening' > *neṣəlēt*, 'ripe brown pods starting to drop' > *nəḳaśīt*, 'brown dried-out pods on the ground' (see also al-Mahri and Boom 2020).

On Soqoṭra, *Dracaena cinnabari* berries were an important dry-season fodder, as well as indicating the health of the tree and its readiness for harvest. Examples of detail for the development of these are (S): *ʕášyuḳ*, 'flowering spike' > *fúʔhu*, 'emerging young green fruit' > *ḥílə*, 'immature green fruit now berry-size' > *ḳarīni*, 'berries turning colour' > *bíśərə*, 'fully ripe red berries'. Other parts of the tree also have specialized terms, such as *séned*, 'dead bark',

ʔīdəḥáʿ, 'processed under-bark', śkeʿámo or éṣlaʿ, 'living leaflet', ṣaʿf, 'dead leaflet', and emṣólo, 'resin'.

Children had to learn specific terms for parts of other significant trees too. For example, in Dhofar, the highly valued foliage of *Boswellia* is (Ś) ṭɛl, that of *Acacia senegal* is (Ś) ʿaźifít and its flowers enśór; the foliage of *Euphorbia balsamifera* is (Ś) ġalfít and its fruit gaʿmút; the flowers of *Anogeissus dhofarica* are (Ś) bīyít and its fruit (Ś) keḏirít. They also had to learn that only the summer foliage of the (Ś) ṭik and (Ś) ġiṣ́ít fig trees is called (Ś) fórog rather than (Ś) ḳolb, the name for the foliage of other trees which come into leaf in the great heat of summer even without rain.

Fauna

Creatures which play a key role in a community are also carefully itemized. For instance, among the Baṭāḥira, who hunted shark to trade for those things they were unable to produce themselves, the most valuable sharks are described according to age, growth stage, when and how many young they bear, the time of reaching Baṭhari waters, from where and in pursuit of which fish. So, for the blacktip shark we find (B): ḥazāzi, 'a mature specimen'; bəkāni or ʿaklūl, 'an immature one'; ḏəmāwi, 'a large specimen'; baʿl miśkōḳ, 'one which can be split lengthways into several sections', an exceptionally large one. Children are taught that it arrives in their area with the summer sardines (hence an alternative name, ber ʿayd, 'the child of the sardines' or bilʿayd, 'with the sardines'), and bears 10–12 young in the winter 'at the time of the ləḥēmer star' (November, December). They learn that in terms of commerce – for the sale or barter of its salted flesh and fins – shark can further be described as mansūf, if larger maṭlūṭ, and if larger still marbūʿ. The turtle, formerly hunted and eaten by the Baṭāḥira as a rare source of meat, is described in even greater detail, especially the different parts of its carcass.

Foodstuffs and drinking

For communities living in an often hostile environment, elements crucial to survival, such as food, pasturage for their animals, and water, are carefully defined.

For example, fat was a vital energy source for people who were often hungry and whose life was hard. On Soqotra, in addition to the general word, śabḥ, 'fat', to describe pericardial, omental, perinephric and mesenteric fat, there are additional terms, such as: ḥigihel di-ʔílbib, 'fat around the heart'; di-ríṣraṣ, 'fat around the abomasum'; śēsíyo, 'fat of the omentum'; maxx / maḥḥ, 'bone marrow'; *di-bērək*, 'fat and gristle of the breastbone'; *kərṣólo di-míʿho* or *fer di-míʿho*, 'fatty part at the extremity of the small intestine' (possibly the terminal ileum); *lášlaṣ (di-ʿayn)* or *mənśówbaḥ di-ʿayn*, 'fat behind the eyes'; *kəhəlá (di-ʿayn)* or *šigídəhān (di-ʿayn)*, 'the tiny amount of fat that remains behind the eye in even the most starved animal', and, after cooking the carcass in water, *ṣiṭálo*, 'layer of fat that congeals on the surface of the cold cooking liquid'.

Equal care is taken in describing an animal in terms of the fat its carcass will yield (S): *rídrid*, 'sickly or starved animal whose meat and fat will be over-soft and slimy'; *mənḳīʿo*, 'carcass with little fat or bone marrow'; *bíkəbak*, 'carcass with little and tasteless fat'; *dímax / dímaḥḥ*, 'carcass with a lot of bone marrow' (and the diminutive, *miyówḥeḥ*, 'carcass with barely any bone marrow'); *ḥagul mes ílbib*, 'carcass with only a little fat around the heart and minimal bone marrow'; *śílihil*, 'carcass with some bone marrow but little fat elsewhere'; *ə́bloġo*, 'carcass with no fat other than some bone marrow'; *ə́bloġo rəhé*, 'carcass with no fat except some in the head'; *nífyiṭ* (lit. 'nasal mucous'), 'animal too starved or sickly to provide anything edible'. Best of all is *rōdi*, 'with so much fat that not only will it "fill all three" (i.e. the *ḥáwro* "large bowel", the *lə́bəhon* "rectum", and the *darṣ* "abomasum"), but there will still be enough left to stuff the various pouches of the *śériś* rumen'.

Drinking: The importance of liquid for survival – and where water was not abundant, of milk derivatives – is reflected in the vocabulary to do with drinking.

For instance, on Soqotra, we find (S): *nésuz*, 'to sip sth. hot'; *níṣaf*, 'to take small sips (usually of milk or buttermilk)'; *ʿə́gər*, 'to drink a long draught, gulp down thirstily'; *máḥaṣ*, 'to take a mouthful; (young) to take milk for the first time' (and from a related root, *imḥáṣiṣin*, 'to drink slowly and deeply'); *mížug*, 'to slurp noisily'; *míšig*, 'to take a sip from a milk bowl before passing it on'; *mə́žar*, 'to take a sip directly from a water- or milk-skin' (√mgr/); *láʿaḳ*, 'to dip a finger into liquid and lick it'; *miṣ*, 'to suck' and 'to dip two fingers into a liquid and suck them'; *ḳáḥaṣ*, 'to wipe the first and second finger around the inside of a container and lick them'; *lúḥuk*, 'to drink from one's hand'; *míśul*, 'to scoop up some liquid and give a little to so. else in the cupped hand'.

Pasturage

Pasturage was crucial to survival for a people with little other than their livestock to support them. On Soqotra, the development of grasses and herbs (S *ḳə́ṣaho*, dim. *ḳəṣúwṣə*, 'fresh green grass or herbs'), and the state of the rangeland as a whole is meticulously classified.

Some examples for grasses are: *midyāmə*, 'with fully developed leaves (though as yet no flowering head)'; *érkaḥ ḳélhem*, 'flowering heads present'; *érkaḥ śémraḥ*, 'fruiting heads present'; *śáʿfur*, 'fruiting heads present but seeds fallen'; *kə́nšfo*, 'chewed down stumps remaining'; *ʿād biḥ ṭarb*, 'stalks remaining'; *ḥōsir*, 'grazed out'.

Examples for *rúʿud, / rógod*[6] 'edible greenery' in general are (S) *ítbib*, 'odd tiny shoot here and there'; *nikéśə*, 'patches of greenery here and there'; *śíśir ḥádəb*, 'faint flush of green across the ground'; *gusíbib*, 'changing colour as the greenery starts to die back'; *yəḳāśaʿ*, 'drying out' > *śáʿar*, 'standing hay' > *iḥiṭímim*, 'nothing but crumbling straw fragments'.

As the flush of rains greenery matures and dies back, the rangeland goes from (S): *ṣōṣ́īyə*, 'greenery everywhere in great quantities' > *ənfígo*, 'pastures in excellent condition and perennial grasses covered in a sugary substance' > *śéṣ́aher*, 'green and flourishing' > *ḥígwəhe*, 'starting to dry out' > *ḥálḥal*, 'yellowing, fading' > *tírihi*, 'drying out but still with some moisture' (considered optimum grazing for cows and goats) > *ḥálkək*, 'half dried' > *ḥeryómo~ḥárihum*, 'only a little greenery remaining'[7] > *śaʿr*, 'standing hay'. If the rangeland is not rested as it should be at this stage, it turns from *ḥōsir*, 'grazed out' > *māṣ́əl*, 'quite bare' (i.e. no *ṣáʿluf*, 'leaves' and no *máḥliṭo*, 'dead leaves on the ground'. Good livestock herders pride themselves on never letting an area become *māṣ́əl*, but instead move their animals elsewhere before this stage is reached) > *ə́ṣlaḥ~míṣlaḥ* 'nothing growing from the ground, no foliage on trees or shrubs, and no trace of earlier herbs and grasses'. *ə́ṣlaḥ ~ míṣlaḥ* also describes an area where all the soil has been blown or washed away, and at this stage, the rangeland is in real danger of irreversible desertification.

Rains grazing is also defined in terms of the livestock grazing it, either in the simplest terms, as (S): *di-sḗrəd*, 'for a lamb or kid' > *di-téʾe*, 'for a sheep' > *di-óʾoz*, 'for a mature goat' > *di-ílǝhe*, 'for a mature cow'; or in greater detail, as *ḳə́śəho di-súwred*, 'enough for a very young lamb or kid' > *śébaʿ di-írǝhan*, 'enough to fill mature goats' > *rǝḥúwḥa*[8] *di-fólihi*, 'enough for a calf to get a lick' > *ḳabṣ́*[9] *di-ílǝhe*, 'enough for a cow to get between its teeth'.

The state of the rangeland

Like pastoralists the world over, people on Soqotra are always asking one another about the state of the rangeland: exactly where had the rain fallen, how heavily and how had it affected the rangeland? Some examples of replies are: *túwʾeh*, 'sth. to eat', i.e. for small stock; *kḗrhe kə́nšfo*, 'little more than grazed-down stumps'; *kḗrhe škófo ḥīdébə*, 'barely adequate for local small stock'; *kḗrhe ṭaʿámo ḥīdébə*, 'barely enough for local small stock to get a taste'; *bə́ṭəl mḳánhim*, 'the necessity of gathering supplementary fodder from shrubs and trees has come to an end'; *śībóʿo diš ḥídəbə ṭúwʿan diš*, 'enough to fill local small stock, and for others with small stock to transhume to'; *ḳəṣəho di-fólihi ṭúwʿan diš*, 'enough grazing for young cattle, and for those with *mə́nḳoʿ* weaned calves to transhume to'; *ḳə́ṣəho di-ílǝhe ṭúwʿan diš*, 'enough green grazing for mature cattle and for those with pregnant and milk-cows to transhume to'. The highest praise is: *ḳālaʿ bə-ṣ̌ādihir wə-ʿa itēbur*, 'rich enough grazing for a clay cooking pot to be thrown to the ground down without breaking'.

Rainfall

In such dry areas, subject to periods of severe drought, people developed an extensive vocabulary to describe rainfall. On Soqoṭra, 'rain' in general is *mése* (and 'less rain', the diminutive, *məlési*), but many other terms elaborate further. Some examples, progressing from the least to the most rainfall, are (S): *kērhe nāṭífo~tənōṭifin*, 'odd drops of rain' > *inʿábdəro oʔōbən* (lit. 'stones become blotched'), 'very light shower' > *tíriho di-oʔōbən* (lit. 'dampness of stones'), 'light shower' > *kērhe giléfo*, 'barely dampening the surface of the ground' > *giléfo*, 'dampening the surface of the ground but not penetrating below' > *rə́ḥo tīri*, '(dampness) has penetrated below the upper surface' (√ʔrḥ, to reach) > *ʾṣiṣəhi* or *di-íṣfer* (lit. 'for birds'), 'light rainfall' > *kērhe mə́ṣəlif*, 'barely enough to form puddles' > *mə́ṣəlif*, 'forming puddles' > *fótḳaḥ éḳəlaṭ*, 'rock pools half filled' > *saʿsáʿa*, 'light drizzle' > *nísas*, 'steady drizzle', or *līso ʿaf ināṭaf máʿbəher*, 'it rained until the lip of the boulder dripped' > *maḥṭúwṭəher*, 'leaving tiny runnels in soft ground' > *mōl di-éḳəlaṭ*, 'filling the rock pools' > *šíʿi ōrəm* ~ *šéʿi di-írəhem*, 'water trickling over hard ground' > *túwgeś* (dim.) 'producing little shoots' > *tígiś~ōtígiś*, 'producing enough shoots to give some grazing' > *ḳélǝm ṣáləhal*, 'gullies flowing' > *ḳélem egḥáyo*, 'streambeds flowing' > *ḳélem egḥáyo lə-mōl*, 'streambeds filled with water' > *ṣ́árbə*, 'rainstorm' (2–3 days of rain) > *ṭhāyif*, 'dangerous flood'.

Ways of naming

Invoking appearance

Some examples in plant species are: (Ś) *aḥṭemút*, (B) *aḥṭəmīt*, (H) *aḥṭəmít*, (S) *aḥtimí*, 'thread, twine', for various *Convolvulus* and other plants with fine stems that trail across the ground; (H) *dənōb d̠-iṯʿayl*, 'fox tail', for a plumed grass; (H) *ḥayṭób ekelbét*, 'bitch's dugs', for various small stumpy *Caralluma* and *Echidnopsis* species. A variety of small clinging plants or plants with burrs are (S) *ləskáno* or *məltúwseḳ*, 'sticky, adhesive', and prickly or thorny plants are (S) *śkaʿinítin*, 'spiky, spiny'. Mosses are known as *eṣerīʾo* (men *mése*), 'residue (from rain)', the denser ones of the central highlands *dówḳəhīn* 'little beard'. (Children peel them off the rocks and wear them as false beards). Related plants are differentiated by the size of their leaves, *ḳīḳəhe* referring to the smaller-leafed variety and *ṣáʿlhal* to the larger-leafed one. So the small-leafed *Kalanchoe farinacea* is *bə́gələhān ḳīḳəhe* and the larger-leafed *Kalanchoe robusta* is called *bə́gələhān ṣáʿlhal*; and the widespread, small-leafed shrub *Croton socotranus* known as *mítrer* becomes *mítrer ḳīḳəhe* in the central mountains where its leaves are better developed, with the larger related *Croton* species of the highlands being called *mítrer ṣáʿlhal*.

Some marine terms are vulgarly illustrative: (S) *žiéb ɛ-rémnem*, 'sea vagina' for starfish, (B) *ʿagerēz lə-gəmōl*, 'camels testicle' for various sea-lemons, (B) *ʿāgərēz lə-kēfər*, 'unbeliever's testicle' for sea hares (known as *məḳəliz di-rínhem*, 'glans of the sea penis' in Soqoṭri on the island of Samḥa), and (B) *gíbər lə-kēfərət* 'vagina of the woman unbeliever' for various Leuconid sponges or sea squirts found on rocks at low tide. The MSAL have similar names for sea cucumbers: (S) *féḥel ɛ-rémnem~ɛ-rébrem* / (B) *faḥl l-ərawnə* / (M) *fēḥəl ḏə-rowrəm~ḏə-rōrəm*, 'penis of the sea'.[10]

Many other names help the listener picture the thing named: (S) *kēr ɛ-ṣúd* 'shaikh of the fish', for goatfish, referring to their chin barbels which look like droopy moustaches; (H) *śaʿtétt*, 'with dull, staring hair' for a very hairy caterpillar; (H) *baʿlít ʿayúntə*, 'full of eyes' for the honeycomb tripe of the reticulum; and (S) *šanṣəhāni* 'butterfly' (< *šə́nṣah*, 'to be spread or split open'). In geology we find (S) *īrét ṭīrīn*, 'hyena's mirror' for fool's gold, a type of pyrite.

Terms for different types of terrain often use of parts of the body to help convey appearance. On Soqoṭra, for example, we find *ʿákərim*, 'hunched' for a ridge; *gimigámo*, 'cranium', for the rounded top of a mountain overlooking the sea; *kóto* 'neck and top of shoulders (seen from the back)', for upper slopes; *ṭādaʿ* 'back', for a flat-topped ridge; *ṭámṭəhīm* 'muzzle, snout', for an escarpment headland overlooking a coastal plain; *śə́ṭəher* 'flesh without bones or fat' for a cleared meadow or area of pure grassland, and *mḥáziz* 'neck of a carcass' (which has little or no meat), for an area just below the head of a watercourse which is lacking in vegetation.

Name sharing

Different plants which share some characteristic often share a name. In the MSAL *Calatropis*, *Datura* and *Ricinis* shrubs, all useless to man or beast (indeed potentially dangerous), are grouped together under the name gɔ́nigɔno ~ gúnigunt ~ žúnijund ~ gɔmēgɔmet ~ gɔnēgɔnet (according to language). This signals to the community that a tree or shrub is of no use as timber or for anything else. On Soqoṭra, ḥárḥeyr is a name given to thorny acacias, as well as to the (related) *Dichrostachys dehiscens* and the (quite unrelated) spiky *Commiphora habessinica*. All plants which produce cucumber-like fruit are called di-ḥśāwɔ ('of the cucurbit'); ḳálḳɔhal is a group name for a wide variety of halophytic plants; mēʕer (pl. meyháʔher ~ meyháʕher) is a general term for various unrelated succulent plants that lessen the thirst of goats browsing on them; šéber is a name for certain plants that exude a milky sap or latex, and mɔléṭɔhe (s. málṭɔhe) is a group name for 'weak' and 'soft-wooded' plants such as *Cissus*, *Jatropha*, *Sterculia*, *Aloe* and various tree *Euphorbias*. While zéydiro is an umbrella term for many prickly, low-growing and clump-forming herbs such as *Indigofera marmorata*, *I. pseudo-intricata*, *Seddera spinosa* and *Campylanthus spinosus*), the same name is also given to stiff perennial grasses such as *Dactyloctenium* or *Panicum rigidum*, and the related term, zídihir, describes the type of terrain on which such plants occur.

Plants that have something in common but are not necessarily related often have names derived from the same linguistic root. On Soqoṭra for example, we find bɔ́ṭaḥ, di-bɔṭáḥun or bɔṭáḥiyun (√bṭḥ) for different Iridaceae and Hyacinthaceae species; írsib, irsíbihon and mɔrsúbɔhān (√rsb) for various Portulacaceae, and lɔséyaḳ, lúwsaḳ or mɔltúwseḳ for a variety of unrelated clinging plants (from √lsḳ, 'to adhere').

Pairs of names

Diminutives

Entities that have something in common often bear related names, one name being the diminutive form of the other.

In Dhofar, (Ś) śxí is the tree *Grewia villosa*, while the smaller shrub, *Grewia erythraea*, is (Ś) śxānítɔ (dim.); (Ś) sīr is the tree, *Boscia arabica*, while the smaller but related *Cadaba* is sīrmár, 'little *Boscia*'. On Soqoṭra, di-ḥowgɔb is a tall Cyperaceae, while smaller ones are di-ḥɔgúbgub; ḳórṣaʔ refers to various perennial grasses of damp areas, while smaller species are ḳerṣáhyun. The tamarind with its edible sour fruit and foliage is ṣúbɔhur, while many species of small sour-leaved plants, chewed for their lemony flavour or used to curdle milk, such as *Begonia* and *Oxalis*, are ṣɔbírbɔher. Out at sea, the sea cucumber is (H) ɔlšīn, 'tongue', while the smaller sea-lemon is ɔlšénút, 'little tongue'; the rock lobster is (Ś) *śīrxót*, and the diminutive form, *śīróxət*, is the name for a shrimp or prawn.

A diminutive form can carry considerable semantic weight. On Soqotra, *ḳáṣ⁽a* or *xélit̞* / *ḥālit̞* is 'a visitor', but the diminutive forms, *ḳəṣó⁽o* and *ḥalút̞ihin* / *xalút̞ihin*, can indicate the way a visitor is to be treated: the host family will ask one another: *ḥáliyat̞ wələ ḥalút̞ihun?*, 'Are they well-regarded visitors or not?', or in the singular, *ḳə́ṣa⁽ wələ ḳəṣó⁽o?*, 'Is he an important visitor or not?' The underlying meaning is understood to be 'Should we slaughter an animal for them/him or not?', because traditionally, out of the ordinary or unfamiliar visitors should be offered fresh meat. If they decide that their visitors are worthy of meat, the hosts will then discuss amongst themselves which animal to sacrifice. Diminutive forms here are a sort of shorthand: do they offer a *di-réken* animal (< *réken*, 'knuckle end of a bone; marrow bone') whose carcass will provide plenty of fat and good marrow, or a *di-rúwken* (dim.), a less valuable animal with little fat and marrow (usually a very young or a very old animal)? Should they offer their visitors an ⁽*agəl*, an animal with fat in either the *ləbəhān* rectum or the *ḥə́wro* large bowel, but not in both? Or an ⁽*ágəli* (dual), one with fat in both the *ləbəhān* and the *ḥə́wro*. Or an ⁽*ə́wgəhel* (dim.), one with little fat and that fat having little flavour or succulence? Or should they offer their visitors the very best, the ⁽*ígəhel* (plural), an animal which will provide fat in the *ləbəhān*, *ḥə́wro* and the *darṣ* abomasum, one that *məló⁽o se* ⁽*ígəhel*, 'fills all the ⁽*agəl*'?[11]

Positive and negative

One name positive and the other negative: pairs of names differentiate between the 'good', i.e. useful, and the 'bad', i.e. useless or harmful, an additional educational aid for children.

On Soqotra, for instance, edible *Caralluma* are *məśhérmhim*, while inedible species are *məśhérmhim di-gírbaḳ*, 'wild cat's *Caralluma*'; and *Edithcolia grandis*, a prostrate succulent with hard spines and a terrible smell, is *di-girbiḳhítin*, 'for wild cats' (wild cats are loathed on the island). In Dhofar, (Ś) *aḥṣəbé* describes cultivated cucumbers, while wild, inedible, often poisonous, cucurbits are (Ś) *aḥṣəbé əlhúti*, (H) *ḥaśwé d̞-elḥēti*, 'cows' cucurbits' or (Ś) *aḥṣəbé ɛ-t̞īrīn*, 'hyena's cucurbits'. The cowpeas (*Vigna unguiculata*), cultivated in Dhofar, are known as (H) *dújur*, but (H) *dújur d̞-āġəréb*, 'raven's cowpeas', refers to the inedible pods of wild legumes such as *Teramnus repens* (the raven is a troublesome predator of weakly livestock).[12] The twining *Ceropegia* whose bulb, flowers and fruit are all edible is (Ś) rōt, while the names (Ś) rōt ε-ġúṣət or rōt ε-ḥōt, 'the snake's rōt plant', or (Ś) rōt ε-ṯīrīn, 'the hyena's rōt plant', denote other twiners which are inedible or toxic. (H) béḏaḥ are the highly valued, edible *Gladiolus* corms, but béḏaḥ esebərō, 'corms of the spirits of the dead', describes inedible or harmful corms and bulbs. The edible *Echidnopsis*, tábaʿš, is contrasted on Soqoṭra with tábaʿš di-tētin, 'sheep's *Echidnopsis*' which are not eaten. (In contrast to women, whose province the sheep are, men on the island tend to have a low opinion of sheep). A common name for unpalatable ferns of the island is di-xáṣəhen / di-ḥaṣáhan' 'of the giant centipede' (*Scolopendra* sp.), while in the pastures of Dhofar, where an area enclosed for rain-fed cultivation is known as (Ś) īšənu, a useless weed with irritant latex, *Gomphocarpus fruticosa*, that spreads across the ground after rain, is called (Ś) īšənu ε-ṯīrīn, 'the hyena's cultivated plot', signalling that it is not suitable fodder for livestock.

In the insect world, (B) hanḏəyōt l-əkfōr, 'the infidels' beetle', is a species which 'bites' people, while hanḏəyɔ̄t l-əməslām, 'the Muslims' beetle' is harmless. Among fungi, the ones that appear on termitaria after the rains were a much sought-after food in Dhofar, but inedible and poisonous fungi are given names such as (Ś) šfṓt ε-ḱéraḥ, 'silent, smelly donkey fart', or (S) ʾīdəhántən di-ṣuwʿīdo, 'ears of the Egyptian vulture', or (H) fahl ḏə-ḥayr 'donkey's penis'.

Names in livestock husbandry

Since for all the MSAL-speaking communities the rearing of livestock played a central role, some livestock husbandry terms are examined in more detail.

Naming livestock

Livestock names can be purely descriptive, as, for cows, (H) šərəbbṓt, 'blotched', (H) jaʿallṓt, 'stout', (H) išxéṣ, 'with the lower legs differently coloured'; (H) magəṯíṯ (jénaḥs), 'with neck and chest differently coloured', (S) di-rúwkes, 'little strong hocks'. Some examples for goats are (S) di-ḥéberbūri, 'with two little blotches of a different colour'; (S) di-šériyiḵ, 'with a flash of white running from an armpit along one side'; (S) di-ḥálkə, 'with one horn curving back towards the eye'; (S) ḥémhīm~ḥamémiyon, 'charcoal-black', and in Dhofar, (Ś) ḱerṭíṭ, 'with one twisted horn', and (Ś) ṣīʿíṯ, 'small-eared'. Colour names for livestock often include other creatures, such as (S) ḥə́wro šílihi, 'black as a Soqoṭra starling', or (S) ḥə́wro ṓġərib, 'raven black'.

An animal can be described by the ownership-markers it bears, as (H) *məkṭíf* or *məkṭíṭ*, 'with a snip taken across the tip of one ear'; (H) *məxajén*, 'with the tip of the ear slit perpendicularly', or 'with the outer edge of the ear slit horizontally'; (H) *məśrēs*, 'with a nick removed from one side of the tip of the ear', and (H) *məkšáˤ*, 'with the edge or bottom of the ear snipped off'. Some names give you other information about the animal, as (H) *enjīdít*, 'frequently aborts'; (H) *səllít* 'takes the mat (on which dried sardines have been put as fodder) in her mouth, and goes off' (< √sll, '(wild beast) to drag prey off in its mouth').

There are also collective names for livestock which indicate their origin or principal grazing grounds. Some Dhofari examples for goats are: (Ś) *ṣubəlúti*,[13] 'from the Ṣolót area' (running from Darbat to Ḥāsik); (Ś) *ḳuṭənúta*,[14] 'from the flat stony plateau area (*ḳaṭn*) partially within the reach of the monsoon'; (Ś) *juzˤóta*,[15] 'of the Mšāyix people above Mirbāṭ'; (Ś) *fəgərúta*,[16] 'of the desert areas' (especially those around Thumrait). For camels (Ś) *ṣubəlúti* is also the group name for those that browse the foothills and wadis of the Ṣolót area, and *fəgərúta* for those who live outside the monsoon-affected areas. There are other designations for camels: for example, (Ś) *śharúti* for those that stay mainly within the monsoon-affected mountains (*śhɛr*); (Ś) *ḥazgúti* for those that feed along the dry foreshore (*ḥazóg*) in the winter and summer months, moving to the shrubbed foothills (*ḥaškík*) for the monsoon and post-monsoon periods. There are even more closely delineated terms, such as (Ś) *jaḥbúti* for the camels of the al-Maˤšani tribe, great camel herders. When their huge herds of camels leave the mountains and come down to the foreshore (*gəḥāb*) to escape the mud and mists of the monsoon months, they are described in this way.

Counting livestock

Livestock owners are notoriously reluctant to reveal the exact number of their animals, and instead make use of a variety of terms to give a rough indication of the size of their herd or flock (see also Watson and Boom in press). Some examples in Hobyōt for goats (H *ḥaywərūn*) are: *ḥaśér*, a small number of milk goats kept close to the homestead (to supply milk for children); *shoṭ*, a small group of goats; *farḳ*, pl. *ḥafrōḳ*, a greater number than *shoṭ* (but this term also refers to 'a goat-owning homestead'); *jizḥút*, pl. *jəzḥóta*, a larger flock than *shoṭ* or *farḳ*; *məġzēl*, pl. *məġáwzəl*, a larger flock than *jizḥút*. And for cows (H *elḥēti*): *keṭəbét* pl. *keṭəbēb* refers to a small herd, some five to ten animals; *jizḥút*, around ten; ġormoṣót, around twenty; ġontəlót, pl. ġəntēl, a larger herd than ġormoṣót. For camels (H həbēʿar): keṭəbét describes around ten animals, and ṭoḥób, around fifteen to twenty.[17]

On Soqoṭra many different terms are used to describe herd or flock size, as shown in Table 2.2:

Table 2.2 Soqoṭri Names Describing Herd or Flock Size

Term	Size of flock or herd
gəmálə	'very plentiful', said to be an old term for 'around 100'
máḥber, pl. máḥbur ~ mḥébəhur	'100' (goats especially, sometimes sheep); said to be more precise than gəmálə above. Both these terms are now overtaken by Ar. miʔa.
maḥbíri (du.)	'200'
fókiyah (di-máḥbir)	'50'
gɛr, pl. ígrud (du. gēri, dim. girírhin)	'large flock of sheep'. Sheep from least to most: məgērid > gerd > ígərid > girírhin > gɛr
dīmi (di-tētin)	'large flock of 80–100 sheep'
tɛwənētin	'handful of sheep (fewer than 10)'
ṭʼuwhítin	'20–50 sheep'
ʿalfə, pl. áʿaluf	'more than 50 goats'
ʿə́ləfo (du.)	'20–30 goats'
ribōdə	'15–20' (goats only)
ḳáṭəbə (dim. koṭóbə)	'a small flock of goats'. Goats from least to most: ʔowziyítin > ʿə́ləfo > ʿálfə > koṭóbə > ḳáṭəbə
rəṣāmə́mo (dim.)	'around 40' (goats or sheep)
rəṣā́məm	'around 50' (goats or sheep)
ʿarf	'a medium-sized herd of cows, 15–20 animals'
dōbə	'a large herd of cows, more than 30' (said to be similar to máḥber for goats, used to describe a large number)
ziké	'large herd of cows, around 40'
ʿáśer, pl. ʿiśárhən	'ten', pl. 'tens' These terms are used if there is a need for greater accuracy than rəṣā́məm above. So '40' could be expressed as úrbaʿ ʿaśárhin (ie. 4 × 10)
ʿáśeri (du.)	'20'

Feeding livestock

When natural graze and browse (rógod / ruʿud) grow scarce, in the dry season or in a time of drought, different terms specify what livestock still find to eat or what their owners give them to keep them going. On Soqoṭra we find śaʿr, meaning that they are feeding on 'hay'; *máḫliṭ*, on 'fallen foliage', often collected for them by their owners; or *ḳównem*, 'foliage and twigs lopped from trees and shrubs' for them. When all these sources are exhausted, livestock are fed on *kídihir*, the pulped branches and even the trunks of trees (such as date-palms, *Sterculia* or *Dendrosicyos*), or on entire plants such as *Eureiandra balfourii* and *Dorstenia gigas* chopped up small. Fodder like this, of little or no nutritive value, is described as *ḥóśoʔ*, 'stuffing for the belly' or, if only available in small handfuls, as *ṭebib di-xa / di-ha*, 'salivation for the mouth' (*ṭebib*, 'salivating', especially on seeing or smelling something delicious).

Naming people

Names and nicknames

It seems that in earlier times certain personal names were often associated with certain tribes or groupings of people, so that knowing someone's name told you something about his or her origin. However, children today are usually given Islamic names, which reveal little other than the religious preferences of their parents.

While parents usually call their child by the name they gave him/her (or an affectionate diminutive) as (Ś) *Munīnúʔt* < *Miné*; *Ṭəfilún* < *Ṭfūl*; *Zēnəbōt* < *Zēnəb* for girls, or, for boys, *Sʕādān* < *Saʕīd*; *Shēlót* < *Shayl*; *Sēlyū́t* < *Sēlim*; *Ḥamīdún* < *Ḥmɛd*; *Mḥīdēn* < *Mḥammad*; *Mḥādót* < *Mḥād*, children give each other joking, often-derogatory nicknames, and some people retain these into adulthood. Some examples of less flattering nicknames are: (Ś) *ḥajfóf*, 'hunchbacked'; *śíḳér*, 'with one eye misshapen' or 'with a squint'; *məgrēr*, 'bees' nest'; *rusḵ*, 'very slow at doing or giving anything'; *ḥarḵún*, 'walks with in-turned toes' or 'limps awkwardly'; *ʕayɛ̃r*, 'blind in one eye', and *ṭīrīn ḵɛrḥít*, 'hornless hyena' (calling someone 'hornless' is always an insult).

Within the extended family, nicknames for girls and women are in general flattering. Some I have noted are (Ś) *ṣgél ʕambér*, 'dripping ambergris'; *śśərér dīriót*, 'flowing greenery'; *gít ɛnúśb*, 'sister of milk' (i.e. pale-complexioned); *ṭaʕr ɛ-ṭēlé*, 'morning shower'; *ɛ̃ṣerdót l-ɛ̃núf*, 'makes her own radiance'; *ɛ̃l aʕayʰn*, 'fills the eye' (i.e. with her beauty); *ɛ̃kɛ̄rdót oxóṭór*, 'drives guests mad' (i.e. with her desirability); and *inḥíś*, 'the mists cleared after the monsoon' (revealing the fresh new greenery). Examples of complimentary nicknames I have noted for men are (Ś): *āḥalíl iyyél*, 'camels' marrow'; *máḥmal ḳəśén*, 'able to carry great loads'; *ḥarfếś*, 'strong and enduring' and *ɛ̃rō*, 'quenches thirst'.[18]

Group names

Man's endless passion for grouping and classifying extends, of course, to people, the name of a group differing according to whether those using the name are members of that group or not. One classification is by how a group lives and where. For instance, in the region east of Mirbāṭ in Dhofar, those who live around the brackish coastal lagoons are referred to as (Ś) *Xabró* (< *xor*, 'lagoon'); those who rely on the sea for their livelihood, owning few goats and with little expertise with animals, are called *Ṣebdó* (< *ṣud*, √*ṣyd*, 'fish'); those of the coastal villages or towns, *Baʿéli Ḥallét*, 'urban people'; those who live along the high escarpment, *Baʿéli Dəhíḵ*, 'people of the high ridges'; and those who live in the area between the shore and the foot of the escarpment (a region called *mekṣért*), *Baʿél Ōḵúṣur*.

There are also eponyms for larger groupings in Dhofar. For example, the people of central Dhofar call those of the settled areas of the coast from Khawr Ṭāqah to Khawr Mugsayl, *Ḥadəbó*; those from Khawr Mugsayl west, *Ḵameró*, 'people of the Qamar mountains'; those of the central monsoon mountains as far as Mugsayl, *Baʿéli Śḥer*, 'those of the monsoon-affected mountains'; those from Mirbāṭ eastwards as far as Ḥāsik, *Enṣeró*, 'those from the east', and those east of Ḥāsik as far as Šarbithāt, *Śeróḵ* ~ *Min Śeróḵ*, 'from the place of the rising sun'.

The Baṭāḥira use birds rather than geographical or occupational features as ethonyms for their neighbours: the *yingayr* heron represents the Śḥaró of the al-Ḥallāniyyāt Islands; the *mʿánḵari* gull the Gəzēli clan of the Janaba; the *sómi* cormorant the Ahkilī of Dhofar; the *bəgarīt* gull the Ḥarāsīs of the central desert, and the *ṣayfərūn* gull, the Baṭāḥira themselves. The Baṭāḥira also group the animal kingdom into 'families' and 'clans': goats, camels, birds, fish, even shellfish. For example, in one shellfish group, the *tḥāś*, a type of limpet, is seen as the 'father'; the *śídəfēt* sea lemon, the 'mother'; the *zikt* rock oyster, a 'daughter', and the *śīnəhāt* chiton another 'daughter'. Among fish, the *terʿān*, a species of pompano (a type of trevally) is the 'head of the family'; the *mənʿášfer*, another species of pompano, his 'sister'; the *fárri*, a flying fish, a 'daughter' and the *mowšəḵāt*, (unidentified), another 'daughter'. The rabbitfish form another fish 'family', with the *śīsənāt* rabbitfish the 'mother'; the *rəgəfān*, another kind of rabbitfish, the 'father', and the *sammǝmōt*, another rabbitfish, the 'daughter'. However, not all fish have 'families': they describe the *ʿakām* barracuda and the *ʿanfəlūs* dolphinfish as being in a class all of their own. This is a designation with which academic taxonomy concurs, the barracuda being the only known genus in the Sphyraenidae family, and the dolphinfish the only one in the

Coryphaenidae family (for MSAL fish terms see Watson, Morris and Anonby, in prep.).

MSAL-speaking communities have their own ways of classifying flora and fauna, the reasons lying behind such classifications not always obvious to an outsider. For example, some trees are said to be 'female' and others (identical taxonomically) to be 'male', and plants from different families are grouped together in a way which bears little relation to taxonomy. Interestingly, all MSAL-speakers agree that the queen bee is male rather than female, and say that the worker bees with no male incharge would not be able to make honey. They call the queen bee (Ś) *sátǝhān di-ʔídbihir di-ʕasǝl*, 'sultan of the worker honeybees'; (H) *ʕanyīb ~ ʕanīb ḏǝ-ʕaḏǝmīt*, 'the large fat male of the worker bees', and (Ś) *ʕamní iź ǝnbéb*, 'the one incharge of the worker bees'.

Naming places (toponomy)

The majority of names for settlements are straightforwardly descriptive, as (Ś) *meṣrób*, 'post-monsoon (< *ṣerb*) quarters', or *ẽstó*, 'winter (< *śéte*) quarters'. Some place names occur again and again: across Dhofar we find many names based around the terms (Ś) *rékeb* 'rock ledge'; *ɛrḳóf* pl. *ɛrḳǝfén ~ ɛrḳefítǝ*, 'with slab(s) of flat-surfaced rock' (useful for preparing food, grinding cereals, serving food and so on); *ṣarfḗt*, 'area of flat bedrock', or the diminutive form, *ṣarfinót*; *dof*, 'large slab of rock'; *śéheb*, 'flat plains area with shrubs, just beyond the range of the monsoon rains'.[19] On Soqoṭra, terms such as *xáderher*, 'shade-giving' and *ṣóyhir*, 'huge slab of rock' (under or beside which a home can be made), occur frequently as place names, sometimes even together, as *xáderher di-ṣóyhir* in the Nōged southern coastal plain.

Place names often refer to a striking feature of the surrounding terrain, as (Ś) *déhek ṭíri*, 'wet cliff'; *daġr ḥōr*, 'black peak'; *ẽdór ~ mídór*, 'deep mud' (this place receives very heavy monsoon rains); *enjǝrót*, 'place of many *nújur* (banks of conglomerate, unstable scree)'; *miśkól ~ íśkól*, 'on a slope'; *kṭérum ~ kṭerū́t*, 'place of *kṭérum* stone' (a soft stone that women used to grind and add to tobacco to make it more pungent), or *ṣaʕéyr ~ ṣaʕếr*, 'place frequented by gazelle'. On Soqoṭra we find names like *ḥámiro di-mǝfélik* (*ḥámiro*, 'small isolated hill'); *mǝfélik*, 'overlooking a low-lying plains area'; *merighǝlítin*, 'place of flat stones'; *di-śaʕníni*, 'place of two peaks'; *di-bin-ṣerfēti*, 'between two ravines'; *di-míśbib*, 'place from which one can look down over the land below' and *di-figífig*, 'at the top of a pass'.

It is very common for names to refer to features of vegetation, as (Ś) *śerbǝtéti*, 'with many thorny "*śerbít*" Maytenus shrubs'; *ʕátinút*, 'with a small "*ʕaytít*" Cordia tree'; *embúʔd*[20] *baʕl iyyén*, 'camel camp with a "*yɛn*" *Moringa peregrina* tree'; *enṣɔʕɔ́t*, 'with many "*ṣaʕb*" *Acacia etbaica* trees'; *sĩrnút* 'with a small "*sĩr*" *Boscia arabica* tree'; *déhek ōtín*, 'cliff of the "*motín*" wild olive'. On Soqotra, we find (S) *dí-ṭik*, 'with a "*ṭik*" *Ficus vasta* tree'; *ətēbəhən*, 'with many "*ítʔib*" *Ficus salicifolia* trees'; *imtēyi*, 'with many "*ímtəhe*" *Euphorbia arbuscula* trees'; *di-lékəhem*, 'with a "*lékəhem*" *Commiphora* tree'; *di-ekéšhe*, 'with many "*ʔíkšə*" *Commiphora ornifolia* trees'; *di-ʕešébək*, 'with many "*ʕášbak*" *Euphorbia schimperi* plants', and *di-eṣgállə*, 'with many "*ṣágəlhiʔ*" '*Metaporana obtusa* shrubs'. From *ṣúbəhor*, *Tamarindus indica*, we find *di-ṣúbəhur*, 'with a tamarind tree', *iṣbírə*, 'with many tamarind trees', or *di-ṣəbərēni*, 'with two tamarind trees'.

Instead of specific plants, a name can derive from vegetation in general, as (S) *di-śákded hámer*, 'hill with patches of greenery'; (S) *zífələ dekəmhinítin*, 'wooded slope with small peaks', or (S) *rōkəb di-saʕdifítin*, 'high pastures with clumps of perennial grasses'. Or a name might refer to a lack of vegetation, as (Ś) *karṣít*, 'with hair trimmed or cut' (i.e. a bare and treeless area), or (Ś) *məkórah*, 'shaved', with the same meaning, or on Soqotra, *gádho di-gúwled*, 'shaved pass or saddle', i.e. bare of vegetation.

It is also common to find names referring to a particular water feature (see Gasparini and al-Mahri, this volume), as (Ś) *ʕāminút*, 'with a small spring'; *aʕnútek*, 'with many small but deep holes in which rainwater collects'; *fekēti*, 'place where water lies close to the surface' (a plural diminutive form of *fókə*, 'pool'). On Soqotra, we find names such as *fʕéyti*, '(between) two watersheds'; *di-hílahəm*, 'place of springs'; *di-dēgub*, 'that drips'; *di-mísron*, 'with many *míssur*', i.e. 'covered waterholes', and *féger di-mísron*, 'edge of a plateau with many *míssur*'.

A name can also describe the man-made environment, as (Ś) *ʕarṣinítə*, 'place of many *ʕarṣót*', (i.e. 'hut of palm fronds', or 'a length of cloth stretched over four poles'); *aʕayrētə*, 'place of stone huts' (built as stores, for livestock, etc.); *hkōb*, pl. of *hokəb*, 'permanent cattle settlement with byres(s)', or the diminutive forms *hakāb* ~ *hakéb*.

Other place names record events, such as (Ś) *men tɛl ʔīnét dótfer*, 'where the women shoved one another' (and one fell to her death) in the Ḥāsik area, or *men tɛl gōji lótəġ*, 'where the two men fought'. Other unusual names are more obscure: what lies behind the name (Ś) *jōt ʔáynet*, 'women's hollow', or (Ś) *ʕagərízi*, 'two testicles'? What is clear is that that such place names have a story behind them, and if this is not known, the name becomes incomprehensible. Sometimes the story behind the name is still remembered. For example, among the Baṭāhira, the place name *śigərēt hāgirít*, 'the pass of the slave woman', recalls the sad story of a slave who, exhausted by the hot, daily treks to distant waterholes, returning with the heavy-filled goatskin on her back, up one steep pass and down the other, and with no expectations of any happier future, decided to end it all and threw herself off a cliff. In the same region, a huge slab of rock by the sea is called (B) baʿlít aṣafərít, 'the one of the plait'. It got its name from the story of a young woman whose father died while fishing: they were in a place far from anyone on whom she could call to carry him away for proper burial. To put him out of reach of hyenas and other scavengers, she hauled him right to the top of the slab of rock by her long plait (ṣafərít).

Naming significant years

In the absence of written records in earlier days, memorable years were given a name that referred to some key event of that particular year. Such events are usually regional, and so are the named years – it is rare to find a name that applies to the whole of Soqotra, for instance. Some examples for Dhofar are: (Ś) ʿonút elhēmér baʿl ɛ-ġoṣór, 'the year when the heavy rains of the elhēmér star brought up a lot of ġoṣór Umbellifera plants'; ʿonút ɛ-dótɛ ɛ-ḳemró, 'the year the summer rains failed in the Qamar area and people from there had to transhume eastwards'; ʿonút ɛ-dótɛ baʿl búndéf, 'the year of the ?flu epidemic at the time of the summer rains' (a year when many died despite good rains) (see al-Manji and Watson, this volume). On Soqotra, we find ʿə́no di-mə́ndoġ, 'the year of pecking' (i.e. a year of such severe drought that the Egyptian vultures found plenty of carcasses to feed on); ʿə́no di-ḥizíz, 'year of cutting throats', another year of severe drought in one area when they slaughtered nearly all of their starving animals rather than see them die (and some islanders say that people were so famished then that they even ate human flesh); ʿə́no di-maḥtighəbítin, 'year when the pregnant animals were nothing but skin and bone'; ʿə́no di-érṭaḥ, 'year of strips of meat', when there was nothing to eat but dried strips of mutton; ʿə́no di-ʔimēti, 'year of Euphorbia arbuscula trees', when goats had nothing to eat but the harvested leaflets of these trees; ʿə́no di-məʿéyib, 'year of skeletal (small stock)', a year when both the winter and summer rains failed and the goats and sheep were stricken with severe diarrhoea and died in great numbers.

Reinforcement of a name through memorable phrase, ditty or rhyme

A name is sometimes reinforced by a ditty or rhyme; this is entertaining as well as helping children recall the creature named. In the insect world, (S) nəfékəhān is a species of click or spring beetle (Elateridae), so called from the sharp click it makes as it leaps high in the air when disturbed or when it lands on its back and tries to right itself. When these beetles appear after rain, children catch one, put it in a scrap of cloth and take it home for the woman incharge of churning to use to ensure that her churn will produce a lot of butter. Some women tie it to the neck of the butter-churning skin, others rub a little ghee or butter on the beetle instead, and then hold it over the churn, repeating the words: *nəfékəhān nəfékəhān, yāṣiṣ bik di-ˤōṣəher*, 'Nəfékəhān beetle, Nəfékəhān beetle, may this droplet of butter strike terror in your heart!' Or *nəfúk nəfākəhen! ḥərútk ˤak di-ˤōṣəher*, 'Little Nəfékəhān beetle, spring up and away! I've greased you with a drop of butter.' Or, using a diminutive of its name: *nəfúk nəfākəhen xózor wə-šənḳalo*, 'Little Nəfékəhān beetle, leap up and away! May tiny globules of fat gather together and the churn produce butter!' The beetle raises and lowers its head and then suddenly clicks and flies off (√nfk, 'to leap from one place to another, to shoot off'). On seeing a solitary potter wasp, (H) *enzaˤnút*, someone might chant: *enzaˤnút enzáˤ tiy*!, 'Oh, *enzaˤnút* wasp, give me a little food from your store!', i.e. of what you have in your *kfeyl* mud nest,[21] a small droplet of matter said to have a sweetish favour. The *ḳāḥáf* beetle (possibly a species of leaf beetle, Chrysomelidae) lays its eggs in the cow-pea plants, and the larvae are extremely destructive. When going through the plants to check them for beetles, a woman chants: (Ś) *ɛ-ḳāḥáf šik ɛxér b-ɛnfés / her ol ˤak thoḏór / bə-tíkən men xɛlés*!, 'Oh *ḳāḥáf* beetle, better that you leave right away than stay to be frightened out of your wits and end up with nothing!' (i.e. when I squash you). The *ḳāḥáf* can reply: in this Hobyōt ditty, the *ḳāḥaf* says: *méken šuk enfés / hum ol txum thaḏōr[22] / wə-tíkən men xɛlés*, 'You have no cares and plenty of room (i.e. leave me alone and go somewhere else!) / If you don't want to sit around while others are working / And achieve nothing at all!'

People working together at a task sang rhythmic chants to ease the demanding labour, the words and music encouraging and synchronizing rhythmic movement. Weeding the rain-fed plots was enlivened by singing such songs as (H): *zəhámk tok rágaś / wə-ˤād el ṣəfórək / ˤasé mən əbˤéli / yōm ṭīt eḏhórək*, 'I come to you with hair uncombed / And as yet unplaited. / Possibly the Lord will permit / That one day I'll be done with it!' (i.e. the weeding). Or *ol təšḥér beh la / w-ol təġalḳ ʾidéh / sen xāməh wə-riḥót / kel tənúkˤan bih*, 'Don't be paralysed at the thought of it, / And don't look at it! / For the five (fingers) and the palm / (Working) together will deal with it!' (i.e. the weeds).

Among birds, there is a very small one[23] of remote areas called *fˤārór*. Children waiting hungrily for the return of those who had left to work at the frankincense harvest or down to a coastal market, hoping for food and perhaps little gifts,[24] would chant (Ś): *ε-fˤārór ε-fˤārór liš l-oġóṯḗš / her ε̃kṯér ḥa-ynféš tfərír / b-her ε̃kṯér o ḥa-ynféš lo sukf*, 'Oh Fˤārór bird, oh Fˤārór bird, on your head (*lit.* neck) be it! / If the group of people is coming back this afternoon, fly off! / And if the group of people is not coming back this afternoon, stay where you are!' (*lit.* 'sit').

Children are amused by the catchphrase: (H) *erxamót ˤamíti hoh bə-kerkém*, 'The Egyptian vulture is my granny made up with turmeric powder!', as well as being reminded that this bird has a yellow face. A less attractive aspect of its scavenging nature appears in the rhyme: (Ś) *erx̃ít šīṯít / té ġob šīˤót*, 'The vulture had an attack of severe diarrhoea, ate the faeces and so filled its belly!'

In Dhofar, when the Abyssinian white-eye, (H) *ˤakəbít εṯób*, 'bird of Loranthus', is seen in a fig tree (*Ficus sycomorus* or *Ficus vasta*), people call out to it: *ˤakəbít εṯób / tentəṯób / éhwə liy / b-aḥfól ḳēṯót*, 'Oh White-eye / Flitting here and there so freely, / Knock down for me / Some small unripe figs!'

The *ḳəfḳóf* kingfisher and the *silwēt ~ səlwót* bird[25] reach monsoon Dhofar just before the onset of the monsoon rains. People say that the *silwēt ~ səlwót* sings: (H) *msē msē yā kerīm*, 'Give us rain! Give us rain, merciful Lord!', but the kingfisher replies: *ḳof ḳof*, 'Stop! Stop!' (i.e. don't give us rain!). Another seasonal visitor to Dhofar is the Dideric cuckoo: it arrives to breed around May, a time when the precious rains of summer sometimes fall. It is said to call out repeatedly: (H) *ṣīṣī ē-kerīm*, 'Light rains, merciful Lord!', and this phrase has now become one of its names. The *ḳəfḳóf* kingfisher also plays a role in cultivation: on seeing it, people call out: (H) *īnə ˤīšεk? díjer mən ḍirrét?* 'What are you going to have for supper? Cow peas or sorghum?' This alludes to the custom of catching this bird before the monsoon rains begin to fall, killing it, setting it alight and wafting the smoke around the rain-fed plot of cowpeas and sorghum as a charm to bring fertility.

The Bruce's Green Pigeon, found in the mountains of western Dhofar at the end of winter, is seen as particularly difficult to approach, let alone catch. It has been given the name (Ś) *o kterór tóʔ dé*, 'Let no-one go for me!', and there is a rhyme which children chant to it: (Ś) *o kterór tóʔ dé / o nhérə b-o(l) ġosəré / ˤak l-iḳér l-əġóhī*, 'Let no-one go for me / Neither by day nor by night. / I need to get back to my brother this evening!'

Because it spends a lot of its time perched in the branches of shrubs and trees around a settlement, the African Paradise Flycatcher, (H) *saˤdé*, is suspected of counting the livestock of a homestead so that it can pass this information on to a sorceress. On seeing it, children call out: (H) *ε-saˤdiyé aḥtēsəb ḥsabš*, 'Oh little *saˤdé* bird, calculate away!'

In the mammalian world, the bat (Ś *nišḥót*, pl. *nišḥíta* ~ *nəšḥāníta*; H *nišḥót*, pl. *nušḥ*) is regarded as bald, and people call out to it: (H) *ɛ-nišḥót ənšáḥ b-śof*, 'Oh bat, grow some hair!' However, a bat was also believed to have the power of influencing the growth of hair: increasing or decreasing it. For this reason, a dead bat was tied to a baby's head to make its hair grow thick and black, but it was also placed in the armpits and crotch of a baby girl to minimize the growth of pubic and axillary hair.[26] There was a song too about rodents (H, but said by the transmitter to be influenced by Mehri): *ʿarḳəbōni serḳ ədōni / el təlóḳaḥ w-el tədōni / saʿd wə-l-erdéhs b-ṣōwer / té tahdōmən əmṯōni*, 'Little rodent, thief of the world / May it not conceive or fall pregnant! / How I wish I could throw a stone at it / And break all (its) teeth!'

Some rhymes are helpful mnemonics. Two examples for plants are (S):

il-ġálġəhal təṅġalġálən / w-il-fɔ́laḳ tənfəlákən,

'Feeding on *ġálġal* foliage brings on a runny nose and chesty cough; feeding on *fɔ́laḳ* makes (an animal) deceptively fat.

wə-il-ḥaṣālilo míṭəhan / śxof wə-ged d-iṣāḳʿas,

But feeding on *míṭəhan* foliage increases milk yield and bestows strength and endurance'.[27]

And:

teʔbilílin ḥeréśim / dārfon intiḳáʿan,

'A stick of *ḥárśim* wood breaks easily; one of *di-ráffan* snaps with a sharp crack.

wə-di-sənémhən márkah / thár ḥá mən meyháxət,

But a stick of *sənémhən* wood leaves a weal right here, where it landed a blow.'[28]

Diachronic change in names

It is important to remember that names can change over time, and that a name recorded today may not be that of earlier times, nor will it necessarily endure. To give some toponomic examples: on Soqotra, the place formerly known as Góʔo Di-Ṣəláṭini, 'the hollow of the Sultans', has today, now that sultans no longer rule Soqotra, become Ḥayy as-Salām. In western Dhofar, the place now known (and officially signposted) as Khaḍrafi was known before as Ḵērf ('flat area on the edge of the steep slopes coming down from the *ḳaṭn* upland plateau'), while in central Dhofar, modern Madīnat al-Ḥaqq is still remembered by the older generation by its former name, Xižól.

In the animal kingdom too, life moves on. Parrotfish are named jokingly (H) *ġaṣabīt həbə ͑ēt*, 'it takes seven people to hold it fast', or (Ś) *meṣarúṭ*, 'noisy farter'. But today, a large multi-coloured specimen is widely known as *filibīni*, 'from the Philippines'. Similarly brightly coloured, the eight-barred grouper is today called *dīsko* (< English 'disco'), and the Indian threadfish is known as *blaywut*, 'plywood' (< English) because it is so two-dimensionally flat (Watson, Morris and Anonby, in prep.).

Name avoidance and suppression[29]

In particular instances names are avoided, obfuscated or deliberately concealed. This can be for reasons of propriety, from fear, to avert evil, or even out of professional reticence.

Spouse name avoidance

There was a tradition of husband-and-wife name avoidance in Dhofar.[30] This was more than the traditional reserve common to much of the Islamic world about revealing a woman's name. The avoidance of mentioning a personal name here was not just in front of strangers, but even within the intimacy of the family home, where it was quite usual for a couple to address each other by terms such as: *ɛ-ḏoh*!, 'Oh that one', or *ɛḏīlīn*!, 'Oh so-and so'. On Soqotra too, a wife commonly addressed her husband as *yáxer* or *šáxer*, literally 'man'. Interestingly, using a diminutive form alters the emphasis: when addressing a little boy, *šúwxar* or *yúwxar* demonstrates great affection, but when addressing an adult it can express mild contempt ('a little man, a poor specimen of a man'). To say *ṭad šúwxar gídaḥ*, 'a *šúwxar* has arrived', implies that the person is either unknown or of little significance, whereas to say *ṭad šáxer gídaḥ*, 'a *šáxer* has arrived' indicates that it is a known man or a man of some consequence. A bridegroom, on claiming his bride, would say: *l-igíḥ tan b-šxar wə-b-ʔə́rəhon*, 'May you bring us fine men and (plenty of) goats!'

Another way of avoiding the use of a personal name is by using instead *ḥéyhi* or *ḥey*, 'someone, a person'. A person arriving at the entrance to living quarters would call out: *íno ḥéyhi b-kā̇nə?*, 'Is there anyone inside?' Like *šúwxar* above, using the diminutive form, *ḥówihin*, can also be disrespectful or disparaging: *ḥówihin* can signify 'an insignificant, unimportant person' (but can also describe a human outline seen at a distance, too far away to determine whether the person is old or young, male or female).

To talk about a married couple without using their names, the term *ḥōd ~ ḥud* can be used. This tends to be used of a recently married young couple, as yet with no children[31] (a long-married, middle-aged couple would be called *śeybíbihon*, the common plural form of *śíbeb*, 'old man' and *śíbib*, 'old woman'). So we find *ḥalf di-ḥud*, 'young couple's place', or *míššin di-ḥud*, 'young couple's sleeping place' for the area screened off from the rest of a cave or single-roomed dwelling to which the couple retire for the night. The diminutive form, *ḥōwəd* or *ḥówdud*, is usually used to refer to a couple of unequal age, commonly where the man is much older than his wife. However, when addressing a married couple directly, even if just married that day, the plural form must be used, never the dual. This is because 'there are people behind them', i.e. they will produce a family, and to address them in the dual would risk casting a blight on their future fertility.

Use of derogatory nicknames

A variant of concealing a name is practised by parents when they deliberately give an ugly or derogatory nickname to their child to protect it from attracting envy, the 'Evil Eye', and falling sick as a result. A woman of the Baṭāḥira gave her only surviving baby son the unattractive name *ḥawrēt*, 'darkness, blackness', to keep him safe: in a lullaby, she sings: (B) *laˁk Ḥawrēt / el yəġtífət w-el yəmét*, 'I beg You (Lord), keep Ḥawrēt safe! May his breath not be extinguished! May he not die!' A mother on Soqoṭra called her baby *handúris*, or a variant, *ḥándis*, a word glossed as: *héyhi al šker wə-di-šírəś wə-ḥátkek*[32] *w-ol šker meyh fānə wələ mákṣə*, 'An unpleasant person with a large belly who is filthy, nosy, and repellent in both face and person.' The Soqoṭri who explained this name to me said 'The man I knew was called this terrible name as a baby so that he wouldn't die.'

Deliberate name concealment

People are sometimes deliberately evasive about giving the real name of something. Experts who treat illness with plant products are not usually prepared to reveal the name of the plant(s) they use. Instead they talk about (H) *herúm enfés*, 'plant for childbed' (*entəfsót*, 'woman to successfully pass the afterbirth'), for example, or (S) *herúm aˁún*, 'plant for conjunctivitis' (*moˁún*, 'conjunctivitis'); (S) *herúm ergifít*, 'plant for fever with rigors'; (S) *herúm ɛ-ḥōt*, 'snake plant' or *herúm aʕúṣ*, 'plant for snakebite' (< √mṣṣ, 'to suck', and, more specifically, 'snake or witch to suck away the lifeblood or life force of a creature'). This is true too for cures for livestock: the plant (H) *herúm ḏ-eṣʕót* is pulled up by its root and tied onto one of the horns or around the neck of a cow which persists in ignoring its new-born calf; another plant, (H) *herúm ḏə-jinbót*, is used in the same way to treat a cow which refuses to suckle its young calf. Traditional veterinary experts also make use of other animals to treat the precious cows: a cow unable to pass the placenta has an (H) *išeróʕ* rock semaphore gecko[33] wrapped in grass placed in her mouth. The shock of feeling the reptile moving around in its mouth is said to be enough for the exhausted animal to make one last effort.

A name can also be inadvertently concealed. Recognized on the mainland and on the island of Soqotra is a fabulous plant known only by the name *ʕabd əl-kasīr ~ ʕūd əl-kasīr*. The plant has a widely known name but the plant itself remains unknown: no-one knows exactly what it looks like or how to get hold of it, though it is generally believed to grow among the highest peaks where only ravens can pluck it. Its magical qualities appear in many stories: the smallest fragment placed inside a butter-skin produces prodigious amounts of the very best butter; an animal that eats any part of it becomes immensely fat and healthy, and produces inordinate amounts of milk.

Name substitution for feared or loathed entities

The name for things that that are feared or loathed is often replaced with some sort of innocuous euphemism. While this phenomenon is especially prevalent when alluding to supernatural creatures, it is also found for living creatures. For instance, on Soqotra, the wild or feral cat, *gírbaḳ*, pl. *girébeḳ*, is loathed because it attacks weak or sickly livestock and kills their young. It was also suspected of being the familiar of demons and sorceresses, so pronouncing its true name risked inviting their attention. So the *gírbaḳ* is given other names like *ḥazōzə*, 'the slaughterer'; *di-gāšaʕ*, 'the twister of necks', *silāwə*, 'causing sickness' (a name given to any wild creature arousing fear or revulsion), or is simply alluded to as *di-ḥádeb*, 'of the land'.

However, name avoidance applies particularly to paranormal phenomenon. Witches, for example, were dreaded on Soqotra, and the word for 'witch', *zéḥirə*, was avoided and replaced by various circumlocutions, as *di-nékir*, lit. 'one who is always angry and full of curses'; *ṣálahil ~ ṣéllə*, lit. 'one who damages'; *ḳiṣādə*, lit. 'one who cuts', or *mirihébo*, lit. 'one always scurrying here and there'. Evil spirits are described as *máʕkaš*, lit. 'one who moves at unusual speed, one who suddenly disappears from sight' or *fídid* / *géhmiš* ~ *gəhémiš*, lit. 'hornless', while a fiend which rides on its victim's back and controls his or her actions is evasively called *máˤdəhe* / *mágdəhe*, 'carried on the back'. The most feared supernatural creature on the island appears as a huge woman who pursues her human prey by making giant leaps on her one iron leg; she slashes at him with her unnaturally long metallic finger and toenails, and tears into him with her long canine teeth. The islanders usually refer to her obliquely as *di-ʔišhəmítin*, 'the shrieker', or as *di-śaf*, 'the one-legged'. In much the same way, one of the harmful supernatural beings in Dhofar is given the equivocal name of (H) *maˤīdēb*, (Ś) *məˤídéyb*, 'the harasser', while a ghoul 'the size of a cow' which makes a swishing sound as it follows its victim, stopping when s/he stops, is called *kərəbrōb*, from √krb, 'to come close'. The terrifying ogre which snatches children, puts them in the pit at the back of its neck and makes off with them to its den to eat is given the understated name of *sēlól* (√sll, '[wild beast] to drag away its prey, to carry its prey off in its mouth').

Name obfuscation around feared or evil actions

Evil actions are concealed behind everyday words. For example, (S) *terōkin*, lit. 'she ties knots', is also used to describe the actions of an evil woman who 'ties knots' against another woman, especially a pregnant one, so that when it is time for her to give birth, she is unable to 'loosen the knot' and deliver her baby. Or *yiráḥaś*, lit. 'he washes sth.', a term also used to describe the actions of the ritual healer of Soqotra, the *mékóli*, when, with the help of his invisible demon assistant, he performs the ritual to 'sniff out' a witch. In everyday speech, *sté* (√twy) means 'she eats', but the same term is used when a witch destroys her victim. *ṭṭōrdən*, 'they chase or pursue', also denotes the actions of the *ṣaʔhéytin ~ ṣahóytin*, bird-like sorceresses who fly screeching across the night sky in pursuit of their maddened victim, the *máṭərid*, ('the pursued'), until he (it is always a man) collapses from exhaustion or until they get close enough to lay a noose of their hair across his path and trap and 'eat' him.

On Soqotra, other strange but invisible creatures cry out at night, some helpfully like the *məkínnə* (< √knn, 'to seek shelter from bad weather') who calls out to warn people of approaching bad weather. Some call this phenomenon *riˤānə*, and claim it is a spirit bird. They say: *ki ṣaˤāro riˤānə nəˤāmer mése íkin*, 'If the *riˤānə* calls out we say it's going to rain', and *riˤānə iṣfirə təˤāmər 'wawáw wawáw' b-axté: igúdiḥin mése*, 'The *riˤānə* is a "bird" that cries "wawáw wawáw" at night: rain will fall.'

However, to the islanders, total silence, ʾɛ́lə, is the most ghastly thing of all. ʾɛ́lə is glossed as: 'no sound, no people, no livestock, no living thing', i.e. no sign of continuing existence. There is a saying which evokes such a terrible state of affairs: ol zéber³⁴ išúʿur w-ol riʿā́nə w-ol mənḥówsis d-íkin b-ṭíyo, 'No orphaned zéber demon-child calling out, nor a riʿā́nə bird from the other world, not even a trickle of earth and pebbles from the cliff above' (which would at least suggest some sort of activity on the part of something or someone). ʾɛ́lə: a name for nothingness, a void.

Conclusion

I have concentrated on giving examples which illustrate the importance of 'bestowing a name', focusing on the natural rather than on the man-made environment. The name is indeed a sign: it instructs; it provides clues; it amuses and entertains; it stimulates the imagination; it demonstrates the significance the thing named has for the community; it encourages careful observation and the development of a retentive memory; it identifies links between different parts of the natural environment and it suggests crucial distinctions. This handing down of expertise and experience is vital to the survival of the next generation: it teaches them to understand, respect and look closely at what surrounds them. Culturally acceptable ways of avoiding or concealing names teach subtle gradations of euphemism, and draw attention to the use of metaphor and metonymy. The 'naming of things' is possibly the greatest gift one generation can pass on to the next.

Notes

1. MSAL Modern South Arabian Languages. Here H = Hobyōt; Ś = Śḥerɛ̄t; S = Soqoṭri; M = Mehri and B = Baṭḥari. For Soqoṭri a slanting line (/) separates western Soqoṭri from central and eastern Soqoṭri.
2. Someone considered to be behaving crazily is described as yəśkōk kərū́d, 'he's skewering human faeces'.
3. I am very grateful to Richard Porter of the Ornithological Society of the Middle East, OSME, for his assistance in trying to identify many birds from my incomplete descriptions.
4. The relevant details for *Boswellia sacra* are available elsewhere (al-Mahri and Boom 2020; Miller and Morris 1988: 70–81, 298–304; Morris 1997: 231–47).

5 Also *ḥaróṣ ed tǝngaśġíś* or *etfǝġóś ḳoṣol*, 'the acacia has put out soft new growth.'
6 In general terms, annuals, all grasses, ferns, aerial parts of bulbs and corms and small perennial plants are *rúʿud / rógod* while trees, shrubs and woody perennial plants are *śírǝhām*. The principal defining characteristics of *rúʿud / rógod* plants are that they come up after rain and then die back in the dry season. For further details on plant characteristics on the island, see Miller and Morris (2004: 17–39).
7 *ḥeryómo ~ hárihum* can also mean 'only a little fresh grazing to have come up after poor rains'.
8 *di-rǝhúwḥa* (√rḥv), *lit.* 'lickable', grass which has grown tall enough to be eaten by young cattle, i.e. they can get their tongue around it.
9 Grass which has grown tall enough for cows to grip between the teeth and wrench away from its roots (at this stage, the grass is on the point of flowering).
10 Soqoṭra however has *ḥfoš*.
11 It will be clear from the above that, as food, an animal is judged by its fat and marrow.
12 On Soqoṭra too, *di-áʿarib*, 'of the raven', is a name for a showy *Crinum* species with unpalatable broad leaves and a poisonous bulb.
13 Short-haired goats of all colours; black and white ones are considered to give the best milk. Although small they are said to have a lot of fat, and are particularly famous for the flavour of their meat and fat, due to a diet of *ḥaróṣ* Acacia and *ʿekǝbēt* and *ʿóḳor* Commiphoras.
14 Mainly belonging to the Shahra and Mahrah people of this region; these goats are regarded as being superior in all ways to the *juzʿótǝ* goats.
15 Large and fat in appearance, once slaughtered they are said to have very little fat.
16 Mainly small, short-haired white goats, said to provide little meat.
17 There are no H terms for larger herds of camels, as these were not common in the areas where Hobyōt is spoken.
18 Flattering nicknames can extend to fish: a large *rēdek* grouper is nicknamed (B) *maḥtāṭ lǝ-serbét*, 'that which ripens many young children', in praise of its plentiful flesh and fat.
19 From *šéheb* we find names for settlements such as *šéheb ɛ-ṣʿáyb*, '*šéheb* area with Acacia etbaica trees', the dim. *šāhāb*, and a plural form, *shētǝ*.
20 *embúʔd*, a general term for a temporary summer encampment on a level area well above a flow-bed.
21 A larger wasp nest is (Ś) *īgʿál ʿarḳáyb*, 'a mouse's large bag' (*migʿál* is a large leather bag in which the woman of the home kept various important possessions, such as salt, clothing, medicines and so on).
22 √ḥdr has both these meanings: 'to be(come) motionless, to do nothing' and 'to be shocked, alarmed'.
23 As yet unidentified.

24 Possibly bringing a kəbrét, i.e. 'a treat', such as a few dates or a piece of sugarcane. Children would call out: zəhámk b-kəbrét śeʔ men zəhámk ḳeśaʕún? 'Have you brought a treat or have you come back empty-handed?' (lit. 'dry').
25 As yet unidentified.
26 'Bat' in (S) is gələmə́no, pl. gilhəminítin, lit. 'unable to see well in bright sunshine' (<√glm, 'to blind, as bright light'); it is considered harmless and has none of the associations with hair mentioned here.
27 'ġálġəhal', Anisotes diversifolius and various Trichocalyx spp.; 'fə́laḳ', Leucas hagghierensis; 'mítəhan', Buxanthus pedicellatus.
28 'ḥeréśim (s. ḥárśim)', various Grewia spp. (shrubs); 'dārfon = di-ráffan', various Hibiscus spp. whose leaves bear fine stellate hairs which cause irritation if they touch the skin; 'sənémhən', Clerodendron leucophloem.
29 We witnessed the powerful effect of the decision made by Prime Minister Ardern of New Zealand to withhold the name of the murderer who killed so many at the Al-Noor mosque in Christchurch on 15 March 2019.
30 It appears that the same is true in north Yemen, and especially around Ṣanʕā (p.c. Janet Watson).
31 They could also be called ḥéyyi ḳaṣlāli (< ḳáṣləhal (m); ḳáṣəlhil ~ ḳáṣləhil (f.), 'having produced no young').
32 As well as 'filthy', ḥátkek also implies 'one who pries and snoops, one always poking his nose into other people's affairs'.
33 Pristurus rupestris, a species of tiny gecko which holds its tail upright or curled back and is widely found in human habitations and caves in Dhofar.
34 A zéber is believed to be either the motherless child of a demon, or the restless and vengeful spirit of someone for whom no funeral feast (tīmed) was held. The zéber is always hungry. It cries and wails for food, and only falls silent if something edible is thrown in its direction. The eerie sound it makes causes a listener's hair to stand on and his flesh to creep. Its persistent wailing is also said to foretell the death of a great man or some other calamity, such as a total failure of the rains.

References

Dunn, C. P. (2017), 'Climate Change and Its Consequences for Cultural and Language Endangerment', in K. L. Rehg and L. Campbell (ed.), *The Oxford Handbook of Endangered Languages*, 720–38, Oxford: Oxford University Press.

Evans, N. (2010), 'Semantic Typology', in J. J. Song (eds), *The Oxford Handbook of Linguistic Typology*, 504–33, Oxford: Oxford University Press.

Leonti, M. (2011), 'The Future Is Written: Impact of Scripts on the Cognition, Selection, Knowledge and Transmission of Medicinal Plant Use and Its Implications for

Ethnobotany and Ethnopharmacology', *Journal of Ethnopharmacology*, 134 (3): 542–55. DOI: 10.1016/j.jep.2011.01.017.

Loh, J. and D. Harmon (2014), *Biocultural Diversity: Threatened Species, Endangered Languages*. Retrieved from WWF Netherlands, Zeist, the Netherlands.

Al-Mahri, S. and A. Boom (2020), *Acacia Tortilis and Baobob*. Paper presented at the MSAL Online Workshops [online].

Miller A. G. and M. J. Morris (1988), *Plants of Dhofar, the Southern Region of Oman: Traditional, Economic and Medicinal Uses*, Muscat: The Office of the Advisor for Conservation of the Environment.

Miller A. G. and M. J. Morris (2004), *Ethnoflora of the Soqotra Archipelago*, Edinburgh: Royal Botanic Garden Edinburgh.

Morris, M. J. (1997), 'The Harvesting of Frankincense in Dhofar, Oman', in A. Avanzini and G. Salmeri (eds), *Profumi D'Arabia: Atti del Convegno*, 231–47, Rome: L'Erma di Bretschneider.

Morris, M. J. (2002), 'Plant Names in Dhofar and the Soqotra Archipelago', *Proceedings of the Seminar for Arabian Studies*, 32: 47–61.

Morris, M. J. (2003), 'The Soqotra Archipelago: Concepts of Good Health and Everyday Remedies for Illness', *Proceedings of the Seminar for Arabian Studies*, 33: 319–41.

Morris, M. J. and Ṭānuf Sālim Nuḥ Di-Kišin (2021), *The Oral Art of Soqotra: A Collection of Island Voices*. Vols. 1–3, Leiden: Brill.

Prance, G. T. (1991), 'What Is Ethnobotany Today?' *Journal of Ethnopharmacology*, 32 (1): 209–16.

Watson, J. C. E. and A. Boom (in press) 'Modern South Arabian: Appraising the Language – Nature Relationship in Dhofar', in L. Souag and M. Lafkioui (eds), *Proceedings of the 47th Annual Meeting of the North Atlantic Conference on Afroasiatic Linguistics (NACAL 47)*, Villejuif: LACITO Publications.

Watson, J. C. E., M. J. Morris, and E. Anonby (eds), *Harvesting the Sea in Southern and Eastern Arabia*, Cambridge: Cambridge Semitic Languages and Cultures.

WWF. (2018), *Living Planet Report – 2018: Aiming Higher*. [Online]. Retrieved from Gland, Switzerland: https://c402277.ssl.cf1.rackcdn.com/publications/1187/files/original/LPR2018_Full_Report_Spreads.pdf?1540487589

3

When Water Shapes Words: Musandam's Kumzari People and the Language of the Sea

Erik Anonby, AbdulQader Qasim Ali Al Kamzari and Yousuf Ali Mohammed Al Kamzari

Much of the Arabian landscape is desolate, but the surrounding waters teem with fish and other marine life. This is especially true of the Musandam Peninsula, located at the north-eastern tip of Arabia.

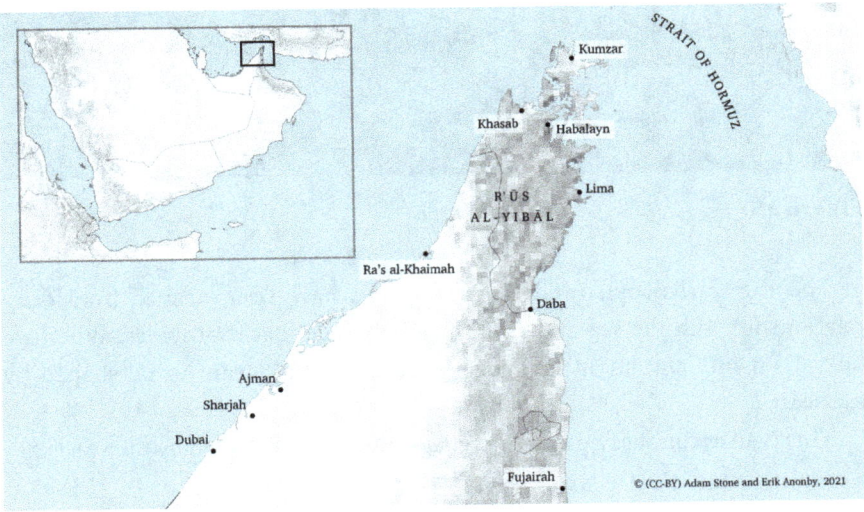

Map 3.1 Kumzar in the context of Musandam Peninsula and the surrounding waters © Adam Stone 2021.

Here, at the very tip of Musandam, right on the Strait of Hormuz, Kumzari people have lived for centuries in the town of Kumzar. From here, they have migrated during the summer each year, by boat, to the regional centres of Khasab and Daba.

Figure 3.1

The Kumzari people, and their language, have been shaped by a deep relationship with the sea and with the sustenance that it provides. When we talk about life, and about language, what does this mean: to be shaped by the sea?

This is an account of how one language, Kumzari, is shaped by the sea.

The sea shapes life

In Kumzar, all of life is oriented to the sea.

Cardinal directions

In English, and in Arabic, there are four cardinal directions:

'north'
A. *šamāl*

'east' 'west'
A. *šarq* A. *ġarb*

'south'
A. *janūb*

In Kumzari, there are two cardinal directions, based on position in relation to the sea:

'upward'
w bāla

'downward'
w ẓērin

Yes, there are Kumzari words for two of the four cardinal directions, borrowed from Arabic: *mašraq* (n.) / *šarqī* (adj.) 'east', *maġrab* (n.) / *ġarbī* (adj.) 'west'.

But if you listen to what people actually say, it's the directions *w bāla* 'up' and *w ẓērin* 'down' that structure the Kumzari world. In hours of recorded oral texts, the words for 'east' and 'west' come up just a few times. In contrast, the directions *w bāla* and *w ẓērin* are frequent.

The cardinal directions *w bāla* 'up' and *w ẓērin* 'down' have two different meanings, one local and one universal – but both are defined in relation to the sea.

The towns of Kumzar and Khasab, the main settlements of Kumzari people, are located on north-south wadis. Inside town, *w ẓērin* means towards the sea, relative to another point, and *w bāla* means up the wadi, within and eventually outside of town.

Figure 3.2

One can continue to travel *w bāla* from either town – although from Kumzar it is only possible to travel by foot – up into the mountains to the south. Just as the beach is true *ẓērin* 'depths' for Kumzari people, the mountaintops are true *bāla* 'height', and the end of the land-based world of Musandam Peninsula.

Outside of Musandam, water still defines the cardinal directions *w bāla* and *w ẓērin*, although in 'absolute' terms they are reversed: when sailing southeast towards Sohar, Muscat, or beyond to Dhofar, you need to travel *w ẓērin* 'downward'. So travel northward within the peninsula is 'downward', but ongoing travel southward, back along the east coast of the peninsula is further 'downward' yet. Travel along the coast to *ab ḍēbī* 'Abu Dhabi', and eventually to *kwēt* 'Kuwait', as the heroes of Kumzari folktales did in days gone by, takes one *w bāla*, although it is a journey in the general direction of the north-west.

Rather than being inconsistent, the local and universal meanings of cardinal *w bāla* and *w ẓērin* are united in their general schematization of *w ẓērin* as towards the greater sea – the Indian Ocean – and *w bāla* as towards the greater landmass of Eurasia, via the peninsulas.

Greetings

The sea works its way into Kumzari greetings.

salām alēkum!	'Peace upon you!'
čābī'ī? xwēšī'ī?	'How are you? Are you well?'
ḥamdilla! š xabar?	'Fine!' (lit. 'Praise God!') 'What news?'
xabar wā tō bē!	'You tell me!' (lit. 'Only you have the news!')
či kawlā?	'What wind is it?'

Because whichever wind there is affects the surface of the sea, and that determines what we'll do today. The most common reply is: *ōfirinin* 'it's a north-west wind', and that means that seas are going to be choppy. We won't travel to the city today ... and we won't go fishing in the afternoon.

Figure 3.3

If we're lucky: *dawqē* 'it's calm', and that's good for fishing.

Figure 3.4

Seasons

Even seasons – the cycle of the year – are defined by the sea:

dimistanin	'it's winter'
āminin	'it's summer'
qēwin	'it's the height of summer'
ūmatin!	'it's sardine season!'

And when the sardines come, all the other work drops, and everyone helps out until the sardines are set out to dry on the beach.

Figure 3.5

Because the sardines are a life-line. They'll get us – and the goats – through the hungry parts of the year.

The sea, the wadi and the mountain

On the edge of the water, Kumzar is known as a fishing village. It's often too hot to stay in the houses, so the centre of community life is on the beach, where people gather.

Figure 3.6

When even the beach is too hot, people climb up into the *sirg* – palm frond-shaded wooden platforms that let the breeze in, away from the radiation on the ground.

Figure 3.7 Sirg shelters, Kumzari quarter, Khasab, by Wolfgang Zimmermann © 1977, reproduced with permission of Wolfgang Zimmermann.

The village is itself shaped by water. It is connected to the mountain by water, or at least, the effects of water. Kumzar is built on an alluvial plain: gravel deposits left behind by *wīji murwānī*, the wadi that comes erratically down from the mountain. The wadi splits the village into two parts, *ēbār* 'this side' and *āmbār* 'that side'.

Figure 3.8 Sirg shelters, Kumzari quarter, Khasab by Wolfgang Zimmermann © 1977, reproduced with permission of Wolfgang Zimmermann.

The rain falls hard enough for the water to flow down from the mountain once every few years – not as often as in the past – but now when it does flow, it often rages: *wīji tay ẓērin* 'the wadi is coming down!' And every two decades or so, the water is so high that homes are washed away.

But even for those living on the mountain, the sea has always been important. Many of the boats used by the local fishing cooperatives are owned by Kumzari *kō'yan* 'mountain people'.

Figure 3.9

When the *kō'yan* still lived in the mountains, before it got too dry, they would bring reminders of the nurturing sea back with them to the mountaintop, at the end of the daily trek down to the water.

Figure 3.10

At the edge of the mountain, by the wadi that comes down to Kumzar: *čōō*, the village well. The only place for miles around where water is guaranteed year-round. Rainwater drawn into clouds from far out at sea, soaking the limestone peaks in its own time, shaping the rocks, trickling through the deep gravels of the wadi, drop by drop, never failing.

Figure 3.11

A water source so reliable that ships would stop in on their way from Basra to India and refill their supplies. The walls of the well have been smoothed into grooves over centuries of ropes, stroking the rock, lowering and raising vessels for the village.

Figure 3.12

Figure 3.13

When red tide – toxic algal blooms – fill the water, and even the desalination plants have to close down, we remember the well that gave us water ever since people have lived in Kumzar. But now, with water from the desalination plant or by ship, the well is neglected. Garbage falls in, and water of the well is becoming salty again. The sea is taking back her own.

The sea shapes language

When your whole life is shaped by
the sea,
and the things you do with it,
and in it,
like the tide, it fills and shapes your language.
It's how you come to know your world.

Species

Of course, the richness and complexity of species in and around the sea provides a wealth of words, systematically ordered as inventories and taxonomies, for example, more than 180 kinds of fish, each with its own name in Kumzari.

Figure 3.14

Seascape

It's not just species in and around the water that have names; every detail of the seascape has a label.

Every island, like the three sister islands that every Kumzari person knows: *mōmur, dīdamur, pānakō!*

Figure 3.15 Aerial view of the three sisters islands of *Mōmur, Dīdamur* and *Pānakō* in the strait to the north of Kumzar, photo by Awf Al Shehhi (Twitter @Awf_Alshehhi) © Awf Al Shehhi 2020, reproduced with the permission of Awf Al Shehhi.

Every inlet on the way from Kumzar to Khasab:

xōran
furṭa
ġōban
xōru ġuẓrō
ġubb
xōr šumm

Figure 3.16 Aerial view of the three sisters islands of *Mōmur, Dīdamur*, and *Pānakō* in the strait to the north of Kumzar, photo by Awf Al Shehhi (Twitter @Awf_Alshehhi) © Awf Al Shehhi 2020, reproduced with the permission of Awf Al Shehhi.

Every fishing cove around the village of Kumzar, and beyond:

manjal
ẓdēf
kōkba
dēqina
ṭaybuba
maysaġ

Figure 3.17

Not just these larger geographical features, but also names of seaside rocks:

ēr suqrō	'osprey bluffs'
ku xāyg	'egg rock', covered with the nests of seabirds
šāratē	'pierced rock'

Figure 3.18

And even rock features:

    šamšir ēlī   'Ali's sword', that cut through the cliffs.

Types of boats

It's true that the shaping of the language by the sea begins in the natural world; but it flows out to all areas of life and culture!

Figure 3.19

Here are some boat terms that you might hear in Kumzari. These aren't terms collected for any study that we did on boat types – they're terms that happened to be used in the folktales we collected!

    ōbur   'boat, vessel' (general term)
    jāẓ   'ship'
    būm   'traditional trading ship'
    battil   'dhow'

salq	'large dhow type'
dādrō	'short dhow type'
lanj	'motorized dhow'
ṭrājē	'motorboat'
ẓōraqa	'small boat'
ōra	'rowboat'
māšuwē	'skiff'
sōntī	'raft'

All of this technology, much of it traditional, some of it modern – and it shows up in folktales! In the shared waters of the Gulf and the Indian Ocean, boat technology is shared in many directions. A careful look at the boat names will show that some of them are shared with Arabic and other languages of the region; other names might be unique to Kumzari people, who call themselves *rōra salqan* 'children of the large dhow'.

Parts of boats and the constitution of culture

Here's the fisherman *Hama Šēx*, Muhammad Sheikh, telling us about all the parts of a boat, using the model that he built.

Figure 3.20

Dozens of boat parts! They fill up the Kumzari lexicon, and they deserve a study of their own.

š	tip of the head of the stem-post
šyō	beams across the main deck on the front side of the mast base area?
andōlō	open, square storage hollow on the starboard (right) side of the mast
aynō	second-to-rear of the four port (left) side pegs to which oars are attached
ap	paddle blade; paddling
ōp	paddle blade; paddling
arrā'an	XX thinner, rearmost portion of the side railings
astur	[lower sail-crossbar?]
ār bandirō'ō	ship's flagpole
ār bandōlō	planks between the mast and the bandal 'open, square storage hollow on the starboard (right) side of the mast'
ār spārō'ō	planks between the mast and the spārō 'open, square storage hollow on the port (left) side of the mast'
isdumi	XX rear section of the keel
ōl	mast, main mast
lyē'ō	frontmost of the four port (left) side tholepins
raw	main section of the keel
risin	oar, paddle
aṣṣ	peg, post
āzaqō	rear wall of the bow raised half-deck
ajabē'ō	rearmost of the three starboard (right) side tholepins
lē	rope; paddle
abī	[joint on a shifting stay?]
albō	ring [of rope?] around the head of the stem-post
amlē	hatch in the forward portion of the stern raised half-deck (poop deck)
arsa	thick rope
a'nag̱	cross-support (boat)
a'nag̱ maklēbit	cross supports across the front portion of the main deck to which the ropes are tied
a'nag̱u dōl	samson-post?
ān sikkānō	tiller (rudder handle)
ubrītō	front wall of the stern raised half-deck (poop deck)

Figure 3.21 An inventory of boat parts in the Kumzari lexicon.

Most of these boat parts are terms that only specialists will know in English, but most older speakers of Kumzari know them well … which shows that they are all specialists! And some terms don't have an exact lexical equivalent in English at all, so a dictionary needs to provide a long description, like 'rearmost of the three starboard tholepins'. In Kumzari, it's simple: ḥajabē'ō!

The list goes on:

Types of nets.

Parts of nets.

Fishing cooperatives, tied to specific bays, and specific boats.

Stories. Kumzari knowledge about nature is transmitted through folktales, and the sea figures strongly in these stories.

The ways men and women relate.

Men and women working together – everyone needs to help when the sardines start swarming. In the village, everyone is a sister and a brother. There is honour in family, and no shame.

Even the goats are defined by the sea. For much of the year, and sometimes for years at a time, when edible plants have all dried up on the land, the goats survive on sardines.

And their meat tastes like fish! So even here, in the festal spread of high days like weddings, the sea takes its place at the table.

Figure 3.22

Changing livelihoods, changing language

The language of nature in Kumzar is the language of water, shaped by the sea.
 But the sea is changing, and the language is changing with it.
 People used to fish for their lives, but now they fish for market. Big markets. Now, most of the fish goes *w bāla* ... up the coast to Dubai.

Figure 3.23

And, there aren't as many fish as there were.
And they're smaller.

Figure 3.24

Livelihood and language have always been shaped by the sea, but now the sea itself is changing.

Last year, the ocean's largest 'dead spot' – a zone of deoxygenated water the size of Scotland – was identified in the Sea of Oman, part of the Arabian Sea that comes right up to the Gulf at the Strait of Hormuz, where Kumzar is located.

Figure 3.25 A news article announcing a 'dead zone' in the Arabian Sea © LiveScience.com 2018. Reproduced on the basis of 'fair dealing for the purposes of criticism and review' or 'fair use for the purposes of teaching, criticism scholarship and research' in accordance with international copyright laws.

Almost every year now, there's a red tide, and the desalination plants have to shut down. They have to bring water into the villages with huge water tankers.

No oxygen for fish, or for anything to live.

With these challenges, with these changing seas, what can you do?
It's only a minority of the men that still fish.
Now, most of them work for the government or collect social assistance.

And what happens when people stop fishing?
They stop going out to sea.
Other activities – school, work, television – replace fishing.
They stop their yearly migration, by boat, from Kumzar to the regional capital Khasab; most families just stay in Khasab now.
They're cut off from the sea, and they forget about the sea, and the species, and the places, and the activities that make life worthwhile … .

… And within a generation, they stop speaking Kumzari. It's already started happening in most homes now.

Why would they need to speak it anymore? And how could they keep speaking it, if they're cut off from the sea?

We lost our words, we lost our world

This is our world, the world of Kumzari people. The things we've been talking about here are just a small selection of a larger story: a witness to the sea at the centre of the traditional livelihood and language of Kumzari people.

But as a new world emerges, there is a push, and a pull.
You're being pushed out of the world you know, because there aren't any fish left to sustain you.
You're being pulled into another world: a world of schools, and television, and jobs, and money, and cola, and mass-produced chicken.

If you're no longer in this world of the sea, and living from it, living with it, you'll lose your connection to it.

We Kumzari people are losing our connection to the sea, and with it,
connection to our whole traditional world,
and the essence of what was unique about us, and important about us:
most of what we as a community, brought to the world as a whole.

You can give a person a fish, and it will feed them for one day.
You can teach a person to fish, and they will feed themselves forever.
But when you take away a fish … when you take away all the fish …
Once that last, small fish is sold,
It's not just the fish that are gone,
it's that their whole world, this world tied to the sea … their whole world dies …
their connection to nature is gone.

And even as we Kumzari people build bigger houses, buy better cars and better phones, we're drifting into a kind of cultural poverty –
we're losing their words, and one day might lose all of our language, too.

We're losing the things that make life worth living: the simple, foundational truth that our lives are nurtured by nature, and that without connection to nature, there is no life.

> The whole world becomes poorer
>   when we lose the wisdom
>   and the world
>   of the Kumzari.

Figure 3.26

We're becoming another factory output bland and empty global culture, where everyone thinks the same, where everyone speaks the same language, goes to the same kinds of schools, listens to the same kind of music on the same model of phone. Is that what life is about?

It's like Bap Eliko's[1] own world in Canada: A world where people no longer know the names of their cousins, or even the names of their neighbours – and this is happening with the families that are building outside of the *hārat* – the Kumzari quarter of the town ...

A world where everyone has lots of stuff, and uses lots of stuff, and becomes isolated and lonely, and contributes to the problem of environmental degradation, and destroys their own livelihoods and those of others, and no one takes the responsibility for fixing things. Because the problems are too big to be fixed by people working alone.

A world that not only might not be *worth* living in,
But a world that might not be *there* for us to live in one day ...
Because we lost the fish, and we lost our words, and we lost the world.

Figure 3.27

Or did we?

The world's not lost yet, though it's fading away, a sound falling out of earshot, like waves subsiding.

Maybe, if we listen to the voices of the past

> The old Kumzari men and their stories and songs
> The old Kumzari women and their lullabies

If we remember our connection to nature,
and we remember our words,
which are a gift from nature,
there will be a tomorrow,
a tomorrow worth talking about.

Dedication

We wish to express our deep appreciation to those people among the Kumzari who generously shared their world with us. This article is dedicated to the past, present and future generations of the Kumzari people. *Waydāra xō aṣṣa!*

Figure 3.28

Acknowledgements

This study was made possible through the support of many organizations and individuals. In particular, we wish to thank Janet Watson and colleagues at the Centre for Endangered Languages, Cultures and Ecosystems (CELCE) at the University of Leeds. Many thanks to Wolfgang Zimmermann for enabling Erik Anonby to revisit Musandam Peninsula and for sharing his historical, geographic and cultural insights about the region in light of his work and experiences, spanning many decades.

Photographs

Unless specified otherwise, photographs in this chapter are by Erik Anonby, © 2020. Please contact the photographer (erik.anonby@carleton.ca) if you wish to reproduce them.

Note

An earlier version of this paper was presented at the 2019 Symposium on the Symbiotic Relationship Between Language and Nature in Arabia, University of Leeds, 24–26 April 2019.

1   Bap Eliko is co-author Erik Anonby's name in Kumzari.

Bibliography

Anonby, Erik (2011), 'Illustrations of the IPA: Kumzari', *Journal of the International Phonetic Association*, 41 (3): 375–80.

Anonby, Erik (2012), 'Stress-induced Vowel Lengthening and Harmonization in Kumzari', *Orientalia Suecana*, 61: 54–8.

Anonby, Erik (2020), 'Emphatic Consonants beyond Arabic: The Emergence and Proliferation of Uvular-pharyngeal Emphasis in Kumzari', *Linguistics*, 58 (1): 275–328.

Anonby, Erik and AbdulQader Qasim Ali Al Kamzari (forthcoming), 'A Typology of Fish Names in Kumzari, a Language of North-eastern Arabia', in J. C. E. Watson, M. J. Morris, and E. Anonby (eds), *Harvesting the Sea in Southern and Eastern Arabia*, Cambridge: Cambridge Semitic Languages and Cultures.

Anonby, Erik, Shahina Ghazanfar, Christina van der Wal Anonby, Yousuf Ali Mohammed Al Kamzari, Ahmad Hassan Ali Salim Al-kumzari, Hassan Suleyman Al-kumzari, and Suleyman Muhammad Al-kumzari (2018), 'Plants and Plant Names in Kumzari and Arabic of Musandam Peninsula, Oman', paper presented at the Workshop on Language and Nature, University of Leeds, 2 July 2018.

Anonby, Erik and Alec Moore (2018), 'Cultural and Linguistic Connections with Fauna in Southern and Eastern Arabia', paper presented at the Symposium on Language and Nature in Southern and Eastern Arabia, University of Qatar, Doha, 18–20 February, 2018.

Anonby, Erik, Christina van der Wal Anonby, and AbdulQader Qasim Ali Al Kamzari (2018), 'The Language of Nature in Kumzari and the Arabic Dialects of Musandam', paper presented at the Symposium on Language and Nature in Southern and Eastern Arabia, University of Qatar, Doha, 18–20 February 2018.

Gasparini, Fabio and Saeed al-Mahri (2023), 'Water and Culture among the MSAL-speaking People of Dhofar', in J. C. E. Watson, J. C. Lovett, and R. Morano (eds), *Language and Ecology in Southern and Eastern Arabia*, London: Bloomsbury.

Harrison, K. David (2007), *When Languages Die: The Extinction of the World's Languages and the Erosion of Human Knowledge*, New York and London: Oxford University Press.

Levinson, Stephen C. (2003), *Space in Language and Cognition*, Cambridge: Cambridge University Press.

van der Wal Anonby, Christina (2015), *A Grammar of Kumzari: A Mixed Perso-Arabian Language of Oman*, Leiden: Leiden University.

van der Wal Anonby, Christina (2014), 'Traces of Arabian in Kumzari', in Orhan Elmaz and Janet C. E. Watson (eds.), *Languages of Southern Arabia: Special Session of the Seminar for Arabian Studies*, Oxford: Archaeopress, 137–46.

Watson, Janet C. E., et al. (forthcoming), 'A Comparative Lexicon of Fish Names in Non-Arabic Languages of Southern and Eastern Arabia', in J. C. E. Watson, M. J. Morris and E. Anonby (eds), *Harvesting the Sea in Southern and Eastern Arabia*, Cambridge: Cambridge Semitic Languages and Cultures.

Weisberger, Mindy (2018), 'Massive "Dead Zone" in the Arabian Sea Is the Biggest in the World', *Live Science*. Available online: https://www.livescience.com/62489-dead-zone-arabian-sea.html (accessed 5 May 2018).

4

Water and Culture among the Modern South Arabian-Speaking People

Fabio Gasparini and Saeed al-Mahri

Introduction

The topic of water has been the object of growing interest from multiple perspectives within the humanities in recent years. The role of issues such as global warming and the threat of water scarcity has given rise to many concerns about the human exploitation of land resources. Great interest has been directed towards the social value of water and how our habits and practices reflect personal and collective beliefs; intensive research in recent years has consistently shown the strong interconnection between cultural practices and the management of water, its use and distribution in ancient times.[1] In this sense, traditional customs adopted by minorities across the world can offer us a chance to confront modern issues – such as environmental crises and the loss of biological and cultural diversity – by developing sustainable strategies.

This chapter tries to portray the place of water within the cultures of the Modern South Arabian languages (henceforth MSAL)-speaking people of the Dhofar Governorate of Oman and the governorate of al-Mahrah in Yemen from an ethnolinguistic perspective. First, we will deal with the way landscape – meaning a man-made system of interpretation of the environment – is created and how the human need to fetch water conditions this process. We then

---

We declare that this chapter represents the joint effort of the two authors. In particular, al-Mahri's contribution is related to paragraph §2.2, while Gasparini is responsible for the remaining contents and text organization. We thank Luca D'Anna and Valentina Serreli for commenting on a draft of this paper.

The contribution from the first author stems from considerations related to the project 'describing the Modern South Arabian Baṭḥari language' funded by Fritz Thyssen Stiftung (ref. 40.20.0.007SL).

examine the occurrence of images related to water in the poetic tradition of the Mahrah by drawing meaningful comparisons with other Arabian groups such as the Dawāsīr of Saudi Arabia surviving in a similar environmental setting in a different part of the Arabian Peninsula.

Water and space

An analysis of the way MSAL-speaking communities relates to their environment from a spatial perspective and the linguistic coding of cultural practices related to water will be the focus of this section. The idea behind this topic stems from our interest in the toponymic system and linguistic encoding of space in the MSAL of Dhofar. In the following section a general assessment of the importance of toponyms and their connection to our topic will be given; an ethnolinguistic analysis of practices related to fetching water will be proposed.

Naming places: The importance of toponyms

Place names – in different areas and times – often allow linguists to trace the origins of languages and to go back to the remote roots of a toponymic system and of a language, offering an opportunity to confirm or to deny theories and hypotheses and to establish an 'onomastic stratigraphy' of toponyms, hydronyms and oronyms. In this sense, through the names of places, wadis and springs, an insight into some aspects of traditional culture in relation to water can be given.

According to Nash (2015: 102), toponyms are 'important cultural and environmental artefacts and events' from an ecolinguistic point of view. They preserve impressions, knowledge and cosmovisions held by the societies that have at some point coined them. Toponyms are the tangible proof of the inseparable functional relationship between humans and environment as realized in the creation of landscape, which 'is not a natural feature of the environment but a synthetic space, a man-made system functioning and evolving not according to natural laws but to serve a community' (Jackson 1986: 68). Human groups become engaged with the environment once they start to assign cultural saliency by assigning names to its constituents: '[e]ngagement gives and is defined by the way we give cultural meaning to the location of our existence – so that even the trees and the rocks mean different things to different people' (David and Thomas 2008: 36).

A well-informed apparatus of toponymic data can be of great interdisciplinary interest, especially in those contexts where historical records are lacking or very poor – as is the case for the MSAL-speaking people. For example, Dostal (1989) observed that Mehri toponyms can be found more towards the northeast of the al-Mahrah province if compared to their current area. This suggests a possible movement of people that more research might eventually be able to verify. While the role of Old South Arabian, an extinct sub-branch of Semitic once spoken in the same area, in shaping the toponymy of South Arabia and Yemen in particular has been (Matthews 1959, 1962) and currently is (Koutchoukali 2020) under investigation and a good amount of field data is available (Glazer 1913, again Matthews 1959; 1962), traditional MSAL toponyms across the area are almost undocumented. Memories of the traditional toponymic system are progressively fading due to the decay of traditional lifestyles and the dramatic environmental changes in the areas around Salalah, the capital of Dhofar. These dreadful phenomena have been taking place during the last thirty years, due to severe over-exploitation of natural resources and leading to progressive desertification in some areas. For these reasons, interest in MSAL toponomastics from a multidisciplinary approach has recently been gaining academic interest; in particular, giving special attention to diachronic approaches in future research (as in Perono Cacciafoco et al. 2015) will surely help scholars to shed new light on the history of Southern Arabia as a whole.

Some place names for inhabited areas make overt reference to the presence of water: the cultural information they encode is directly related to the availability and physical manifestation of water itself. Some examples are the Mehri names for the villages of *Nūṭəf* ('dripping water'), close to Ḥāsik, to the east of Salalah, *Aġayṣat* ('abundant water') on the mountains east of Salalah and *Muṣay* ('water seeping from underground'), located in the Najd to the north of Salalah. Without any doubt further studies will produce further evidence of the relation between less overt toponyms and the environment.

It is now time to focus our attention on how the people of Dhofar (with special attention to the formerly nomadic and semi-nomadic population) managed to satisfy their need for water. Cultural practices related to fetching water and how they relate to the landscape will be considered.

Finding water

Sedentary lifestyles based on agriculture and water management developed in Northern Oman as early as during the Iron Age, as archaeological data on the *aflāj* system (water channels used for irrigation and water distribution) testifies

(Tikriti 2002). On the other hand, most of the inhabitants of Dhofar maintained a semi-nomadic lifestyle, preferring pastoralism to agriculture. It might seem too obvious to state the difficulties in accessing water experienced by those living in the desert areas of Arabia; however, the case of the Baṭāḥira tribe is particularly illustrative in that throughout their history they have faced what could be considered to be among the hardest conditions experienced by those living in southern Arabia.

Fetching water with the Baṭāḥira

Incessant water shortage was experienced in the past by the Baṭāḥira. Living in the easternmost coastal area of Dhofar – a desertic and harsh environment offering almost nothing in the way of fresh water to its inhabitants – the Baṭāḥira did not enjoy the abundant rain of the monsoon season (Baṭḥari *xarifīt*) of Salalah and the surrounding mountains. As a consequence, drinkable water was even more vital: many of the narratives gathered by Gasparini as well as those collected by Morris (in prep.) during their respective fieldwork with the Baṭāḥira stress how hard it was to quench their thirst (*əmōh ykūn lə śūrī lā əmoh / mɛlḥēt / ykūn mɛlḥēt w-ikūn ṭayf / śay mɛlḥēt w-nəḵuy* 'The water was not good, the water / salty / it was salty and it was bitter / it was salty and we would throw up' (Gasparini 2018: 143)). The tribe could not find what they needed in order to survive in their immediate area, so the tribeswomen were forced to go off daily to fetch water. The Baṭāḥira spent most of their time settled[2] along the coast, so they could harvest the sea. The only water resources were springs (*ʕayn*) or occasional small natural pools of non-porous rock (*śterīr*) filled with rainwater on the mountains surrounding Gəzərēt[3] and Šarbithāt, the two main areas of settlement of the tribe. The lack of reliable water sources (together with other social factors which go beyond the topic of this chapter) inevitably had a severe impact on the life of the tribe, since it did not allow them to rely on pastoralism as much as the other Dhofari tribes did (and still do): only goats and a few camels were bred, whereas cows would not have survived in such a harsh environment.

Fetching water with the Mahra[4]

The other nomadic tribes scattered across Dhofar were blessed with lands offering greater opportunities of finding water, be it from the ground (permanent) or from rainfall (temporary), as explained in alMahri (2015). Since rearing animals was the priority, desert dwellers could not spend the whole year in the vicinity of groundwater sources as they had to move from one place to another in search of better pastures – notwithstanding the fact that in desert areas groundwater can rapidly come to shortage. Periodic migrations from the desert to the green mountains around Salalah and back were therefore a necessary tradition. Cloud movements were carefully observed by those in desert areas in order to predict where rain might fall, so to lead the herd. The dark *ʔafōr rəmnay* ('cloud from the sea') would bring heavy rain, whereas the white *ʔafōr nəgday* ('cloud from the interior') would not. Clouds were also distinguished by size: the *zəḥfīf* clouds would completely cover the whole sky, whereas the *ġamlēl* and the *ġamṭār* would be of more modest extension. Seasonal rains would leave natural water pools (*maḥlīḵ*) scattered across the desert making it easier for herds and those in-charge of them to cross the desert. A scout was usually sent ahead of the group in order to check whether the rainfall was sufficient for the tribe's needs.

The mountains were preferred in order to avoid attacks from raiders and whenever there was the need for more abundant water. Natural pools of water seeping in from the rock (*fōḳa*) would be available especially during and right after the rain season; water could be collected from rocks in any season, thanks to springs and dripping underground water.

In the Najd of Dhofar, the wadis of Andur[5] (near Jabal Samḥān, north of the town of Mirbāṭ) and Habrut[6] (in the western mountains of Dhofar) were the two most important places for nomadic groups, both for their crucial position and wealth of natural resources[7]: these permanent waterholes are surrounded by natural oases providing abundant water, food and dates and shelter from the merciless heat of the desert, as described also by Bertram Thomas in his famous book Arabia Felix (1932). Even today, these wadis are still used for tribal meetings.

Still, fetching water was far from easy and the unpredictability of natural resources forced the nomadic tribes to invent ingenious techniques for collecting and conserving water. One of the strategies adopted by the inhabitants of the Najdi desert consists in creating a waterscrape (Mehri *maḥṣāt*, Shẹrēt *maḥisi*). A hole in the ground would be dug to access underground water, usually at the head of a wadi. To determine a valid place to dig, a heavy stone would be lifted and dropped down. The echo produced by this thud would be evaluated to determine the presence and depth of underground water. If the presence of water was confirmed, a waterhole would be dug with simple digging tools such as wooden poles or rocks and using milk bowls (Mehri *ḵālīw*) as shovels up to two metres below the surface. Again, milk bowls would be used to extract the water, which would be carried in waterskins made from the complete hide of a goat (common MSAL *nīd*).

Even such inhospitable and dry places as the desert offer unexpected possibilities for gathering water: by covering a tree with a textile, dew drops could be collected for drinking and cooking purposes. Troughs built beneath big trees such as the widespread *tik̠* (fig tree) collected monsoon rain dripping from tree branches.

Other strategies for collecting water were also developed, such as digging wells or cisterns (Mehri *bēr*, Śḥerēt *ġōr*) and building dams (Mehri *krayf*) in order to collect rainwater at the bottom of a valley. In this case, clayish soil was required to prevent seepage for a long period of time. Access to these resources was not equally granted to all: it often happened that a tribe claimed the ownership of one of these and felt entitled to water their animals first. It is not irrelevant that a popular Śḥerēt saying states that *ɛ bedər i-šɔk̠* 'he who comes first, waters his animals'.[8] This is said to praise someone's promptness at carrying out an action and this person's subsequent gain, in contrast to someone else who did not act as promptly and effectively (al-Shahri 2000: 74, 242; Castagna, 2022).

The practices described so far are remnants of a world lacking direct access to water, prompting its inhabitants to find different ways to survive in this environment. These specific skills do not appear to be useful on a daily basis anymore, due to urbanization and ease of access to water – much to everyone's relief. The availability of water parallels the widespread process of cultural (and linguistic) impoverishment of minorities known to be taking place around the world. However, the recording of such skills and other similar examples of traditional expertise and their integration into current scientific studies could lead to innovative solutions to water management and help mitigate future hydrologic crises.

Water and poetry

In the previous paragraphs we examined the human-landscape interface in southern Arabia, focusing on its ethnographic peculiarities. But what is the impact of landscape on the imaginative world of its inhabitants? Is water a salient element in literature?

From a comparative perspective, water – with its endless imaginative potential (Douglas 1973) – is a recurrent element in the creation of metaphors at multiple levels and in different cultural systems of the world. One might rightfully wonder about the 'universalities in human experience' given the widespread use of the image of water in religious rituals to symbolize spiritual 'congregation', processes of transformation and the generation of life itself (Strang 2008: 124). We shall demonstrate how specific allegories about daily life are developed in an Arabian environment.

We want to stress a recurrent motif of Arabian poetry regardless of poetic genre and prestige, social occasion, intended audience and – more importantly – tribal affiliation and cultural heritage. Taking as a primary object of examination Mehri poetry (al-Barami, al-Mashikhi and Liebhaber, this volume; Liebhaber 2018),[9] we will try to create a dialogue between different traditions of the Arabian Peninsula by reading them from a synchronic perspective. Questions about historical connections and transmission will not be dealt with here, since such a discussion is not pertinent to the topic of this chapter (some answers can be found elsewhere).[10] Instead, we will navigate from Mehri to Arabic poetry on an arbitrary basis, and let thematic parallelisms take the lead in the following paragraphs.

Rainstorms and floods: A history of violence

Within the *ʔōdī we-krēm krēm* Mehri genre, which is 'felt to encapsulate the codes and customs of traditional Mehri society and to preserve its official tribal history for posterity [...] using the Mehri language's unique poetic formulations' (Liebhaber 2018), the so-called *faṣīḥ* poems stem from a formulaic structure, also dear to the Arabic tradition: the poet observes the landscape from an elevated vantage point, with the gentle *mdīt* wind blowing from the sea. The poet then explains the escalating violence which brought the tribes close to conflict through the use of allegoric images: '[t]he atmospheric tumult and transition from day to night mirrors the poet's emotional turmoil as he anticipates a shift from social stability to conflict and upheaval' (Liebhaber 2010: 229). This ultimately leads to a war described with the recurrent rainstorm and flood motif and its allegorical implications as an element of rites of passage and religious purification (Liebhaber 2013: 133).

Consider the following passage:

fōn eġawreb ezernīw / bāl ezōyed ḏe-ġbēr / zehmōten le-ġrūb | eḏhībeh yeṭmūm / le-ġdēd ebelyōt / we-k-ṣamt yekbūb | we-ġżāb eżeymet ḳā / we-ġyīm l-ḥārwāh / w-hel men eṭma ksūb 'I've known from before the thundering rain clouds / the one that brings great quantities of dust / sheets of rain from water-buckets | Its flood covers the earth / even up to the ancient highlands / with violence (the flood) rolls down | Its roiling surge encompasses the land / sending clouds over all of humankind / and snatches away everything that is valuable'.[11]

In this prototypical passage the poet stands *ṭār ḳāṭen w-ṭarbūt* 'atop the peak of Ṭarbūt' feeling the *mdīt* 'sea breeze' and pondering about past clashes he has witnessed. The tribal army (the thundering rain clouds) does not spare anything on its path of destruction (the subsequent violent flood rolling down). This *topos* is common to both Mehri and Arabic tradition – even though it is not as frequent in the classical *qaṣīda* (Stetkevych 1993: 278). Rainstorms are thus associated with uncontrolled and devastating fury and the intimidating strength of the tribe during the assault, as we see in the traditional poetry of the Bedouin Dawāsīr tribe of central Saudi Arabia. Their odes to tribal power and strength regularly propose images such as the following *nawwin ḥadar gāmat tigaṣṣaf rʕudih / amṭar ʕala Yāmin b-suww al-ʕaḏābi* 'a large cloud came down from the sky with loud thunderclaps, / releasing a deluge that brought death and destruction to Yām' (Kurpershoek 2002: 656–7).

The tribesmen army always stand proud *we-ṭṭərēf el yehyūb* 'and they do not fear the other side' (Liebhaber 2018).[12] Their fierce nature cannot be tamed and they do as they please:

> la nāḏ barrāg al-wsāmi tibiʕ nāh/ w-in nāḏ barg aṣ-ṣēf sannad ḏaʕanna | inna ćima nawwin sibag bārǵih māh/ min ṭāh fi diglātna ma šaḥanna 'we follow the flicker of the winter rains' lightning/ the flashes of late spring send our pack-camels up-country. | We are like a rainstorm that is announced by lightning, / indifferent to the fate of those who are swept up by us'.[13]

Total annihilation of their opponents is the ultimate goal of their attack:

> tanahhaḏat min jarr Ṣabḥa maxīlah / b-sēlin yiṭimm al-ʕirǵ wi-l-ʕadām / ṣabbat w-anṣibat w-inṣabb māha w-ṣabṣibat / bi-mšawwakin yašḏi silīb iʕḏām 'from Ṣabḥa's watercourse a dark mass of clouds arose, / unleashing a torrent that flooded the dunes and undulating sands / pouring down its waters relentlessly and persistently, / in a hail of bullets that splice and shatter the enemy's bones'.[14]

An impending rainstorm can also foreshadow imminent catastrophe or a lurking menace (Liebhaber 2013: 141): *bālī teḥfīf eśśēr / men ezōyed we-ġṣūt | nōwet eds ettənāyū / w-ṭerefs ber ǵtūt* 'Lord, lessen the evil between the people, stay its increase and overwhelming darkness. | Rain clouds are yet darkening the sky, but they have begun to disperse at their edges' (Liebhaber 2013: 139).

It must be noted that this kind of poetry is far from being a 'dead' genre; to the contrary, any event worthy of memory can trigger the poetic occasion, such as the case of an accidental gun fight between armed Mahra and a group of North Yemeni troops in the port town of Nišṭawn, referred to as the *Ḥadīthat Nishṭūn al-dāmiyya* 'Nishṭūn's Bloody Incident' (al ʕAhdal 1999: 111), which took place in 1997. Here an allegorical and apparently cryptic narrative is favoured due to the sensitive political topic and the need to avoid explicit reference to the central government:

neğm ertəbūb w-hen / men ḥōmer ḏ-ḥeklī / nēweh ʾādeh ān ṭbūt | ḥemlet arḵās / men erems̆ ḏe-ks̆ē / yeḥlīlen ebyūt | ār ḫlūṭem s̆eh nğūm / men ʾāṣef ḏe-ryiḥ / we-tḵawleb ḏ-bīlōt 'The rain-star about to burst and thunder / at the edge of the eastern clouds / the downpour is about to come | They fall upon Arḵās / from mouths of the black thunderheads / they come through the roofs of the houses | Other rain-stars have arrived with them / on the storms of winds / that become like those of desert'.[15]

Here the *nğūm* represent the Mahra intervening in the gun fight one after the other, beckoned by the gunshots.

Water as a blessing

Not only the wild and potentially destructive side of water is represented in poetry: we should always remember the universal relationship between water and life. Invocations are made, appealing to the mercifulness of God, manifested through the blessing of rain on the drying land: ʕasa dārhum ʕugb ar-ribīʕ tṣāf 'may their homeland be blessed with rains in spring and summer' (Kurpershoek 2002: 516–17) and s̆mīmet enṭərōr / teh bālī ks̆ē | ys̆eṭṭem ḥarḵ / we-ryiḥ we-lḥēb 'would that God might give us rain / in the canyon of S̆mīmet Neṭrōr | It has struggled against the drought, / the wind and fire for long enough' (Liebhaber 2018).[16]

Caton (1991: 316) states that fixed formulas are frequently used based on the ideas of 'rain falling from the sky, lightning flash, and the wadi in flood' in traditional *zāmil* poetry of northern Yemen. These formulas function as intensifiers of a greeting/thanksgiving and can be extended according to speakers' needs and will. This use has a clearly apotropaic function:

yā dhī badaʕt al-gōl ḥayyā mā tanazzal / maznah fiy ignāf al-ʕamān | marḥab jamiʕ aḏ-ḏēf mā yirʕad wa sayyal / mā raḥbah al-jabrī wa yām[17] 'O you who composed the saying: greetings as great as the rain that falls / from the black cloud, | welcome to all the guests, [a welcome] as powerful as the lightning | and as turbulent as the flood, / as the Jabri and Yam'[18]

And again:

salam[a] l-ak ma lamaʔ barg-ah wa ma sabbal | min rus[a] l-agnaf[a] w-amsa r-raʕda hannani 'greetings to you [as many times as] His lightning flashes and rain falls; | From the mountain peaks all night long the thunder claps'.

(Caton 1991: 295)

Compare these to the following Dawāsīr thanksgiving from Kurpershoek (2002: 440–1), where the allegoric augmentative value of the raindrops perfectly echoes the previous greeting: *sallim ʕalēh ʕdād wablin miṭarha* 'Salute him as many times as drops of rain fall from the sky'.

Poetic impetus (sometimes seen as the fruit of inspiration from the spirit *ʕafrīt shiʕr*) is said to assail the poet *miṯl sēlin ḥadar min rūs šiʕbāni / la ja ʕḏātin b-wasṭ aš-šiʕb yazwīha* 'like a torrent rushing down from the higher valleys, / sweeping up any tree that happens to stand in its course' (Kurpershoek 2002: 652–3); or it cascades on the *nabaṭi* poet *kina marāhiš ba ṣ-ṣēf* 'like summer rainstorms' (Holes 2011). Both metaphors rely again on the unpredictable nature of weather phenomena and on the uncontrollable strength of waterstreams. Yet such inspiration can be elusive: *wet ṭwōren thākawb / beyn ərāmel we-ḫtāt / hēs əbīr messənūt* 'Sometimes the "muse" migrates / between the sandy plain and the pasture land / like a spring from which people habitually draw water' (Liebhaber 2018).[19]

Conclusions

The ultimate aim of this chapter was to provide a critical account of the place of water among the MSAL speakers of southern Arabia. We showed how a specific environment pushes its inhabitants towards the development of cultural practices to enable them to survive and, at the same time, how the experience of a similar environment by different human groups impacts their imaginative poetic use of language.

We hope we have succeeded in explicating some, if not all, of our initial premises and that the ideas explored here will inspire academic debate and encourage further study: *al-waʕd ka-r-raʕd wa-l-īfā ka-l-maṭari* 'a promise is like lightning and fulfillment is like rain'.[20]

Notes

1   See Strang (2008) for an exhaustive overview of the literature on the topic from an archaeological and anthropological perspective.
2   See Morris (2017: 15–19) for an account on the concept of 'home' in the various MSALs.

3   The Baṭḥari name for the better known Ashwaymiyyah.
4   We will be referring to Mahra customs throughout this paragraph; however, such practices are common also among the other nomadic tribes in the area.
5   Possibly from the root *NDR, from which Mehri *hǝndūr* 'to sever at a stroke' but also 'to suckle' (Johnstone 1987: 280–1). Also locally called Wādi Nṣawr.
6   Possibly from the root *BRW, from which Mehri *hǝbrō* 'to lift; to climb right up; to jump; to shield oneself under' (Johnstone 1987: 54).
7   In the light of the tentative etymological connections proposed in the two preceding footnotes, the names for these two wadis might refer to two fundamental properties of a desirable shelter: safeness and protection (i.e. a place safe enough to suckle babies with no danger).
8   It is also worth mentioning that pragmatic equivalents to this saying can be found among many different cultures, and that the rewards for being the first on the scene give us significant details about their *weltanschauung*: compare with one of the many Italian similar idioms *chi prima arriva meglio alloggia* 'the one who arrives earlier receives a better accommodation (lit.)' and the English *first come, first served* or *the early bird gets the worm*.
9   This freely accessible online resource gives a vivid and engaging portrait of contemporary Mehri poetry gathered by its author between al-Mahrah and Dhofar during the last twenty years.
10 Liebhaber (2010; 2015) offers a detailed discussion on the connections between Mehri and *Nabaṭī* poetry (vernacular poetry from the Arabian Peninsula).
11 Liebhaber 2018. http://whenmelodiesgather.supdigital.org/wmg/atop-the-peak-of-arbt (accessed 3 June 2020).
12 Ibid.
13 Kurpershoek (2002: 220–1).
14 Kurpershoek (2002: 674–7).
15 Liebhaber (2018). http://whenmelodiesgather.supdigital.org/wmg/gunfight-in-nisawn (accessed 8 September 2020).
16 Liebhaber (2018). http://whenmelodiesgather.supdigital.org/wmg/the-dog-days-of-summer (accessed 8 September 2020).
17 It must be noted that Caton's Arabic transcriptions do not follow the academic standards of Semitic studies. They are hereby reported unchanged, apart from the /ʔ/ and /ʕ/ phonemes.
18 Caton (1991: 315–16). Jabri and Yam refer to two ancient tribes of Yemen famous for their generosity.
19 http://whenmelodiesgather.supdigital.org/wmg/the-battle-of-kbbt (accessed 29 September 2020).
20 Cf. Caton (1991: 57).

References

Al ʾAhdal, Ḥ. M. (1999), *Muḥāfaẓat al-mahra: Ḥaqāʾiq wa-l-ʾarqām*, Sanaʾa: al-Ḍiyāʾ li-l-Ṭibāʿa bi-l-Kambyūtur.

al-Barami, K., A. al-Mashikhi and S. Liebhaber (2023) 'Orature and Nature in Southern Arabia', in J. C. E. Watson, J. C. Lovett and R. Morano (eds), *Language and Ecology in Southern and Eastern Arabia*, London: Bloomsbury.

alMahri, S. (2015), *Traditional Water Sources in Dhofar*. Water@Leeds blog. Available online: https://wateratleeds.wordpress.com/2015/02/18/traditional-water-sources-in-dhofar/ (accessed 29 September 2020).

Castagna, G. (2022), A Collection of Jibbali/Śḥerēt Proverbs from Ali al-Shahri's Publication 'The Language of Aad'. *Old World: Journal of Ancient Africa and Eurasia*, 2(1): 1–89.

Caton, S. C. (1991), *'Peaks of Yemen I summon': Poetry as a Cultural Practice in a North Yemeni Tribe*, Berkeley: University of California Press.

David, B. and J. Thomas (2008), 'Landscape Archaeology: Introduction', in B. David and J. Thomas (eds), *Manual of Landscape Archaeology*, 27–43, Walnut Creek: Left Coast Press.

Dostal, W. (1989), 'Mahra and Arabs in South Arabia: A Study in Inter-ethnical Relations', in I. Moawiya (ed.), *Arabian Studies in Honour of Mahmoud Ghul: Symposium at Yarmouk University December 8–11, 1984*, 27–36, Wiesbaden: Harrasowitz.

Douglas, M. (1973), *Natural Symbols*, London: Random House.

Gasparini, F. (2018), *The Baṭḥari Language of Oman. Towards a Descriptive Grammar*, PhD diss., Naples: Università degli Studi di Napoli 'L'Orientale'.

Glaser, E. (1913), *Reise nach Mârib*, Wien: A. Hölder.

Holes, C. (2011), 'Nabaṭī Poetry, Language of', in L. Edzard and R. de Jong (eds), *Encyclopedia of Arabic Language and Linguistics*, Leiden: Brill. Available online: https://referenceworks.brillonline.com/entries/encyclopedia-of-arabic-language-and-linguistics (accessed 12 September 2020).

Jackson, J. (1986), 'The Vernacular Landscape', in E. Penning-Rowsell and D. Lowenthal (eds), *Landscape Meanings and Values*, 65–81, London: Allen and Unwin.

Johnstone, T. M. (1987), *Mehri Lexicon and English–Mehri Word-List*, London: Routledge.

Koutchoukali, I. (2020), *Toponyms of South Arabia: From ESA to Arabic*, Lecture for the Semitics Twitter Corona Conference, online 31 March 2020.

Kurpershoek, M. P. (2002), *Oral Poetry and Narratives from Central Asia, Vol. IV (A Saudi Tribal History – Honour and Faith in the Traditions of the Dawāsir)*, Leiden: Brill.

Liebhaber, S. (2010), 'Written Mahri, Mahri Fuṣḥā and Their Implications for Early Historical Arabic', *Proceedings of the Seminar for Arabian Studies*, 40: 227–32.

Liebhaber, S. (2013), 'Rhetoric, Rite-of-passage and the Multilingual Poetics of Arabia', *Journal of Middle Eastern Literatures*, 16 (2): 118–46.

Liebhaber, S. (2015), 'Mahri Oral Poetry and Arabic Nabaṭī Poetry: Common Core, Divergent Outcomes', *Arabian Humanities*. Available online: http://journals. openedition.org/cy/2973 (accessed 23 August 2020).

Liebhaber, S. (2018), *When Melodies Gather: The Oral Art of the Mahra*, Stanford: Stanford University Press. Available online: http://whenmelodiesgather.supdigital. org/wmg/stanford-up/index.html (accessed 3 October 2020).

Matthews, C. D. (1959), 'Non-Arabic Place Names in Central South Arabia', in H. Franke (ed.), *Akten des vierundzwanzigsten interionationalen Orientalisten-Kongresses, München, 28. August bis 4. September 1957*, 259–62, Wiesbaden: Franz Steiner.

Matthews, C. D. (1962), 'Again on Non-Arabic Place Names in Central South Arabia', in E. G. Gafurov (ed.), *Trudy XXV mezhuarodnogo kongressa vostokovedow, Moskva, 9–16 August 1960*, 1, 548–54, Moscow: Vostočnoj Literatury.

Morris, M. J. (2017), 'Some Thoughts on Studying the Endangered Modern South Arabian Languages', *Journal of Afroasiatic Languages and Linguistics*, 9 (1–2): 9–32.

Morris, M. J. (in prep.), *A Collection of Baṭhari Texts*. Wiesbaden: Harrassowitz.

Nash, J. (2015), 'Placenames and Ecolinguistics: Some Considerations for Toponymists', *AAA: Arbeiten aus Anglistik und Amerikanistik*, 40 (1/2): 99–103.

Perono Cacciafoco, F., F. Cavallaro and F. Kratochvíl (2015), 'Diachronic Toponomastics and Language Reconstruction in South-East Asia According to an Experimental Convergent Methodology: Abui as a Case-Study', *Review of Historical Geography and Toponomastics*, 10 (19–20): 29–47.

AlShaḥrī, ʿA. A. (2000), *Lughat ʿād*, Abu Dhabi: al-Muʾassasa al-Waṭaniyya li-al-Taghlīf wa-al-Ṭibāʿa.

Stetkevych, S. (1993), *The Mute Immortals Speak: Pre-Islamic Poetry and the Poetics of Ritual*, Ithaca: Cornell University Press.

Strang, V. (2008), 'The Social Construction of Water', in B. David and J. Thomas (eds), *Handbook of Landscape Archaeology*, 123–30, Abingdon: Routledge.

Thomas, B. (1932), *Arabia Felix: Across the Empty Quarter of Arabia*, London: Jonathan Cape.

Tikriti, W. (2002), 'The South-East Arabian Origin of the Falaj System', *Proceedings of the Seminar for Arabian Studies*, 32: 117–38.

5

A Botanical and Etymological Approach to Plant Names in Southern Arabia

Shahina A. Ghazanfar and Leonid Kogan

Introduction

Human dependence on plants cannot be overstated. Plants provide not only food for human consumption, but also shelter and medicine and have done so for millennia. Humans have taken plants along with them wherever they have travelled to and settled. Be it for food, timber, medicine, shelter, fragrance or ornament, plants have been intimate companions to humankind.

In the Old World, domestication of crops known from archaeological and archaeobotanical evidence suggests that by 10,000–8000 BCE annual cereal grasses such as einkorn, emmer free-theshing wheat and barley together with several pulses such as pea, lentil and chickpea (lentil – *Lens culinaris*, pea – *Pisum sativum*, chickpea – *Cicer arietinum*) begin to appear in the Levant and northern Fertile Crescent of southwest Asia (Jordan, Palestine, Syria, Turkey) (Fuller and Stevens 2019; Zohary et al. 2012: 1–2). In the Near East, during the Bronze Age indigenous forests were replaced with cultivated crops such as olive, grape and fig; date palm appears to have been cultivated since more than 5000 years BCE.

Through global human expansion, crops and animals favoured by humans along with non-domesticated plants and animals spread globally. Evidence

---

Royal Botanic Gardens, Kew, TW9 3AE, UK.

National Research University HSE, Moscow, Russia. Kogan's contribution to this chapter has been financed in the framework of the project 20-012-41005 of РФФИ/RFBR.

seen from translocated crops, as well as linguistic data relating to tree crops and boat technology shows cultural contacts between societies in East Africa, South Asia, Arabia and Southeast Asia (Fuller et al. 2011). During 2000–1500 BCE trade existed between northeast Africa, India and Arabia, and by the end of the third millennium BCE sea trade was established between the Persian Gulf and the Red Sea. Trade with Egypt was established from 4000 BCE, and from 2000 BCE trade was prevalent between India and the Persian Gulf region (Boivin and Fuller 2009). The Harrapan civilization (Indus Valley Civilization, mature period from 2600 to 1900 BCE) was involved in sea trade with Oman, Bahrain and Mesopotamia in the second half of the third millennium BCE (Boivin and Fuller 2009).

The recognition of useful and harmful plants has always been a keen objective to human civilization. Plants have been given names and classified wherever they have been used or proved harmful for consumption. Consequently, hundreds of names can exist for the same plant in different languages or dialects. Wherever plants were transported to, domesticated and cultivated, either new names were given to them or the original names retained. Adopted in different languages, names of plants changed overtime sometimes beyond recognition of the original name. An analysis of the etymology of the drugs mentioned in Al-Kindī's (c. 801–75 CE) book on medicine, Aqrābādhīn, showed that 31 per cent of the names were derived from ancient Mesopotamian pharmacology transmitted later in Aramaic or Persian; 23 per cent came from Greek; 18 per cent from Persian; 13 per cent from India; 5 per cent from Arabic itself; and 3 per cent from Egypt (Levey 1966). With established maritime and inland trade between Arabia, Africa, India, Iran and China many plants and animals and other objects were known to the peoples of the Arabian Peninsula and adjacent regions, even if they were not cultivated or originated there.

In this chapter we explore the names of fifteen selected plants that are common and well known to the peoples of southern Arabia. These plants (except *Citrus*) are native to southern Arabia (Oman, Yemen and Saudi Arabia) and commonly found there, used for food or medicine sourced from the wild. For each plant we list its Classical Arabic name side by side with vernacular names used in the Arabian Peninsula (both dialectal Arabic and Modern South Arabian), trace their etymology and outline their cultural-historical context (Table 5.1).

Table 5.1 Fifteen Common South Arabian Plants with Names in Arabic and Other Semitic Languages

Taxon [Family]	Common English name	Classical Arabic	Hebrew	Syriac	Akkadian	South Arabian: Dhofari Arabic (DA) Ḥarsūsī (H) Jibbāli (J) Mehri (M) Soqoṭri (S)
Aloe dhufarensis A. *praetermissa* A. *vera* [Asphodelaceae]	Aloe	ṣabr-, ṣabir-, ṣibr-	ʔăhālōt	ʕalwā ṣabrā	ṣibaru	ṭayf (M, S), ṭuf (J) ṣubr (J) sikil (J), sēkel (DA)
Ficus carica [Moraceae]	Fig, ficus	tīn-	taʔēnā	tettā	tittu	tik (J), tek (S)
Flemingia grahamiana [Fabaceae]		wars-		wʔrsʔ		waras (H)
Lawsonia inermis [Lythraceae]	Henna	ḥinnāʔ-	kōpär	ḥennā		ḥine' (J)
Nannorrhops ritchiena [Aracaceae]	Dwarf palm					ʕazaf (DA) and ṣaʕf leaflets ʕarfēt, zerbēt (J) ārfit (M)
Olea europaea [Oleaceae]	Olive	zayt- (oil), zaytūn- (tree)	zayit	zaytā	serdu	môtin (J) mûṭayn (M)
Peganum harmala [Nitrariaceae]	Wild rue; Syrian rue; African rue	ḥarmal-				ḥadgēt (M), also fruit of *Citurllus colocynthis* (DA ḥarmal is used for *Rhazya stricta*)

Taxon [Family]	Common English name	Classical Arabic	Hebrew	Syriac	Akkadian	South Arabian: Dhofari Arabic (DA) Harsūsi (H) Jibbāli (J) Mehri (M) Soqoṭri (S)
Tamarix aphylla [Tamaricaceae]	Tamarisk, salt cedar	ʔaṭal-	ʔēšāl	ʔtlʔ	ašlu	íʔitel (S)
Vachellia (Acacia) nilotica [Fabaceae]	Acacia	ṭalḥ-, sanṭ-	šiṭṭā		šamṭu	ṭalḥ, qurut̠, t̠emmar (DA) t̠ūr (J), ṭalḥ (M)
Withania somnifera [Solanaceae]		saykarān-, waraq aš-šīfā, burdat-		šakronā	šakirû	genēgeneh (DA)
Ziziphus spina-christi [Rhamnaceae]	Christ's thorn, lote tree,	sidr-, ḏāl- (tree), nibq-, nabiq- (fruit)	ṣäʔǟlīm	ʕālā		ẑōt̠ (M) ẑed (J) ẑáʔed (S) ʕilb (DA)
Juncus socotranus; J. rigidus [Juncaceae]	Reed, rush	ʔasal-			Ašlu	íʔishɛl (S)
Phoenix × dactylifera [Arecaceae]	Date palm	tamr- (dates), naḫl- (trees)	tāmār	tmartā (date), deḵlā (tree)		temrêt (date), naḫlêt (tree) (J) tōmer (dates), neḫlit (tree) (M) tōmer (dates), têmre (tree) (S)
Dracaena cinnabari [Asparagaceae]	Dragon-blood tree	damu l-ʔaḫawayni				šenɛ́bhɛr (fruit) (S)
Citrus aurantium [Rutaceae]	Bitter orange	ʔutruǧǧ-, ʔutrunǧ-, turunǧ-				tenéẑe (S)

Plants, plant products and their names

Aloe [*Aloe dhufarensis, A. vera, A. praterissima* – Family Asphodelaceae]

Aloe vera[1] has been used medicinally since ancient times. The medicinal part of the plant are its succulent leaves from which juice and gel are removed, boiled and the water evaporated to produce a blackish, hard, shining residue which is called, not unlike the plant itself, ṣabr-, ṣabir-, ṣibr- in Classical Arabic (Lane 1645).[2] Easily transported, it has been exported from Arabia to the Middle East and Egypt for its healing properties as a laxative and emollient.

A. dhufarensis and *A. praterissima* are found in southern Arabia, the former endemic to Dhofar (McCoy 2019: 135, 305; Miller and Morris 1988: 182–4).[3] On Soqoṭra, another endemic species, *A. perryi*, is widespread and highly prominent in the island's ethnobotany (see extensively Miller and Morris 2004: 297–303). The Soqoṭri name for *Aloes* is ṭayf (LS 203, CSOL I 689), whose cognates are limited to other MSA: Mhr. ṭayf (ML 414), Jib. ṭuf (JL 282).

A. vera, native to southwest Yemen and Saudi Arabia, is widely cultivated in gardens more or less throughout the world and is grown commercially for the production of *Aloe vera* creams, shampoos and soaps, etc.

Fig [*Ficus carica* – Family Moraceae]

Ficus carica[4] is one of the few classical fruit trees that are associated with the beginning of horticulture and plant domestication in the Mediterranean region. The earliest evidence that figs were consumed as food/fruit comes from Pre-Pottery Neolithic sites in the Jordan Valley and the Upper Euphrates. It is conceivable that around 9,700 BCE cultivation of figs may already have started (Fuller and Stevens 2019). Fossil pollen evidence suggests that fig was in cultivation during the third and fourth centuries BCE at Ramat Rahel, near present-day Jerusalem (Langgut et al. 2013).

In the wild, edible figs or 'true figs' are produced on female trees only if they are pollinated by fig wasps (*Blastophaga psenes*) from the caprifigs.[5] Under domestication, female trees can develop parthenocarpically, that is, without pollination (Zohary et al. 2012: 127). Parthenocarpic figs produce sweet fruit without the formation of seed and have to be propagated vegetatively, giving an advantage to cultivators as they can be grown in regions where the natural pollinator does not occur.

Fig is native to the Middle East and Western Asia; it has been in cultivation since ancient times. Their domestication predates that of wheat, barley and legumes, and suggests that the fig may be the first known plant in the history of agriculture (Zohary et al. 2012: 129). The Eastern part of the Mediterranean basin has the closest relatives to the cultivated fig, suggesting that southern Turkey and the Aegean belt may be where the original stock of the cultivated fig came from.

Cuneiform tablets indicate that figs were grown in Mesopotamia from 2500 BCE (Postgate 1987: 117). Its Akkadian designation *tittu* (CAD T 435) goes back to Proto-Semitic *taʔin-at-* (Kogan 2012: 254), first attested in the lexical lists from Ebla as *ti-i-tum*, equated to Sumerian GIŠ.PÈS (Catagnoti 2008: 181). The Hebrew designation *təʔēnā* (HALOT 1675)[6] goes back to the same source, as does Arabic *tīn-* which, however, in view of the lack of the glottal stop, is likely a Hebraism or an Aramaism (Jeffery 1938: 96–7). The Arabic word is attested, *inter alia*, in the famous Quranic surah of the same name (*at-tīn*), in the peculiar combination *wa-t-tīni wa-z-zaytūn* 'I swear by the fig tree and the olive!', probably referring to a mystical tree growing in the Paradise.

Numerous species of figs are known from the Arabian peninsula, among which five are attested in Dhofar (see an extensive survey in Miller and Morris 1988: 204–9). Of particular interest from the etymological point of view is *ṭik*, the Jibbali name of *Ficus vasta* (ibid. 208). Together with its Soqotri cognate *ṭek* (Miller and Morris 2004: 637), it closely resembles Beotic Greek τῦκον (Attic σῦκον) and Armenian *t'uz* (Frisk 818) and must belong to the same, hitherto unknown, ancient source.

In Egypt, the earliest record of figs dates back from 2000 BCE to 1000 BCE (Fuller and Stevens 2019). It is one of the most common fruits shown on reliefs, tombs and paintings. The Egyptian name for 'figue' is *dȝb* (Wb. 5 417), remarkably similar to Hbr. *dəbēlā* 'pressed figues'. According to Laufer (1919: 410), fig was not introduced in China earlier than the Tang Period (618–907 CE). The Chinese names *a-ži*, *a-yi* correspond to the Persian term *anjīr* whose Old Iranian etymon means literally 'flower-less' (EDPL 1 286–7).[7]

Dried, pressed and strung on rope, figs are available throughout South West Asia and regraded as a blessed fruit beneficial to health. The medicinal uses of figs are many and the uses have been recorded since ancient times. Figs are mostly used as a health tonic being rich in magnesium and potassium, as a laxative in suppositories and as a wound dressing (Ghazanfar 1994: 147, 148; Manniche 1989: 102). The rough leaves have been used as scourer for cleaning pots.

Wars [*Flemingia grahamiana* – Family Fabaceae]

Wars (Lane 2936) is a red powder obtained from the dried pods of *Flemingia grahamiana*. It is widely used in parts of Africa, especially in Ethiopia and southern Arabia (Yemen and Oman), as a dye and made into a paste applied on face as ornament and to prevent skin diseases (Schopen 1983: 192). It is also used as a dye for fabrics, dyeing bamboo for baskets and making coloured ink. *Flemingia grahamiana* is found from Tropical and south Africa to the Arabian Peninsula, south India, south China (Yunnan) to Indo-China (POWO).

The word *wars* has been used as early as in pre-Islamic Arab poetry (King 2015: 514). It has been borrowed into Syriac as *wrwš*, *wʔrš*ʔ, *wryš*ʔ, *wrš*ʔ (LSyr. 186), as well as into the Ethiopian Semitic language Harari as *wärsi* (EDH 161) and as *waris* into Somali (DSI 614). As one can judge from Lane's dictionary, the word is deeply incorporated into Arabic morphology and has produced various verbal and nominal derivates, such as *warīs*- 'garment died with *wars*', *warrasa* 'to die with *wars*', *ʔawrasa* 'to put forth *wars*'.[8]

Wars was not known to early medical authors such as Dioscorides nor Galen and is not mentioned in their works. However, it is mentioned in early Arabic sources as a yellow pigment found in Ethiopia, Yemen and India (Amar and Lev 2017: 127–9; Jansen 2005). Forsskål documented *Flemingia grahamiana* during his excursion to Yemen during 1772, but recorded the name *safarjal* for it, a name used for quince in Arabic (Provençal 2010: 68). In Oman *safarjal* is used for a sweet orange grown locally in northern Oman (Ghazanfar 2007: 122) and one can surmise that Forsskål may have given that name because of the colour that *wars* gives when made into a paste with water which is a yellowish orange, the colour of the rind of the Omani *safarjal*. *Wars* was exported from Arabia to Sicily as a dye for silk and other fabrics during the early Islamic era.

In Southern Arabia, *wars* has been used mainly as a cosmetic for women, made into a paste and applied to face and body to treat skin diseases such as itching, eczema, abscess, boils and for the treatment for discolorations of the skin. A root decoction has been used as a treatment of diarrhoea and dysentery in Zimbabwe and Malawi (Jansen 2005). It has also been used topically to make the body strong, especially after childbirth. In Oman, *wars* has been used to colour the body yellow for celebrations, solely or in mixture with turmeric; in the UAE and Oman it was also used with hair oil. In Dhofar, *wars* was applied on legs below the knees (Schönig 2002: 304). *Wars* is still used in southern Yemen and amongst the Harsūsī women of central Oman where they know only the powder (not the plant) that comes from Yemen (Ghazanfar and Al Sabahi 1993).

Schönig (2002: 297) gives the names ʕanbar and ġumra⁹ which, she notes, is the name of a liniment extracted from the plant much loved by Arabian women. Schönig (2002: 298) states that *wars* is best known in the Hadhramaut region of Yemen where it is used widely by the women. She also notes the plant is rare in Yemen, the area where it grew wild taken up by plantations of coffee or qat. Wood (1997: 162) also noted the rarity of the plant, which has been confirmed via a recent inquiry to a senior botanist from Yemen (pers. comm. with Dr Abdul Wali AlKhulaidi, July 2020). The *wars* powder in Yemen mostly comes from Ethiopia and Somalia (possibly also India).

Flemingia grahamiana was first described by Wight and Arnott in 1834 in *Prodromus Florae Peninsulae Indiae Orientalis* (vol. 1, p. 242). The description was based on specimens collected in India by R. Wight, nos. 803 and 816, the former housed at the Kew Herbarium (K) and duplicate at the Gray Herbarium, Harvard University (GH).

Henna [*Lawsonia inermis* – Family Lythraceae]

The Arabic name *ḥinnāʔ* (Lane 654) for *Lawsonia inermis* has no known etymology. Related terms are attested only in Aramaic, cf. Syr. *hennā* (LSyr. 243), but the nature of their relationship (Aramaism in Arabic or vice versa) cannot be easily established.

The Hebrew name for henna is *kōpär* (HALOT 495), attested several times in the Song of Songs, but with no direct reference to dyeing. It is traditionally derived from the verbal root *kpr* 'to smear, to coat'.

In the Sanskrit lexicography henna is called *mendhī, mendhikā* (MW 833). Comparable terms are attested in many modern Indo-Aryan languages such as Hindi, Urdu, Bengali as *mehādī, mēhdī* and similar (Turner 1966: 596).

Henna has been used as dye for hands, feet and hair since ancient times. There is evidence that ancient Egyptians dyed their finger nails red, and some Egyptian mummies were found to have their hair dyed red which may have been henna. Henna leaves have been found in Egypt in tombs of the Late Period (*c.* 664 BCE–*c.* 332 BCE) (Manniche 1989: 114).

The Romans have used the plant to dye hair as it is still used in many countries today as a dye for hair. Moroccan Jews use henna in their traditional ceremonies, in particular weddings, where elders of the family smudge henna on the palms of the bride and groom to symbolically bestow the new couple with good health, fertility, wisdom and security (Ghazanfar in press, 2023). This tradition is still practised in India and Pakistan and is meant to give the bride and groom a good life in marriage. Henna is believed in tradition to protect the couple from demons. In most Muslim countries, but with growing popularity in the Western countries as well, palms of hands and soles of feet are decorated in intricate patterns for festivities such as *Eid al Fitr* and *Eid al Adha*, marriages and birthdays. In traditional medicine the leaves and paste made from powdered leaves have been used for cooling fevers, as a local anaesthetic, an anti-inflammatory, a sun screen, and for treating mouth ulcers and nose bleeds (Ghazanfar 1994: 134).

Figure 5.1 'Lawsonia inermis – Arb. ḥennā. ḥinnāʔ.' Illustration by Sue Wickison for *Plants of the Qu'ran* by S.A. Ghazanfar, Kew Publishing. © Sue Wickison 2021. Reproduced with the permission of Sue Wickison.

Henna was given the botanical Latin name *Lawsonia inermis* by Linnaeus in 1753 in Species Plantarum (1753: 349), based on a plant from India and Egypt. The specimen (LINN. 496/1) on which this name is based is present at the Linnaeus Herbarium at Burlington House in London. *Lawsonia* was named after Dr Issac Lawson (d. 1747), a eighteenth-century naturalist and traveller, a friend and patron of Linnaeus – the specific name, *inermis* means unarmed referring to the stems being without prickles. It is native to north-east Tropical Africa, and from the Arabian Peninsula to India; elsewhere introduced and cultivated.

Dwarf palm (*Nannorrhops ritchieana* – Family Arecaceae)

The dwarf palm is a small shrubby palm with a short trunk and greyish-green fan-shaped leaves. It is found from eastern Arabia to Iran, Afghanistan and Pakistan; in the Arabian Peninsula it is native to southern Oman, UAE and south-east Yemen, found in desert wadis and sandy depressions where it grows gregariously, often forming large clumps several metres across (Ghazanfar 2018: 8). In central and southern Oman, this palm was of great importance, and was used extensively by desert Bedouins for making ropes, twine and tackle for camels. Strips of leaves were weaved to make baskets covered with leather for household use, and bowls for milking camels with the base covered with leather to make them waterproof (Miller and Morris 1988: 224).

In the Arabic dialects of the south of the Peninsula, the tree is called *ʕazaf* (GD 2289, Behnstedt 825, Piamenta 325, al-Iryani 750–1).[10] A clearly related verb *ʕzf* 'to plait, weave (wicker)' is also attested there, but it is hard to judge whether it is primary and the botanic term is denominative, or rather vice versa. The corresponding Jibbali designations are *ʕarfét* and *zerbét* (Miller and Morris 1988: 224, JL 15).

Olive[11] [*Olea europaea* – Family Oleaceae]

The olive is one of the oldest plants found in cultivation in the Old World (Stager 1985). Ancestry of the cultivated olive has been lost through years and years of cultivation, but it is assumed that it may have arisen from *Olea chrysophylla* in northern Africa.[12] Estimates show that the cultivation of olive trees began more than 7,000 years ago; definitive signs of olive cultivation are attested in Palestine and the Jordan valley where carbonized olive stones and wood have been recovered date back to 3500 BCE; in Crete olive is known to have been cultivated around 3000 BCE (Zohary et al. 2012: 117–20).

The Phoenicians and Greeks probably introduced olive cultivation into the West Mediterranean basin in the first millennium. Apparently, the olive was not cultivated in a major way in Egypt, but the export of olive oil from Palestine to Egypt is well documented in the Bronze Age (Schweinfurth 1886). Finds of olive date back to the eighteenth Dynasty (1550–1549 BCE) (Newberry 1889) and the New Kingdom (1550–1070 BCE) when wreaths and garlands of various plants included olive leaves; garlands and collars of olive leaves have been found in Tutankhamun's tomb (d. 1323 BCE) (Manniche 1989: 129). The origin of the Egyptian word for olive and olive oil *bꜣk* is uncertain (EDE II 93–4). The olive cannot grow in Mesopotamia for climatic reasons; accordingly, the corresponding Akkadian word *sirdu* is rather rarely attested (Stol 2003–2005: 32, CAD S 311).[13]

The Arabic words for olive (*zaytūn-*) and olive oil (*zayt-*) are likely borrowed from a North-West Semitic language, such as Aramaic or Hebrew (Jeffery 1938: 156–7), even if the ending *-ūn-* does not lend itself to an easy explanation.[14] Both words are well attested in the Quran, most famously in the *āyat an-nūr* (24:35) which speaks of the Divine Light whose oil (*zayt-*) goes back to a 'blessed tree, an olive which is neither Oriental nor Occidental' (*min šaǧaratin mubārakatin zaytūnatin lā šarqiyyatin wa-lā ġarbiyyatin*). The corresponding lexemes in the Semitic languages of the Levant are known from Ugaritic *zt* (DUL 984) onwards.

Olive oil has been used medicinally since ancient times for muscular pain and sprains, and for abdominal problems. In the Arabian Peninsula the fruits of the wild olive are not eaten, being mostly bitter to taste, nor used for extracting oil, but at certain locations on the western Al-Ḥajar Mountains in the Sultanate of Oman and in Saudi Arabia, the fruits are sweet and edible (Ghazanfar 2015: 131). The wood is resistant to termites and has been used for building, making utilitarian implements, firewood, and for making charcoal (Miller and Morris 1988: 216). The branches have been used for making 'throwing sticks' used as a weapon in Dhofar in southern Oman and foliage is lopped for fodder for livestock. The Jibbali term for the – feral? – *Olea europea* is *móṭín*, whose Soqoṭri cognate *míṭhan* designates quite a different plant, viz. *Buxanthus pedicellatus* (Miller and Morris 2004: 472).

Olive was given the Latin name *Olea europaea* by Linnaeus in 1753, with the specimen (LINN 20.1) on which this name is based, held at the Linnaean Herbarium at Burlington House, London.

Wild rue, African rue, Syrian rue [*Peganum harmala* – Family Nitrariaceae]

Wild rue, also known as the African or Syrian rue, is called *ḥarmal* in much of the region where it grows: from north Africa and southern Europe, the Arabian Peninsula, Turkey, through Iraq, Iran and Afghanistan to eastern Mongolia and northern China (POWO). It has been introduced and naturalized in many warm and arid regions of Southwest Asia and the Middle East, and it tends to be weedy in several regions. It is a plant that has been used medicinally since ancient times and has been introduced to many countries for its use in traditional medicine and as a ritual plant with magical powers. Seeds of *ḥarmal* are bitter to taste and when crushed have a heavy unpleasant smell. Smoke from burning the seeds has been traditionally used in driving away evil spirits. A concoction of powdered seeds with water has been used as a vermifuge, narcotic and for removing kidney stones (Ghazanfar 1994: 216; Schopen 1983: 30).

The Arabic word *ḥarmal-* (LA 11 181) is of uncertain etymology. Greek ἁρμαλά is thought to be borrowed from a Semitic source (Frisk 143).

Peganum harmala is known as *espand, sepand, esfand* in Modern Persian, going back to Middle Persian *spand* and, eventually, Avestan *spənta-* 'holy, pure' (EDPL 198–9), reflecting its medicinal and ritual significance. In Urdu it is called *ḥarmal* or *ispand*, and is known as *spalanay* in Pashto (Ghafoor 1974: 7).

Peganum harmala is not known from Oman and is uncommon in eastern and northeastern Arabia. Interestingly, there, the name *ḥarmal* is used for a different plant, *Rhazya stricta* [Family Apocynaceae] native to the Arabian Peninsula, Iraq, southern Iran to north-west India.[15] Why and how *Rhazya stricta* got to be known as *ḥarmal* in some areas of the Arabian Peninsula cannot be ascertained: apparently, the medicinal use of *Rhazya stricta* has been similar to that of *Peganum harmala* (mistaken identity is unlikely in this case as the two plants look very different from each other). Indeed, *Rhazya stricta* has been one of the chief medicinal plants in Oman (Ghazanfar 1994: 28). In Dhofar it was collected and sold by the people living in the desert areas to the mountain dwellers and also to the sea traders on the coast. It was regarded highly for both its medicinal and supernatural powers (Miller and Morris 1988: 34).

Tamarisk[16] [*Tamarix aphylla* – Family Tamaricaceae]

Tamarisk is an Old World genus with about fifty-four species distributed in the arid and semi-arid regions (Baum 1978: 75). *Tamarix aphylla*, commonly referred to as tamarisk, is one of the most commonly found tree in the Arabian Peninsula.

The Arabic term ʔaṭal- (Lane 21) is a generic name for tamarisk trees, but most commonly used for *T. aphylla* (Ghazanfar 2003: 121). The word is once attested in the Quran (34:16). In the Arabic dialects of Yemen, it is recorded as ʔiṭl (Piamenta 3) or ʔaṭl id. (Behnstedt 8). The Arabic word goes back to a deeply rooted proto-West Semitic *ʔaṭl- or *ʔiṭl- (Kogan 2012: 235), attested in Soq. íʔiteḷ (Miller and Morris 2004: 696), Mhr. hōṭəl (ML 9), Hbr. ʔēšäl (HALOT 95), JBA ʔtlʔ (Löw 1881: 65), Sab. ʔṭl (SD 9, Sima 2000: 181–4).

In Dhofari Arabic *Tamarix aphylla* is called bēneh (Miller and Morris 1988: 282). Together with Jibbali ben (ibid.), it continues a very old Proto-Semitic term for tamarisk, first attested in Ebla as ì-zu ba-ne, ba-nu /baynu(m)/ = Sum. GIŠ.ŠINIG (VE 395, Krebernik 1983: 15). It is continued by bīnu in Mesopotamian Akkadian (CAD B 239) and Syr. binā (LSyr. 69), perhaps in Akkadism.

In Arabic and other languages of the Peninsula, PS *bay(a)n- (Kogan 2012: 238)[17] came to designate another tree, *Moringa peregrina*: Arb. bān- (Lane 278, Piamenta 47, Sima 2000: 198), Sab. bn (SD 33, Sima 2000: 198–9), Jib. yēn (Miller and Morris 1988: 210). The shift is apparently due to the fact that the branches of *Moringa* are leafless and somewhat resemble the apparently leafless branches of tamarisk.

In the Modern South Arabian language Jibbali *Tamarix aphylla* is designated as ʕarʕeyr (Miller and Morris 1988: 282). Comparable terms with the same meaning are also attested in Ugaritic ʕrʕr 'tamarisk' (DUL 178) and Syriac ʕarʕurā 'tamarisk resin', ʕarrā 'tamarisk' (LSyr. 544, SL 1141, 1133). Interestingly enough, elsewhere in Semitic the reflexes of *ʕarʕar- (Kogan 2012: 242–4) designate quite a different, coniferous tree, namely the juniper (*Juniperus procera* and other species): Mhr. ʕarʕōr (Sima 2009: 200), Hbr. ʕarʕār/ʕărōʕēr (BDB 792, HALOT 887), Arb. ʕarʕar- (LA 4 644, Lane 1990, Behnstedt 819, al-Iryani 746), Sab. ʕrʕr (Stein 2010: 200, 203, 720). The shift is undoubtedly conditioned by the external similarity of tamarisk leaves to the needles of conifers. *Tamarix aphylla* has been a popular tree in cultivation in Mesopotamia as it was widely used for its termite-resistant timber and for making utilitarian objects such as ladles and stools. It has been used in Babylonian and early Greek medicine for the treatement of various conditions. Its many uses are best attested in the Sumerian debate poem between the date palm and the tamarisk where each tree boasts of its superiority to the other and their usefulness to humans (Cohen 2013: 177–98; Streck 2004).[18]

Tamarisk does not have an ancient history of cultivation or use in Southern Arabia. Its foliage is not necessarily a choice browse for camels, though they will browse on fresh shoots. The timber, though, has been popular for building animal and human shelters as it is resistant to termites. It is not an important medicinal plant, but in southern Oman a concoction of dried leaves has been used to ease difficult childbirth, and dried leaves have been used to treat saddle sores and rope burns in camels and donkeys (Miller and Morris 1988: 282, 333).

Most of the species of *Tamarix* are tolerant of saline soils and excrete salt through their leaves; this feature has been used in times of salt shortage as a salt substitute.

Tamarix was given the Latin name *Thuja aphylla* by Linneaus in *Centuria I. Plantarum* 32-3 (1755), based on a plant from central Asia, which is present in the Linnaeus Herbarium at Burlington House, London (LINN. 1136.3). The generic name was transferred to the genus *Tamarix* by Karsten in 1882 in *Deutsche Flora, Pharmaceutisch-medicinische Botanik* (p. 641).

Acacia[19] [*Vachellia (Acacia) nilotica* – Family Fabaceae]

The Arabic word *ṭalḥ* (Lane 1865) is a term used for a number of *Vachellia* (*Acacia*) species found in northern Africa and the Arabian Peninsula (Ghazanfar 2007: 11).[20] It is once attested in the Quran (56:29), in a description of the Gardens of Paradise: *wa-ṭalḥin manḍūdin* '(Those of the Right Side will stay among) acacias growing in rows'.

There are six species referred to as *ṭalḥ* or *ṭulḥ* in the Arabic dialects of the Arabian Peninsula, Iraq, Syria, Palestine, Jordan, Egypt and Libya (Ghazanfar 2007: 11):

- *Vachellia gerardii*, called *ṭalḥ* in Oman, Saudi Arabia, Yemen, Jordan and Iraq.
- *V. nilotica* subsp. *kraussiana*, known in Saudi Arabia and Oman, also called *ḵuruṭ* in Dhofari Arabic (Miller and Morris 1988: 178).
- *V. nilotica*, also called *sanṭ-* (Lane 1445), well known as the Egyptian gum tree in Egypt and Arabia. The word is borrowed from Ancient Egyptian *šnḏ.t* (Wb. IV 520-1, DELC 267).[21]
- *V. seyal*, found in Saudi Arabia and Egypt, also called *seyyāl* (Behnstedt 604, Piamenta 242).

- *V. raddiana* and *V. tortilis*, found in Saudi Arabia and Libya [*V. tortilis* also called *ḥaroṣ* in Jibbali and *samra* in Dhofari Arabic (Miller and Morris 1988: 176)].
- *V. senegal*, also known as *ṭūr* in Jibbali in southern Oman and *ṭemmar* in Dhofari Arabic (Miller and Morris 1988: 180).

Vachellia nilotica is one of the most widespread species found from South Africa north to Iraq and east to India. It is a majestic tree, both in flower and fruit, often planted in villages for its shade, evergreen habit, and mildly fragrant flowers. The pods contain tanin and have been used for tanning since ancient times. In Pharaonic times the wood was used for timber, the bark for tanning and the leaves and pods in medicine. Its tanning and medicinal properties are well known and used commonly in south-west Asia.

The Greek word ἀκακία is used by Dioscorides in *Materia Medica* (Book 1, 133). It is also mentioned by Theophrastes in his *Historia Plantarum* (referring to *Acacia nilotica*). Ishbili's description and uses of *ṭalḥ* (Bustamante et al. 2010: 792) are very similar to that given by Dioscorides. Maimonides (Rosner 1995: 213) describes the juice of pods (*qaraḍ-*, Lane 2518) as beneficial for coughs.

Indian ginseng[22] [*Withania somnifera* – Family Solanaceae]

The Arabic name *saykarān* (Lane 1392) has an immediate parallel in Syr. *šakronā* (LSyr. 777, Löw 1881: 381). Both are thought to be derived from Proto-Semitic **škr* (> Arabic *skr*) 'to be intoxicated, inebriated', alluding to the properties of the plant to induce sleep. One cannot rule out, however, that we are dealing with an ancient *Wanderwort* only secondarily contaminated with that Semitic root.[23] Other Arabic names of the plant are *waraq aš-šifā*, referring to its curative and healing powers, and *burda* 'cooling, soothing' (Piamenta 25).

W. somnifera is a small woody shrub widely distributed in the drier parts of tropical and subtropical regions of the Old World, from the Canary Islands, South Africa, the Middle East, Sri Lanka and India to China (Hepper 1991). It is unpalatable to livestock and therefore commonly found in Southern Arabia (Ghazanfar 2015: 43; Wood 1997: 229). It is known as the 'Indian Ginseng' due to its multiple medicinal uses and long use in traditional medicine. In Sanskrit it is known as *áśva-gandhā* (literally 'horse-smelling', MW 115) and in India it is grown as a medicinal crop, with the whole plant or its different parts used in Ayurvedic and Unani systems of medicine; it is mentioned as an official drug in Indian Pharmacopoeia-85 (Dar et al. 2015). In Arabia pounded leaves are applied as a poultice on burns and sunburnt skin; mixed with garlic, it is applied on stings and bites (Ghazanfar 1994: 201).

Withania somnifera is much regarded for its stress elevating properties and has been widely used as a narcotic and sedative (Kulkarni and Dhir 2008).

Christ's thorn, Lote tree [*Ziziphus spina-christi* – Family Rhamnaceae]

The Arabic name *sidr* (Lane 1331) is used for *Ziziphus spina-christi* throughout the Arabian Peninsula, Jordan, Palestine and Iraq where it is found wild (Ghazanfar 2007: 98; Taifour and El-Oqla 2017: 141). However, in eastern Saudi Arabia and Iraq this name is applied to two species, *Z. spina-christi* and *Z. nummularia*, the latter native from the Arabian Peninsula to India (Chalabi-Ka'bi 1980: 436; Mandaville 1990: 206). The word is several times attested in the Quran: 34:16, 53:14.16, 56:28.[24]

While the origin of the Arabic word *sidr-* is unknown, there exists another, deeply rooted Proto-West Semitic designation of *Ziziphus*, viz. **ṣaʔl-* (Blau 1998: 189–92), attested in Hbr. *ṣäʔälīm* (HALOT 992),[25] Syr. *ʕālā* (LSyr. 503), Arb. *ḍāl-* (Lane 1816) and, with dissimilation of the lateral *l*, in Mhr. *ẑōṭ* (ML 478), Jib. *ẑed* id. (Miller and Morris 1988: 242, JL 327), Soq. *ẑáʔed* (Miller and Morris 2004: 660, LS 359).

Ziziphus spina-christi is one of the most common trees in Arabia, found in the foothills, wadis and gravel deserts, and is widely cultivated. It is also one of the most useful trees, especially in Yemen and Oman (Ghazanfar 2007: 98). Its timber is highly valued as durable roof beams; spoons and ladles and other utilitarian objects are made from it; its leaves provide good fodder for goats and camels, being also used as a soap substitute for washing hair and scalp; it yields edible fruit, and provides abundant shade (Ghazanfar 2012: 163–80).

Theophrastus (4, 3, 3) (ed. Hort 1948) described the plant and fruit in detail and said it to be abundant throughout the Nile Valley. Fruits of *sidr*, called *nibq-* or *nabiq-* in Arabic (Lane 3027), have been found in underground storage rooms of Zoser at Saqqara (Lauer et al. 1951). The name *nbs* 'Ziziphus fruit' (Wb. II 245–6) in Ancient Egyptian occurs amongst funeral offerings in all eras in Egyptian history.

The fruit of *Ziziphus* has been found in ancient tombs in Palestine and is mentioned as medicinal by Ibn al Bayṭār (1197–1248), an Andalusian Muslim pharmacist, botanist and physician. In the Christian tradition, *Ziziphus spina-christi* is identified with the crown of thorns Jesus was crowned with before his crucifixion (Matthew 27: 28, 29; John 19:5, Mark 15:17), hence the second part of its scientific name ('Christ's thorn').

Ziziphus spina-christi was placed in the genus *Rhamnus* with the name *Rhamnus spina-christi* given by Linnaeus in *Species Plantarum* (1753: 95) with the specimens (LINN-HL262–36) housed at the Linnaean Herbarium at Burlington House, London, UK. It was transferred to *Ziziphus* by Willdenow in 1798 (Sp. Pl. ed. 4 [Willdenow] 1(2): 1105).

Figure 5.2 'Ziziphus spina-christi – Arb. *sidr*.' Illustration by Sue Wickison for *Plants of the Qu'ran* by S.A. Ghazanfar, Kew Publishing. © Sue Wickison 2021. Reproduced with the permission of Sue Wickison.

Reed [*Juncus socotranus*; *J. rigidus* – Family Juncaceae]

The Proto-Semitic designation of common reed, *ʔašal-* (Fronzaroli 1969: 276, 289, 299, Kogan 2012: 235), is among the most archaic and deeply rooted botanical terms in the Semitic linguistic area. First attested in Ebla as *a-sa-lu* = Sum. Ú.NINNI5 (VE 300, Krebernik 1983: 13), it is continued by Mesopotamian Akkadian *ašlu* (CAD A$_2$ 449), Arabic *ʔasal-* 'rush' (Lane 59, LA I 17) and, importantly, Soqoṭri *íʔishɛḷ* (Miller and Morris 2004: 389).

The genus *Juncus* is almost cosmopolitan in distribution (rarer in the tropics). Two species, *Juncus socotranus* and *J. rigidus*,[26] are widely distributed, the former from the Middle East to Iran, and the latter, more widely, from Africa to southern Pakistan and Turkmenistan (Ghazanfar 2018: 14–5). Both species are found in Southern Arabia, by permanent fresh water or brackish pools and on fringes of streams, in gravelly wadi beds and on landward sides of sea inlets.

Reeds have been used to make pens for writing since ancient times. *Juncus rigidus* has been identified as a good possibility for making pens with chiselled nibs in Egypt dating back to 6th–19th dynasties (2345–1189 BCE) and the Greco-Roman times. Reeds have been (and still are) used to make mats, brooms, baskets in the Arabian Peninsula, though their use has declined in recent years due to the introduction of plastics.

Juncus rigidus is a perennial herb, up to 1.5 m, often gregarious and seemingly tufted, with a creeping branched rhizome (underground stem). The stems are rigid, often with a spiny tip. First described scientifically by Desfontaines in 1798 – the specimen on which this name is based is present at the Herbarium at the Muséum national d'Histoire naturelle, Paris.

Date palm [*Phoenix dactylifera* – Arecaceae]

Proto-West Semitic **tam(a)r* (Fronzaroli 1969: 291, 279, 300) testifies to a fairly ancient knowledge of the date palm and its products. Representations of this common term in individual West Semitic languages are uneven and can be classified into the following groups.

- Both the tree and the fruits are designated by the same word: Hbr. *tāmār* 'date palm' (HALOT 1756), 'date-palm; date' (Jastrow 1679).[27]
- There are different derivations for the tree and the fruits: Soq. *témre* 'date palm' vs. *tómer* 'dates' (Miller and Morris 2004: 393, LS 443), Gez. *tamart* 'date palm; date' vs. *tamr* 'dates' (CDG 576, LLA 555).

– The term applies only to the fruits, whereas the tree is designated by an unrelated term: Syr. *tmartā* 'date' (LSyr. 828) vs. *deḵlā*, Arb. *tamr-* 'dates' (Lane 317) vs. *naḫl-* 'date palms', Sab. *tmr*, Min. *tmr* 'dates' (Sima 2000: 246) vs. *nḫl* 'date palms', Mhr. *tōmer* 'dates' (ML 402) vs. *neḫlīt* 'date palm', Jib. *temrét* 'date' (JL 271) vs. *naḫlēt* 'date palm'.

It goes without saying that the date palm has been of greatest economic importance throughout the Arabian Peninsula and the Middle East and has been known here since ancient times. Rock carvings dating back to more than 8,000 years BCE at Jebel Umm Salim at Jubba in Saudi Arabia show fruiting dates palms (and some animals), illustrating its prominence in prehistoric Arabia (Murad 1980).

Dates and date gardens are mentioned in Sumerian and Akkadian cuneiform sources dating back to 3000 BCE, where dates are recorded in relation to the supply of dates, indicating established cultivated gardens at that time (Landsberger 1967; Nesbitt 1993; Volk 2003–2005). The date palm is one of the first trees to be domesticated in the Old World. From the Bronze Age onwards (3500 to 1700 BC) date cultivation is documented to be well established in deserts of the Near East (Zohary et al. 2012: 134).

The entire plant is used variously and has been since long. The fact that date palms can withstand a hot and dry climate, moderately saline soils, and produce an abundance of sugary fruit which can be stored, has contributed much to the success of this species in the Middle East and North Africa. The old Arabic saying 'the uses of the date palm are as many as the days in a year' is true today as it was in olden times. The trunk and fronds are used as building materials, basketry and making other utilitarian objects; the fruit, date, is used in various forms, both as food and as medicine.

Phoenix dactylifera, the date palm, is a dioecious plant (with the male and female flowers borne on separate trees). It produces basal suckers which are used in vegetative propagation or cloning to keep the varieties of dates true. Wild populations are pollinated by wind and produce an equal proportion of male and female individuals. In cultivated date gardens, pollination is carried manually, and usually one male to 25–50 female trees are planted in a date grove. This tradition was already in practice in Mesopotamia (Iraq) during 1792–50 BCE, being registered, *inter alia*, in the Codex Hammurabi (§§ 64–5).[28]

The original location of the date palm in Southwest Asia is obscure, but recent evidence shows that it could be the Arabian Peninsula (Jennings et al. 2015). Wild populations of dates are found throughout the region, where they have been cultivated and are still cultivated today. The wild forms of *P.* ×*dactylifera* produce smaller, more fibrous fruit than the cultivated forms, and some produce inedible fruit.

Date palm was given the Latin name *Phoenix dactylifera* by Linnaeus in *Species Plantarum* (1753: 1188). The Latin name for the genus *Phoenix*, to which the date palm belongs, is borrowed from Greek φοῖνιξ 'Phoenician', referring to the Levantine background of the plant (Frisk 1032); *dactylifera* means 'date-bearing'.[29]

The dragon-blood tree [*Dracaena cinnabari* – Asparagaceae]

There is abundant literature on the dragon-blood tree, a virtual botanical symbol of the island of Soqoṭra whose prominent role in the traditional lifestyle of its inhabitants is impossible to overestimate (Miller and Morris 2004: 324–32). The Arabic name *damu l-ʔaḥawayni*, 'blood of two brothers', refers to the red sap that it exudes.

Dracaena cinnabari is endemic to Soqoṭra, Yemen; this species, together with five other trees in the genus *Dracaena*, are considered to be remnants of the Mio-Pliocene Laurasian subtropical forests. These forests are now almost extinct because of the climate changes of late Pliocene that caused the desertification of North Africa (Mies 1996: 83–105).

What will interest us here is the etymology of the second element of the scientific name of the tree – *cinnabari*. It is not difficult to find out that it goes back to Greek κιννάβαρι (Frisk 855), borrowed in this way or another into a variety of Western languages such as Latin *cinnabaris*, English *cinnabar*, French *cinabre* or Russian *киноварь*. The Greek word is thought to go back to an Iranian source, such as Old Persian *si^nkabru-* > Neo-Persian *šangarf* (EDPL 1913–14). It has not been previously noted, however, that a conspicuously similar lexeme is present in the Soqoṭri language itself, viz. *šenébhɛr* 'fruit of Dracaena cinnabari' (Miller and Morris 2004: 325). Given the fact that palatalized *k is one of the sources of Soq. *š*, the underlying form *kinabar* is nearly identical to the attested Greek lexeme, a coincidence which can scarcely be accidental.

Lieutenant Wellsted of the East India Company first described the Dragon-blood tree in his *Memoir on the Island of Socotra* which was published after his survey of Soqoṭra in 1834 (Wellsted 1835: 198). Later, *Dracaena cinnabari* was formally described by the Scottish botanist Balfour in the Transactions of the Royal Society of Edinburgh (Balfour 1882: 623).

Bitter orange [*Citrus aurantium* – Rutaceae]

The Soqoṭri name of the bitter orange *tenéže* (Miller and Morris 2004: 672) has a long history behind it. Its earliest traceable source is Sanskrit *mātuluṅga-* 'citron (tree)' (KEWA 620), itself of uncertain origin. Undoubtedly related are Middle Persian *wādrang* and Neo-Persian *bādrang* (EDPL 862–63, Ciancaglini 2008: 105). From an Iranian source the word has reached Arabic as ʔutruǯǯ-, ʔutrunǯ-, turunǯ- (Lane 301, Dozy I 146, Piamenta 51) and then, eventually, Spanish and Portugese as *toranja*, *toronja*. The exact origin of the Soqoṭri word – Iranian, Arabic or Portuguese – cannot be easily established since each of the alternative sources known to us displays an -*r*-, thoroughly missing from the Soqoṭri form.

The Bitter or Seville orange (*Citrus aurantium*) is native to Southeast Asia and spread to the rest of the world through humans. It is cultivated in warm temperate countries for its essential oil used in perfumes and as a flavouring in foods and sweets. It is widely used in the production of marmalade.

Notes

1 The generic name *Aloe* in the Western languages goes back to Greek ἀλόη, considered to be borrowed from an 'uncertain Oriental source' (Frisk 77). The Hebrew term ʔăhālōt undoubtedly goes back to the same, hitherto unknown source (Noonan 2019: 43–4). Numerous phonetically similar terms in Arabic, Aramaic and Ethiopian Semitic are, in the wake of Nöldeke 1910: 43, usually considered borrowings from Greek, even if the presence of ʕ in them is not easy to explain within such a hypothesis: Syr. ʕalwā (LSyr. 526), Gez. ʕalwā (CDG 62).

2 With numerous variants in the spoken dialects of the South of the Peninsula: ṣabar, ṣabur, ṣabār, ṣibīr (Behnstedt 699, Piamenta 275–76, al-Iryāni 659–60). Related designations are attested also in Syriac: ṣabrā, ṣabbārā (LSyr. 620, Löw 1881: 295, 426). The earliest attestation is, probably, Akk. ṣibaru (CAD Ṣ 155), widely attested in medical texts as a drug against, *inter alia*, 'excessive bile' (see further Thompson 1949: 129–30). Among Arabs, ṣabr 'aloe' is closely associated with the verbal root ṣbr 'to be patient', and it may be for that reason that *Aloe vera* is often planted in graveyards in northern Oman (pers. obs.): it may help the defunct to be patient on his journey from life on earth to afterlife. It is hard to say whether, in this case, we are faced with a 'true' or 'popular' etymology.

3 Another species of *Aloe* found in Dhofar is *A. inermis* (Miller and Morris 1988: 184). Its local names are *síḳil* in Jibbali, *sēḳel* in Dhofari Arabic. Their etymology is somewhat controversial. Phonetically close terms in Classical Arabic (such as

ʔisqīl-) designate the 'sea onion' (*Drimia maritima*), quite a different plant rather dissimilar from *Aloe*. Together with Syr. *sqyl?* (LSyr. 494), the Arabic word is clearly borrowed from Greek σκίλλα, of uncertain etymology (Frisk 731), but coming close to the Akkadian plant name *sikillu* (CAD S 243), in turn apparently borrowed from Sum. *ú.sikil* 'pure plant'.

4   The Latin name *Ficus* was given by Linnaeus. According to a widespread opinion, it is an early borrowing from Hebrew *pag* (HALOT 909), but this is not acknowledged or even explicitly rejected by the modern etymological dictionaries of Latin (WH I 492, EM 232). The word *fig* first came into English early in the thirteenth century, brought by the Norman conquerors from the Old French *figue*, itself from Latin *fica*. The second element, *carica*, is a geographic epithet, referring to Caria, a region of western Anatolia where figs were cultivated. The locality of the specimen on which the name *Ficus carica* is based is not known; the specimen, however, is preserved and is housed at the Linnaean plant collection herbarium at Burlington House in Piccadilly, London.

5   The pollination of fig is through a complex symbiotic relationship with the fig wasp, *Balastophaga penes*. Although species of fig wasps are specific to the fig species they pollinate, studies on fig pollination have shown that the same species of fig wasp may pollinate different but related species of fig.

6   There is a special Hebrew term for the so-called 'early fig', appearing in March or April and ripening in June: *bikkūrā* (HALOT 130). The late figs, which sometimes ripen after the fall of the leaf, and occasionally remain on the tree during the winter months, were called *taʔēnā*, which is also the generic term. Finally, the young, unripened figs having little juice but still suitable for consumption were called *pag* (HALOT 909). See further Dalman (1928: 378–81). Fresh figs were dried and pressed into cakes called *dəbēlā* (HALOT 209).

7   In the fig tree, male and female flowers are not visible as they are produced within the 'fruit', the fig, which is a fleshy receptacle called a synconium. The synconium is a specialized structure, a highly modified flowering branch bearing very reduced male and female flowers within.

8   Mandaville (2011: 217) reports the word *wāris* used by desert bedouins in eastern Saudi Arabia for the stage of flowering of *Cornulaca arabica* (Ar. *hāḏ*) when the yellow anthers protrude from joints (reduced flowers), which may refer to the similarity of the colour of *wars*.

9   For the latter, see further Piamenta 359.

10 For some post-Classical written attestations v. Dozy II 125.

11 The English word *olive* is derived from Latin *oliva*, in turn borrowed from early Greek *ἐλαιϝā, of uncertain origin (EM 460, Frisk 480, WH II 205).

12 For *zabbūg* or *zanbūg* as a designation of the wild olive in Maghreb v. Dozy I 578, 605 (originally a Berber word). This tree is mentioned, *inter alia*, by Maimonides (Rosner 1995: 101).

13 The etymology of the Akkadian word is unknown, but it bears a certain similarity to *salīṭ-*, designating vegetable oils in Classical Arabic and especially in the dialects of Yemen (Lane 1406).
14 A fossilized masculine plural ending? In Hebrew and Aramaic, the corresponding terms are indeed used with such an ending in the plural (Hbr. *zēt-īm*).
15 Outside the Arabian Peninsula, *Rhazya stricta* is known by other names, such as *lūwiza* (Iraq, Southern desert), *ešwarak* (Persian), *sihar, hisawarg* (Urdu).
16 The generic Latin name, *Tamarix*, is etymologically uncertain, for various hypotheses v. WH II 646, EM 676. The second element *aphylla* 'leafless' describes it as being apparently without leaves.
17 It is hard to say whether Soq. *bóyhən* designating *Sterculia africana* (Miller and Morris 2004: 694) etymologically belongs to the same root.
18 It is not without significance that some sort of contamination between 'tamarisk' and 'juniper' is attested already in the Antiquity and the Middle Ages. Thus, the Hebrew word *ʕarʕār*, commonly translated as 'juniper' by modern Hebraists, has been understood as 'tamarisk' by LXX (Greek μυρίκη). Even more interesting is the tradition reported (unfortunately, without source) in Kazimirski's dictionary according to which *ʕarʕar-* 'juniper' 'est réputé ennemi du palmier et tenu à distance de ce dernier' (BK 2 224). This tradition undoubtedly goes back to the famous Ancient Mesopotamian debate poem (*munāḏara*) 'Date Palm and Tamarisk', where the two trees are presented as outspoken opponents (Streck 2004).
19 The generic name *Acacia* originates from Greek ἀκακία. According to Frisk 50, this is a loanword from uncertain source, possibly influenced by Greek ἀκίς 'sharp point'.
20 In the Sidamo region of southern Ethiopia, the name *tallaha* is given to another tree, *Polyscias fulva*. This is a woodland tree found in semi-humid and humid highland forests throughout Africa and has been reported more recently on the mountains in Yemen (Cheek 2009; Hedberg et al. 1989: 537).
21 The same is true of Hbr. *šiṭṭā* (Noonan 2019: 208–9; Parkhurst 1829: 525).
22 The generic name *Withania* given by Pauquy in 1825 is believed to have been in honour of Henry Witham (1779–1844), a British geologist and palaeobotanist. The specific epithet *somnifera* refers to the plant's sleep-inducing properties.
23 Cf. Akk. *šakirû* 'henbane' (CAD Š$_1$ 167), thought to be borrowed from Sum. *šakira* (Lieberman 1977: 475).
24 Each example is of considerable cultural-historical and religious significance. Thus, 34:16 refers to the break of the Marib dam (*saylu l-ʕarimi*) because of which the Saba lost their two wonderful gardens and got instead tamarisks and 'a bit of Ziziphus' (*šayʔan mina s-sidri*). In 56:28, 'those of the right side' are described to stay in the Paradise among 'Ziziphus trees without thorns (*fī sidrin maḫḍūd*)'. But by far the most famous is 53:13–16, where a Ziziphus tree is described, in somewhat mystical terms, as one of the places where Gabriel appeared to the

Prophet: 'He saw him descend another time * Near the Ziziphus of the Extreme End (ʕinda sidrati l-muntahā) * Near which is the Garden of Abode * And the Ziziphus was covered by what it was covered (ʔiḏ yaġšā s-sidrata mā yaġšā)'. It is not surprising, therefore, that the tree has been sometimes considered 'holy' by the Muslims of the Middle East (Dafni et al. 2005). Muslim rosaries are made from Ziziphus seeds (Wickens 1980).

25 In Job 40:21–22, as the habitat of Behemoth: 'Under the lotus plants it lies, in the covert of the reeds and in the marsh. The lotus trees cover it for shade, the willows of the wadi surround it'.

26 Synonyms: *J. arabicus*; *J. maritimus f. rigidus*; *J. maritimus* var. *arabicus*.

27 There is no reference to fruits in the Biblical corpus, hence the necessity to rely on the data from Rabbinic Hebrew.

28 On the Akkadian verb *rukkubu* 'to pollinate' and its sexual connotations v. extensively SED I No. 60$_v$. The male form was called *zikarum* 'man' in Akkadian, and in Soqoṭri the term *miʔšer* 'billy-goat' (ultimately related etymologically) is in use up to now.

29 From Greek δάκτυλος 'date'. According to Frisk 345, there is no etymological connection between this term and δάκτυλος 'finger', which have been secondarily associated by popular etymology due to the oblong shape of the fruits.

References

Amar, Z. and E. Lev (2017), *Arabian Drugs in Medieval Mediterranean Medicine*, Edinburgh: Edinburgh University Press.

Balfour, I. B. (1882), 'Botany of Socotra', *Transactions of the Royal Society of Edinburgh*, 30: 623.

Baum, B. B. (1978), *The genus Tamarix*, Jerusalem: Israel Academy of Sciences and Humanities.

Blau, J. (1998), *Topics in Hebrew and Semitic Linguistics*, Jerusalem: Magnes.

Boivin, N. and D. Q. Fuller (2009), 'Shell Middens, Ships and Seeds: Exploring Coastal Subsistence, Maritime Trade and the Dispersal of Domesticates in and around the Ancient Arabian Peninsula', *Journal of World Prehistory*, 22 (2): 113–80.

Bustamante, J., F. Corriente and M. Tilmatine (eds) (2010), *Abū al-Khayr al-Ishbīlī. Kitābu 'umdati ṭ-ṭabīb fī ma'rifati nabātin li-kulli labīb*, Madrid: CSIC.

Catagnoti, A. (2008), 'Il lessico dei vegetali ad Ebla. 2. La frutta (parte I). Uva, fico, mela', *Quaderni del dipartimento di linguistica*, 18: 175–87.

Chalabi-Ka'bi, (1980), 'Rhamnaceae', in C. C. Townsend and E. Guest (eds), *Flora of Iraq*, 4 (1), 435–7, Kew: Royal Botanic Gardens, Kew.

Cheek, M. (2009), '*Polyscias* (Araliaceae) not *Brucea* (Simaroubaceae) Is Native to the Arabian Peninsula', *Kew Bulletin*, 64: 581.

Ciancaglini, C. (2008), *Iranian Loanwords in Syriac*, Wiesbaden: Reichert.
Cohen, Y. (2013), *Wisdom from the Late Bronze Age*, Atlanta: SBL.
Dafni, A., S. Levy and E. Lev (2005), 'The Ethnobotany of Christ's Thorn Jujube (*Ziziphus spina-christi*) in Israel', *Journal of Ethnobiology & Ethnomedicine*, 1: 8–11.
Dalman, G. (1928), *Arbeit und Sitte in Palästina*, Gütersloh: Bertelsmann.
Dar, N. J., A. Hamid and M. Ahmad (2015), 'Pharmacologic Overview of *Withania somnifera*, the Indian Ginseng', *Cellular and Molecular Life Sciences*, 72: 4445–60.
Duke, J. A. (2008), *Duke's Handbook of Medicinal Plants of the Bible*, Florida: CRC Press.
Fronzaroli, P. (1969), 'Studi sul lessico comune semitico. V. La natura domestica', *Accademia Nacionale dei Lincei, Rendiconti*, VIII/XXIII (7–12): 267–303.
Fuller, D. Q., N. Boivin, T. Hoogervorst and R. Allaby (2011), 'Across the Indian Ocean: the Prehistoric Movement of Plants and Animals', *Antiquity*, 85 (328): 544–58.
Fuller, D. Q. and C. J. Stevens (2019), 'Between Domestication and Civilization: The Role of Agriculture and Arboriculture in the Emergence of the First Urban Societies', *Vegetation History and Archaeobotany*, 28 (3): 263–82.
Ghafoor, A. (1974), 'Zygophyllaceae', in E. Nasir and S. I. Ali (eds), *Flora of Pakistan*, 76, 7, Karachi: Karachi University Press.
Ghazanfar, S. A. and A. M. Al-Sabahi (1993), 'Medicinal Plants of Northern and Central Oman (Arabia)', *Economic Botany*, 47 (1): 89–98.
Ghazanfar, S. A. (1994), *Handbook of Arabian Medicinal Plants*, Boca Raton: CRC Press.
Ghazanfar, S. A. (2003), *Flora of the Sultanate of Oman, Vol. 1, Piperaceae-Primulaceae (Text + photo CD-ROM)*, Scripta Botanica Belgica 25, Belgium: National Botanic Garden of Belgium, Meise.
Ghazanfar, S. A. (2007), *Flora of the Sultanate of Oman. Vol. 2, Crassulaceae-Apiaceae (Text + photo CD-ROM)*, Scripta Botanica Belgica, Belgium: National Botanic Garden of Belgium, Meise.
Ghazanfar, S. A. (2012), 'Medicinal Plants of the Middle East', in Ram Singh (ed.), *Genetic Resources, Chromosome Engineering and Crop Improvement*, 163–80, Boca Raton: CRC Press.
Ghazanfar, S. A. (2015), *Flora of the Sultanate of Oman, Vol. 3, Loganiaceae-Asteraceae (Text + photo CD-ROM)*, Scripta Botanica Belgica 55, Belgium: National Botanic Garden of Belgium, Meise.
Ghazanfar, S. A. (2018), *Flora of the Sultanate of Oman, Vol. 4, Hydrocharitaceae-Orchidaceae (Text)*, Scripta Botanica Belgica 56, Belgium: National Botanic Garden of Belgium, Meise.
Ghazanfar, S. A. and S. Wickison (2023), *Plants of the Quran*, London: Kew Publishing (in press).
Green, P. S. (2002), 'A Revision of *Olea* L. (Oleaceae)', *Kew Bulletin*, 57: 91–140.
Hedberg, I., O. Hedberg, T. B. G. Egziabher and S. Edwards (1989), *Flora of Ethiopia and Eritrea. Vol. 3, Pittosporaceae to Araliaceae*, Addis Ababa: The National Herbarium & Uppsala: Uppsala University.

Hepper F. N. (1991), 'Old World *Withania* (Solanaceae): A Taxonomic Review and Key to the Species', in J. G. Hawkes, R. N. Lester, M. Nee and N. Estrada (eds), *Solanaceae III: Taxonomy, Chemistry, Evolution*, 211–17, London: Royal Botanic Gardens Kew & Linnaean Society of London.

Hepper, F. N. (1992), *Illustrated Encyclopaedia of Bible Plants*, England: Inter Varsity Press.

Hort, S. A. (1948), *Theophrastus Enquiry into Plants and Minor Works on Odours and Weather Signs*, London: William Heinemann Limited.

Jansen, P. C. M. (2005), 'Warus', in P. C. M Jansen and D. Cardon (eds), *Plant Resources of Tropical Africa* (PROTA), *Dyes and Tannins* 3, 81–3, Leiden: Backhuys.

Jeffery, A. (1938), *Foreign Vocabulary of the Qur'an*, Baroda: Oriental Institute.

Jennings, R. P., J. Singarayer, E. J. Stone, U. Krebs-Kanzow, V. Khon, K. H. Nisancioglu, M. Pfeiffer, Xu Zhang, A. Parker, A. Parton, H. S. Groucutt, T. S. White, N. A. Drake and M. D. Petraglia (2015), 'The Greening of Arabia: Multiple Opportunities for Human Occupation of the Arabian Peninsula during the Late Pleistocene Inferred from an Ensemble of Climate Model Simulations', *Quaternary International*, 382: 181–99.

Johnston, P. (trans. & ed.) (1998), *Ibn Qayyim al Jawziyya, Medicine of the Prophet*, London: The Islamic Texts Society.

King, A. (2015), 'The New materia medica of the Islamicate Tradition: The Pre-Islamic Context', *Journal of the American Oriental Society*, 135 (3): 499–528.

Kogan, L. (2012), 'Les noms de plantes akkadiens dans leur contexte sémitique', in N. Pat-El and R. Hasselbach (eds), *Language and Nature. Papers Presented to John Huehnergard on the Occasion of His 60th Birthday*, 229–67, Chicago: Eisenbrauns.

Krebernik, M. (1983), 'Zu Syllabar und Orthographie der lexikalischen Texte aus Ebla. Teil 2 (Glossar)', *Zeitschrift für Assyriologie*, 83: 1–47.

Kulkarni, S. K. and A. Dhir (2008), '*Withania Somnifera*: An Indian Ginseng', *Progress in Neuro-Psychopharmacology and Biological Psychiatry*, 32 (5): 1093–105.

Landsberger, B. (1967), *The Date Palm and Its By-products According to the Cuneiform Sources*, Graz: Selbstverlag.

Langgut, D., Y. Gadot, N. Porat and O. Lipschits (2013), 'Fossil Pollen Reveals the Secrets of the Royal Persian Garden at Ramat Rahel, Jerusalem', *Palynology*, 37 (1): 115–29.

Lauer J.-Ph., Laurent-Täckholm V. and Åberg E. (1951), 'Les plantes découvertes dans les souterrains de l'enceinte du Roi Zoser à Saqqarah (iiie dynastie)', *Bulletin de l'Institut d'Égypte*, 32: 121–57.

Laufer, B. (1919), *Sino-Iranica. Chinese Contributions to the History of Civilization in Ancient Iran, with Special Reference to the History of Cultivated Plants and Products*, Chicago: Field Museum of Natural History.

Levey, M. (1966), *The Medical Formulary or Aqrābādhīn of al-Kindī*, Madison: University of Wisconsin Press.

Lieberman, S. (1977), *Sumerian Loanwords in Old Babylonian Akkadian*, Missoula: Scholars Press.

Löw, I. (1881), *Aramäische Pflanzennamen*, Leipzig: Engelmann.
Mandaville, J. P. (1990), *Flora of Eastern Saudi Arabia*, London: Kegan Paul International.
Mandaville, J. P. (2011), *Bedouin Ethnobotany*, Tucson: The University of Arizona Press.
Manniche, L. (1989), *An Ancient Egyptian Herbal*, London: British Museum Press.
McCoy, T. (2019), *The Aloes of Arabia*, Temecula, California: McCoy Publishing.
Miczak, M. A. (2001), *Henna's Secret History: The History, Mystery and Folklore of Henna*, Lincoln: Writers Club Press.
Mies, B. (1996), 'The Phytogeography of Soqotra: Evidence for Disjunctive Taxa, Especially with Macronesia', in H. J. Dumont (ed.), *Proceedings of the First International Symposium on Soqotra Island: Present and Future*, 83–105, New York: UN.
Miller, A. G. and M. Morris (1988), *Plants of Dhofar, the Southern Region of Oman: Traditional, Economic, and Medicinal uses*, Oman: Office of the Adviser for Conservation of the Environment, Diwan of Royal Court.
Miller, A. G. and M. Morris (2004), *Ethnoflora of the Soqotra Archipelago*, Edinburgh: Royal Botanic Garden.
Murad, A. S. (1980), 'Prehistory in the Arabian Peninsula', *Paleorient*, 6: 237–40.
Nesbitt, M. (1993), 'Archaeobotanical Evidence for Early Dilmun Diet at Saar, Bahrain', *Arabian Archaeology and Epigraphy*, 4: 20–47.
Newberry, P. E. (1889), 'On Some Funeral Wreaths of the Græco-Roman Period, Discovered in the Cemetery of Hawara', *Archaeological Journal*, 46 (1): 427–32.
Nöldeke, T. (1910), *Neue Beiträge zur semitischen Sprachwissenschaft*, Straßburg: Trübner.
Noonan, B. (2019), *Non-Semitic Loanwords in the Hebrew Bible*, Winona Lake: Eisenbrauns.
Parkhurst, J. (1829), *A Hebrew and English Lexicon without Points: In Which the Hebrew and Chaldee Words of the Old Testament Are Explained in Their Leading and Derived Senses. . . . To This Work Are Prefixed, a Hebrew and a Chaldee Grammar, without Points*, London: Thomas Tegg.
Postgate, J. N. (1987), 'Notes on Fruits in the Cuneiform Sources', *Bulletin of Sumerian Agriculture*, 3: 115–44.
POWO = Plants of the World Online portal. Royal Botanic Gardens, Kew. https//:www.plantsoftheworldonline.org
Provençal, P. (2010), *Arabic Plant Names of Peter Forsskål's Flora Aegyptiaco-Arabica*, Copenhagen: Det Kongelige Danske Videnskabernes Selskab.
Rosner, F. (1995), *Maimonides' Medical Writings. The Glossary of Drug Names Translated and Annotated from Max Meyerhof's French Edition*, Haifa: The Maimonides Research Institute.
Schönig, H. (2002), *Schminken, Düfte und Räucherwerk der Jemenitinnen: Lexikon der Substanzen, Utensilien und Techniken*, Würzburg: Ergon-Verlag.
Schopen, A. (1983), *Traditionelle Heilmittel in Jemen*, Wiesbaden: Franz Steiner.
Schweinfurth, G. A. (1886), 'Reise in das Depressionsgebiet im Umkreise des Fajum', *Zeitschrift der Gesellschaft für Erdkunde zu Berlin*, 21: 96–149.

Sima, A. (2000), *Tiere, Pflanzen, Steine und Metalle in den altsüdarabischen Inschriften*, Wiesbaden: Harrassowitz.

Sima, A. (2009), *Mehri-Texte aus der jemenitischen Šarqīyah*, Wiesbaden: Harrassowitz.

Stager, L. E. (1985), 'The First Fruits of Civilization', in J. N. Tubb (ed.), *Palestine in the Bronze and Iron Age*, 172–88, London: Institute of Archaeology.

Stein, P. (2010), *Die altsüdarabischen Minuskelinschriften auf Holzstäbchen aus der Bayerischen Staatsbibliothek in München*, Tübingen: Wasmuth.

Stol, M. (2003–2005), 'Öl, Ölbaum. A. In Mesopotamien', *Reallexikon der Assyriologie*, 10: 32–3.

Streck, M. (2004), 'Dattelpalme und Tamariske in Mesopotamien nach dem akkadischen Streitgespräch', *Zeitschrift für Assyriologie*, 94: 250–90.

Sung, C. K. (2006), 'The History of Aloe', in Y. I. Park and S. K. Lee (eds), *New Perspectives on Aloe*, 7–17, Boston, MA: Springer.

Taifour, H. and A. El-Oqla (2017), *Plants of Jordan: an Annotated Checklist*, S.A. Ghazanfar (ed.) Royal Botanic Gardens Kew: Kew Publishing.

Thompson, R. (1949), *A Dictionary of Assyrian Botany*, London: The British Academy.

Turner, R. L. (1966), *A Comparative Dictionary of the Indo-Aryan Languages*, London: OUP.

Volk, K. (2003–2005), 'Palme', *Reallexikon der Assyriologie*, 10: 283–92.

Wellsted, J. R. (1835), 'Memoir on the Island of Socotra', *The Journal of the Royal Geographical Society of London*, 5: 129–229.

Wickens, G. E. (1980), 'Alternative Uses of Browse Species', in H. N. Le Houérou (ed.), *Browse in Africa: the Current State of Knowledge*, 155–82, Addis Ababa: ILCA.

Wood, J. R. (1997), *A Handbook of the Yemen Flora*, Kew: Royal Botanic Gardens.

Zohary, M. (1982), *Plants of the Bible: A Complete Handbook to All the Plants with 200 Full Color Plates Taken in the Natural Habitat*, Cambridge: Cambridge University Press.

Zohary, D., M. Hopf and E. Weiss (2012), *Domestication of Plants in the Old World. The Origin and Spread of Domesticated Plants in South-West Asia, Europe, and the Mediterranean Basin*, 4th Edition, Oxford: Oxford University Press.

Abbreviations of lexicographic tools

al-Iryani: M. al-Iryani. *Al-muʕǧam al-yamanī fī l-luġa wa-t-turāṯ*. S.l., 2012.

BDB: F. Brown, S. R. Driver, Ch. A. Briggs. *A Hebrew and Aramaic Lexicon of the Old Testament*. Oxford, 1906.

Behnstedt: P. Behnstedt. *Die nordjemenitischen Dialekte (Glossar)*. Wiesbaden, 1992–2006.

BK: A. de Biberstein Kazimirski. *Dictionnaire arabe-français*. Paris, 1860.

Biella: J. C. Biella. *Dictionary of Old South Arabic, Sabaean Dialect*. Chico, 1982.

CAD: *The Assyrian Dictionary of the Oriental Institute, the University of Chicago.* Chicago, 1956–2010.

CDG: W. Leslau. *Comparative Dictionary of Geʕez (Classical Ethiopic).* Wiesbaden, 1987.

CSOL I: V. Naumkin, L. Kogan et al. *Corpus of Soqoti Oral Literature.* Volume One. Leiden, 2014.

DELC: W. Vycichl. *Dictionnaire étymologique de la langue copte.* Leuven, 1983.

Dozy: R. Dozy. *Supplément au dictionnaires arabes.* Leiden, 1881.

DSI: Francesco Agostini, Annarita Puglielli, Ciise Moxamed Siyaad. *Dizionario somalo-italiano.* Roma, 1985.

DUL: G. del Olmo Lete, J. Sanmartín. *A Dictionary of the Ugaritic Language in the Alphabetic Tradition.* Leiden, 2003.

EDE: G. Takács. *Etymological Dictionary of Egyptian. Volume Two. b-, p-, f-.* Leiden, 2001.

EDH: W. Leslau. *Etymological Dictionary of Harari.* Berkeley, 1963.

EDPL: M. Hassandust. *Etymological Dictionary of the Persian Language.* Teheran, 2015.

EM: A. Ernout, A. Meillet. *Dictionnaire étymologique de la langue latine.* Paris, 1959.

Frisk: H. Frisk. *Griechisches etymologisches Wörterbuch.* Heidelberg, 1954–1972.

GD: C. de Landberg. *Glossaire daṯinois.* Leiden, 1920–1942.

HALOT: L. Koehler, W. Baumgartner, J. J. Stamm. *The Hebrew and Aramaic Lexicon of the Old Testament.* Leiden, 1994–2000.

Jastrow: M. Jastrow. *A Dictionary of the Targumim, the Talmud Babli and Yerushalmi, and the Midrashic Literature.* New York, 1996.

KEWA: M. Mayrhofer. *Kurzgefasstes etymologisches Wörterbuch des Altindischen.* Heidelberg, 1956–1980.

JL: T. M. Johnstone. *Jibbāli Lexicon.* Oxford, 1981.

LA: Ibn Manẓūr. *Lisānu l-ʕarab.* Bayrūt, 1990.

Lane: E. W. Lane. *Arabic-English Lexicon.* London, 1867.

LLA: A. Dillmann. *Lexicon linguae aethiopicae.* Leipzig, 1865.

LS: W. Leslau. *Lexique Soqoṭri (Sudarabique moderne) avec comparaisons et explications étymologiques.* Paris, 1938.

LSyr.: C. Brockelmann. *Lexicon Syriacum.* Halle, 1928.

ML: T. M. Johnstone. *Mehri Lexicon.* London, 1987.

MW: M. Monier-Williams. *A Sanskrit-English Dictionary.* Oxford, 1899.

Piamenta: M. Piamenta. *Dictionary of Post-Classical Yemeni Arabic.* Leiden, 1990.

SD: A. F. L. Beeston, M. A. Ghul, W. W. Müller, J. Ryckmans. *Sabaic Dictionary (English-French-Arabic).* Louvain-la-Neuve, 1982.

SED I: A. Militarev, L. Kogan. *Semitic Etymological Dictionary. Volume One. Anatomy of Man and Animals.* Münster: Ugarit.

SL: M. Sokoloff. *A Syriac Lexicon.* Winona Lake, 2009.

Wb.: A. Erman, H. Grapow. *Ägyptisches Handwörterbuch.* Berlin, 1921.

WH: A. Walde, J. Hoffmann. *Lateinisches etymologisches Wörterbuch.* Heidelberg, 1938.

6

Traditional Knowledge and Vocabulary around Weather and Astronomy in Qatar

Kaltham Al-Ghanim

Introduction

There is considerable interest in recent years in local knowledge as a resource for enhancing governmental and societal mechanisms for regulating the environment and making the best and most sustainable use of resources (cf. Fischer 2000; Turner et al. 2000). Localized traditional knowledge has become the object of research in many societies in order to ensure that environmental provisions are optimized, given that 'these forms of knowledge have formed the basis for societal growth in many regions able to deal with the constraints that the environment imposes' (Vedwan 2006: 6). This involves combining traditional ecological knowledge with the sciences, something which can greatly assist in the battle against climate change and its effect on soil, atmosphere and crops. There are a few basic rules to improvise from in traditional knowledge that can produce great benefits administratively that accord with logic and can facilitate the relation of traditional ecological ideas to scientific findings (Moller et al. 2004: 2). Thus, indigenous peoples can proffer alternative ideas on climate variation based on their own knowledge and practice and drawing on local resources. This traditional ecological knowledge also plays a decisive role in the individual and collective understanding of climate change among those indigenous peoples (Leonard et al. 2013). Indigenous knowledge is part of traditional culture and the United Nations in general (and UNESCO in particular) consider culture the fourth pillar of sustainable development (cf. UCLG 2010). Thus, heritage has ascended to a place of importance, as has conserving and sustaining it as a native, popular source of knowledge and experience and as an indicator of cultural diversity that has become a prerequisite for implementing policies (UNESCO, WWF & Terralingua 2003).

Language is a key aspect of culture and part of identity. When languages disappear, cultures do too, changing this sense of identity forever. A recent study indicated that between 50 and 90 per cent of languages spoken today may become extinct within a century (Austin and Sallabank 2011: 1). UNESCO believes that language is both an essential diffuser and a source of heritage and traditional knowledge (UNESCO, WWF & Terralingua 2003; UNESCO 1996).

While interest centres on vernacular spoken languages threatened with extinction and on cultures at risk of dissolution into a hegemonic culture, field-oriented research, such as the present work, is significant in its consideration of language as a source of local knowledge. It focuses on wisdom shared by its native speakers who are themselves the transmitters of this language to new generations (Skutnabb-Kangas 2011: 177–8). This type of study is beneficial in that it newly documents material found in linguistic expressions which are themselves the bearers of that type of localized knowledge. It is especially true since language is the prime vehicle for absorbing and transmitting knowledge, information and conceptualization in every localized culture, being something shared by its native speakers who are the transmitters of this language to new generations (ibid.).

The spread of Modern Standard Arabic (MSA) in the media and education has posed a severe threat to Qatari language varieties since the middle of the nineteenth century. While the eldest generation of Qataris has retained usage of their native language, it is nonetheless evident today that most of the younger generation is no longer well-versed in the spoken varieties (cf. Ingham 1997; Milroym and Dean 2013). Preserving the region's linguistic varieties has become known as the key to discovering climate solutions rooted in important indigenous terms and expressions that embody the inhabited landscape.

UNESCO has urged popular education, training and awareness on the interaction between environments, cultures and languages, forewarning citizens of the importance of preserving human heritage in every regard, reviving sustainable development and preserving Qatar's cultural and natural heritage (UNESCO, WWF & Terralingua 2003: 6). The language of older generations is important, just as are their environment and cultural values. UNESCO's 2003 report warns that today's changing world presents people, youth included, with serious challenges in relation to language Linguistic roots are not merely an academic issue but are indeed important for the future of human development itself. When respect for cultural heritage is encouraged, it also encourages respect for our biological and material environment.

Gathering data on intangible culture under threat of disappearance is only the first step. It is also important to examine the context of usages and the derivational history as far as possible. To clearly understand the extent to which Qatari intangible culture is threatened, a more thorough survey conducted with the younger generation is needed. However, one of the aims of the study is to analyse the collected terms and the principal lexica in relation to indigenous knowledge. Focusing on terms related to weather and seasons has a particular importance for the region, especially because it is characterized by an arid climate with challenging living conditions. Recording and preserving local knowledge relating to the environment and land management are essential to develop, for example, more sustainable ways of territorial control and grazing. In such an arid region as the Arabian Peninsula, finding new systems are critical in view of climatic changes. There has also been a heavily marked decline in usage of such terms due to social and economic changes, e.g. the introduction of more technological tools for breeding, harvesting and land management.

This study is pioneering the research into the relationship between language and nature in the region, specifically looking at lexical data concerning seasonal changes, weather and stars. It will contribute to the improvement of our understanding of this relationship in the Arabian Peninsula and also to the preservation of old expressions which encapsulate traditional knowledge linked to the environment and threatened with extinction.

Methodology

The collection and analysis of dialectal expressions and native knowledge require interaction with the local communities, a good knowledge of the language of the indigenous population and the ability to communicate with it effectively. The methodology employed involves the qualitative analysis of primary linguistic data: in particular, the content analysis of local expressions relating to meteorologic phenomena, names of seasons and local knowledge usually transmitted orally from generation to generation. These data were drawn from interviews conducted with four local experts of Qatari heritage. In addition to this, some written documents relating to Qatari traditional knowledge have been used for comparative purposes, especially pertaining names of winds, seasons and weather. The methodology employed builds on disciplines such as sociolinguistic and anthropology, which uses interviews and observation respectively as main tools of research. This method has been furthermore shaped by Grounded Theory as first formulated in Glaser & Strauss (1967), which entails an inductive process, i.e., first formulating the theory or the hypothesis and then finding the evidence in the data.

Data collection, documentation, categorization and analytical methods

Published databases were drawn upon, such as dictionaries, published studies, books on popular culture and descriptive narrative studies. The material includes proverbs and sayings, poetry, festival material, pearl divers' songs, work songs, traditional children's tunes and games. Fortunately, there is also a rich vein of documentation for a number of expressions used in the Arabian Peninsula related to the stars, and knowledge of the seasons, including storm patterns. Examples include pioneering works on the categorization of the seasons (Al-Zajjāj 2006; cf. Ibn Qutayba 1956; Quṭrub 1985). Likewise, there have been studies in the Gulf region on the stars such as those of Nash & Agius (2011), Ibn Khamis (1985) and Al-ʾUjayri (1986). Regional poetry and popular sayings and proverbs were also a rich source.

Categorization of expressions and information

Two approaches were adopted to categorization, one focusing on information specific to weather-related phenomena, heavenly bodies, vegetation and animals, and another related to the type of textual genre: story, popular proverb, poetry, song, narrative text and so on. The research team also used descriptive, analytical and exploratory methods to analyse the linguistic expressions after categorizing them according to topic area (Baptiste 2001).

Two-stage analysis

The analysis was conducted in two stages. Firstly, the environmental phenomena were correlated with the explicit, metaphorical and underlying meaning of the terms and expressions and also the practical application of such related knowledge. A table of such expressions was compiled. Secondly, linguistic analysis was conducted according to the category to which the various linguistic expressions belong (in Classical Arabic). The study drew on original sources from

Classical Arabic dictionaries: Ibn Manẓūr's *Lisān al-ᶜArab* (1956); Al-Fīrūzbādī's *Al-Qāmūs al-Muḥīṭ al-Wasīṭ* (n.d.); the *Al-Muᶜjam al-Wasīṭ* dictionary[1]; the *Al-Maᶜānī* dictionary; and Al-Ṣaġānī's *Al-Takmilah*. These terms and expressions were categorized by their morphology, derivational sources and their relationship to Classical Arabic meanings. The same process was conducted with regard to related proverbs, sayings and so on. The purpose was to compile linguistically based information as primary data for a future compendium of environmentally related terms. The comparison with terminology in Classical Arabic sources is deemed important for this work in order to investigate and clarify the original meaning or its use in poetry of weather-related nouns in Qatari culture.

Observations

The usage of the gathered terms and expressions was in more frequent use in the past of Qatar when the principal sources of inhabitants' income came from the sea, animal husbandry and certain limited forms of agriculture. The rhythm of social and economic life was to a great extent in tandem with the seasons (Al-Ghanim 2011; Al-Ghanim 2014; Varisco 1990). Common means for articulating social customs and values, especially in Arab Bedouin communities, were poetry, commonly established sayings and simple, popular songs. These have been preserved and handed down from parent to child and are used either spontaneously in the course of daily life or on particular occasions with a religious, social, economic and commemorative character.

The strong relationship between humans and their environment has led towards the development of a fundamental set of related knowledge systems, for example, whether rain might come, which prevailing wind will blow, what specific outcomes particular periods for farming and animal husbandry will have, when the fish are ready for catching depending on their variety and times and areas where they breed, and when pearl fishing should begin and end. It also provides information for the various diving seasons and their relation to storm patterns and prevalent wind varieties, temperature trends, water depth and the best areas where oysters breed. Moreover, it informs decisions on when the season for animal husbandry commences and where it should be done, the right type of fodder to feed each species of animal, when to transport them, whether to travel by sea or by land, the right degree of wind velocity and its relation to astronomical phenomena. This kind of information has been a basic form of knowledge over the centuries for men and women, settled or Bedouin (Al-Ghanim 2011). As a result, a vocabulary of the Qatari vernaculars has been developed in order to encapsulate that knowledge. Many of these expressions are peculiar to Qataris, though some are also used across the Arabian Peninsula in other dialects.

This leads us onto the analysis of particular lexical items derived from this heritage and which are expressive of humans' relationship with their environment.

Language and storm patterns, seasons and winds

The vital relationship between humanity and its environment-based knowledge helps people knowing when rain is about to come in otherwise very arid climates. Such knowledge is linked to other forms known collectively as *al-ʾanwāʾ* (or 'seasonal knowledge', such as that related to rain and precipitation, storms, and wind direction). The Arab and Islamic scientific heritage on this subject relates changes in rain and in weather patterns to the movement of the stars and the lunar stations, since most of the calculations in the ancient tradition are based on lunar rather than solar trajectories. Interest in the relation between stars' positions in the sky, their movements, ascents and absences from view due to weather conditions (rain, winds and seasons) emerged as a field of study in very early Islamic civilization. The most famous scientific work that compiled the local knowledge of desert dwellers was Ibn Qutayba's (d. 276/879) *Kitāb al-ʾAnwāʾ fī Mawāsim Al-ʿArab*. This book became the original source reference for other astronomy in Islamic culture.

Arabs in the Peninsula take into great account the times of the stars' appearance and disappearance in the sky and the star themselves, to the point that they use some of the stars' names for their children, such as *al-Jawzāʾ* (Orion) for girls. The Arab poet Al-Bāriq Al-Huḍalī (600–660 CE) relates the rise of *Al-Jawzāʾ* to November which is the month of *Al-Wasm* rain in the region. *Al-Wasm* rains (16 October–15 December) are very important to the people of the region. Al-Kabbabī (2014: 23) records this example:

> *saqā al-raḥmānu jizʿā nubayyātin min al-jawzaʾi ʾanwāʾan ġizāra*

The poet asks God for rain to fall at the time of the appearance of the *al-Jawzāʾ* star in a place called *Nubayyāt* where his beloved people live.

Ibn Al-Ajdābī (1233 AD), in a chapter entitled 'On the Meaning of *al-Nūʾ*' from his book *Al-Azmina wa al-ʾAnwāʾ* ('The Times and Seasons'), says:

> The [movements of the] celestial bodies that relate to storms are the twenty-eight phases [lit. 'dwellings'] of the moon. The meaning of *nūʾ* is the descent

of the star in the west in the morning, while the night remains in full darkness and another arises to encounter it that hour in the east. That which storms from these two in reality is the ascendant (star) because *al-nūʾ* in the language [means] the ascendancy

(cited in Ibn al-Ajdābī 2006: 120)

Another school of thought is that storms are a divine presage for the times of the rain, just as the month of *Kānūn* means the onset of cold and the months of *Ḥuzayrān* and *Tammūz* drought.

In Tables 6.1 to 6.4, the names of stars employed for indicating seasonal phases are given. For each star is indicated the name in Arabic script, the dates of appearance and disappearance, and the constellation they belong to with indication of the corresponding season.

Table 6.1 Spring Phases

	Star name	Arabic	Start–End	*burj* – 'Constellation'
1	Saʿd al-Axbīyah	سعد الأخبية	21 March–2 April	al-Hamīmīn (Spring)
2	Al-Farġ al-Muqaddam	الفرغ المقدم	3–15 April	al-Hamīmīn (Spring)
3	Al-Faraġ al-Muʾaxxar	الفرغ المؤخر	16–28 April	al-Ḍurāʿayn (Spring)
4	Baṭn al-ḥūt	بطن الحوت	29 April–11 May	al-Ḍurāʿayn (Spring)

Table 6.2 Summer Phases

	Star name	Arabic	Start–End	*burj*
5	Al-Šaraṭān	الشرطان	12–24 May	Ṭurayyā (Summer)
6	Al-Buṭayn	البطين	25 May–6 June	Ṭurayyā (Summer)
7	Al-Ṭurayyā	الثرياء	7–19 June	Ṭurayyā (Summer)
8	Al-Dabarān	الدبران	20 June–2 July	Tuwaybaʿ (Summer)
9	Al-Haqʿah	الهقعة	3–16 July	al-Jawzāʾ (Summer)
10	Al-Hanʿah	الهنعة	17–28 July	al-Jawzāʾ (Summer)
11	Al-Ḍirāʿ	الذراع	29 July–10 August	al-Marzam (al-Šaʿra al-Yamāniya) (Summer)
12	Al-Naṯrah	النثرة	11–23 August	al-ʾiklīl (Summer)
13	Al-Ṭarf	الطرف	24 August–5 September	Suhayl (Summer)

Table 6.3 Autumn Phases

	Star name	Arabic	Start–End	burj
14	Al-Jabhah	الجبهة	6–19 September	Suhayl (Autumn)
15	Al-Zubrah	الزبرة	20 September–2 October	Suhayl (Autumn)
16	Al-Ṣarfah	الصرفة	3–15 October	Suhayl (Autumn)
17	Al-ᶜAwwāʾ	العواء	16–28 October	Wasm (Autumn)
18	Al-Simāk	السماك	29 October–10 November	Wasm (Autumn)
19	Al-Ġafr	الغفر	11–23 November	Wasm (Autumn)
20	Al-Zubānā	الزبانا	24 November–6 December	Wasm (Autumn)

Table 6.4 Winter Phases

	Star name	Arabic	Start–End	burj
21	Al-Iklīl	الإكليل	7–19 December	Marbaᶜāniya (Winter)
22	Al-Qalb	القلب	20 December–1 January	Marbaᶜāniya (Winter)
23	Al-Šawlah	الشولة	2–14 January	Marbaᶜāniya (Winter)
24	Al-Naᶜāʾim	النعائم	15–27 January	al-Šabaṭ (Winter)
25	Al-Baldah	البلدة	28 January–9 February	al-Šabaṭ (Winter)
26	Saᶜd al-Ḏabīḥ	سعد الذبيح	10–22 February	al-ᶜAqrab (Winter)
27	Saᶜd Bulaᶜ	سعد بلع	23 February–7 March	al-ᶜAqrab (Winter)
28	Saᶜd al-Suᶜūd	سعد سعود	8–20 March	al-ᶜAqrab (Winter)

Local knowledge related to winds as manifested in linguistic expressions

There is an evident relation between environmental knowledge and the organization of the economic activity aided by it, bearing in mind the paucity of resources available to enhance the productivity and protection of animals. This knowledge determines the approach to and times for planting and harvesting, fishing, pearl diving, transferring animals to pasture and travel by sea and land is necessary (Al-Ghanim 2014; Varisco 1989). As a result of that, a rich lexicon has emerged for the terms and expressions in the Qatari dialects. Some of these lexemes are widely used in the Arabian Peninsula or in other vernacular dialects, though many of them are distinct to the people who live in Qatar. The lexical items that we have collected reveal a diverse taxonomy for wind names, as we explain below.

Some winds are named according to their direction:

1. *Šamāliyyah* ('northerly'): A cold winter wind with the temperature increasing with the approach of summer. In June they name it *al-Bawāriḥ*, where the wind is hot and active and stirs up dust. In the diving era, their dhow ships stop sailing due to wind speed.
2. *Šamāliyyah Ġarbiyyah* ('north-westerly'): A dry wind which blows most of the year and is turbulent with a high velocity.
3. *Junūbiyyah* ('southerly'): It is also called *al-Sēli*. The word *sēli* means 'running water'. This type of wind was called *Sēli* because it contributes to the accumulation of clouds and will lead to the fall of the torrential rains that flow into the valleys. This wind is often hot since it originates in the desert. They also call it *al-Hayfiyyah*, which means the warm one. It is pleasant in winter, and the saying goes that *nisnās al-sēli awhab nisnās* ('*al-Sēli* is the greatest gift of the breezes'). Reference to this phenomenon can be found in popular songs.
4. *Junūbiyyah Šarqiyyah* ('south-easterly'): It is known as the *Nakbah*. It is regarded as pleasant because it brings rain and moisture with it. Qatari people are known to chant: 'If the *nakbah* blew day and night, the dry valley must be flooded.'
5. *Šarqiyyah* ('easterly'): It is known as *al-Kaws*. According to the lexicon of the *Al-Muʿjam al-Wasīṭ*, the meaning of the word *kaws* is linked to the sound of the strong sea raging, and since the sea is eastward in the region, the eastern winds are called *kaws*. These are usually loaded with moisture that accumulates in the clouds during the fall and winter seasons.
6. *al-ʿInāšī*: It is a north-easterly wind coming from the direction of *najm Banāt al-Naʿš* which is the *Ursa Minor*.

Other winds are named according to their speed:

7. *al-Rākid*: a low velocity wind that allows people to settle in a specific location without being disturbed by it;
8. *al-Nisnās*: a light breeze;
9. *al-Nasīm*: a gentle, cool and refreshing wind;
10. *al-Salaf*: a very high velocity wind;
11. *al-ʿĀfūr*: whirlwinds that swirl up the dust;
12. *al-ʿĀbūs*: a powerful, dust-laden wind;
13. *al-Lāhūb*: a powerful, hot wind;
14. *al-Sumūm*: a dry, hot south-westerly wind;
15. *al-Dālūb*: gale-force winds that co-occur with thunderstorms, or that descend from cumulus clouds.

Vocabulary related to winds

Research has shown us that Qatar has rich traditions of indigenous knowledge about winds because of their importance to local people in determining the seasons, transportation, agriculture and so on. There are many terms related to knowledge of the winds. An example is the word *walm*, a term that divers used in the past.

This kind of knowledge and intimate contact with the environment has helped the local population in forecasting the weather generally and the winds specifically. For example, often if they anticipate a possible sudden change in the way *Al-Sēlī* wind is blowing from south to north, they will cite another popular saying:

> lā taʾmin al-dunyā wa-lā taʾmin al-iʿdāʾ, wa-la taʾmin al-sēlī yadūr šimāl
>
> 'Do not be sure of the world, do not be sure of enemies and do not be sure of *al-sēlī* turning north.'

Another highly important research finding is that most of the expressions have different linguistic forms and usages. Each of these words may be uttered in a different way, by, for example, rearranging or adding to its root consonants. One such word *walam* may have its consonants re-arranged and the insertion of an *alif* to produce *wālam*, meaning 'ready' or 'someone who is ready or prepared'. According to dictionaries, the meaning of the word *walam* is the completion or confluence of a thing. Meanwhile, *wālam* is normally used in the context of travelling and departure. It is notable that the word *wālam* is still used, so, for example, someone may say to a colleague *antā wālam* (if to a male) or *antī wālmah* (if to a female), meaning 'you are ready', to which one replies *ay, wālam(-ah)*, meaning 'yes, [I am] ready'.

The major constellations

al-Nuʿāyim ('the Ostriches')

This is a constellation of eight third-magnitude stars. They together form a rainbow-like arc (*al-Rāmī*) comprised of two slightly misshapen rectangles. *al-Qaws al-Junūbī* ('the southern Arc') shines in the lower rectangle and *al-Nūnkī* in the upper. Arabs in the past called the easternmost rectangle *al-Nuʿām al-Sādir* ('the Departing Ostrich') and the westernmost *al-Nuʿām al-Wārid* ('the

Incoming Ostrich'), as they imagined it forming the outline of the bird as if drinking water from the Milky Way. It was also known as *al-Nāqah* ('the She-Camel'), with a ninth star added to it called *Sinām al-Nāqah* ('the She-Camel's Hump'). It appears in the sky after sunset for thirteen days between 15 and 27 January in the fourth lunar station of winter. It is accompanied by a cold northerly wind and a popular adage has it that *al-Nuᶜāyim yuwāqiz al-nāᶜim* ('*al-Nuᶜāyim* awakes the sleeper') since people cannot sleep when it prevails due to the extreme cold. The temperature falls during this time and frost and fog occur, with clouds passing rapidly overhead. The male palm trees' pollen (*al-fuḥūl*) and early palm shoots appear, and hoopoes appear.

al-Marbaᶜāniya

This is a constellation made up of *al-Iklīl*, *al-Qalb* and *al-Šawlah*. These stars appear at the beginning of winter for thirty-nine days from 7 December to 14 January, the coolest period in the winter season.

Ḍarbat al-ᶜAjūz ('the Old Woman's Punch')

There is a popular folktale about a twenty-six-day phase of Spring from 8 March to 2 April that is characterized by strong, cold, northerly winds that follow a warm period called 'the Old Woman's Punch'. The story reports that an old woman, feeling that the weather was warm, decided to shear her sheep. A cold northern wind blew though, and the sheep died. Hence, this wind was named the 'Old Woman's Punch'. A familiar expression – 'Do not be like the old woman who sheared her sheep' – forewarns an ill-informed person who believes that a cold spell is over. This folktale is used to convey knowledge about spring weather fluctuations in order to counsel caution as to sudden, cold northerly winds.

al-Sarāyāt ('the Night Travellers')

al-Sarāyāt relates to sudden weather changes due to the rapid through-passage of a climatic depression. Spring is the season for *al-Sarāyāt*, between 20 March and 21 July, and the winds blow either at noon or during the night, with thundercloud formations accompanied by strong, sometimes destructive, depression winds. They are called *al-Sarāyāt* because they occur intermittently and often at night, as if they are night travellers. After the *al-Sarāyāt* end, the temperature rises and the *al-Bawāriḥ* season begins.

al-Bawāriḥ

Al-Maʿānī defines *bāriḥ* as 'severity, severe torment, agony'. The word has come to be associated with the severely hot winds at the end of summer, again showing the relation between such terms and the role of seasonal information in daily life. *al-Bawāriḥ* (singular *al-Bāriḥ*) are the strong and hot northerly summer winds that blow in June and July, when the Arabian Peninsula and the Persian Plateau are affected by the Indian monsoon. *al-Bāriḥ Al-Ṣaġīr* ('the Minor Ill-Omen') or *Ṭāliʿ Al-Baṭīn* blows from 25 May to 6 June when the brisk north-westerly winds prevail. The period of *al-Bāriḥ al-Kabīr* or *Bāriḥ al-Jawzāʾ* (*Ṭāliʿ Al-Turayyā*) is between 9 June and 16 July. It includes a sub-period called *al-Tuwāybah* (20 June to 2 July), during which the winds are hot. The period 3–15 July is called *al-Jawzāʾ al-ʾŪlā*, which is the period also of *Ṭāliʿ al-Haqʿah* (three stars are close together at the top of the constellation Orion, which is one of the homes of the moon), when the *Al-Sumūm* winds increase and there is a distinct intensification of the summer heat. The period 16–28 July called *al-Jawzāʾ al-Ṯāniyah* features the last of *al-Bawāriḥ* and *Ṭāliʿ al-Hanʿah* and is *Jamrat al-Qayz*, the fierce heat. The period between 29 July and 10 August is *Al-Marzam*, during which *Ṭāliʿ al-Ḍiraʿ* features *Jamrat al-Qayz*, and there are record temperatures.

al-Ṯurayyā ('the Chandelier')

It is located between *al-Baṭīn* in Aries in the west, and *al-Dubarān* in Taurus in the southeast. This constellation is called *al-Ṯurayyā* ('The Chandelier', i.e. the Pleiades) because of the great density of stars within it. *al-Ṯurayyā* is the most renowned cluster of stars, known since ancient times, with six or seven visible to the eye and fourteen through an astronomical telescope. The appearance of *al-Ṯurayyā* lasts twenty-six days (12 May–19 June) and it is visible in the morning (at dawn) on the eastern horizon from 7 June. The Arabs have been familiar with *al-Ṯurayyā* since the pre-Islamic period. It has been a recurring feature of ancient poetry and was used to measure eyesight.

The poet Al-Mubarrad says:

iḏā ma aṯ-ṯurayyā fī al-samāʾi taʿarraḍat	*yarāhā al-hadīdu l-ʿayni sabʿata ʾanjami*
ʿalā kabdi al-jarbāʾi wa-hya kaʾannahā	*jabīratu durrin rukibat fawq miʿṣami*

If Al-Ṯurayyā is exposed in the sky	the sharp-eyed beholder sees it as seven stars.
On the liver of Al-Jarabā˒² as if it were	a splint of pearls that was attached to a wrist.

Astronomy's impact on the determination of time periods, humans and language

Qataris used to determine their days, months and years according to the lunar system and associated phenomena such as the times of new moons and religious occasions such as the Ramadan fast, Eid al-Fitr, the rituals on ᶜArafāt and the Ḥajj, Eid al-Adha, the month of Muharram, and the month of Šaʿbān. They would also garner information about tides from their monitoring of the lunar stations. At the beginning of each month in the summer there is a great swell tide and they would fix the commencement of the diving season accordingly, calling the phenomenon *ḥaml rās* (bearing a head, meaning the tide at the beginning of the month is always higher than other days). There is also another tide related to the culmination of the full moon with which their movements and sea transportation activities are coordinated (Al-Ghanim 2011: 24).

People in Qatar depend on the Qatari Calendar of Shaykh Al-Ansari[3] which still provides some of the best documentary testimony to the importance of the lunar system and of astronomy generally in the lives of people in Qatar and in the region more widely. An example from the wider region is the Al-Ajiri calendar in Kuwait. Shaykh Al-Ansari's Calendar contains many local dialect terms and traditionally shared knowledge from that particular society and the wider region also. It is considered one of the most important pieces of documentary evidence in relation to the determination of and nomenclature for dates, phases and seasons, as well as recording certain aspects of a predominantly oral heritage. This documentation is systemically based on the phases of the moon and draws on the Arab and Islamic heritage of fourteen centuries in the field of astronomy and remains well known across the Gulf region. It reveals local knowledge of the weather and the use of stars as markers for the seasons (Varisco 1990). Knowledge of the movements of the stars, the moon and the sun were existentially important in various types of environment and for the forms of production conducted within them. The old calendar was one of the keys for determining the seasons based on astral and lunar trajectories, the latter being described as lunar stations (or mansions of the moon). It was known to the Islamic sciences of astronomy, with variations, throughout the region as well (Varisco 1991).

One indicator of the importance of the lunar system and astronomy is the extent of their reflection in many terms in the local dialect and traditional knowledge in the life of society. Significantly, this calendar divides the Islamic *hijrī* year into time periods related to seasons and in turn related to the stars. It also provides data related to times, dates, cultivation seasons, and the variety of trees and vegetables suitable for agriculture at any one time, fruit ripening seasons, and other agriculturally related information of relevance for the region. It is furthermore a source for Islamic astronomy and traditional knowledge about omens, spells, winds, and seasons, fruit picking, grazing seasons, breeding, pollination and so on. This calendar has been the source of much day-to-day practical knowledge. The stars have a great significance for the lives of the peoples of the region and for life in particular in the desert, which experiences tumultuously hot summers, cold winters and little rain. The indigenous peoples relate astronomical phenomena to the character of tempests, dry and rainy seasons, agriculture and many other phenomena (Badr 1982: 13). It is noteworthy that localized dialects mostly use commonly accepted names for stars drawn from the Arabic language, but that each dialect has its own names and expressions, for example, for the name of the star, Sirius, the brightest in the sky. The seafaring people of the Arabian Gulf call it *al-Tīr* and the people of Al-Bādiyah in the Najd region call it *al-Murazzam*. The same is the case with Qatar and most Arab Gulf societies. Sirius is the renowned star of good fortune associated with date palm tree maturation and indications of date ripening. Sirius (*al-Murazzam*) is mentioned in the Quran: 'He alone is the Lord of Sirius' (Surat al-Najm: 49). Some have even taken Sirius for a god to worship. Here, one can perceive seasonal knowledge intertwining with religious knowledge in particular regions in particular periods. There are many oral traditions that reveal the importance of this star and its connection with certain seasonal knowledge related to agriculture, especially dates, as well to the religious and metaphysical imagination.

The Polaris or Polar Star is *al-Jadī*, though some regions call it *al-Jāh, al-Yāh* in Qatari dialect. Since it maintains the same position in the sky throughout the year, it has often been used for directions, such as towards the southern star, *Suhayl*.

The star *Suhayl* – diminutive form of *sahl* – is without doubt the most familiar in the regional popular imagination. It is also known as *Suhayl al-Yamanī* ('Yemeni Suhayl') since it appears on the southern horizon in the direction of Yemen. Its appearance on 23 August signals the end of summer and the beginning of autumn, the season of the rains, before it disappears from sight in March. Its reappearance heralds the end of the arid and arrival of the rainy season. Due to the importance of rain in the lives of the desert dwelling peoples, the appearance of the *Suhayl* star is a source of elation for the people of the region. They set their schedules by the time of its appearance and speak of times 'from *Suhayl*'s ascent' and times 'since *Suhayl*'s descent'.

The local inhabitants have embedded *Suhayl* into vernacular expressions of their feelings and have linked the blowing of its southern winds with reminders of their beloved. Many popular myths and folk tales incorporate numerous astronomical phenomena such as the legend of the *Banāt Naʿš* ('daughters of the coffin'): an Arab man named *Naʿš* was killed by another named *Suhayl*. *Naʿš* had seven daughters who mourned the death of their father and swore not to bury his body until they had killed *Suhayl* and hence had secured their father's revenge on him. *Suhayl* learned of this and fled to the southeast, so the daughters decided to pursue him, with four of them bearing their father's body and the other three following behind the coffin. Of these latter three, one was dragging her younger sister along and the third was either lame or pregnant and walked behind them slowly. The legend has it that from time immemorial they chase *Suhayl* while carrying their father's coffin, while *Suhayl* flees from them to the south, leaving the sisters unable to catch up with him nor take revenge for their father nor bury him and rest. A song lodged in the popular imagination also relates to this legend: *Banāt Naʿš* ('daughters of Naʿš') *šaylāt naʿš* ('carrying a coffin') *man qāla-hā sabʿa amrār* ('who said it seven times') *mā akalat wāliday-hi an-nār* ('hellfire will not consume his parents') (Al-Ghanim 2015: 30). Thus, legend has it that whoever says 'coffin daughters, coffin shawls' seven times will spare their parents hell. Qataris would often tell their children to observe the constellation on clear nights when *Banāt Naʿš* shine in the sky, likened to a casket. The song includes the heritage and knowledge about the stars, and they linked them to family values such as love and prayers for parents.

Conclusion

The research has revealed that Qatar has a rich tradition of indigenous knowledge about the seasons, local weather and astronomy. There are also many lexemes that have themselves become a source of knowledge since they incorporate local wisdom, some still in circulation and some belonging to the past. This research project has represented an opportunity to collect vocabulary relating to nature and environment which is threatened with extinction due to economic, social, technological and climatic change over the last century.

The study found many items of vocabulary with multiple usages. It has shown that reference to natural phenomena is made in order to express feelings, as part of processes of socialization, and sometimes with explicatory value for certain phenomena. These terms have also been used for organizing social schedules, activities, occasions and traveling, with a cognitive and practical interchange in the relationship between language and nature. Through such research it is possible to gather local knowledge, understand cultural identities in their diversity, and identify key aspects of language and its richness. Since the collected vocabulary represents only a limited part of that which characterizes our heritage, and since there were resources that we were unable to access due to the lack of time and the demanding student timetable, the project remains for us an ongoing one.

Acknowledgements

This publication was made possible by a grant from the Qatar National Research Fund (QNRF) under its undergraduate research experience programme award number UREP19-091-5-014. Its contents are solely the responsibility of the authors and do not necessarily represent the official views of the QNRF. The authors would like to thank Qatar University students Nourhen ben Abedlaziz, Duha al-Bander, Fatheih Saber, Ward el-Ghalayeeni and also Prof. Daniel Varisco, Dr Okasha El Daly and Dr Mohammad Mostafa Saleem for their efforts to guide and train the students so that they could find suitable information for the study.

Notes

1. Official Arabic dictionary of the Arabic Language Academy in Egypt, founded in 1932.
2. Al-Jarabāʾ here means 'the sky'.
3. https://qatarch.com/

References

Al-Dhahri, A. (1983), *Al-Ajman and Their Leader Rakan bin Hathleen*, 1st edn, Riyadh: Al-Yamamah Publishing House.

Al-Fayadh, A. and S. Al-Mannai (2003), *Badāʾiʿ* (Qatari Folk Poetry). *The Poem of Saeed bin Salem Al-Badid. ʿIndi min al-Ġarami Dalīl* (My Love Signs), Qatar: The National Council for Culture and Heritage.

Al-Fīrūzābādī, M. Ibn Y. (n.d.), *al-qāmūs al-muḥīṭ wa-al-qābūs al-wasīṭ al-jāmiᶜ li-mā ḏahaba min luġat al-ʿArab al-šamāṭīṭ*, 2.

Al-Ghanim, K. A. (2011), *Al-ʾIḥtifālāt al-Jamāᶜiyyah fī Mujtamaᶜ al-Kaws* (Mass Celebrations in the Pearl Diving Community), 2nd edn, Doha: Marine Festival.

Al-Ghanim, K. A. (2014), 'Contradictory Forces in the Gulf Environment: Old and New Cultural Values and Knowledge', in P. Sillitoe (ed.), *Sustainable Development: An Appraisal from the Gulf Region*, 481–96, Oxford: Berghan Books.

Al-Ghanim, K. A. (2015), *Aṣāṭīr min Turāṯ Qaṭar* (Myths from Qatari Heritage), Doha: Qatar Museums Authority.

Al-Kabbabi, R. (2014), *Rain Images in the Poetry of Al-Huḏaliyīn*, MA Thesis, Makkah: Umm Al-Qura University.

Al-Maᶜānī Dictionary [online]. Available online: https://www.almaany.com/

Al-Ṣaġānī, H. (1971), *Al-Takmilah w aḏ-Ḏayl w aṣ-Ṣilah li Kitāb Tāj al-Luġah w Ṣiḥāḥ al-ᶜArabiyyah* ('The Crown of Language and the Correct Form of the Arabic Language'). Available online: https://shamela.ws/book/18254

Al-ᶜUjayri, Salih ibn Muhammad (1986), *Al-Ihtidāʾ bi-l-Nujūm fī al-Kuwayt*, Kuwait: Al-Nadi al-ᶜIlmi.

Al-Zajjaj, A. I. (2006), *Kitāb Al-ʾAnwāʾ*, Damascus: Academy of the Arabic Language.

Austin, P. K. and J. Sallabank (2011), 'Introduction', in P. Austin and J. Sallabank (eds), *Cambridge Handbook of Endangered Languages*, 1–24, Cambridge: Cambridge University Press.

Badr, A. (1982), 'On the Arabs and the Stars', *Arab Heritage Journal*, 7: 13–35.

Baptiste, I. (2001), 'Qualitative Data Analysis: Common Phases, Strategic Differences', *Forum Qualitative Sozialforschung*, 2 (3). Available online: http://www.qualitative-research.net/fqs/https://www.qualitative-research.net/index.php/fqs/article/view/917/2003 (accessed 27 March 2021).

Fischer, F. (2000), *Citizens, Experts, and the Environment: The Politics of Local Knowledge*, Durham: Duke University Press.

Franzosi, R. (1989), 'From Words to Numbers: A Generalized and Linguistics-Based Coding Procedure for Collecting Textual Data', *Sociological Methodology*, 19: 263–98.

Franzosi, R. (1998), 'Narrative Analysis-Or Why (and How) Sociologists Should Be Interested in Narrative', *Annual Review of Sociology*, 24: 517–54. Available online: http://www.jstor.org/stable/223492

Glaser, B. and A. Strauss (1967), *The Discovery of Grounded Theory: Strategies for Qualitative Research*, Chicago: Aldine.

Hijazi, M. F. (1985), *Al-Madxal al-Luġawī li-Dirāsat al-ᶜĀdāt wa-al-Taqālīd wa-al-Maᶜārif al-Šaᶜbī* (The Linguistic Entrance Point for Studying Popular Customs, Traditions and Knowledge). Doha: Markaz al-Turāṯ al-Šaᶜbī li-Duwal al-Xalīj al-ᶜArabiyyah.

Ibn Al Ajdābi, Abu I. (2006), *Kitāb al-ʾAzminah w al-ʾAnwāʾ*, Azza Hassan (ed.), Beirut: Dar Al Raed Al Arabi for Printing and Publishing.

Ibn Khamis, 'A. bin M. (1985), *Rāšid al-Khalāwī: Ḥayātuh – Šiʿruh – Ḥikmatuh – Falsafatuh – Nawādiruh – Hisābuh al-Falakī* (Rashid al-Khalawi: His Life, Poetry, Wisdom, Philosophy, Anecdotes, Astronomical Assessments), Saudi Arabia: Al-Yamamah Publishing House.

Ibn Manẓūr, M. ibn M. (1956), *Lisān al-ʿArab*, Dār Ṣādir.

Ibn Qutayba, Abu M. 'A. (1956), *Kitāb al-ʾAnwāʾ* (The Book of the Stars), Hyderabad: Matbaʿāt Majlis Dāʾirat al-Maʿārif al-ʿUṯmāniyah.

Ingham, B. (1997), *Arabian Diversions: Studies in the Dialects of Arabia*, Reading: Ithaca Press.

Leonard, S. et al. (2013), 'The Role of Culture and Traditional Knowledge in Climate Change Adaptation: Insights from East Kimberley', *Australia Global Environmental Change*, 23 (3): 623–32.

Moller, H. et al. (2004), 'Combining Science and Traditional Ecological Knowledge: Monitoring Populations for Co-Management', *Ecology and Society*, 9 (3): 2.

Nash, H. and D. Agius (2011), 'The Use of Stars in Agriculture in Oman', *Journal of Semitic Studies*, 56 (1): 167–82

Quṭrub, Abu ʿA. M. (1985), *Kitāb al-Azminah wa-Talbīyat al-Jāhilīyah* (The Book of Times and the Satisfactions of the Al-Jahiliyah Period), Al-Zarqaʾ: Maktabat al-Manār.

Skutnabb-Kangasm, T. (2011), 'Language Ecology', in J. Ostman and J. Verschueren (eds), *Pragmatics in Practice*, 177–98, Amsterdam: John Benjamins Company.

Turner, N. J. et al. (2000), 'Traditional Ecological Knowledge and Wisdom of Aboriginal Peoples in British Columbia', *Ecological Applications*, 10: 1275–87.

UCLG. (2010), 'Culture: Fourth Pillar of Sustainable Development the Committee on Culture'. Available online: https://issuu.com/uclggold/docs/gold_ii_eng

UNESCO (1996), 'Universal Declaration on Linguistic Rights'. Available online: https://culturalrights.net/descargas/drets_culturals389.pdf

UNESCO, WWF and Terralingua (2003), 'Sharing a World of Difference: The Earth's Linguistic, Cultural and Biological Diversity'. Available online: https://terralingua.org/shop/sharing-a-world-of-difference/

Varisco, D. M. (1989), 'The *Anwāʾ* Stars According to Abu Isḥāq al-Zajjāj', *Zeitschrift für Geschichte der Arabisch-Islamischen Wissenschaften*, 5: 145–66.

Varisco, D. M. (1990), 'Folk Astronomy and the Seasons in the Arabian Gulf', *Al-Ma'thurat al-Ša'biyah*, 19: 7–27.

Varisco, D. M. (1991), 'The Origin of the *Anwāʾ* in Arab Tradition', *Studia Islamica*, 74: 5–28.

Vedwan, N. (2006), 'Culture, Climate and the Environment: Local Knowledge and Perception of Climate Change among Apple Growers in North-Western India', *Journal of Ecological Anthropology*, 10 (1): 4–18.

7

Plant and Animal Terms in Ḥaḍramī Arabic Idiomatic Expressions, Proverbs and Chants

Abdullah Hassan al-Saqqaf

Introduction

Ḥaḍramawt

It is known that Ḥaḍramawt in the older times was the route of trade of many goods brought from China, the Indian subcontinent and other eastern regions to the Middle East and Europe. These included silk, spices and precious stones. But the most important of all was the trade of incense. Lewcock (1986: 21), in a short but comprehensive study on Wādi Ḥaḍramawt, maintains that 'the growth of settled life in the Wādi is still shrouded in the mists of time'. Evidence from the inscriptions of the kingdoms to the west, however, suggests that the towns evolved as entrepôts controlling an increasingly valuable trade route, probably dealing mainly in aromatic incenses.

To have a simple glimpse on the trade of incense in the ancient world and the role it played on the prosperity of Ḥaḍramawt, one could quote nobody but an ancient historian like Pliny (xii: 42, in Lewcock 1986) who wrote: 'Let us take into account [also] the vast number of funerals that are celebrated throughout the whole world each year, and the heaps of odours that are piled up in honour of the bodies of the dead. ... It is the luxury of man, which is displayed even in the paraphernalia of the death, that has rendered Arabia thus "happy".

At present, people of coastal Ḥaḍramawt, or as it is often called *as-sāḥil*, refer to the *wādi*, simply, as Ḥaḍramawt. The geographical description of the *wādi* is as follows (Collins 1969):

> For the Wādi Ḥaḍramawt is the most distinctive feature of the entire south-western area of Arabia. It is the main Wādi which splits the high plateau *jōl* and

mountains of that area. It extends for more than 200 miles parallel to the coast. It is a broad well-defined valley and is described by W.B. Fisher in his Geography of the Middle East, in this manner 'the Wādi Ḥaḍramawt, which is parallel to the coast some 120 miles inland and extends for a distance of 200 miles before making a sharp turn south-westward and cutting through the coastal ranges to reach the Indian Ocean near *Sayḥūt*. The valley is much broader at its western end far inland than at its point of entrance into the Indian Ocean. This fact gave Fisher the idea that it is the result of intricate river capture.

Ḥaḍramawt is defined by Beeston (1971: 53) in the Encyclopaedia of Islam as 'the deep valley running parallel to the Southern coast of Arabia from roughly 48 E to 50 E. In a more extended sense, however, the name Ḥaḍramawt has always been applied to a much larger area, comprising the district to the north and south of the Wādi Ḥaḍramawt proper, together with an area on the west'.

Until 1967, the date of independence of South Arabian sultanates, which later became known as the People's Democratic Republic of Yemen (PDRY), Ḥaḍramawt was made up at that time politically of two sultanates, namely, the Quᶜaytī Sultanate of which Mukalla was the capital, and which covered all the coast and part of the interior, and the Kathīrī Sultanate, of which Seiyun (pronounced locally as *sēwūn*) was the capital, and which covered only a small area of the Wādi. The inhabitants of Ḥaḍramawt are called Ḥaḍramī. In 1990 PDRY unified with the Yemen Arab Republic (YAR) and became the present-day Republic of Yemen.

Ḥaḍramawt had a long history as a centre of religious teaching in the region. The inhabitants come mainly from a Qaḥṭānī descent. Some are also from an ᶜAndānī descent (i.e. tribes of Ḥijāzī or North Arabian origin). Some people in the interior have Asian blood mixtures (Indonesian, Malay and Chinese) while in coastal regions, there is African blood (al-Shāṭrī 1972: 22).

Western explorers such as Stark (1939, 1940) and Robert Serjeant (1951, 1964) describe some of the flora and fauna of Ḥaḍramawt. Among modern detailed studies are Bin Qadīm (2018) and Bā Saywud et al. (2019). The FAO (2016) report on The State of the World's Biodiversity for Food and Agriculture has a detailed bibliography and information about flora and fauna in Yemen.

The variety of Arabic spoken is known as Ḥaḍramī Arabic (henceforth, HA). The question regarding whether present-day HA is a descendant of the ancient language of the Ḥaḍramites (the inhabitants of old Ḥaḍramawt) or not is questionable. For more details, see Serjeant (1951: xii).[1]

Now, present-day HA has witnessed many changes as the effect of language contacts with other neighbouring Arabic dialects as well as emigration of

Ḥaḍramīs to different parts of the world has led to important changes at different linguistics level of the dialect, especially the lexicon. The dialectal variation in HA includes Coastal HA, Wādi HA and Bedouin (or ṣaḥrāʾ) HA.

The variation can be phonological like pronouncing the <jīm> as <y> in some parts of Ḥaḍramawt. At the level of lexis, there are some variations. For example, the word for 'owl' in Wādi HA is *dmēmih* while in Coastal HA it is *ninih*. The word for 'cat' in Wādi HA is *hirr* (m.) / *hirrih* (f.), *ʾahrār* (pl.), while in Coastal HA it is *ᶜurrī* (m.) *ᶜrārī* (pl.) and *ḍēwin* (f.)/ *ḍwāwin* (pl.).

The word for 'camel' in Wādi HA is *bᶜīr* while in Coastal HA it is *bᶜār*. Sometimes, words are the same in both varieties when they are in their singular form, but they differ in their plural as in *ḍānih* 'ewe' which is pluralized in Wādi HA as *ḍawēn* but *ḍūn* in Coastal HA.

HA allows initial consonant clustering. Thus, Standard Arabic polysyllabic words of which the first syllable contains a *kasrah* /i/ or a *ḍammah* /u/ vowel such as *bilād* 'country' or *ṣurāx* 'screaming' are rendered monosyllabic *blād* and *ṣrāx*, respectively. But in a word like *kalām* 'speech', Wādi HA does not cluster the first two consonants (as they are separated by a *fatḥah* vowel /a/). For the final syllable clusters of a word like Standard Arabic *baḥr* 'sea', HA splits the cluster by using an epenthetic vowel [ə], i.e. *baḥər*. As this chapter is not concerned with the phonology of the dialect, I adopt a transliteration system which does not show minutiae phonetic details such as the central vowel [ə] that splits final clusters.

Other aspects of pronunciation of HA and the transliteration of words in this chapter are as follows:

- Classical Arabic <qāf> is rendered *g* (as the <g> in Eng. *guard*).
- <jīm> is [dʒ] (as the <j> in the Eng. *jump*), [ɟ] (as the <g> in the Eng. *give*) or [j] (as the <y> in the Eng. *yes*) depending on the educational level of the speaker, the register of his speech, or the type of lexical items. Thus, speakers tend to pronounce religious words with a [dʒ] realization rather than [j].
- <ḍ> and <ḏ̣> are realized in Coastal HA as [dˤ] (velarized <d> as in Eng. *dust*)[2] while in the interior HA, they are realized [ðˤ] (velarized <th> as in Eng. *thus*).

For detailed description of HA, see al-Saqqaf (1999, 2006) and al-Quᶜaiṭī (n.d.).

The importance of studying idioms and proverbs in language

If you say *nazal mxirriṭ* instead of *nazal yxub* 'he went away quickly', this is an idiom. The word *mxirriṭ* means that 'he cannot get control of the speed of his bicycle because its chain around the gear became loose (*inxaraṭ il-gēr*), and the gear system cannot function properly'. The meaning of an idiom is different from the actual meaning of the words used. *kul gurṣak w dxul xulṣak* 'Lit. Eat your loaf and enter your hole!' is a proverb which advises one to lead a peaceful life by not being involved or interfere in other people's matters. Proverbs are old but familiar sayings that usually give advice. The treasury of HA idioms and proverbs come from registers related to social, religious, military, agricultural and other phenomena related to flora and fauna. They cover all the natural and geographical environment, including the coastal region, the valleys, the mountainous regions and the desert. In coastal regions, you may hear a proverb like: *zgul b-ᶜēdih yātīk ḥūt* 'Throw a sardine fish, you would win a big fish', meaning that if you sacrifice something less valuable in order to win something better, you will get it in the end.

Water

Clouds, lightening and rain

In Ḥaḍramawt, a relatively arid region in comparison with north-western plateau of Yemen, children rejoice and enjoy themselves with playing outside when it starts drizzling:

jāt iṭ-ṭašših fi ᶜēni
naxl abūy bā yišrab
'A drop of rain came into my eye
[A sign that] my father's palm trees will be watered'.

ʾiḏā bargat fi il-giblih, traffaᶜ fōg ya ṭārif
If lightning flashes in the west, you (who dwelt on the foot of the mountain) should ascend upward (to avoid being drowned by the upcoming torrential floods)

(From a poem by Hussein Al-Miḥḍār)

Other water-related proverbs include:
il-bīr bīrnā w il-māʾ l-ġērnā

'The well belongs to us, but the water goes to other people', said when someone does not benefit from his property. Instead, all the revenue goes to others.
bīr (well; orchard; field of palm trees watered on a well).

Proverbs and sayings related to the constellations of the zodiac with reference to agriculture

Before modernization, farmers used to memorize lots rhymes and proverbs that deal with instructions regarding what to plant in each season:

štāk b il-baldih w burrk il-ḥūt 'Your sorghum should be planted in the *najm* (zodiac star) of *Baldah*, and your wheat to be planted in the *najm* of *Ḥūt*.'
štāʾ is the sorghum that is planted in summer (*Najm al-Baldah*) to be harvested in *aš-šitāʾ*, i.e. winter. *ṣēf* is the sorghum that is planted in winter (*Najm al-Ḥūt*) to be harvested in *aṣ-ṣēf*, i.e. summer.

sabiᶜ fi š-šōl yithaḍḍa il-rāᶜī
'In the seventh day of *Najm* 'star' *al-Shawl*, the shepherd should wear his sandals (meaning that it is getting hot)'.

saᶜd xbāʾ, yā gafaz gafz id-ḍbāʾ,
yā xalla al-ᶜajāwiz ṣbāʾ
Lit. 'The Najm Saᶜd Khibāʾ, either jumps like a gazelle or it makes the old young, where the metaphor here is old women become (like) young women': The *Najm Saᶜd Khibāʾ*, either passes unnoticed, with no rain, or it may come with heavy rain that transforms the 'old' palm trees into 'younger' ones.

Plants

gaṣab 'soghum stalks'
mā maᶜnā illā ʾgālīd il-gaṣab 'We have nothing except the keys of stores of sorghum stalks.'
When sorghum is harvested, dry stalks are stored to be used as forage for animals like oxen and camels. Because of the low value of stalks, their stores need not be locked with strong keys. This saying is used when people complain that their valuable properties are in control by other (powerful) people, and what is left to them is simply, the trivial things. Note that, for goats, *gaḍib* 'clover' or *šjar* 'grass' are used.

Cereals

ḥabb 'cereals'

burr 'wheat'
zaraᶜt il-burr w ṣarabtuh
w bukrah bā ṭraḥ baᶜduh
baṭāyn maxrafī
'I planted wheat and I harvested it, and tomorrow I will sow the seed of sorghum (that can yield in *Kharīf* harvest season)'.[3]

lā tgūl burr alla lammā ykūn bēn iš-šwā w iṣ-ṣurr 'Do not say (what you have eaten) is really "wheat" until it is between your stomach and your belly button.'
The saying means that you should make sure that the things you were promised to be given are truly given and not merely 'lip-service'.
jiljil 'sesame'
tuxx 'left over of sesame seeds, known locally as *jiljil*, after extracting oil from them' (See example of *bᶜīr* below.)

ᶜilb / pl. *ᶜulūb* 'Christ's thorn tree'
rubuṭ b-ᶜilb 'Tie with a *ᶜilb* tree', meaning that if you want to start on any successful business, you should make a good start that would ensure success; it is like when want to tie your domestic animal, you should tie it to a strong trunk of a *ᶜilb* tree in order to guarantee that it would not escape.

dōmah / pl. *dōm* 'Christ's thorn tree fruit'
ṣōmah ṣōmah w ifṭir b-dōmah 'Fast and fast and eat with a single *dōm* fruit', meaning that one should not live on a tight budget, and at the same time cannot see the benefit of this in the long run.

ᶜajrah / pl. *ᶜajr*, noun: 'Christ's thorn tree fruit stone', verb: *yiᶜjur* 'to eat the fruit and leave its stone for further use'. See *ḥalūl* below.
kama l-ᶜajrah fī ṭ-ṭabag. 'Like a *dōm*-fuit stone (moving from one side to another) in a straw-woven tray'. The proverb is used when things or people are not stable.
gāᶜdīn yiᶜyirūn ġallagaw iṭ-ṭabag kulluh. Here the verb *yiᶜjur* is derived from the noun *ᶜajrah*. The expression means that they sat eating the *dōm* fruits, throwing their stones till they finished the whole plate.

For the sake of completion, one could add words like *ḥālūl / ḥālīl* (seeds of dried *dōm* fruits) roasted together sesame seeds and other nuts and eaten by people as snacks, or *ḥatī* 'dried *dōm*' ground and mixed with water or milk and eaten as a light meal in the older times.

ġussih also called *ljin*, dried Christ's thorn tree leaves used like shampoo in the old days, hence the verb *ġassat* means she washed her hair.
il-ᶜarūs ġassat šᶜarhā 'The bride has washed her hair (using *gussih*)'
Bees collect their nectar from different species of trees. The best of which are the Christ's thorn tree *ᶜilb* '*Ziziphus spina-christi*'. Others include *salam* '*Acacia ehrenbergiana*', and *sumur* '*Acacia tortilis*'.

Palm trees

Palm tree pollination songs

Serjeant (1964) described the process of palm trees pollination in Wādi Ḥaḍramūt. In February 1954, he heard a farmer in his garden in Seiyun, singing the following song. Here, we have the mention of bees, birds and game (*qanṣ* – known locally as *ganīṣ*):

yā ṭyūr il-xalāʾ
w iṣ-ṣēd w in-nūb
yā xēr maṭlūb
'O, birds of the open country,
Game, and bees,
O, what an excellent thing to ask'

(Serjeant 1964: 64)

'... the allusion to birds has probably a significance that is at present unknown to me, but the reference to game at once brings the ritual Ḥaḍramī hunt to mind, and honey has properties next to magical' (Serjeant 1964: 64).

Farmers also sing a longer ditty when performing palm trees pollination like the one quoted in Serjeant (1964). Below, are a few lines from a ditty which I personally heard from a farmer in Seiyun:

rabb is-samāʾ yaḥmīh
li bšagguh w li ḥawālēh
w bā farārah mā yjīh
May Lord of the Heaven protect it,
Together with its neighbourhood and (other trees) around it.

May the flying beetle (*bā farārah*) not approach it

...

Palm trees

naxlih / pl. *naxl* 'palm tree'
iṭ-ṭūl ṭūl naxlih w il-ᶜagl ᶜagl raxli 'He is high as a palm tree, but his mind is like a small she-lamb'.

*jiḏi*ᶜ 'trunk of palm tree'
bġā tamrah raṣnōh b-jiḏᶜhā 'He wanted just one date, but they tied him forcefully with the palm tree trunk'. This proverb is used when people exaggerate in their generosity.

karbah / pl. *karab* 'dried root of a palm leaf'
dīf dīffi il-karab w il-līf 'Hit and hit on the dry parts of a palm tree like *karab* and *līf*', i.e., much ado about nothing.

saᶜfih 'palm leaf'
kul ṭēr ᶜala saᶜfih (see *ṭēr* below)

guṣum 'dry palm tree leaf'
šēbih šᶜaruh kuḍuh alla guṣum 'an old man with white hair like a dry palm leaf'. The dry part of the palm tree leaf is whitish in colour, so *guṣum* is used humorously to describe one's hair to show the degree of old age.

līfih / pl. *līf* 'the dry tissue layers around the stem of palm leaf'
šᶜarhā štgūl līfih 'Her hair is as dry as a *līfih*'. The dry tissue layers around the palm tree stem of the leaf used like a sponge for cleaning; here it is used figuratively to describe dry hair.

maṭmar /pl. *maṭāmir* 'stalk with date cluster; date-palm panicle, branch stripped of its leaves'
bā niṭᶜam xarīfak yā madīnī i-šabab
ᶜād alla al-maṭāmir w il-xbar w il-xūṣ
'We want to taste your yield, O, palm tree of young Madīnī (tree),
But (alas!), what has remained is only the dry stalk, the straw-woven bags and dry palm leaves'.

kirzām 'often eaten: the stalk of male palm tree fertilizing flower *fuxṭah*'
zēnih kama il-kirzām 'She is as beautiful as *kirzām*'

dubdubah /pl. *dubdub* 'tiny early date fruit; date buds'
mᶜuh ġarfat ᶜyāl ṣġār kama id-dubdub 'He has a lot of small children like *dubdub*.'

bisrah /pl. *bisr* 'green, unripe dates, but could also be yellowish or red in colour, depending on the type of the palm tree'
šufuh yitšawwaf ᶜyūnuh štgūl bisr 'Look at him gazing. His eyes are so red as if they were *bisr*.'

maḥlih / pl. *maḥl* 'rotten unripe dates'
faḥl jāb maḥl 'A good male palm tree brought unripe rotten dates', used when describing someone who is not as good as his father.

garᶜah /*garᶜ* 'half-ripened date, considered by many is the best stage of the fruit, known in some parts of Yemen as *manāṣif*:
yā ḥaḍramī šūwig l-ḥaḍramūtak
šuwwig l-garᶜ iš-šōl lā yfūtak
'O, Ḥaḍramī [who lives in the Diaspora]!
Long for your Ḥaḍramūt!
Long for it, otherwise, you will miss [the tasty] half-ripe dates Of the *šōl* star season.'

madīnī 'Madīnī dates' (known in Ḥijāz as *ᶜajwat al-madīnah*)
wēš lak fi il-madīnī yā mšinnig ᶜyūnak 'What is your concern, you who are glancing furtively, towards the Madīnī ripe dates hanging from the palm tree?' This is said to describe something one cannot get or afford.

ᶜaljūm / pl. *ᶜajam* 'date stone'
yā ᶜaljūm gaᶜ naxlih 'O, date fruit stone, be a palm tree!' It is said as a piece of advice meaning that planting a palm tree is not an easy thing, it is not just sowing a date stone. It is laborious work

ḥašfih / pl. *ḥašaf* 'dried unripe dates used as forage for animals'
ṣām w faṭar ḥašfih 'He (took pains) in fasting but, (alas) he broke his fast by eating a dry (non-delicious) date.'

tamrah, 'palm tree date' / pl. *tamr* 'freshly harvested or preserved date fruit'
māšī kamā it-tamr fi d-dār 'Nothing like preserved dates in the house.' i.e. one needs to keep dates at home as nutritious food reserve.

Other date-fruit related terms include

ṣaḥlih / *ṣaḥl* (dried unripe sweet dates) used together with other dry food as snacks, or used as an ingredient of *faḍxah*, which is used in cooking.

faḍxah, verb: *yifiḍḍix*
A *faḍxah* is a small ball of dried ingredients made of *ṣaḥl*, onions, dried onions and spices preserved and kept for cooking. The verb *yifiḍḍix* is used figuratively, to mean eating the best food, thus depriving others.
  Other date-related words are:
  raṭab (fresh ripen dates. Pronounced in Standard and Gulf Arabic as *ruṭab*)
  For the sake of completion, one could add some other date-related words like: *faḍḥah* / pl. *faḍḥ* 'red or yellow dates that can be clearly seen on the tree', hence <fḍḥ> means disclose or make something apparent, clear', *ḥašfih* / pl. *ḥašaf* 'dry dates, normally used as forage for animals' and *xamgah* / pl. *xamg* 'rotten ripe date fruit'.

ḍīrih adj. 'tender; slender'
yā ġuṣn fī šijritak ḍīrih 'O, bough of a tree! How tender, slender and beautiful, you are!', a well-known line of verse describing a beautiful woman.

līmih 'lime tree' pl. *līm*
kama ṭyūr il-līmih 'Like birds (singing) in a lime bush', said when a group of in a social occasion sit together and prattle, where nobody can understand the other.

bagl 'radish'
kul min il-bagl w lā tinšid ᶜalā min baggaluh 'Eat the radish and do not ask who planted it,' i.e. do not be too curious about things; you must be realistic.

baṣal 'onion'
māḥad dārī b-sᶜādih fī sūg il-baṣal 'Nobody cares about Saᶜādah in the onion market', i.e. nobody would care for her; after all, the whole market smells onion and she would smell onion too.

ᶜšar 'Calotropis procera'
See *zunbuᶜ il-ᶜišar* below under **Insects**.

gšār 'coral'

min yāt gšār ja ḏa (Coastal HA *min yāt gšār yeᵓ deᵓ*) 'Which part of the coral reef did this [strange] fish come from?' Talking about a strange-looking person whom one met all of a sudden.

Animals

Wild animals and man-eating animals

The Arabian leopard (*Panthera pardus nimr*)
(Pronounced in HA *nmir*)
The striped tiger, *al-babr*, does not exist in Arabia. It is common in other habitats in Asia like South and Southeast Asia. Many people in the Arab world confuse the English word 'tiger' for the 'Arabian leopard'. The reason for this confusion is due to the fact that the Arabic word *namir* is used in Arabic to refer to both species, although some people who are aware of such a difference use the Farsi word *babr* to refer to the tiger.

In HA people refer to some wild animals like ᶜ*asad* 'lion', *nmir* 'leopard' and *ḍab*ᶜ 'hyena' in their proverbs and poetry. In the following *zāmil* (a military chant), soldiers or tribesmen are chanting slogans praising their Sultan:
gafa ṣulṭānina niddirij miṯl is-saḥābah
w hu miṯl in-nimir w in-nimir kullin yahābah
'We are supporting (following) our Sultan (and we) surround him like a cloud
He is like a leopard, and the leopard is feared by everybody'.

*ḍab*ᶜ 'hyena' / pl. *ḍbā*ᶜ
*sib*ᶜ *walla ḍab*ᶜ 'A lion or a hyena' a proverb asked when people want to know the result, i.e. is it good or bad. See also *ṣagr walla* ᶜ*afandaš* below.

ḏīb 'wolf' / pl. *ḏyābih*
Wolves are still around in rural areas. They may attack livestock, especially goats and lambs. They normally attack at sunset when herdsmen take their animals back home. A *ġūnih* (twilight) wolf is supposed to be very hungry. In the following examples, a mother is talking about her son who came back home hungry:
iz-zagr ḍawa wahš kama ḏīb il-ġūnih: dala ᶜ*ala gaṣ*ᶜ*at it-tamr, mā ḥaṣṣal šī* 'the boy came back home very hungry like (a hungry) wolf in the twilight. He went

to a date container, but he did not find anything in it' (*waḥš* 'Lit. predator' is used here in HA metaphorically as 'hungry').

ṭiᶜl 'fox' / pl. *ṭᶜālih*
il-jūᶜ ṭiᶜil w iḍ-ḍamaʾ wiᶜl 'Hunger is bearable and thirst is not.'

il-gāmah gāmat wiᶜl w il-fiᶜl fiᶜl ṭiᶜl 'The frame is like an ibex, but the deeds are like a fox.' It means do not be misled by the outer look of things or how people look as the importance is in the essence.

wiᶜl male ibex, pl. *wᶜālih*, female: *ṣēdih*, pl. *ṣyad*
qabaḍnā l-wiᶜl laḥmar, kassarnā grūnuh 'We caught the red ibex and broke its horns', said when people defeated someone and took his weapons.

Domesticated animals

bᶜīr / Coastal HA *bᶜār* 'camel'
bānšūf rās il-bᶜīr yōxḏ naḥnā fēn 'We will see where the head of the camel will take us to.' This proverb is said when one has not decided yet what to do next.

bᶜīr yiᶜṣur w bᶜīr yōkul it-tuxx 'A camel is working in the sesame mill, while the other is eating the *tuxx* (dry peat-like left-over of sesame seeds after extracting oil from them).'

burrik jamal tissbaᶜ 'Let the camel lie down and be slaughtered and you will get a lot of fat.' The proverb means that if you spend more of your reserves, and not become stingy, you will enjoy life.

gāflih bala jammāl 'A camel caravan without a leader', said when people need somebody who can organize them and act as a team leader.

jamal dāsī w mitḥimmil w intī ᶜā gyāsik tiglī ʾaw xiffifī '(I am) like a camel from Bā-Dās area, patient and strong. As for you (my beloved), it is up to you; you can increase the load or make it lighter.'

ṭōr / *bagrah* 'ox / cow'
gulnā ṭōr gāl ʾiḥlibūh 'We said: it is an ox, but he said: milk it, though!' This proverb is said when one insists on doing something although it is clear that what he asks is impossible.

nṭaḥ yā ṭōr w hū ᶜalā garnak 'O, ox, butt (and the harm will be on) your horn', said when thankful that he could defeat someone who is superior to him.

kabiš, 'ram', for female, see *ḍānih* below
int māšuft min il-kabš alla ḏēluh 'You haven't seen from the *barbari* ram except his tail'. i.e. you will see more of it for your satisfaction. See also *barbarī* 'ram from Barbarah, Somalia' below.

šāh 'female goat'/ *tēs* 'belly goat'
iš-šāh šāt sālmīn w il-laban l-sīduh 'The goat belongs to Salmīn, but the milk goes to his master.' This is said when people of power deprive poor people from making use of their own properties by confiscating them.

ḍānih 'ewe', pl. *ḍawēn* (Wādi HA), *ḍūn* (Coastal HA)
ḥsibtak rajjāl ṭliᶜt ḍānih 'I thought you were a man, but you came out to be an ewe', i.e. I thought you were brave enough, but you turned out to be a coward.

bā illā blādī
bā ᶜīš šāwī w rāᶜī ḍūn
'I want to go (and stay) in my homeland,
and will live as a shepherd caring for goats and sheep' (from a song by Ḥusain Al-Miḥḍār)

Domestic animals

hirr / *ᶜirrī*, also *ᶜurrī* 'cat'
hadiyit il-ᶜirrī ḥanaš 'The gift of a cat could be a snake or the like'.
It is said when one should not expect a good deed from someone who is not generous enough.

kalb 'dog'
jidd il-klāb wāḥad 'The grandfather of dogs is the same.' This proverb is said when one should not expect good deeds from a family or a tribe who have a bad reputation because it is possible that they got such characteristics from their forefathers and ancestors, and therefore, one should keep away from them.

juwiᶜ kalbak yitbaᶜak 'If you give less food to your dog, it will follow you.' If you are firm with someone, they will obey you.

Other animals

rubbāḥ / gird 'monkey'
wēš ᶜarraf ir-rubbāḥ b ʾakl it-tuffāḥ 'How on earth can a monkey know how to eat apples?' This is said when someone lacks basic skills.

ṣbur ᶜala girdak lā yjīk ʾagrad minnuh Lit.: 'Be patient towards your monkey, otherwise you will get another one which is worse.' You must be patient and accept what is in your hand, otherwise, things may get worse.

Rodents

jraḏ 'rats and mice'
jraḏ ḏī is-sanih ṭarad jraḏ il-ᶜām 'The rat of this year kicked the rat of last year', said if nothing changes, e.g., corrupt officials take power one after another.

jraḏ w mazkūm 'A rat and having a cold'. Said when one is complaining about something they are not supposed to complain about.

trayyaḏ yā jraḏ lā tᵉinkir lak sgayih 'O, rat! Slow down, so that you will not be stumbled by a public fountain.' This proverb is used to describe someone who overestimates himself, or by being over ambitious.

Reptiles

Snakes

ḥanaš 'snake'
faḏx il-ḥanaš 'the smashing (of the head) of the snake' which means 'the last dinner in the month of Shaᶜbān on the eve of Ramaḍān'.

il-yōm bā yifḏaxūn il-ḥanaš 'Today they are going to have the last dinner in the month of Shaᶜbān on the eve of Ramaḍān.' This meal is taken outside the house in a picnic.

hām 'serpent'
hām kala hām 'A serpent has eaten another serpent', i.e., you are brave and noble, but you cannot compete with somebody who is brave and good like you.

rās hām xēr min zamālat jirdān 'A head of a serpent (though poisonous) is better than the company of rats', meaning that one should be concerned with important rather than trivial matters.

dafan 'sand viper'
A very poisonous snake that buries itself in the sand (*tadfin nafsahā fī t-turāb*) *ida gabaṣak id-dafan girrib il-maʾ w il-kafin* 'If you were bitten by a sand viper type snake, you should bring water (for the burial wash) and cloth (for your coffin).' The proverb is said when someone is affected by a big problem, and he may not escape it.

Birds

ṭēr 'bird' / pl. *ṭyūr*
kull ṭēr ʿala saʿfih 'Every bird is on a palm leaf.' Said when people are scattered, busy in their places and businesses.
lā dīk yiṣrax w lā kalb yinbaḥ 'No dogs bark and no cocks cry.' A deserted area where you can find no one.

ṣxēriyyih 'a small variety of brown pigeon (female),' pl. *ṣxēr*
gūrī 'male of all pigeon species'[4]

ya l-ʿōl lī f-is-samā mʿillī
lā taḥsabēna kadā naʿsān
'O, wild pigeons who are flying in the sky, do not think that I (am not aware of you) in slumber.'

gūrī
il-gūrī aʿzam ʿa ṣ-ṣxēriyyah
lī tġirrid fōg šarj axḍar
'The *gūrī* has invited the *ṣxēriyyih*,
Which is singing on the green field'

ʿōlih / pl. *ʿōl* 'wild pigeon', *gūrī* 'male of all pigeon species'
A beautiful woman can be described as a *ʿōlih* or *ḥamāmih*. Here the poet says:

    gāl bin hāšim ana galbī slī
    ṣāḥbī ḥibbuh wala yintasī

gid našadt il-ᶜōl minnuh w il-ḥamām,
hayyaḍn galbī xaḍīrat il-wišām

'I (the Hāšimī poet) said: My heart is rejoicing,
I love my beloved one and I will never forget her,
I have asked both, the sedentary and wild pigeons about her.
O, my heart is becoming weak because of the beautiful women who wear green *wašm* tattoos'.

ṣagr 'falcon'
lī mā yiᶜrif iṣ-ṣagr yiswīh 'He who does not know what a falcon is, may think it is an ordinary bird, and therefore, roast it.' Said when one does not know the real value of things.

durrah 'parrot'
ḏā faṣl ḏāᶜat ᶜalay durrah
fi l-ʾarḍ min šānhā bā dūr
b asʾal ᶜalēha w bā duwwir lhā fī kul bandar
yā zēn kullīn yitmannāk

'Once upon a time, I missed a lovely small parrot
I will travel around to look for her.
I will look for her in every city.
O, beautiful one, everybody wishes to get you!'

The parrot (or any other parrot-like bird) is not indigenous to Ḥaḍramawt, but reference to it in the folklore is quite common. It could be one of the migrant birds that appear in some seasons. The use of the word *durrah* could be neologism from other neighbouring dialects (e.g. Aden Arabic). The Standard Arabic word for it is *babbuġāʾ*.

ᶜafandaš 'vulture'
ṣagr wallā ᶜafandaš 'A falcon or a vulture'.
This proverb is said when someone asks about the achievement of an errand that someone has been sent to, i.e. is it good or bad.

jidāmih / kāḥil (m.) *jidām* (collective pl.) and *ḫlāʾ* pl. *ḥalāyāʾ*, Arabian *bulbul* 'nightingale'
il-ḥalālāya w il-jidām mā jxallēn ḥad ynām 'The bulbuls and sparrows do not give people a chance to sleep.' A children's song.

Insects

jaradih collective n. *jarād* 'locust'
jarādih b-īdi xēr min ʿašr fārrāt 'a locust in my hand is better than ten flying.'

zinbuʿ il-ʿšar 'Usherhopper', *Poekilocerus bufonius*
'Appendage of ʿUšar tree'. A large locust-like insect found [feeding] on ʿUšar trees.
šakluh štgūl zunbuʿ il-ʿšar 'It looks like *zunbuʿ il-ʿšar*.'

faxṣūs / faxṣūs 'cockroach', pl. *fxāsīs*
tfaxsas tislam, tʿagrab tugbaṣ 'Be like a cockroach, you will be safe. Be like a scorpion, you will be bitten.' A proverb said to advise someone to lead a safe life and not interfere in other people's matters or to be harsh towards other people.

aḥmad ḥmuddih yā mširrig il-xūṣ,
ummak šawat lak ʿagrab w faxṣūs
'O, little Ahmed, you who are sitting splitting the leaves of palm tree, your mother has roasted for you a scorpion and cockroach.'
It is believed by some people that if they eat a roasted scorpion in their childhood, they would develop immunity against scorpion bites when they grow up.
ʾilla l-fxāsīs 'Only cockroaches!' Said when one fears the sudden appearance of something he or she does not like.
tfaxsas tislam 'Become a cockroach, you will be safe.' Said to someone who cannot stand his opponents.

ḏbāb 'fly'
jufnih ʿasīd ʿaṭṭalhā ḏbāb 'A tray of ʿasīd (sweet porridge), how nice it is! But, alas, it was spoilt by flies.'
A proverb said describing something beautiful, but it has some flaws, i.e. nothing can be perfect.

ḏibrih / pl. ḏbir 'wasp'
ʿala xēš iḏ-ḏbir min bġā l-haddih ylāgī 'It is all about 'nest of wasps' (i.e. tribal disputes) and he who wants to fight, should come forth and join (us).'
māḥad gid dabas xēš iḏ-ḏibir 'No one has ever got honey from a wasp nest (thinking that it is a beehive),' i.e. Do not expect that you can get something useful from someone who usually do wrongdoing.[5]

gamlih / pl. *gaml* 'louse'
mā ygubbuṣak alla gamil ṯōbak 'you will not get stung except from the lice from your clothes'

nūbah / *nūb* 'bee'
Ḥaḍramawt is well known for its good honey. The famous types of Ḥaḍramī honey are the Dawˤanī (Wādi Dōˤan) and Jirdānī (Wādi Jirdān, now in present-day Shabwah). Reference to honey is found in many proverbs and sayings and folk poetry, as in the verse below. The word ˤ*asal* 'honey' is always associated with its collocations like *jibḥ* 'beehive', *baġīyih*, the best type, which its collection starts from the seasonal star of *xarf*, starting from October, and lasts for forty days.

ḏā faṣl ḥinn yā n-nūb laxḍar
xarmān ba tsammaˤ ḥanīnak
ġibtih ˤalay fī yāt wādi
dawarit lak fī kull bandar
lānā gatīlak
min yōm ġabbatnā ṣwātak
ruḥtih ˤamī la smaˤ walā šūf

'O, now sing you green bees!
I am longing for your humming.
In which valley did you disappear and leave me alone?
I looked for you in all towns,
As if though I am your (killed) victim.
When your sounds became lost,
I became deaf and blind.'

Conclusion

Do historical plant and animal idioms remain in language even after environmental and ecological changes?

The Ḥaḍramī Arabic literary heritage is full of reference to nature. Being mainly agricultural or Bedouin society, nature is reflected in their poetry and proverbs. Now with urbanization and modernization, the referents of lexical items of plants and animals are diminishing. The reasons behind such changes can be diverse; they include, among other things, the fact that with climate changes, changes in lifestyle of people, the introduction of modern technology and contacts with other people in neighbouring countries and in the world as well as the spread of mass media, all led to linguistic changes. Many young people may not know many of names of these plants or animals because, simply, they do not exist anymore. However, thanks to the spread and use of modern mass media where people are trying to write, in nostalgia, about the old days and about values like bravery, honesty and simplicity of life, people are trying to use such proverbs and idioms in their everyday speech and, most importantly, by contemporary folk poets who are increasingly using them in their poetry.

Notes

1. Serjeant defines the language by quoting the following observations from the Ḥaḍramī scholar ᶜAlawī b. Ṭāhir al-Ḥaddād, the then Mufti of Johore in Malaya (now Malaysia) who was an authority in the field:
'The language common to-day in lower Ḥaḍramawt, i.e. where the Kathīrī and Nahdī element is greater, is not the language of (the tribe) Kindah or (the tribe) Ḥaḍramawt, because the two peoples, Kindah and Ḥaḍramawt, were overcome, and most of them emigrated from Ḥaḍramawt to Lower Yemen (ʾAsfal al-Yaman) and Baiḥān. Some went to Ṣaᶜīd of Egypt and Waddān (sic.) by Barqah, and some accompanied the Banī Hilāl to the Maghrib, but remnants of them remained scattered in the villages of Dawᶜan. Also, most of the people of al-Ṣadaf in the Wādī Dawᶜan emigrated to Egypt and al-Andalus at the beginning of Islam. Those remaining in the mountains of Dawᶜan, consist partly of Kindah, though they are but few, and the majority are those who claim descent from Ḥimyar al-ʾAṣghar and those known as ʾUmmat Ḥaḍramawt ... In the language of the workmen (ᶜummāl) of Tarīm, etc., are the remains of the language of Ḥimyar. The language of the Kathīrī places is Ḍannī, Qaḥṭānī. They and the people of Tarīm and Nahd have a ḍannī dialect (lughah), but what predominates over them is the dialect of Najd, because their first dwelling was near Najd ... As for the language of the settled parts (Ḥawādir) of Dawᶜan, it is free from any trace of Quḍāᶜah (taqquḍḍuᶜ).'
2. i.e. when the word dust is pronounced with a lamino-alveolar /d/ as it is the case in some varieties of British or American English (see for example Abercrombie 1967:53).
3. Kharīf (xarīf) in Ḥaḍramī Arabic means the 'season of harvest' or 'the ripe fruit itself, especially dates'. xufrit iš-šijrah means 'the tree has yield (fruit)'.
4. Cf. qumrī in other dialects.
5. The Classical Arabic term dibs means 'date syrup' or any honey-like syrup, i.e. molasses. However, in HA, the root is used to refer to the process of honey collection, hence, yidbis 'to collect honey', dābis 'honey collector; beekeeper'.

References

Abercrombie, D. (1967), *Elements of General Phonetics*, Edinburgh: Edinburgh University Press.

Beeston, A. F. L. (1971), 'Ḥaḍramawt', in P. Bearman, Th. Bianquis, C. E. Bosworth, E. van Donzel and W. P. Heinrichs (eds), *The Encyclopaedia of Islam*, 53, Leiden: Brill.

Bin Qadīm, M. S. S. (2018), *al-nabātāt al-ṭibbiyyah fī flōra wādī dōᶜan w wādī al-ᶜayn, Ḥaḍramwt, al-Yaman wa ᵓahamu istixdāmātihā al-šaᶜbiyah* 'Medical Plants of the Flora of Wādī Dōᶜan w Wādī al-ᶜAyn, Ḥaḍramwt, Yemen', PhD thesis, Al Neelain University.

Collins, B. B. (1969), 'Ḥaḍramawt: Crisis and Intervention 1866–1881', unpublished Ph.D. Dissertation, Princeton University.

FAO (2016), *Yemen's Country Report Contributing to the State of the World's Biodiversity for Food and Agriculture*. Republic of Yemen Ministry of Agriculture and Irrigation Agriculture Research and Extension Authority National Genetic Resources Center.

Lewcock, R. B. (1987), *Wādī Ḥaḍramawt and the Walled City of Shibām*, Paris: UNESCO.

al-Quᶜaiṭī, Ḥ. S. (n.d.) *xaṣāᵓiṣ al-luġah al-ḥaḍramiyyah* (The Characteristics of the Ḥaḍramī Tongue), (edited with an introduction and comments by al-Saqqaf, A. and M. Basalamah (forthcoming), Cairo: Dār al-Wifāq.

al-Saqqaf, A. and M. Basalamah (eds) (forthcoming), 'A Treatise on the Phonetics of Ḥaḍramī Arabic by Saif bin Ḥusain al-Quᶜaiṭī, (n.d.) entitled: *xaṣāᵓiṣ al-luġah al-ḥaḍramiyyah* ("The Characteristics of the Ḥaḍramī Tongue", with an Introduction and Comments by the Editors)', Cairo: Dār al-Wifāq.

al-Saqqaf, A. H. (1999), *A Descriptive Linguistic Study of the Spoken Arabic of Wādī Ḥaḍramawt*. Ph.D. Thesis, University of Exeter.

al-Saqqaf, A. H. (2006), 'Wadi Hadramawt Arabic', in K. Versteegh et al. (eds), *Encyclopaedia of Arabic Language and Linguistics*, 4, 687–99, Leiden: Brill.

Bā-Saywud et al. (2019), 'A Comparative Study of Bee Rangeland Vegetation in Madar and Shohouh Valleys in Hadhramout', (in Arabic), *Hadhramout University Journal of Natural & Applied Sciences*, 16 (2): 251–63.

Serjeant, R. B. (1951), *South Arabian Poetry I: Prose and Poetry from Ḥaḍramawt*, London: Taylor's Foreign Press.

Serjeant, R. B. (1964), 'Some Irrigation Systems in Ḥaḍramawt', *Bulletin of School of Oriental and African Studies*, 27: 33–76.

Serjeant, R. B. and G. R. Smith (1995), *Farmers and Fishermen in Arabia: Studies in Customary Law and Practice*. Variorum. Hampshire: Aldershot.

al-Shāṭrī, M. (1972), *ᵓadwār it-tārīx al-ḥaḍramī*, Jeddah: ᶜĀlam al-Maᶜrifah.

Stark, F. (1939), *The Southern Gates of Arabia*, London: John Murray.

Stark, F. (1940), *A Winter in Arabia*, London: John Murray.

Part Two

Arabia: Narratives and Ecology

8

The Language of Kumzari Folklore

Christina van der Wal Anonby

Folklore references indigenous knowledge systems

Folklore is a repository for the shared knowledge of a cultural community, and oral traditions in Kumzari are no different. Kumzari folktales are brimming with references to the natural world. Equally important as what is *said*, is what is left *unstated* as information that is already understood by both narrator and audience. There exists a rich and deep connection between the Kumzari language and their natural surroundings on Musandam, because of their dependence on their knowledge of nature as a means of survival in a challenging environment.

The present chapter explores these connections as they emerge from Kumzaris' direct experience with their environment, especially the mountains and the sea, from their livelihood in both fishing and date cultivation, and from their shared understanding of familiar natural concepts and spaces.

Firstly, this chapter on the Kumzari language is dedicated to the master storyteller, Aliko Abdullah Shobubu al-Kumzari. Aliko passed away two years ago, but not before he had passed along his wealth of knowledge of Kumzari folklore to the scientific record of his language.... *wasalamun aalayhi* (and peace be upon him). Folktales quoted in this chapter are from van der Wal Anonby (2015), referred to by an initial letter followed by a time-stamp in recorded seconds (see appendix).

Direct experience with the environment

The Kumzari language has been shaped by its speakers' close experience with their environment. Directions are indicated by their perspective of being either toward, or away from, the mountains or the sea. Kumzaris distinguish a dichotomy of space: the inward-facing *mountain*, as the place where girls play and women gather firewood, and the outward-facing *sea*, where boys play on the shore and men go out to fish. The Kumzari cultural world is structured according to the natural world, as nature is intertwined with cultural categories.

In *Rōran Šēxō*, a Kumzari folktale about the seven sons of a sheikh, the *čāf* 'shores' of the wadi are connected to the cultural categories of the two family clans, *Aqali* and *Ghosbani*:

raft inča pi čāf ğušba =ā n ↗
raft inča wā=aqil =ā ↗
rēsid ba sar ğēlila. ↘
'Going like this from the Ghoshbani clan's shore, ↗
going like this toward the Aqali clan ['s shore], ↗
he arrived at the cape of the lagoon.' ↘

(R342)

The language reflects this direction of movement, as seen in this text from the tale: as the youngest brother in the story ascends the shores of the wadi, the first two clauses have the subordinating enclitic *ā* and rising intonation. Then the resolution of the boy arriving at the mountain top overlooking the lagoon is marked by the independent clause and falling intonation.

Directions are based on the centre ground of the wadi that connects the mountains to the sea and transects the village both socially and geographically. Space is conceived of as being directly tied to nature just as is time. The Kumzari language uses the form of the abstract plural to generalize from the particular to a common state or time period. Represented by the suffix *-an*, the abstract plural occurs especially in descriptions of weather, natural states, days and seasons (see Table 8.1).

Table 8.1 Abstract Plurals and Natural States

bang	'sunset'	bang-an	'dusk, eventide'
āfur	'wind sp.'	āfur-an	'windy sp. weather (state)'
ğātal	'storm'	ğātal-an	'stormy weather (state)'
ḥēriq	'dry heat'	ḥēriq-an	'hot, dry weather (state)'
īd	'holiday'	īd-an	'holidays' (the place/time of *eid*)
dimistān	'winter'	dimistān-an	'wintertime'
šartağ	'storm'	šartağ-an	'stormy weather (state)'
bāram	'rain'	bāram-an	'rainy weather (season, place, period)'
kawl	'wind sp.'	kawl-an	'windy sp. weather (state)'

The form of words with the abstract plural encompasses the entirety of time and space for that semantic notion. The abstract plural signifies Kumzari's attunement to the timing of nature and the centrality of the sun, rain and wind in their cultural sphere.

Kumzari figures of speech expressing time and space are joined by animal metaphors, symbolic of their closeness to the environment. Animal metaphors are stand-ins for well-known characteristics in Kumzari. *mār aqrab* 'snakes, scorpions' is a phrase that depicts something that is surprising and horrible. In the *Pačaxčēō* tale, a boy buys a treasure chest at great cost without knowing its contents. He notes that it might have been filled with snakes and scorpions, but instead it contained a great quantity of gold and a girl genie 'whose beauty made the world turn' (P173). The tale of the orchard *Bāǧ al-Mowẓ* has a horse flying with a boy on his back, who warns the boy about the people on the ground: He [the horse] said to him, 'They are coming for you now. Some [of them] will turn themselves into snakes and some [into] scorpions' (B614). In contrast, a dove in Kumzari is used to denote a beautiful woman. A boy who finds his way to the fabled city of Khor Shet'ane wins over its princess; the tale indicates that she engages herself to the boy with the phrase *yāyi ṭēr ḥaṭṭu ra'sī alā ẓandī* 'a bird came to him and laid its head on his arm' (U398).

Lexical interaction with livelihood

The language also carries semantic ties to nature in Kumzari identity and subsistence activities. The Kumzari lexicon has extensive inventories referring to species of fish and plants, types and stages of dates, kinds and parts of a boat, astronomy, tides and weather. These semantic categories are all essential shared knowledge in their livelihood as fishers, gatherers and date cultivators.

References to the sea in Kumzari folktales are inevitably tied to boats and fishing, and always mentioned in relation to the effect of nature on a character's livelihood. In the folktale *Sōntyō*, the sheikh's daughter does not want to marry, and instead asks her father to build her a boat to live on as she goes out to sea.

The text from later in the folktale, shown in Table 8.2, demonstrates that the princess knows enough about the geography of the sea to tell her father exactly where to release her boat where the tides will carry her far away. After the girl travels for a year or so, the boat becomes enveloped in barnacles and algae, and docks on a distant shore. Her presence in the new land is identified by her boat that is covered in the detritus of a life at sea.

Table 8.2 Geography of the Sea in *Sōntyō*

Kumzari (S173–235)	English
xālaṣ tŏat=ā	82 'When it is finished,
bō kard mē dirya-ō	83 go and plunge me into the sea.
kard-ī mē dirya-ō=ā	85 Plunging me into the sea,
bar mē ba mōmur wākiš mē	87 carry me to Momur Island, [there] release me.
ar jāga br-um	90 I shall go anywhere.'
bard-in yē āw-an	172 They carried [the dhow] to the water.
wa dār-iš yē ba lenj-ō	173 And [the sheikh] gave [his daughter] to the dhow,
bard-in yē ba mōmur	
wākid-in yē	174 They carried it to Momur Island.
abāra … āw-ō ŏgar-ē =ā	177 [There] they released it.
dug-a yē ba quxayg	179 Like … the ebbing tide goes out,
wa āw-ō čōt bāla purya =ā	183 it took her to Quxayg Rock and
tēbur-a yē ba sar mistō	185 the flowing tide comes in,
wa lenj-an tēmuš-in yē	187 it carries her to Cape Misto.
č-in ba yē rāy-in na abaša yē	190 When dhows see it [the boat],
tk-in na	191 they go to it, they cannot catch it.
rāy-in na sī-in yē nēxan na	193 They cannot bring it aboard,
gap-ē na =ā?	195 it being such a big one! you know?
xall gid-iš	197 it was covered with green algae,
mṣaww gid-iš	199 It was covered with barnacles,
maḥḥar gid-iš	200 It was covered with oysters, and
wa ğazara gid-iš inda āw-an	203 It was covered with water,
yē wa āw-an sātē tā-ē=in	204 sinking until it was one [level] with the water.
inča xall ba yē	207 Like this, there was green algae on it
wa maḥḥar ba yē wa	208 and oysters on it and …
mād laba si-mā-an	212 time went by, about three months,
čār mā-an dirya-ō	213 four months, she was at sea,
čār panj mā-an	214 four or five months.
ammū ādamī jīr-in yē	215 All the people saw it.
ar čōt ba yē=ā	217 [but] of anyone who went to it [to look at it],
kas tāt-a yē na	218 no one wanted it.
ka byō nāšī būr	220 Then it came about that there was a storm wind. A nor'easter.
nāšī	
nāšī-ō āmad	222 A storm wind blew up, [the boat] became beached in a country,
ḥamya wābur inda walēyit-ē	
inda lēmē inda jāgēē ya'nī	229 in Lima, in somewhere, that is to say.
ḥamya wābur ba čāf-ō	231 [The boat] became beached on the shore,
nāšī-ō wād-iš yē	232 the storm wind brought it,
ḥamya gid-iš bāla ba āw-ō	233 beached it high on the spring tide.
gābanō-ō	
araṭa yē gid-iš	235 It [the storm] stuck it [the boat].
āw-ō čōt pi yē ẓēran	237 Water flowed down from it.

(S173–235)

In this short text, we find numerous lexical items of specific meaning to sea-dwelling people, some unique to the geography of Musandam: boat terminology, specific local place names, types of sea creatures and plants, and lexicon pertaining to tides and weather:

lenj 'dhow'
mōmur 'island place name'
ōǧar 'ebbing tide'
quxayg 'rock place name'
purya 'flowing tide'
sar mistō 'cape place name'
nēxan 'aboard (boat)'
xall 'green algae'
mṣaww 'barnacles'
maḥḥar 'oysters'
lēmē 'settlement place name'
nāšī 'nor'easter storm wind'
ḥamya 'beached (boat)'
čāf 'shore'
gābanō 'spring tide'

As the narrator relates her journey about the sea, the tides and the storms, and about the boat covered in barnacles and algae, the audience can picture every detail, because they know these places, they know these plants and animals, they know these times. The narrator and the audience, as well as the characters in the tales, have a shared knowledge of the lexicon of their indigenous natural environment.

Kumzari livelihoods ensure they encounter familiar places in the folktales. As nomadic pastoralists they are traditionally mobile by sea between coastal fishing villages in winter and date orchards in summer, with intermittent stays on sea islands to pasture goats. Travel to the high mountains and deserts of the peninsula is also a common activity.

Throughout Kumzari folktales, customary places for trade follow the coastline, sea routes, mountain settlements and desert interior. A boy in the tale *Pačaxčēō* leaves his land and his grandmother to go and work in Kuwait. When he makes his fortune, he journeys as a pilgrim to Mecca. Later he travels through the deserts and over mountains in search of his wife, who has become the sheikh of a faraway city.

Settings in the folktales reflect the generic 'here', and mention common places where the local economy converges with nature: the beach, the orchard, mountain pastures for goats, islands in the sea and clifftop acacia copses where firewood is gathered.

In one tale set in an orchard and on a mountain, an almond tree serves as a sign for where a mother should look for her kidnapped son. As he is taken away by the sorcerer, the boy shouts to her,

> *ida ya'nī bādam-ō išk wābur pi wā=ǧarbī, yē jōr-ē mē pi wā=šarqī. ida bādam-ō šarxit yē išk wābur pi wā=šarqī, yē jōr-ē mē pi wā=ǧarbī.*
>
> 'If, I mean, the almond tree has become dry from the west, then search for me in the east. If half of the almond tree has become dry from the east, then search for me in the west.'
>
> (B254)

Destiny is often revealed through an intersection of natural elements. A poignant instance in the tale *Kan'ēdō* finds the boy waiting for a sign by sitting in a fig tree (*lētab*) beside a water reservoir (*ḥasī*) under a full moon (*mētāw panḍa*) (K155).

In another tale, a clever thief covers his shoes with tar in order to discreetly pick up the sheikh's gold coins from the ground, then travels to the wilderness (*xalwat*) and to a high mountain peak (*sar-ō*) to discover a secret place to bury them (A681).

Sensing the intersection of natural and supernatural

Beyond the practical considerations of making a living, daily life for Kumzaris is infused with references to the blurred line between natural and supernatural. Their folktales recognize this intersection of nature and magic by referencing direct encounters through the characters' and listeners' senses.

The Kumzari language has a set of three clause-initial evidentials to mark the source of information for a statement. Firsthand information is indicated by the sensory evidential, *tamna*. It can refer to information that has been seen, heard, or felt, and it is also used to label the narrator's and audience's shared interaction at the appearance of something that is surprising or magical, such as in the clauses shown in Table 8.3.

As seen in these examples, in most instances of magic noted by the sensory evidential, a concrete aspect of nature is involved. Encounters with magic happen

Table 8.3 The Sensory Evidential *tamna*

tamna ... a sorcerer descends from the sky in the form of an albatross (R978)
tamna ... a meadow of *kinb* and *tumi* trees uprooted by a giant (K293)
tamna ... a gazelle with fawn inside as the answer to a riddle (U188)
tamna ... a huge snake that thwarts men from fulfilling their destiny (R209)
tamna ... seven women eating magic pomegranate seeds (B131)

in the context of nature. The sensory evidential serves to connect the natural world that can be *directly* seen with the human eye, to *indirect* observations of the supernatural world.

In the folktale *Kanēdō*, a boy must retrieve his pearl that he found in a fish, by catching some magic horses. The magic horses can only be found under a full moon, in the mountains, at a water reservoir, beside a wild fig tree.

lakin inčka jō'ar-ō xō tāt-ī=ā
burwā inda kō-ō
asp-an insī-an ar inda kō-ō asp-an insī
asp-an insī-an byār ba mē=ā
byō īn tō dō-um ba tō jō'ar tō
sā asp-an insī-an tār-a
filḥāl mād šēx-ō bāla kin šām xōr
wa brō mētāw panḍa
brō ūnī ba ḥasī-ō
ba ḥasī-ō ba čō-ō ya'nī
sā čō-ō ēwō īn-ō ba yē
lētab-ē gap yē raftništ qummit īn-ō
qummit lētab-ō
šaw wābur=ā
***tamna**=ā asp-ē rēsid*
di-ta rōr wā yē
asp-ē insī rēsid wa di-ta rōr wā yē
sā āw txōr-in pi ḥasī-ō=ā
yē=ā asta asta asta=ā rukbō kin ba mām-ō
pi lētab-ō ya'nī
'Since like this you want your pearl,
run to the mountains.
The magic horses which are
in the mountains,
magic horses: bring me the magic horses,

then I will give you your what's-it-called.
Your pearl.'
Now, he [the boy] would bring the
magic horses.
But [firstly] anyway, he stayed with
the sheikh,
he went up and ate supper,
and [then] he left! It was a full moon.
He went and sat at the very top
of the what's-it-called:
at the top of the wild fig tree.
When night fell,
tamna a horse came, two foals with it!
A magic horse came, and two foals with it.
Now [as] they were drinking water from
the pool,
this [boy], he slowly, slowly, slowly
mounted the mare.
From the wild fig tree, that is to say.

(K139)

In this case, the boy catches sight of the magic horses. The *tamna* lends a here-and-now effect to the folktale at this point in the story. In addition, the evidential compels an explicit description of the boy's experience as he is perching on the tree in the moonlight and discovers the horses. It functions to bring the listeners into the experience of nature that can be seen, heard or felt.

Another evidential, *ēka*, is based on inferred information source. Shared interaction with the land and sea is in play, because the inferred evidential can only be used when certain pieces of information are already known between speaker and hearer. In this case, the information held in common intersects both geography and culture: a place on Musandam called Sar Kardēo, and a type of boat built for navigating the sea around that point. The audience can identify the place and artefact that is marked by the evidential, based on cultural landmarks they know.

raft māšuwē-ō gid-iš ba xō, māšuwē swuk, **ēka** =ā inčka ādamī-an sar kardēʾō=ā, ...
'He went and built himself a skiff – a lightweight skiff, **you know**, just like the people here in Sar Kardeo have – '...

(K62)

Beyond evidentials, the tales' characters relate to their natural surroundings as marks in the narrative. They encounter animals, often with magical powers, at turning points in the plot. In the tale *Ǧrābō*, a boy supports his grandmother by building thorn-bush fences around their mountaintop wheat fields to deter goats from eating the crops. One day, the boy is surprised to find their wheat eaten but no apparent culprits except a large crow in a jujube tree. The boy must make a long journey into the mountains, chasing the crow into a cave to catch it. Once he has captured it, the crow propels him to success by uttering truth-revealing 'caws' in critical situations.

The tale of the seven brothers, *Rōran Šēxō*, features a fearsome snake that represents the divergence of perspectives between the older brothers and the youngest, who is castigated as being 'weak'. The six strong brothers, embarking on a journey on horseback, cower when the snake lunges at them and prevents them from continuing on the path. When the youngest brother catches up to them on his donkey, his transformation into a grown man is so complete that they do not recognize him as he strikes down the snake. Overcoming the trials of nature earns him the right to travel alongside his brothers as they seek their fortunes, and the defeat of the snake is the challenge that initiates him into a series of triumphs that improve his standing.

A similar storyline develops in the tale of the fisher-boy. In each instance the mention of a natural element at first seems to be peripheral but emerges as a signpost to the fate of the main character. The boy in *Kanēdō* learns to make a meagre living through fishing and selling his catch to the sheikh. One day he captures a kingfish with a pearl inside it, and both the boy and the sheikh lay claim to the treasure. The rest of the tale is spent battling over the pearl, but ultimately the boy brings it home along with all the other marks of success he has attained: the sheikh's crown, servants, a wife, gold and magic horses.

Other fortune-turning animals abound. A clairvoyant camel in the tale *Aḥmad Tka* has the shrewdness of a police dog, able to sniff out the thief who has stolen the king's treasure and poisoned ten of his guards. A gazelle and fawn in the tale *Abūyi salaḥnī Ūmmī rakabnī* are the focus of a riddle a boy uses to win the heart of a princess; she turns herself into a bird and sets her bridal diadem on his pillow. Sorcerers in Kumzari tales are known to turn themselves into albatrosses. The sorcerer in *Bāǧ al-Mowẓ* uses the form of the bird to snatch up the boy he conceived out of pomegranate seeds, and in *Rōran Šēxō* the albatross screeches down to earth to begin a battle the boy is waging over the country's water supply and human sacrifices the sorcerer demands.

Each of these appearances of animals infuses the variability of natural forces into the cultural landscape to bend the direction of the narrative. The tales bring together environment and society to voice Kumzari shared identity through their common lived experiences.

Narrative and nature

The language of the folktales describes contexts where nature and culture meet. Folklore references an indigenous knowledge of nature that is recognized, and taken for granted, by both the narrator and the audience. Kumzaris depend on this collective knowledge for communication in the same way that they depend on the natural environment for their livelihood and well-being.

References

van der Wal Anonby, C. (2015), *A Grammar of Kumzari: A Mixed Perso-Arabian Language of Oman*, Leiden: Leiden University.

Appendix. Abbreviations of Folkloric Text References

(Initial letter is followed by a time-stamp in recorded seconds)
    A   *Aḥmad Tka*
    B   *Bāğ al-Mowẓ*
    G   *Ğrābō*
    K   *Kanẽdō*
    P   *Pačaxčēō*
    R   *Rōran Šēxō*
    S   *Sōntyō*
    U   *Abūyi salaḥnī Ūmmī rakabnī*

9

Orature and Nature in Southern Arabia

Kamela al-Barami, Ahmed al-Mashikhi and Sam Liebhaber

Introduction

The convergence between the fields of literary ecocriticism and postcolonial studies highlights the manner in which the written word – prose, poetry and other genres of literary expression – has alternately reinforced and resisted the hierarchical and patriarchal premise of human exploitation of the environment (Heise 2010: 251–8). Absent from this school of critique are non-written modes of orature such as oral poems, songs, proverbs and riddles which, in an ironic turn, are arguably closer to the actual praxis of word-power (Foley 1992: 275–301) amongst the communities and individuals most affected by the legacies of globalization and environmental exploitation. Instead, we must turn to scholarship in the field of linguistics and language documentation which has noted that ecological and linguistic diversity and resilience go hand-in-hand: where linguistic diversity has held on in the face of imposed linguistic monocultures, so too has biological diversity (Gorenflo et al. 2011: 8032–7). And yet, scholarship in this field tends to give short shrift to the power of word-art and orature by focusing on the quotidian rather than the numinous: word lists and recorded conversations instead of poems, songs and prayers.[1]

In this chapter, the co-authors will address how the figurative language of poetry and song in the Mehri and Śḥerēt (a.k.a. Jibbāli) languages circulates ecological knowledge about seasonal weather patterns: a formerly stable system currently threatened by changes to the South Asian monsoon cycle (Turner and Annamalai 2012: 587–95).[2] The focus of analysis lies on emotional expression: poets composing in the endangered Śḥerēt and Mehri languages rely on the shifting seasons for the metaphors that articulate the richness of their inner lives. The use of figurative language drawn from the environment gains a particularly nuanced resonance in the contrast between two poetic genres in the related Mehri and Śḥerēt languages. In the public facing tribal ode from the Mehri language – known as the *ōdī we-krēm krēm* genre – the twinned motifs of diurnal winds and the seasonal arrival of the monsoonal *mdīt* wind communicate the themes of abrupt social change and political turmoil. In the *nānā* genre of poetry in the Śḥerēt language – a genre that attracts the finest talents amongst female poets from Dhofar – the arrival of the monsoon and accompanying onshore breeze (*bōbet*) signals a refreshing sense of renewal and calm. However, the bedrock of this cultural practice remains the same: poets in both languages express their sentiments and thoughts on personal and social issues through imagistic motifs drawn from the natural environment, especially the wind.

Finally, in drawing attention to the scope of meaning in a single suite of figurative motifs, the authors will foreground the value of orature in documenting and circulating environmental knowledge in languages whose speakers find themselves assimilating to a linguistic superstrate at the very moment that weather patterns have entered into a state of flux.

The monsoonal wind in the Mehri tribal ode

One of the chief thematic formulas of public-facing, vernacular poetry from the Arabian Peninsula – in Arabic or in any of the Modern South Arabian languages (MSAL) – is the introductory mountaintop-ascent trope. At the beginning of a conventional oral poem, the poet depicts his arrival at the top of a mountain peak to declaim a poem. The physical exertion, dramatic setting and social isolation entailed in this trope function as a metaphorical correlate to the numinous aura that coalesces around the act of poetic creation on the Arabian Peninsula. Further, the symbolic separation of the quotidian from the otherworldly through this trope frames – to use a concept highlighted by Richard Bauman and subsequent performance ethnographers – a heightened sensitivity on the part of the listener to the immanent word-power of an oral performance.[3] Linked to the mountain-top formula in South Arabian vernacular poetry is the associated figure of an evening wind that gusts around the poet in counterpart to the poet's labile emotional state. This wind is generally named as the southerly *mdīt*, which is also known in southern Arabia in Arabic and the MSAL as the *kaws*.

In meteorological terms, the *mdīt* wind arises at the end of the South Arabian summer when the burgeoning heat of summer (*ḳeyẓ*) gives way to the monsoon season (*kharīf*). This season has historically lasted from mid-June to September, although the *mdīt* blows most strongly in September when the temperature differential between the sweltering interior of the southern third of the Arabian Peninsula and the cooler waters upwelling from deep in the Gulf of Oman and the Arabian Sea is at its greatest. The *mdīt* wind accompanies the surge of cooler, humid air that pushes northwards and westwards off the ocean in the morning and evening, and as it runs up against the escarpment of the South Arabian highlands, it releases its burden of moisture as light rain and fog.[4] Along with the precipitation that it carries and the fearsome oceanic breakers that arise along with it, the *mdīt* wind is one of the most emblematic manifestations of seasonal change in southern Arabia, occurring as it does at the height of the transition from the stillness of the torrid summer months to the meteorological dynamism of the monsoon. At a smaller scale, the *mdīt* arises in the early morning and dusk and thus further correlates to a sense of personal and social liminality that exists at the cusp of poetic creation.

It would be a mistake, however, to understand the related tropes of the mountain top ascent and *mdīt* wind in strictly literal terms: not every poem is composed at the onset of the monsoon or while facing the *mdīt* wind, nor is every poet a mountain climber.[5] Given the frequency of the trope and its undoubted counter-factuality in many instances, the audience is made to understand the linked tropes of the mountain top and the *mdīt* wind are a figurative rendering of the poet's emotional and psychic state – not an indicator of actual location in time and space.[6]

The following opening lines are from a traditional poetic narrative of a type known as *ōdī we-krēm krēm* and can be taken as exemplary of the genre:

1) *'ōdī wə-krēm krēm / ṭeyr edōreb ḏ-ānkīd / hēl eṣāber yešteyb*
2) *hēl tḏūleh emdīt / ṭeyr ḥalles tekhōb / hīs feyṣel meġreyb*
3) *tefrīren b-'āfōr / yeṭfīfen ṭeyr ekā / yeġyīben w-yekkeyb*

---

1) I begin with the Generous and Munificent / atop the path of 'Ānkīd / where the lofty peaks loom.
2) Where the southerly breeze arises / and arrives at its usual spot / as though the evening were its season.
3) It scatters the clouds / which float over the land / they disappear into the ravines and draws.[7]

The poet begins with the conventional pious invocation: *ōdī we-krēm krēm*; this phrase also serves as the metrical template for the poem and as a melodic mnemonic.[8] The poet next locates himself at the top of the mountain of ʾAnkīd. By stationing himself atop the mountain, the poet claims a panoptic vantage point from which to witness the events unfolding below. The poet puts figurative distance between himself and the quotidian, human realm: in short, the poet adopts a celestial perch from which to observe, document and judge human society. The poet continues: stationed on the mountain's peak, he catches the *mdīt* wind as it blows from the ocean and watches as the moisture-laden air coalesces as fog and rain and then disperses into low clouds. The poet remarks on the timing of the wind: it arrives at the setting of the sun (*meġreyb*), the transitional period between the afternoon (*al-ʿaṣr*) and night (*al-ʿishāʾ*). The third line is composed entirely of a series of verbs that convey a sense of movement and dispersal across space – *tefrīren, yeṭfīfen, yeġyīben* and *yekkeyb* – which depict the clouds as they retreat into the deep canyons and ravines of the coastal escarpment. A sense of dynamic movement and change echoes throughout this opening sequence; what was formerly stable has been rendered dynamic, fluid and mercurial.

These linked qualities of movement, change and transition – expressed through the *mdīt* – arise as a regular feature in the opening lines of Mehri narrative and historical poetry. In view of the limited oral formulaicism in Arabian vernacular poetry – particularly at the lexical level – the pious invocation *ʿōdī we-krēm krēm* and the evocation of the *mdīt* wind stand as two of the few definitive oral formulas of the Mehri oral poetic tradition.[9] For instance, another poem begins with the following lines:

1) *ʾōdī we-krēm krēm // śōbī ṭeyr eġižwəlūt*
2) *ke-mġawnī ḏe-ḥyōm // ġsīreyyen ettəhūt*
3) *we-hlats ṭamḥeyt // sebḥawt ekkerdəfūt*
4) *we-mdīt men emṭəlā // emhawġes enkəśūt*
5) *heġs lād yġōwī śīs // wel ʿaynī haġfūt*

---

1) I begin with the Noble and Generous: climbing to the top of a hill
2) When the sun sets in the evening and its light fades,
3) Darkness spreads, swimming over the *wādī*'s edge,
4) Then the sea breeze from the South stirred up strong feelings
5) That do not subside when the wind dies, my eye cannot sleep[10]

In this introduction to a much-longer historical narrative poem, we find all of the same elements of the previous example. In the first line, the poet mounts a low rise: not a mountain exactly but something more fitting to the interior steppe of al-Mahrah from whence this poet hails. The second line brings the liminal nature of the timing of the poem to the fore: the poem situates the audience at sunset (as in the previous poem), when the harsh light of the late afternoon (*ġsīreyyen*) begins to attenuate. The poet introduces another motif that locates the poetic act at the liminal threshold between day and night: the 'creeping shadow' (*hlats tamḥayt*) that moves across the landscape and appears most visibly under the lip of the *wādī's* edge. The *mdīt* arises, although this far inland it has been stripped of its cargo of moisture and precipitation. Yet it still fulfills its emotional purpose: as it blows across the landscape it inspires the poet's passion, yielding a poem whose recitation extends into the gloaming.

The fact that the *mdīt* wind is metaphorically correlated to a transitional state is rendered in clear terms in the opening lines to a well-known narrative historical ode by the poet Saʻīd bir Laʻṭayṭ from the district of Qishn in al-Mahrah:

1) *ṭār kāten w-ṭarbūt* // *hel mġawrī ḏ-rīheyn* // *wet ġmūzem w-klūb*
2) *we-ṭwōren emdīt* // *beyn edōṭa we-rbē* // *feyṣel ḥawlī klūb*
3) *ṣrōme mehhəbīb* // *ṭār elēhen mātlīm* // *ān ewakb ertəkūb*

---

1) Atop the peak of Ṭarbūt // at the place of the paths of the winds // when they blow furiously and are joined together.
2) Sometimes (there comes) the sea breeze // between the stars of Dōṭa and Rbē // (when) the first season has come [or finished, lit. 'happened'].
3) Now I'll compose a *habbōt* // atop a well-crafted melody // if the rhymes fit together.[11]

This poem begins with a straightforward example of the formulas already illustrated in this chapter, but the transitional timing of the *mdīt* is given explicit notice: the poet describes the wind as arriving between the seasonal marker stars of *dōṭa* and *rbē* as one season ends and another begins. In this example, a temporal liminality is foregrounded, which – unless recitation of this poem is actually restricted to this brief window of time – the audience experiences a metaphoric reference to social instability and emotional unease.

In addition to serving as a metaphoric correlative to socio-political affairs in al-Mahrah, there is likewise a figurative relationship between the *mdīt* wind and the act of poetic composition in southern Arabia.[12] As we have seen in the previous examples, the appearance of the *mdīt* wind corresponds to the poet's emotional state: just as the atmospheric stillness of the summer gives way to the climatic volatility of the monsoon season, so too does the poet's emotional quiescence give way to emotional lability. The timing of the wind – falling in between the appearance and disappearance of calendrical stars, heralding the beginning and end of the seasons, and arising daily at dawn and dusk – recapitulates a transition in the poet's own status and behavior. Formerly disengaged, the poet must now intervene with his people before whatever conflict he perceives on the horizon reaches home. Not surprisingly, poems that begin in this fashion often conclude with a call for a restoration of calmer minds to leadership roles: people such as himself who will apply the balm of wisdom and persuasive rhetoric to whatever plagues the commonweal.

The breeze (*bōbet*) in the Śḥerēt *Nānā*

The *nānā* is considered the spoken artform best suited to expressions of emotional conflict and passion in the Śḥerēt language. The *nānā* genre is sung by an individual or a chorus of singers without any rhythmic accompaniment; instead, the sole instrument is the voice of the singer who chooses a location to sing on the basis of its resonant and echoing acoustics. This fact secures the close conceptual relationship between the *nānā* poetic genre and its natural surroundings: the voice of the singer is experienced as an echo carried by the wind as it ascends the narrow ravines that are carved down the steep flank of the coastal highlands. The *nānā* poetic genre evolved to take advantage of a key topographical feature of Dhofar and it has emerged as its vocal embodiment: the physical terrain of Dhofar and the seasonal wind patterns that reach it are inseparable from the composition and reception of lines of *nānā* verse. Reflecting on this phenomenon, Tabook says the following:

> The day comes when one will hear a woman or a man singing from a valley, a hill or in a dwelling on the eastern side of the province, while a similar man or woman can be heard on the western side of the province singing an identical song with the same lyrics in an almost identical voice, to the extent that anyone who is not familiar with the custom might imagine that it is the same person in both places, or that it is an echo.[13]

Nānā poems may take the form of stand-alone stanzas or they may take the form of dialogic poetic couplets (*rajaz maraddāt*) exchanged between two poets or a group of poets on the same topic. In some circumstances, a poet might generate the first couplet – called a *ḥarf* on the basis of its final rhyming letter – leaving other poets to add a second, rejoining couplet. This mode of composition is arguably the most difficult to master insofar as it requires an astute hermeneutical capacity to unravel the poet's intended meaning – often wrapped in layers of metaphor and the granular lexicon of environmental kenning – and thence to compose a relevant response. The two poets examined in this section on the *nānā* genre, 'Īdāl bint Suhayl al-'Amrī and Ṭufūl bint Muḥammad Bāqī ('Bish Ḥaqf'), are highly regarded *nānā* poets and their lyrics are widely esteemed for their eloquent composition, hidden meanings and capacity for narrative within the space constraints of the *nānā* form.

As mentioned earlier, the genre of *nānā* poetry draws pre-eminent female poets towards its composition.[14] The fact of there being prominent female poets is hardly noteworthy for the people of Dhofar and southern Arabia; indeed, the very concept of poetic inspiration in southern Arabia is personified by the feminine figure of 'Halīla'. While many personify 'Ḥalīla' as supernatural figure who bestows poetic inspiration on fortunate poets, Bish Ḥaqf describes 'Ḥalīla' in more instrumental terms as the 'imaginary horizon' (Ar. *al-'ufuq al-khayālī*) of a poet, saying:

> The poet's imaginary horizon is what distinguishes him from other poets. We find poets who possess such a broad imaginary horizon and cultural knowledge that they may match and challenge other poets without flagging. Others who possess a closer imaginary horizon can continue up to a certain point and travel a certain distance before they must cut their intentions short ... [There are poets such as herself] who possess a broad imaginary horizon, like broad and deep canyons and valleys that have no obvious boundaries, and there are poets whose horizons are much closer, like narrow ravines with small streams whose channels never extends beyond their close confines.[15]

As a poetic reflex to the valleys and wind of Dhofar, the *nānā* genre is suffused with an abundance of naturalistic vocabulary and imagery. This, indeed, may be related to the gender of the poet; as al-Ghadeer notes, female poets working in the closely related *nabaṭī* tradition place pastoral imagery at the forefront of their poetic works:

> [Their] poems blossom in pastures, rain clouds, and patches of lavender. Bedouin women compose poetry in the desert and about the desert, offering vivid images drawn from life around them. Their poetry displays many extraordinary images of animals ... The repository of wildlife includes lizards, snakes and hedgehogs, as well as plants and the weather. Some poems have a power motif of lightning,

which usually arouses the woman's longing. When lightning flashes in the sky, memory opens up and silence is interrupted."[16]

In a similar vein to their *nabaṭī* counterparts, *nānā* poets boast of their ability to harness naturalistic vocabulary in rendering different meanings in the bodies of their poems. In the *nānā* couplets composed by ʾĪdāl al-ʿAmrī and Ṭufūl Bāqī ('Bish Ḥaqf') selected below, we find *nānā* poets utilizing the monsoon season, rain bearing and non-rain bearing clouds, the breeze and the verdant flora of monsoonal Dhofar to express a sense of peace and contentment. In contrast, they utilize the sun, heat, profound darkness, storms, violent waves and glowering thunderheads to express their anxieties, frustrations and fears.

ʾĪdāl al-ʿAmrī

ʾĪdāl bint Suhayl bin ʿAlī al-ʿAmrī was born in the district of Mirbāṭ in the province of Dhofar and is currently considered one of the region's most distinguished *nānā* poets. She composes her poetry according to the highest degree of craftsmanship and goes toe-to-toe with the most famous *nānā* poets in exchanges of *nānā* couplets. Additionally, she has achieved fame for circulating poetic couplets (*ḥarf*) and challenging other poets to respond to them. ʾĪdāl al-ʿAmrī's abundant use of the lexicon of the Dhofari monsoon reflects a gendered relationship to the conventional poetic idiom, insofar as cultural mandates of female modesty require a circumspect mode of lyric personal expression. Unlike her male counterparts who have greater license to speak directly to their sentiments, ʾĪdāl relies on a more figurative and recondite idiom that draws from her natural surroundings: the wind, weather and mountainous terrain. In doing so, ʾĪdāl achieves a degree of plausible deniability: her verses may be interpreted as imagistic meditations should she be called to account for the personal meanings embedded in her verses.

1) *qalā khōref henī leḥaymel balqōfi*
2) *bel ʿābēṣ ʿōmer ēn esnēn enzōfi*
---
1) Leave me the monsoon and let me bear it as I will
2) In payment for my age and all the years that have bled away

These lines articulate the emotional state of the poet: she describes someone dear to her as the monsoon season and appeals to her folk to let her enjoy his company as she wishes and to enjoy the life that she had previously denied herself. In these short lines, the poet acknowledges that carrying on a relationship with this beloved individual will compensate for whatever the previous years have taken from her while she waited for him to resume their relationship.

In the following *nānā* poem, ʾĪdāl al-ʿAmrī welcomes her guests to an evening social gathering. Even as she extends her hospitality, the poet slyly asks about one member of the group who typically comes with them and yet is missing this time around.

1) *lawb ār aġmēd khōraf mēd aġlēl shōbeh*
2) *dōn śī dōl lektēmel bōl ḥasan asbēbeh*

---

1) Nightfall during the monsoon envelops us with its fog and clouds.
2) But one thing is unknown: the reason something remains incomplete.

Expressing the joy she feels at the arrival of her guests, ʾĪdāl al-ʿAmrī describes the celebrants as the monsoonal clouds since they infuse her immediate surroundings with their generosity and blessing. However, the joy is incomplete because one person from the group is missing and the poet cannot fathom the reason for this person's absence. The pleasure ʾĪdāl experiences at the party is tempered by the regret that the one person whom she was especially looking forward to seeing is unexpectedly absent.

In the following *nānā* couplet, ʾĪdāl al-ʿAmrī offers an alternative kenning to the rain-laden, monsoonal clouds. In these couplets, the rainclouds take on a decidedly negative meaning: the clouds are so thick that the local folk are incapable of distinguishing between night and day.

1) *hēr adōmk ġōber beṣēb men ʾejrōmed*
2) *āl ʾāk foz thāzer ḳrēb kōn ʾamġōmed*

---

1) When thunderheads collide with a downpour from the rainclouds:
2) So dark! No one can distinguish between sunrise and sunset.

Here, ʾĪdāl al-ʿAmrī uses the terms *adōmk* and *ʾejrōmed* to convey the sense of shadowy darkness cast by rain-bearing clouds. In doing so, ʾĪdāl al-ʿAmrī obliquely references unsettled circumstances that are dimly understood by 'the folks on the ground'. While the precise circumstances are unstated by the poet, it is safe to assume that the lines contain a social and political valence: dark machinations have clouded the public's capacity to fathom current affairs.

Bish Haqf

Ṭufūl bint Muḥammad Bāqī, known as Bish Ḥaqf, was born in the western mountains of the Dhofar region and has garnered acclaim amongst the contemporary poets in the region. Bish Haqf's poetic interventions are usually social and political responses to poetic challenges. In her own words, Bish Ḥaqf contends with 'serious issues of public concern that challenge the attitudes of the people and give rise to the difficulties and dangers that face society as a whole'.[17] While the surface 'text' of her couplets may appear to be strictly sentimental in nature, the underlying intentions are typically expressions of political and social engagement and require social and political knowledge in order to decode them. This is the chief pleasure of the *nānā* genre for its audience: its hidden meaning is slowly unwrapped through a heuristic exercise that relies on the listener's imagination, familiarity with the poetic tradition, environmental knowledge and awareness of local and regional issues, concerns and personalities.

As can be seen in the following *nānā* couplet, Bish Haqf incorporates social and political commentary in an imagistic scene based on the monsoonal rainclouds and seasonal winds.

1) āl śayfak ār khōref heyr ʾaġmōṭer ġaydel
2) b-bōbet ʾat ʿayneh ʿād be-dheyḵ y ʿaddel
---
1) I could never love anything but the monsoon that brings the rain clouds.
2) And the breeze which pushes them up and over the high mountains.

In this couplet, Bish Haqf expresses her yearning for the monsoon and the accompanying rainclouds, and the verdant greenery and personal tranquility that they bring. The second verse of the couplet describes how the mild monsoonal breeze lifts the clouds past the highest peaks of the ocean-facing escarpment onto the dry plateau beyond. While this couplet could be heard as a descriptive meditation on natural beauty and emotional bliss, the *nānā* genre does not allow its listener the comfort of an initial impression. Instead, the listener is meant to apply local environmental knowledge to the puzzle: the precipitation of the monsoonal fog cannot reach the plateau without the aid of the monsoonal breeze. This knowledge transforms the image into an expression of gnomic wisdom: the blessing of moisture requires a vehicle – in this case, the breezy *bōbet* – to those who need it. And insofar as the monsoonal precipitation is a boon to all who live along the coastal escarpment and the highlands, this *nānā* couplet takes on a social meaning: communal welfare and prosperity requires the collective work of people of good will. It is possible to extrapolate a further meaning that carries a political undertone: the monsoonal breeze may be understood as a single, powerful figure who, once resolved to bring development or aid to an underserved region, ensures that it arrives at its intended destination.

1) ʾabōbet eḏ khōref berot heyr ʾamhōfī ḥaṣart alkims
2) w-hat heyr šenḳōṭek teylī ʾār amśōḳeṣ ʿād fōz yġims

---

1) The monsoon breeze has crossed beyond the mountains, offering itself to the desert folk.
2) And you: if this gentle breeze rudely awakens you, just wait until dawn and face the dry wind!

As in the previous *nānā* couplets, Bish Ḥaqf uses the monsoon and the monsoonal breeze – the *bōbet* – in a figurative sense for happiness, prosperity and ease. In this specific couplet, the Dhofari listener recognizes that the *bōbet* rarely reaches beyond the escarpment to descend into the dry gullies and canyons on the inland side of the coastal range. However, the end of the line expresses the notion that the folk who live in the rain shadow of the mountains do not appreciate the munificence that has come their way, whether it is physical comfort, personal happiness or social services. Speaking sardonically, Bish Ḥaqf tells them that if the gentle, moisture-laden breeze 'rudely awakens' them, they can simply wait until the dawn of a new day brings the blistering *simūm* to which they are accustomed. The object of this critique is open to multiple possibilities: in addition to the aforementioned ungrateful people who reject kindness and generosity, the listener may also interpret the 'you' of the second line as referring to folk who believe the blessing of the *bōbet* should stay with them. According to this latter interpretation, Bish Ḥaqf criticizes individuals who hoard public services and support for themselves out of fear that it will be enjoyed by other people.

Conclusion

Insofar as the metaphorical language of the seasonal winds and breezes supplies the primary idiom for emotional and sentimental expression in poetry in the Mehri and Śḥerēt languages of al-Mahrah and Dhofar, this chapter poses a question: what will happen to personal expression when the seasonal meteorological patterns inevitably shift in response to global climate change?

This question is a pressing one, since both the Mehri and Śḥerēt languages are oral languages indigenous to Southern Arabia and thus bear an intimate and inalienable relationship to the environmental milieu that shaped them. In the absence of a common experience with the *mdīt* wind amongst younger Mehri speakers, it remains to be seen how poets will articulate their inner turmoil to their audiences. Without the regular onshore *bōbet* wind, the ravines and canyons will lose their ability to carry the voices of Dhofari poets upwards and inland; the speaking landscape will fall silent at the same moment its poets do. While the authors of this chapter recognize that the consequences of climate change transcend the realm of human perception and experience, they hope to draw attention to the fact that climate change will necessarily alter the human repertoire of personal expression – a fact doubly true for those communities whose languages and orature remain in close, unmediated contact with their native terrain and environment.

Notes

1 This critique lies at the heart of Moneera al-Ghadeer's *Desert Voices*, a study of Bedouin women's poetry from the Arabian Peninsula: 'Scholars of modernity and critical theory seem to overlook popular poetic forms ... [accordingly], Bedouin poetry remains the focus of very few studies by anthropologists, folklorists and ethnographers' (al-Ghadeer 2009: 16). Al-Ghadeer provides a critical literary perspective on *nabaṭī* poetry and furthermore, restores women *nabaṭī* poets to the heart of the *nabaṭī* poetic tradition – an intervention that the authors of this chapter hope to build on.
2 The Śḥerēt language is also known as the Jibbāli language amongst native speakers. The Śḥerēt language has approximately 30,000–50,000 native speakers based primarily in Dhofar and elsewhere in Oman (Rubin 2014: 3). The Mehri language is primarily spoken in al-Mahrah in Yemen and Dhofar in Oman and has anywhere between 100,000 to 180,000 native speakers (Watson 2012: 1).
3 See Bauman (1975: 290–311).
4 Al-Ḥamādī (2016).
5 This is a reference to the *nabaṭī* poet al-Dindān, whose poetic persona is described as an 'assiduous climber of mountains' by Marcel Kurpershoek (Kurpershoek 1993: 41) in contrast with his actual, enfeebled physical condition. Although it may, at times, be understood literally, as Tabook does: 'A third way of composing a lyric is to go to the mountains, listen to the wind in the tress and meditate, whilst the others are anxiously waiting and composing poems so that they can be sung with the new lyric' (Tabook 1997: 241).

6   I have previously analysed the mountain-top ascent and *mdīt* formulas in Arabic vernacular (*nabaṭī*) and Mehri poetry from a structural standpoint, to wit, how the latter formula has displaced the former in southern Arabia (Liebhaber 2015).
7   The entire poem can be found here: http://whenmelodiesgather.supdigital.org/wmg/conventional-invocation (Liebhaber 2018).
8   Salim Tabook provides an excellent clarification of the *ōdī we-krēm krēm* introductory formula, suggesting that it serves as a call for God's attention rather than an explicit call for human intervention, which is the purview of the closely related '*sam'īn sam 'īn*' genre (Tabook 1997: 261).
9   While the groundbreaking work of James Monroe (1972) and Michael Zwettler (1978) uncovers elements of oral formulaicism in early Arabic poetry, their conclusions also highlight the manner in which the oral formulaicism of early Arabic poetry deviates from the lexical and phrasal oral formulaicism of Balkan and Homeric epic poetry as demonstrated by Milman Parry and Albert Lord, respectively. This is not to say that lexical and phrasal formulaicism does not exist in early and vernacular Arabic poetry; but rather, such formulaic utterances are restricted to introductory and transitional points in the poem. Instead, formulaic patterns in early and vernacular Arabic poetry more characteristically occur at the level of the motif, theme and topic.
10 The entire poem can be found here: http://whenmelodiesgather.supdigital.org/wmg/a-three-way-conflict (Liebhaber 2018).
11 The entire poem can be found here: http://whenmelodiesgather.supdigital.org/wmg/atop-the-peak-of-arbt (Liebhaber 2018).
12 This sense of poetic inspiration and release is personified in the imaginary persona of 'Ḥalīla', a female djinni 'who inspires the poetical imagination' (Rodionov 1996: 120) and a poetic muse who 'grants access to aesthetic brilliance, enabling poets to produce immediate, ad-hoc verses that may be eloquent, penetrating, and at times verbally dazzling' (Miller 2007: 297).
13 Tabook (1997: 241).
14 In addressing the *nānā* genre of poetry from Dhofar, it is no coincidence that Tabook lingers on poetry composed by women, giving particular attention to three famous female poets (Atslom Bint Slim ʿAfor, Bint ʿAbēdān and Auʿort) and dedicates a substantial portion of his chapter on poetry to their verses (Tabook 1997: 226–67).
15 Personal communication with al-Mashikhi, 14 June 2020. Bish Ḥaqf's definition of *ḥalīla* as the imaginary faculty intrinsic to a poet departs from the commonly found conception of 'Ḥalīla' in Arabic sources as a feminized power that stands outside of the poet, whom she visits at moments of poetic composition (Baziġ 2012).
16 al-Ghadeer (2009: 21–2).
17 Personal communication with al-Mashikhi, 14 June 2020.

References

Al-Ghadeer, M. (2009), *Desert Voices: Bedouin Women's Poetry in Saudi Arabia*, London: I.B. Tauris.

Al-Ḥamādī, H. (2016), 'Mūnsūn'... tajdab riyāh al-kaws lil-Dawḥa', al-ʾIttiḥād', 25 July. Available online: https://www.alittihad.ae/article/33948/2016/--تجذب--موسون رياح-الكوس-للدولة (accessed 22 August 2020).

Bauman, R. (1975), 'Verbal Art as Performance', *American Anthropologist*, 77 (2): 290–311.

Bazīġ, K. (2012), 'Shayāṭīn al-shiʿr', *Dīwān al-ʿArab*, 28 February. Available online: https://www.diwanalarab.com/شياطين-الشعر (accessed 22 August 2020).

Foley, J. (1992), 'Word-Power, Performance, and Tradition', *The Journal of American Folklore*, 105 (417): 275–301. Available online: https://www.jstor.org/stable/pdf/541757.pdf (accessed 22 August 2020).

Gorenflo, L. J. et al. (2012), 'Cooccurrence of Linguistic and Biological Diversity in Biodiversity Hotspots and High Biodiversity Wilderness Areas', *Proceedings of the National Academy of Sciences of the United States of America*, 109 (21): 8032–7. Available online: https://www.pnas.org/content/109/21/8032 (accessed 22 August 2020).

Heise, U. (2010), 'Afterword: Postcolonial Ecocriticism and the Question of Literature', in B. Roos and A. Hunt (eds), *Postcolonial Green: Environmental Politics and World Narratives*, 251–8, Charlottesville: University of Virginia Press. Available online: https://www.jstor.org/stable/j.ctt6wrkp7.18 (accessed 22 August 2020).

Kurpershoek, M. (1993), *Oral Poetry and Narratives from Central Arabia, Volume 1: The Poetry of ad-Dindān: A Bedouin Bard of the Southern Najd*, Leiden: E.J. Brill.

Liebhaber, S. (2018), *When Melodies Gather*, Redwood City: Stanford University Press. Available online: http://whenmelodiesgather.supdigital.org/wmg/index (accessed 22 August 2020).

Miller, F. (2007), *The Moral Resonance of Arab Media: Audiocassette Poetry and Culture in Yemen*, Cambridge: Harvard University Press.

Monroe, J. (1972), 'Oral Composition in Pre-Islamic Poetry', *Journal of Arabic Literature*, 3 (1): 1–53. Available online: https://www.jstor.org/stable/4182889?seq=1#metadata_info_tab_contents (accessed 22 August 2020).

Rodionov, M. (1996), 'Poetry and Power in Ḥaḍramawt', *New Arabian Studies*, 3: 118–33.

Rubin, A. (2014), *The Jibbali (Shaḥri) Language of Oman*, Leiden: E.J. Brill.

Tabook, S. (1997), 'Tribal Practices, and Folklore of Dhofar; Sultanate of Oman', PhD diss, University of Exeter.

Turner, A. and H. Annamalai (2012), 'Climate Change and the South Asian Summer Monsoon', *Nature Climate Change*, 2: 587–95. Available online: https://doi.org/10.1038/nclimate1495 (accessed 22 August 2020).

Watson, J. C. E. (2012), *The Structure of Mehri*, Leipzig: Harrassowitz Verlag.

Zwettler, M. (1978), *The Oral Tradition of Classical Arabic Poetry: Its Character and Implications*, Columbus: Ohio State University Press.

10

Climatic Disasters and Stories of Resilience in Southern and Northern Oman

Suad Al-Manji and Janet C.E. Watson

Oman has a climatic system marked by unpredictable, aperiodic, catastrophic events, such that local Omani communities are unable to have regular culturally engrained movements within the landscape to synchronize with the climate, in contrast to the way in which, for example, transhumance works. Instead, resilience is enhanced traditionally by telling stories of the catastrophic effects so that these effects become culturally engrained, thereby changing people's behaviour. Speaking through the voices of consultants from the Al-Ḥajar Mountains in northern Oman, and Dhofar in southern Oman, this chapter examines narratives to shed light on people's perceptions of particular events, nomenclature and metaphors used around such events, and acts of community resilience.

We begin by discussing our fieldwork. We then briefly describe Oman and our focal research regions. Through the voices of our community-member consultants, we consider instances of local resilience during climatic events that affected northern Oman and southern Oman, respectively. Here we include a brief discussion of the traditional role of climatic events in southern Oman for dating. We end the chapter with a transcribed, translated and annotated text in Mehri describing pastoralists searching for grazing land during the period of drought immediately preceding the cyclone of May 1959, and sheltering during the cyclone. In our conclusion, we suggest personal and historical narratives in a society in which storytelling is engrained and had the power to admonish

Thanks are due to the Leverhulme Trust for the project grant RPG-2012–599 awarded to Janet Watson during which time the Modern South Arabian material discussed in this chapter was collected. We are very grateful to Abdullah al-Mahri, Umm Abdullah and Saeed al-Mahri for discussing aspects of this chapter with us. We also thank our consultants for trusting us with their stories, and Miranda Morris for pertinent comments on an earlier version.

dangerous behaviour and promote resilient behaviour. The move, however, from a traditional society in which people communed with the natural environment to one marked by urbanization and reliance on digital technology means that future narratives will lack the potency and immediacy of those of the past.

Fieldwork

Fieldwork in Dhofar on the Modern South Arabian languages (MSAL), Mehri and Śḥerēt, was conducted by Watson in collaboration with Miranda Morris between 2013 and 2019, principally during a Leverhulme Trust-funded project on the Documentation and Ethnolinguistic Analysis of Modern South Arabian (DEAMSA). The project recorded and archived from the five mainland MSAL, Mehri, Śḥerēt, Ḥarsūsi, Hobyōt and Baṭḥari, some 200 hours of audio material and fifteen hours of audio-visual material relating to traditional cultural activities and the exploitation of traditional ecosystems in Dhofar in Oman and al-Mahrah in Yemen.[1] The digital material was collected primarily from men and women with no or little education born around or before the cyclone of May 1959. To maintain anonymity, consultants are given code names beginning with M for Mehri speakers and beginning with J for Śḥerēt speakers: thus, the first Mehri speaker to be recorded has the code name M001, and the first Śḥerēt speaker the code name J001. Audio material was collected either on an Olympus LS-11 digital recorder or on a Marantz PMD661 solid-state recorder with an external Audio-Technica microphone, and saved in WAV format at 44 kHz, 14-bit. Audio-visual material was collected on a Canon HDXA20 video recorder with an external Audio-Technica microphone and saved as either MOV or MTS files. The material can be accessed from Watson and Morris (2016a, 2016b).

Fieldwork in northern Oman in the Dākhiliyyah and the Sharqiyyah was conducted by Al-Manji and Watson in January 2020, where we interviewed men and women who had experienced, or had local knowledge of, particular climatic events. Code names for these consultants begin with the village name followed by the number of the consultant; thus, Sinaw01 is the first speaker to be recorded from Sināw and Ibra01 the first speaker to be recorded from Ibra. Audio recordings were collected in WAV format on an Olympus LS-11 digital recorder, and audio-visual recordings in MTS format on a Sony HDR-PJ410 Handycam.

Oman

The Sultanate of Oman is located in the south-eastern part of the Arabian Peninsula. Its shoreline extends from Hormuz in the north to the Republic of Yemen in the south. The total area of the Sultanate of Oman is approximately 309.5 thousand square kilometres, much of which is covered by a vast gravel desert plain, with a coastal plain and mountain ranges along the north (Al-Ḥajar Mountains) and to the south (Dhofar).

Climatological natural hazards have become a critical problem in arid and semi-arid areas (Hughes and Diaz 2008; Middleton and Sternberg 2013), causing a wide range of economic losses and social impacts (Almazroui et al. 2012; Middleton and Sternberg 2013; Ravi et al. 2010). With its dry climate and extreme temperatures (AlSarmi and Washington 2014), limited seasonal rainfall and a vast expanse of desert (Almazroui et al. 2012), Oman is susceptible to multiple climatic hazards (Middleton and Sternberg 2013), with cycles of droughts and cyclones. In this section, we present brief descriptions of the northern Al-Ḥajar Mountains and Dhofar, and then examine the general effects of drought and cyclones in Oman.

Northern Oman (Al-Ḥajar Mountains)

The Al-Ḥajar Mountains are located on the south-eastern edge of the Arabian Peninsula, extending along the Gulf of Oman in the form of a curved arc from Ra's Musandam in the north to Ra's al-Ḥadd in the east (Al-Ḥaṭrūshi 2014). The mountain range is approximately 800km long, and ranges in width from 30km in the northern and eastern extremities to 130km in the middle part averaging approximately 80km. The height of this series reaches approximately 3,000 metres in the Green Mountain (Al-Jabal al-Akhḍar). The mountain range is divided into the Western Al-Ḥajar Mountains and the Eastern Al-Ḥajar Mountains, which are separated by a natural passage, the Samā'il Pass (Al-Ḥaṭrūshi 2014). The climate is extremely hot in the summer season (from mid-April to October), with temperatures occasionally surpassing 50°C. At lower elevations, the humidity may be as high as 90 per cent. In the winter, the weather is mild, with the temperature ranging between 15°C and 23°C.

Inhabitants of the Al-Ḥajar mountain villages speak various dialects of Omani Arabic. They traditionally depended on agriculture and livestock. They grew different types of crops, with a focus on date palms. During severe weather, such as severe drought and storms, the dates, in particular, were heavily affected.

Southern Oman (Dhofar)

The southern province of Dhofar extends from Raʾs al-Šarbithāt on the coast of the Arabian Sea south-west of the Oman–Yemen border, dividing topographically into the coast and the coastal plain. The plain, which is approximately 64km long, and ranges in width from 1.5 to 9.5km; the mountains, from west to east are: Jabal Qamar, Jabal Al-Qarāʾ and Jabal Samḥān, which range in height from 1,500 to 2,000 metres (Al-Ḥaṭrūshi 2014); the central plateau; the gravel desert; and the sand desert. The main towns are situated along the coast, including Salalah, the provincial capital, Dhalkūt, Rakhyūt, Raysūt, Ṭāqah, Mirbāṭ and Ḥāsik. The large desert of stony plains and sand dunes to the north-east contributes to the isolation of the region from northern Oman. Dhofar differs significantly from northern Oman in enjoying a more temperate climate and four distinct seasons: the monsoon period between early June and early September during which time the sun is scarcely seen; the post-monsoon period from early September to late November; winter from early December to late February; and the hot period, from early March to early June.

Culturally, the inhabitants of Dhofar traditionally spoke one or more of the now-endangered MSAL; in order of number of speakers, these are: Mehri, Śḥerēt, Hobyōt or Baṭḥari. The MSAL are maintained in the region as oral languages today, although, through urbanization and education, Arabic plays an increasingly important role in the communities (Watson and al-Mahri 2017). The traditional lifestyle was one of fishing and commerce on the coast, pastoralists in the mountains and gravel desert (Ball, Macmillan et al. 2020), some rainfed agriculture in the mountains, focusing on cereals and legumes (Watson and Boom in press), cultivation of coconuts, bananas, guava, sugar-cane, papaya and Indian almonds along the coast, and frankincense harvest in eastern Dhofar, around Sadḥ, and in parts of the central plateau and gravel desert. The Mahrah, speakers of Mehri, were mainly nomadic pastoralists, although some settled on the coast. In the past, the people of the coast enjoyed a symbiotic relationship with those in the mountains, with fishers moving up to the mountains to work on seasonal agriculture during the monsoon period when the sea was 'closed' due to high monsoon winds, and mountain dwellers coming down to the coast to barter animal products, cereals and legumes in exchange for dried fish and imported goods such as rice, tea and sugar. Due to this symbiotic relationship, the people of Dhofar were traditionally multilingual; in regions where they are in close contact, it is still common, for example, for Mehri speakers to speak Mehri, and Śḥerēt speakers to respond in Śḥerēt and for both to understand the other adequately.

Climatic events

Drought

Rainfall in Oman is limited, tends to fall over small areas (Birks 1978), and is insufficient to support dryland cultivation (Speece 1981). Irrigation water is obtained primarily from shallow aquifers and from the flow of underground dry flow pathways. These water sources can be significantly affected by prolonged drought, a recurring feature of the arid climate. Large areas of the country lack water resources and, in the north, can only be obtained from the depths by traditional human-made water channels known as *falaj* (Speece 1981). During the drought period in 1974–5, about eight villages in Wādi al-Ḥawāsina in northern Oman were severely affected, with lack of rain causing drought and severe reduction in underground water (Birks 1978).

Drought has a variety of impacts in the arid and semi-arid areas, which can be categorized into meteorological, hydrological, economic and socio-economic (Spinoni, Vogt et al. 2019; Wilhite and Glantz 2009). In Oman, the impacts of drought waves have not been well documented; the documents that do exist include ones describing a severe drought at the end of the First World War, and a letter from Sultan Faisal bin Turki[2] to Sultan Ali bin Hamood, the Sultan of Zanzibar, mentioning a severe drought between 1903 and 1911.

In northern Oman, people suffered from mega-droughts several times during the course of the last century. Prolonged drought periods caused water demand stress in many villages in the Al-Ḥajar Mountains, having severe impacts on agriculture and livestock husbandry (Birks 1978), and leading many people to migrate in search of water (Barlow et al. 2015). With low water security, agriculturalists tried to keep their palm trees alive, because dates can be stored for a long time. In southern Oman, periods of severe drought affected pastoralists, who lost many of their camels, cattle and goats to starvation due to lack of pasture (see below).

Cyclones

The location of Oman in the Arabian Sea and the Indian Ocean puts the country at severe risk from tropical cyclones and storms (Byju and Kumar 2011; Evan and Camargo 2010; Membery 2001). The affected coastal areas run from Muscat in the north to the southern border with the Republic of Yemen, with exceptional cases extending to the coastal areas bordering the Sea of Oman. Cyclones are usually accompanied by high-speed winds, with high sea waves leading to severe flooding, which can cause significant loss of life and substantial damage to infrastructure. For example, in 2007, as a result of hurricane surges, cyclone Guno, which was recorded as the first cyclone to reach the fifth degree in the Arabian Sea in the past 100 years, caused nearly four billion dollars in losses and approximately 100 deaths. Guno was followed three years later by cyclone Phet, which also caused significant damage to the infrastructure.

The first record of a severe cyclone affecting northern Oman was that of 1890. This cyclone took an unusual path to the sea of Oman and then entered directly into the Western Al-Ḥajar Mountains. The storm caused extensive destruction and human loss of life, with the death of 727 people and the collapse of about fifty houses in Muscat alone. With heavy rains estimated at 285 millimetres, the cyclone of 1890 caused losses to the Omani economy estimated at nine million dollars. The floods swept away approximately 100,000 palm trees, particularly from Al-ʿĀmirāt, Samāʾil and villages scattered on the Al-Ḥajar Mountains in the Bāṭinah, leading to the collapse of the date industry, an essential economic resource at the time.

On 24 May 1959, a severe tropical cyclone passed through the coastal area south of the city of Salalah with winds of about 90 knots and heavy rains. The storm caused significant damage to infrastructure, as torrential rains washed away the road between Raysūt and Salalah. The high waves wrecked the ship, al-Samaḥa, which was returning from Zanzibar, drowning all 141 people on board, mostly women and children; another ship was sunk off the coast without any loss of life. At the end of this chapter, we provide a narrative in Mehri describing searching for pasture at the end of the drought period immediately before the tropical cyclone of May 1959. In more recent times, Makuno in 2017 was one of the most severe cyclones to hit southern Oman as the eye of the cyclone crossed the coast of Dhofar near the port of Raysūt. Makuno was classified as category three, with maximum wind speed while crossing estimated at 115 knots. It caused heavy rains recorded at 505 millimetres, resulting in severe flooding in Dhofar province, with significant damage to infrastructure and housing. Table 10.1 presents the most critical cyclones that affected Oman and the resulting social and economic losses from 1890 to 2018.

Table 10.1 Most Critical Cyclones, 1890–2018

Date	Disaster	No. killed	Damage	Cost (US $)
5 June 1890	Tropical cyclone	727	Palm trees, boats and houses collapsed	9 million
24 May 1959	Tropical cyclone	141	Two ships coming from Zanzibar sank in the Arabian Sea	NA
13 June 1977	Tropical cyclone	105	Buildings damaged in Masirah Island, including the military base	NA
10 August 1983	Tropical storm (Aurora)	NA	NA	NA
10 May 2002	Tropical storm	7	Hundreds of cattle drowned and several cars swept away	25 million
6 June 2007	Super cyclone (Guno)	50	Damage to 25,419 houses and over 13,000 vehicles	4.2 billion
3 June 2010	Tropical cyclone (Phet)	16	Roads and power lines damaged	780 million
2 November 2011	Tropical storm (Kyla)	14	Flash flooding caused damage to roads and buildings	80 million
31 October 2014	Cyclone (Nilofar)	4	Flash flooding caused damage to vehicles, roads and buildings	NA
12 June 2015	Cyclonic Storm (Ashobaa)	NA	Flash flooding caused damage to vehicles, roads and buildings	NA
25 May 2018	Cyclone (Mekunu)	7	Massive damages to infrastructure and buildings	1.5 billion in Oman and Yemen

Source: S. Al-Manji, *Planning for resilience to extreme weather events in Oman, 2000–2015* (PhD diss., 2018).

Stories around climatic events

In al-Manji and Watson (2019), we describe the role of cultural narratives in the resilience wheel approach to climatic hazards. This section introduces stories and anecdotes from northern and southern Oman around severe climatic events. Cultural narratives demonstrate the way in which people visualize the events, both in terms of the words and phrases used to name the events and the figurative language to describe their effects, and the way in which narrative content may promote particular behaviours to bolster social resilience. They also show how climatic disasters are situated in respect of well-known socio-political events.

Fieldwork and interviews conducted from the mountain villages of Sināw, Qafīfah and Tanūf in northern Oman, and in the gravel desert village of Rabkūt and in Salalah, the provincial capital in southern Oman, elicited narratives around loss, coping and recovery during periods of drought.

Northern Oman

All recordings from northern Oman were conducted in the local Arabic dialects. We interviewed a man in Qafīfah, Ibra, who talks about a long period of drought, locally known as *maḥall al-arbaʕat ʕašar* 'the Drought of Fourteen' and named as such due to the fourteen-year period of the drought. It occurred around ten years after the severe eleven-year drought of 1918–28.[3] The drought had a severe impact on water security, agriculture and livestock, and many villages in the Al-Ḥajar Mountains are described figuratively as having 'died' (*mōtan*). The 'death' of the villages caused three types of migration: internal, permanent external and temporary external. Thus, people in the affected villages either moved locally to other villages further up the mountains, or entire families emigrated on a semi-permanent basis to East Africa, in particular to Tanzania, Zanzibar and Kenya, or men emigrated individually on a temporary basis to, in particular, Bahrain, Saudi Arabia and Kuwait for work purposes.

The following stories describe the importance of conserving grain during drought periods, and the internal and external migration that resulted from the Drought of Fourteen. During that period, the people were described as being *ʕalā l-swād* 'in blackness'. The villages low down on the mountains were said to have *mōtan* 'died'. With few exceptions, dates for such events are not provided by our speakers; however, approximate dates can be ascertained through triangulation with co-occurring events mentioned: from the narratives, the

Climatic Disasters and Stories of Resilience in Southern and Northern Oman 221

Drought of Fourteen can be dated to around 1939 as Ibra01 says it occurred shortly before young people emigrated to Zanzibar, and Ibra03 says it coincided with his father migrating to the African coast, and on arrival learning that the Second World War had broken out.

We start with a story told by Ibra01, which describes grain conservation and internal migration during the Drought of Fourteen. Ibra01 is a member of the Manji tribe, aged around sixty-three. He was born in Qafifah, a village in Ibra province, used to work as an agriculturalist, and has basic literacy skills. The story he tells here was one he remembers hearing from his parents.

> *Ibra01:* One of the young people from our maternal uncles and our mothers' grandfathers say that they were in darkness, ʕala l-swād. They used to call it *maḥall al-arbaʕat ʕašar* 'the Drought of Fourteen'. It was just before the young people emigrated to Zanzibar.[4]
>
> *Ibra01:* At that time there were very few seeds, because of the severe drought, and they saved a bag of wheat seeds in the stored straw walling. They stored it there for about fourteen years. After fourteen years, they ploughed the land in Al-Jaḥlah. They used bulls to plough land in Al-Khubb (a place in the village). And then after fourteen years they saw a small cloud in the sky. A man told his son to take the bull and the ploughing materials.[5] During the night it started raining, and the whole area was swept by rain and floods. They removed the sack of wheat from the storehouse and sowed it, and it became fertile from those days of rain.
>
> *SM:* How did people describe that rain? Was there severe wind?
>
> *Ibra01:* There was lightning and wind. A thunderstorm hit the villages. The villages Qafifah and Al-Khadid were covered in dust and muck.
>
> *SM:* After fourteen years.
>
> *Ibra01:* After fourteen years it began to rain a little, just enough to make the weather a little cooler.
>
> *SM:* Did anyone come to the village during that time?
>
> *Ibra01:* Yes, a group of mountain pastoralists[6] came from other villages that had completely dried out at that time, because the villages higher up in the mountains are better.

The water remains there for some time, unlike the villages further down. All those villages had 'died' at that time. This is as much as the old people told us. The Bedouin all came to Qafifah and helped in the harvest in exchange for some dates.[7]

> *SM:* Ok, the people at that time of severe drought, what did they have to eat when there was so little food?

Ibra01: They ate dates and bread, but no rice at that time.
SM: But there was no flour, no wheat, so how did they make bread?
Ibra01: There wasn't much bread at all. There weren't many people either, most of them had emigrated to Zanzibar and Bahrain. They left Oman and only a very few people stayed.

Story 2: Water management

From Story 1, we see that dates were of vital importance to survival in the Al-Ḥajar Mountains. In Story 2, Ibra02 describes how people conserved water to focus on preserving some of the date palms. Ibra02 is a member of the Manji tribe, aged over ninety, and had no formal education. He was born in Qafīfah and never moved out of the village. He worked as an agriculturalist and, despite his age, has a prodigious memory. The stories he told were from his own personal experience.

SM: What kind of crops you were growing at that time.
Ibra02: We grew everything ... dates, garlic, onion, wheat and lemons.
SM: And when the long drought happened, how were you able to irrigate the crops?
Ibra02: The water was limited. We tried to collect water in the *falaj* canals, in small areas known as *ḥuwayrāt* within the canals, and then we used the water to irrigate two or three palms. Other crops died because there was no water to irrigate the land.

Story 3: Food conservation

Ibra03 is a member of the Manji tribe. He was born in 1948 in Tanzania to first-generation immigrant parents, and came to settle in Oman in 1971. While in Tanzania, he worked in the rice fields. In Oman, he worked in the Air Force for about thirty-seven years. Bilingual in Arabic and Swahili, he is also fluent in English, and received his MA in logistics management from the University of Cardiff in 2002.

Ibra03 describes the need to conserve grain during the Drought of Fourteen. He also describes the affected farms as having all but 'died' due to the drought. The narrator says the event happened at the time his father migrated to the African coast, and on arrival he heard about the Second World War.

Ibra03: I remember my father telling me: It was a very long drought season, and our farms 'died' except for a few palms. A man from the village took a bunch of wheat grain and stored it inside the wall. He saved the wheat for the rainy season because they would need the grain to build up the farms again. Without grain, they would not be able to survive even during the rainy season.[8] When it started raining a few years later, he asked his son to dig the wall to bring out the grain. His wife became very angry because he had allowed them to suffer from hunger, although wheat was available. He told her that this wheat would not have been enough to stop their hunger for a long time, but it would be essential to cultivate the fields again.

SM: When did this happen?

Ibra03: It was after my father migrated to the African coast, and when he reached there, they heard about World War II.

Story 4: Livestock

As well as the direct effect of the drought on the water and food supply, the drought decimated the livestock of the mountain pastoralists due to lack of grazing and drought-related diseases. In Tanūf, a village in Nizwa province, we interviewed an old woman who recalled the drought. Tanuf02 is a member of the Jāmūdiyyah tribe, aged around eighty-one, and received no formal education. She was born in Bahla, and on marrying her first husband moved to Tanūf. During her working life, she was a goat-herding pastoralist:

Tanuf02: During that severe drought, I was a strong woman at the time. We came down from the mountains to the village in Tanūf because it was extremely dry and there was no water for our goats. When we arrived at Tanūf our goats became sick, and they got goat pox. I lost about 100 goats, and had only ten left.

Southern Oman

In southern Oman, the main periods of drought in the twentieth century are known locally as *ʕuyun ɛ-xēt* 'the Years of Paucity', *ʕōnut ɛ-ḳaṣrɛri* 'the Year of Dried Stalks' (~1905), *ʕōnut ɛ-ḳamro* 'the Year of the People of Jabal Qamar' (~1951), *snay ḏ-əḳahəṭ* 'the Years of Drought' (1947–8) and *ʕōnut ɛ-ḥśerēt* 'the Year of Destruction' (1958–9). The first three and fifth terms are in Śḥerēt, as these events particularly affected Śḥerēt-speaking regions in the western mountains. *snay ḏ-əḳahəṭ* 'the years of drought' is given here in Mehri, and affected the entire region of Dhofar. Nomenclature for climatic events was derived either according to the people affected: ʕōnut ɛ-ḳamro 'the year of the people of Jabal Qamar', which refers to the year in which drought and famine caused the people of Jabal Qamar in western Dhofar to migrate in search of food; or to the effect of the event. These latter include: ʕuyun ɛ-xēt 'the Years of Paucity', a period when the monsoon rains failed; ʕōnut ɛ-ḳaṣrɛri 'the Year of Dried Stalks', the year there was so little moisture that strange dried stalks emerged, and on the fall of the post-monsoon rains previously unknown plants appeared; and ʕōnut ɛ-ḥśerēt 'the Year of Annihilation', when much of the mountain livestock died, in particular the cows, so valued in Dhofar. J004, a cattle herder in his late 30s from the Shahri tribe and brought up in Ḥalḳot, a village in the central mountain region, described so many cows dying during ʕōnut ɛ-ḥśerēt that cattle herders bought up more and more goats, as they required less water. Once the rains and pasture returned, they replenished their cattle herds. M001, a member of the Bit Ikḥor subtribe of Bit Thuwār born in 1993 and brought up in Rabkūt,[9] tells of Wabr, a Mehri man who was believed to have lived until he was 140. M001 says Wabr described significant numbers of people and camels dying of starvation during snay ḏ-əḳaḥəṭ 'the Years of Drought'. So little pasture was said to be available that pastoralists set tree trunks on fire to provide charcoal as fodder for the camels, and when the camels were milked the milk came out black. Such stark images remain engrained in popular memory.

Cyclones, storms and floods

Cyclones, storms and floods frequently follow long periods of drought, and have caused significant socio-economic damage in both northern and southern Oman. As mentioned above, the first tropical cyclone recorded to have hit Oman occurred in 1890, causing massive damage in northern Oman in the social and economic sectors, killing about 727 people, and sweeping away approximately 100,000 palm trees (Membery 2001). This did severe damage to the date trade in the late-nineteenth century, and had deep-reaching social impacts: due to the large number of Omani deaths and consequent drop in the labour force, the slave trade increased significantly to provide sufficient labour to work the date palms (Hooper 2016).

The main floods and cyclones recalled by our consultants in the Al-Ḥajar Mountains are: *jarfat bašārah* 'the sweeping away of Bashārah' (1979), *jarfat al-muġāyirah* (1957), also known as *jarfat al-sabʕīn* 'the Flood of the Seventies', and *jarfat barġūš* 'the sweeping away of Barġūš'. Nomenclature around the floods and cyclones refers either to the time of the event, as in *jarfat al-sabʕīn* 'the Flood of the Seventies', known as such because it occurred in 1377 AH, i.e. during the seventies of the Hijri year, or the people affected: Bašārah was a woman from the village of Qafīfah who was swept away during the flood known as *jarfat bašārah*; *al-muġāyirah* refers to the tribe most affected by *jarfat al-muġāyirah*; and Barġūš was a pastoralist from Qafīfah who lost around 100 of his goats when they were swept away during the floods of *jarfat barġūš*.

Stories from northern Oman

The stories given below from northern Oman are translated from the Arabic originals. Sinaw02 is a member of the Maḥrūqi tribe and was born in Sināw in 1363 AH, making him around seventy-one. Sinaw02 worked as an agriculturalist, and has basic literacy skills. He moved to Zanzibar for around two years, after which time he returned to Oman. In the story below, he describes the floods associated with *jarfat al-sabʕīn* 'the Flood of the Seventies' also known as *jarfat al-muġāyirah*. The narrative serves as a warning both not to build near the wadis or camp in the wadi basin, and to listen to local advice.

> *Sinaw02:* It was in the night when the rain started in Sināw and the surrounding villages. The rain was in different places and caused severe flash floods from Wādi ʕAndām to Sināw. In an arid area when a severe storm occurs, it can cause a disastrous flood, so that's why we no longer build our houses near to the wadis. What happened is that there was a group of Bedouin who came to Sināw for the date season. They erected their tents in the wadi. They didn't expect a flood to come at that time. Some locals from Sināw told them it was dangerous, and that they should move out of there, but they did not listen. During the night, a massive flood reached them and about half of the people died. It was a real tragedy. People in the villages know about the risk of living near flood areas, and you will find that most old villages were built in places far away from the Wadi.

In around 1955 CE, another extreme event happened in Sināw, known locally as *sanat al-maḥṣi* 'the Year of Hail'. Sinaw02 tells this story, which is also confirmed by another male consultant, Sinaw03.

> *Sinaw02:* It was the afternoon when it started to become darker because of the clouds. The rain started in the village with extreme rain and hail. I never saw hail like that again. There was a huge amount of hail, and it caused damage to the two *falaj* in Sināw, Falaj al-Muštaq and Falaj Bū-Manīn. When the rain and hail stopped, the locals went to check the damage to their palm trees and the *falajs*.

The hail was 3 metres high in the *falaj* canals. The people had to work for several days to clear the *falaj* canals.

The Year of Hail caused significant agricultural damage, due to not only the hail but also the winds. Sinaw02 said: 'Many people lost their palm trees because of the severe wind, but no one died because of this storm, and there was no damage to the houses.'[10]

Sinaw03 is a member of the Ṣawāfi tribe. He was born in 1363 AH, making his age around eighty-one. He is well educated, working as a history teacher in the 1970s and in the municipality for a few years after that. Through travel with his work in the municipality, he witnessed the effect of the drought in the eastern Al-Ḥajar Mountains.

> *Sinaw03:* The hail hit Sināw during the days of Mohammed bin Abdullah Al-Khalili,[11] and it was also called *al-xarsah*[12] because many people were affected. It happened in the summer and the palm farms were affected and the dates were affected. This was in the summer, and there were Bedouins living in huts. But thanks be to God, there were no deaths, although the people were affected. That was in 1363 AH. I was born two years earlier. I was born in 1361 AH. The falaj was washed away, the hard, packed ground (known locally as *ṣilāfah*) where the *falaj* walls were built collapsed. The *falaj* here is open to the wadi.[13] The roofs of the *falaj* collapsed, and the community members worked hard to repair it. Six people from our village were killed during the repair of the *falaj*.
>
> *SM:* What was the name of the *falaj*?
>
> *Sinaw03:* Falaj al-Mišuq. Six people died in it, mainly young men, one middle-aged, and one at the beginning of a youthful life. That happened in the year 63 AH.

Stories from southern Oman

Until the 1970s in Dhofar, southern Oman, calendrical dates were rarely used to indicate events such as birth, death, marriage and stages of life (Watson and al-Mahri 2017; Boom, Wilson and Watson 2020). Dhofar lay very much at the socio-political periphery, and it was not until the 1980s, for example, that official birth certificates were commonly issued. For people who maintained a nomadic life, the issuance of birth certificates came later still. Instead, people would refer to their birth in relation to a particular climatic event. This meant that lifetime events were not referred to linguistically through the use of numerals, but rather through naming. In response to a question about a person's date of birth, death or marriage, we are often told the person in question born at the time of, for example, 'the Year of Alḥaymar', in Mehri snēt ḏ-əlḥaymər, in Śḥerēt śɔ̄nut əlḥīmər (1947). Another will say they were old enough to stand on one leg and balance a milk bowl on their thigh to milk a camel at the time of 'the Year of Drowning', in Mehri snēt ḏ-əġarḳayyət, in Śḥerēt śɔ̄nut ɛ-ġarḳɛ̄t (1959).

The main floods and cyclones recalled by our consultants in Dhofar are: snēt ḏ-əlḥaymər 'the Year of Alḥaymar' (1947), snēt ḏ-əġarḳayyət 'the Year of Drowning' or snēt ḏə-ḥmaymət 'the Year of Ḥumaymat' (1959), and snēt ḏ-əbit fərgīś 'the Year of the Fərgīś family' (1975), with names provided here in Mehri.

Cyclonic events were named either according to the aftereffects of the event: snēt ḏ-əġarḳayyət 'the Year of Drowning', the year when two ships capsized off the coast of Dhofar and all but three people drowned; or after the person or people affected: snēt ḏə-bit fərgīś 'the Year of the Fərgīś Family' is named after the family of Shayl bər Fərgīś al-Mašaykhi, who almost all drowned during the floods of that year; or, as certain stars are traditionally associated with particular weather patterns,[14] according to the star at the time of the cyclone, as in: snēt ḏ-əlḥaymər 'the Year of Alḥaymar', snēt ḏə-ḥmaymət 'the Year of Ḥumaymat', snēt ḏə-ḥḥəmyēmɔ̄t 'the Year of Small Ḥumaymat' (in reference to an event that had less magnitude than that in snēt ḏə-ḥmaymət).

The Year of Alḥaymar is known as such due to the heavy rains and floods that occurred during the c. thirteen-day period of the Alḥaymar star in the late the post-monsoon period (late October) in Dhofar. Rains associated with the əlḥaymər star are known to be strong and accompanied by rainstorms, especially in comparison with rains associated with the pre-monsoon stars: dɔ̄ṭa at the onset of the hot period (March), and ḥmaymət at the end of the hot period (May) (see 20130306_ShehretCJ_J004_non-xorfstars in Watson and Morris 2016b). Names of affected individuals further help communities to remember events: the floods of the Year of Alḥaymar are etched in popular memory through Sēnyaḥ, a strong cattle herder from the Maʿšani tribe in the eastern part of Dhofar, who, according to J004, M001 and his mother, M010, died due to the strength of rain and wind while pushing his cows towards shelter.[15]

The story associated with snēt ḏə-bit fərgīś 'the Year of the Fərgīś Family', which according to several Mehri consultants occurred around four to five years after Sultan Qaboos bin Said Al Said overthrew his father in 1970, warns of the unpredictability of flash floods; like Story 2 by Sinaw02 above, it also warns against camping in the wadi basin at any time. The story was told by M010, a monolingual Mehri speaker from the Bit Blēḥ subtribe of Bit Thuwār, who was brought up around Wādi Nṣawr and lived as a nomadic pastoralist before settling in Rabkūt in the early 1990s. In conversation with her son, M001, she describes the story as follows (translated from the Mehri original):

> Shayl bər Fərgīś al-Mašaykhi's two wives each had around fourteen children, and some of his children already had their own children. The family went to Wādi Ṣālaffan near the wadi village of Dhahbūn on their way to the mountain village of Gabgabat. They all camped in the bottom of the wadi apart from two of the man's daughters and two of his sons and their goats. The two daughters and two sons found no place in the wadi, so they went up above the wadi to camp. They saw the clouds of the monsoon rains. At night the flood came. When they awoke, they did not realise there had been a flash flood because they had felt no rain. All the tents and the people and livestock had been swept away. They went and shouted for help. People rushed to help from Gabgabat and other places. They found the body of the man, Shayl bər Fərgīś, and his books with his debts written in. Then they found a woman and then a boy, and then someone else, and they buried them all.

A personal narrative

The following personal narrative describes a group of Mehri nomadic pastoralists moving in search of pasture at the end of a dry period, and sheltering during the subsequent floods associated with the cyclone of May 1959. The speaker, now living in the village of Rabkūt, is a member of the Bit Iḵhōr subtribe of Bit Thuwār and a monolingual speaker of Mehri, and had no formal education. At the time of the event he was a young adult pastoralist. He was interviewed by Janet Watson in Mehri in Rabkūt in October 2013. The full text, transcription and translation can be accessed by entering in the search box of the ELAR Mehri archive (Watson and Morris 2016a) the file name: 20131018_MehriRabkut_M018_headingforwaterstory.

We provide the text in its near-complete form as it demonstrates a depth of recall in place names, and expertise in anticipating rains and what pasture they will bring up, knowledge of winds and sources of water. One of the messages of this narrative is that people should trust the advice of those who are more knowledgeable than them about rains and pasture. Significantly, the only numbers used in the narration are for 'one' and 'two': for the one goat that fell ill, the one camel that kicked a goat and confirmation that two boats capsized during the cyclone.

> M018: *xaṭrāt / xaṭrāt / xaṭrāt nhah bə-śhayr / ḥāl bāti ḏiddūr / əkā ḏakməh həmməh ḏiddūr / hamaś / wə-śərḥawm u-mṣā nagd / śərḥawm / bāti ftaxayt*

/ hamaš / wə-šīn bēr / wə-tōli āmūrən nəḥōm nənśah / nəḥōm nənśah / bēr
wə-rawn / wə-nōśən / wə-ḵīṯōy /
Once, once, one time we were in the mountains. In the region of
Dhiddūr. That place is called Dhiddūr. Do you hear? And downstream they
had had rains in the Najd. They had had rains in the region of Ftakhayt. Are
you listening? And we had camels. Then we said we want to head for water.
We want to head for water with the camels and goats. So we set off. And it
was during the hot period.

JCEW: ḥād fnōhən yəṭawf / ḥād fnōhən yəṭawf /
Did someone scout beforehand? Did someone scout?

M018: yəṭawf / lā / fnōhən haman āmūr ḏ-ərhəmēt əgidət / wə-ṭōfən lā / wə-
nūśən iftaxayt u-mṣa? / iftaxayt / wə-həlḥōḵən həbēr / həlḥōḵən / ahā māna
ḏə-nḥōm nənśah / həlḥōḵən / həlḥōḵən mən ḥalakməh həbrōkən / wə-
nakam bīsən śśōḏəb tā həbrōkən əśāmər ḏə-ḏkūr / wə-mən ḥalakməh gihmā
həbrōkən / b-ūṭawm / ḥəwōdi / ḥəwōdi ṭwaylət ūṭawm / wə-kənḥən bə-ṭəra:fs
ət-tā gihma həbrōkən hāl əbərāṣāṣ / boh hāl əbərāṣāṣ /
No-one scouted. We first heard they said the rain was good, so we didn't
scout. We headed downstream towards Ftxayt, Ftxayt. And we followed
with the camels. We followed. Yes, that means we meant to seek pasture.
We followed, we followed from there then we couched the camels. We took
them to Slōdhab then couched them at the end of Dhukūr wadi. Then the
next day, we couched by Uṭawm, the wadi, Uṭawm is a long wadi. Then we
headed back on ourselves by the side of it until we camped at Abarāṣāṣ, here
by Abarāṣāṣ.

M018: wə-tā wišlən ərhəmēt / kūsan ərhəmēt əl-sēh mēkən lā / ərhəmēt / əl-sēh
gidət lā / xawr mtwē wə-ḥəmoh xawr / wə-ḥābū ḵīṯōy / ḥarḵ / šīn sīyəryōt śī
lā / śī sīyəryōt lā / wə-śxūlōlən ḥalakməh / ūḵōn sbūʕ / kūsan rḥāmāyən xawr
/ məḥṣāt / tġayrəb məḥṣāt / məḥṣāt bərk əbaṭḥ / ḥmoh bərk əbaṭḥ /
Until we reached where it had rained, and we found it had not rained
much. The pasture wasn't good, there was only a little pasture and only
a little water. And it was the hot season. It was very hot, and we had no
vehicles. There weren't any cars. So we stayed there around a week. We
found a little water, a waterscrape. Do you know what a waterscrape is?
A waterscrape in the soft ground. Water in the soft ground.

M018: yḥaṣyəm tēs / nhayṣəs / wə-ḥmoh bərk əbaṭḥ wə-yəmṣawś yəmṣawś ār
mən əbaṭḥ aʕīnat aʕīnat / ūḵōn sbūʕ / wə-təmm ḥəmoh / āmūr nəḥōm nkəlēb
/ aġawf / mānat nərdēd hōbah nʔawmər nḥah nkəlēb əkā? / aġawf / ahā /
mən ḥalakmah / raddən / bərk ḥawōdi / bərk ḥawōdi ḏikm ūṭawm / hamak
/ nḥah / ār ḏə-rikbən ṯār həbēr / ḏə-rikbən ṯār həbēr / wə-šīn ḥārawn mən
sərīn / šīsən ḥaynēṯ / hamak / wə-šīsən ḥōz ṭayt / əḏ-gəlwō:t /

They scrape it out, we scrape it out. And water is in the ground and it seeps in, it seeps in from the ground little by little, for around a week. Then the water finished. We said we should go up, we should go back up, and from there we went back up the wadi, in that wadi, Uṭawm. Do you hear? We rode on camels. We rode the camels and the goats were behind us with the women. Do you hear? We had one goat that fell ill.

M018: *gəlwōt ād midri mən hēśən / wə-ḥārawn barsən fənwīn / wə-hīs bə-ḥallay kūsan ḥōz ḥalakməh ḏə-rdoh bīs / mtōt ḥōz / wə-lḥākən ḥārawn wə-hbēr tgaryən bə-ḥārawn groh həbēr / wə-gū[rən] həbūrən / tā bə-ḥawōdi ḏikməh / əlḥak həbrōkən / həbrōkən /*

She fell ill, I don't know with what. The goats were in front of us. At night we found the goat there that had been thrown away. The goat had died. And we caught up with the goats and went in front of them with the camels in front of the goats. The camels were in front. And we crossed that wadi and couched upstream. We couched the camels.

M018: *bə-ġārīt / bə-ġārīt / ḳiṯōy śī ḥəbūr lā / həbrōkən tā::: k-sōbəḥ / wə-gəhma həlḥōkən lḥak / həbrōkən bə-ḥawōdi mśəġrēt / (y)ʔamrəm hīs ṣālaffən / ṣālaffən / hamak / wə-t-tā həbrōkən ḥalakməh tā k-ṣōbəḥ / gəhma hūrōdən ḥəmoh ḏkūr / yʔamrəm hīs ḏkūr /*

In the open, in the open. It was the hot season, so there wasn't any cold. We stayed there until the morning and the next day we went upstream. We spent the night in the next wadi, that they call Ṣālaffan. Ṣālaffan, do you hear? And we stayed there until the morning. The next day we watered by Dhukūr. They call it Dhukūr.

JCEW: *hūrədkəm mən ḥə̃h / hūrədkəm mən məḥlōk aw hūrədkəm ... /*

Where did you water? Did you water from rock pools or from ... ?

M018: *lā lā ḥəmoh ḥəmoh əgūt / wə-mət nūka mūsē / ykūn bīs ḥəmoh sēt / tmōna krayb əl-snēt wal ār xass / tmōna ḥəmoh / əgūt hənōb / əl-sēh ḥəmoh awd lā / ār ḥəmoh ār aywah ār mwakkatəh / ār mʔakkət /*

No, no, from a water hole. When the rain comes the water stays a long time. It remains for almost a year or a bit less. It holds the water. A large water hole, it's not permanent water, just water that comes temporarily, just temporarily.

M018: *wə-hūrōdən mən ḥlakməh / śbūbən wə-lḥakayn ḥārawn / wərūd / ḏə-bāti ḥārawn / hīs barən bark ənēḥar ḏakm aġawf / ḥārawn bār ṣdūr / həlḥawk ḥārawnən / wə-nḥah ḏə-gāyən / əbēli ḥaybīt ṭayt tdəfdūf ḥōz / adəfdəfats bə-ḥayd ūṭoh /*

And we watered from there. We went up and the goats caught up with us. The goats drank. When we got above that smaller wadi branch, the goats had come up from drinking. We caught up with our goats. We were hungry, and through God one of the camels kicked a goat with its forelegs. It kicked it with its foreleg like that.

M018: *wə-shāṭən / mtōt wə-shāṭən / w-allah ḏə-hōh aṣədḵi / [laughter] / wə-shāṭən / w-ātaśyən tēs / hamaś / wə-ttā ḥaḵ həbrōkən / w-ūxāfən / wə-tā wṣalnā / gəhma / ḥaṣawfən aġawf tā / boh hāl / šāh rkəfōf yʔamrəm hēh / aġawf / bə-śhayr / hamak / kūsan / əḵā bih mtwē fōna / bih mtwē / mtwē ḏə-hawrət / tġayrəb əhhawrət / ahā hawrət aw rhəmēt nḥah nʔōmər hawrət /*

We slaughtered. It died and we slaughtered. By God, I'm telling the truth! We slaughtered and ate it for supper. Do you hear? We camped upstream and spent the night. The next day we went up to Shāh Rkəfōf they call it. Up in the mountains, do you hear? We found land that had grazing from before. Dried up grazing. *hawrət* grazing. Do you understand *hawrət*? Yes, either dried out grazing or fresh rains grazing. We say *hawrət*.[16]

M018: *ahā / əhhawrət / hām śī mūsē nūka lā / mətwē ḏə-hhawrət / ahā / wə-həbrōkən āṣər āṣəri ṭroh / w-ūḵōt ərhəmēt xōṭər / xōṭər / xōṭər mən hāl əśhayr xōṭər /*

Yes, pasture that remains when there is no rain. Pasture after a period of no rain, yes. We camped for one or two nights, and rain had fallen down below. Below. Below the *śhayr* mountains.

JCEW: *rēḥaḵ / aw ḵərayb /*

[Did it come from] far away or nearby.

M018: *xwēṭār rēḥaḵ lā / aywah / hām / āmūr nhōm nhakfd h-ərhəmēt / āmərk hōh ərhəmēt ḏīməh / bīs mtwē xaybət / wə-bawməh kūsan mtwē nhōm nśxawwəl bawməh / āmūr lā nhōm ār ərhəmēt / šāmīni lā hōh /*

A little way down, not far. Yes. They said we want to go down to the rain. I said that rain won't bring much pasture, and here we've found pasture, so we should stay here. They said, no, we want to go towards the rain. They wouldn't listen to me.

M018: *həḵfōdən tā rhəm[ēt] tā yaxah ərhəmēt / kūsan / hīs / hərūm ʕaśś / āmūr uṭīyōməh / barh ḏ-inḵərṣawm / ənḵərṣawm ūṭōməh ḵayśa ḵrayb / mətwē śī lā / wə-hbēr kənhūr fəġśaytən wə-śxūlōlən ḥalakməh l-ād bīsən / śxōf śī lā / ham[ak] w-ūbūdən xass / wə-śxūlōlən / hīs barsən həbēr / l-ād bīsən əśxōf lā w-ūbūdən xass / ṣabbən aġawf / raddən ū-boh aġawf / aġawf əḵāṭən /*

We moved down towards where the rain had fallen, and we found that when the plants had come up, they had come up shrivelled and almost dry, like that. There was no proper pasture, and while the camels had plenty of milk we stayed there as long as they still had some. Then there was no more milk, do you hear? And things got worse for us. We stayed there as the camels no longer had any milk and we did poorly. We went back up. We went back there up to the Qāṭan plateau.

M018: *ḏōməh / ḏōmə nʔōmər hēh nḥah ḳāṭən / wə-xōṭər / əśḥayr / wə-mən əḵāṭən ū-boh / ənagd / ahā wə-hēh ḳāṭən ḏōm / hamaš / u-mən ḥalakməh śxūlōlən / śxūlōlən ṭoh wə-btadyən agawf axayr / śxūlōlən śxūlōlən / wə-ḥmoh xawr / ḥəmoh xawr / hīs əmtəlēn / wə-nəhrūd ār rēḥaḵ ūṭoh /*

This, this we call the Qāṭan [the central plateau]. And further down are the mountains and from the Qāṭan that way is the Najd desert. Yes, and that is the Qāṭan. Do you hear? And then we stayed put. We stayed there and did better higher up. We stayed and stayed. There wasn't much water, and we ended up having to go a long way for water.

M018: *hāl əgəbgabət mənṣāwən / ḥəmoh yʔamrəm hēh / əməḥāzīr / əməḥāzīr / ahā / nəhrūd ḥalakməh / wə-nāṣadrən agawf / hōba śḥayr [sic] əḵāṭən / hīs barən / ṭār waḵt / nkōt ərīyēḥ / ərīyēḥ tgərb ərīyēḥ /*

Downstream from Gabgabat was water. They call it Maḥāzīr, Maḥāzīr, yes. We watered from there and then went back up towards the Qāṭan. After a while winds came. Do you know the word *rīyēḥ*?

M018: *xərūb / hēh wə-hzēz mən bawməh / nʔōmər hēh rīyēḥ / xərūb / wə-hēh wə-nūka mən śḥayr nʔōmər hēh mdīt / wə-mən nagd əbəlēt / ḥall ḏə-śētū əbəlēt / wə-ḥall ḏ-aṣayrəb arīyēḥ / ərīyēḥ ykūn ḥarḵ wīyən lā /*

Hot desert winds, *xərūb*. When it is wind from here, we call it *rīyēḥ*, *xərūb*, and when it comes from the mountains, we call it *mdīt*. And the *bəlēt* winter wind is from the Najd. In the winter, there is the cold winter wind, and in the post-monsoon season the *rīyēḥ*. This wind isn't very hot.

M018: *ah / ḥall əś-śētū bəlēt wə-məṭṭawr tkūn ḥəbūr ḳāṣəm əbəlēt / wə-śxūlōlən ḥalakməh / tōli nūka rīyēḥ ḏakməh rīyēḥ ḏakməh śafḥ mənwōt / hamak / wə-nūka rīyēḥ ḏakm hamak u-mən ṭār nhōri ṯrayt nūka āṣf / mənwōt / ū-bīs āṣf / həzayz ū-mūsē /*

The winter wind [known as *bəlēt*] comes in the winter, and sometimes it is very cold, the winter wind. And we stayed there, then that *rīyēḥ* wind came, that wind, and it turned out to herald rain. Are you listening? And that wind came, do you hear, and two days later a storm came. Wind and rain.

M018: *mūsē ḳway / hamak wə-nḥah / wə-nḥah wə-hbēr bərk ṣayga? / knōnən bərk ṣayga / knōnən / nʔōmar knōnən / knōnən bərk aṣayga ḏakməh / wə-t-tā:: nkōt əmūsē / ṯalāṯ īyām / śīləṯ yōm /*

Really strong rain. Are you listening? And we were with the camels in a cave. We sheltered in a cave. We sheltered. We say *knōnən* 'we sheltered'. We took shelter in that cave while the rain came. Three days. Three days!

JCEW: *wə-śīləṯ yōm w-atēm bərk aṣayga /*

And for three days you were in the cave.

M018: *wə-nḥah bərk əṣayga / mūsē mēkən / nʔōmər hīs / yʔamrəm hīs ḏhīb / yʔamrəm hīs ḥābū snē(t) ḏ-əġərḵayyət /*
We were in the cave. There was lots of rain. We call it ... We call it floods. People call it [that time] the Year of Drowning.

M018: *ġərḵəm / bərk sənbūḵi ṯrayt / ġərḵəm / əlyakm kall /*
They drowned. In two ships. They drowned. They all [drowned].

JCEW: *ḏīməh sēh snēt ḏ-əġərḵayyət /*
And that was the Year of Drowning.

M018: *ḏ-əġarḵayyə / əġərḵayyət / wə-ḥābū əlyakməh kall ġərḵəm wə-mōtəm / w-əlyakməh əbwāxər ġayrəḵ / ṯrayt / ahh / śīnəš həzayz ḏakm əḵway / yəṯūbər hərmayt / āṣf / yəṯūbər hərmayt ətyēḵ w-əryēś tġərəbhəm ətyēḵ w-əġyēṣ́ /*
Of Drowning. And those people all drowned and died. And those ships were wrecked. Two. Yes, do you see that strong wind? It destroys large trees with the storm. It brings down large trees such as *Ficus vasta* and *Ficus sycamorus* (Miller and Morris 1988: 345). Do you know *Ficus vasta* and *Ficus sycamorus*?

M018: *əlyōmah tkūn bə-śhayr / yənōka həzayz yṯūbər əlyakməh / əgənzēf ḏə-l-hīs ūṯōməh yəfrərsən ūḵōna tā sār ḏēk / ahh / wə-mġōrən wīḵa / ʕəśś amaray / wīḵa xayr wə-faġś /*
Those are in the mountains. The wind came and tore them down. The trunks that were like that [gestures their large size] it sent them flying like that and piled them one on top of the other. And then the pasture sprang up and there was goodness and good pasture.

JCEW: *wə-bād śīləṯ yōm ftəkkəm mən əṣayga /*
And after three days you came out of the cave.

M018: *ahā / ftūkən mən əṣayga bād śīləṯ yōm / wə-śxūlōlən / b-əḵāṯən ḏakm ū-boh / hāl ḏiddūr m-boh / bə-ḵāṯən / śxūlō:::lən / w-əmōl əflēḥ / wə-həbēr aymət əśxōf / w-əmōl aymət əśxōf / wə-ḥābū rtāḥəm / hamak /*
Yes, we came out of the cave three days later and stayed on the Qāṭan, by Dhiddūr on the Qāṭan. We stayed and the livestock did well, and the camels gave milk, and the small livestock gave milk, and people were happy. Do you hear?

M018: *wə-ḥābū yəməkrəm / mākənay mən ḥārawn / həbēr yəməkrəm mənsēn lā / ah ġrəbš tēsən lā / yəməkrəm ār mən ḥārawn w-əbḵār / wə-śxūlōlən waḵt / wə-nūka xarf / xarf /*
People churned milk, but just from goats. People don't churn camel milk. Didn't you know that? They churn just from goats and cows. And we stayed for a while. Then the monsoon period came, the monsoon.

M018: *nḥah hīs bərk xarf / nūka xxarf ḵayrəb əxxarf / kənḥən bərk ḥawōdi ū-boh ūmṣa? / ūmṣā / twōli nagd / mən xarf / hamak / kənḥən / əmsyōl ḏakm wə-mṣā kūsan əḵā rayf /*
When the monsoon came, when it was about to come, we returned to the wadi downstream towards the Najd desert, towards the Najd, to shelter from the monsoon. Do you hear? We went back to the wadi bottom and downstream we found the land had good pasture.

Conclusion

In this chapter, we presented personal and historical narratives around personal and community experience of climatic events in northern and southern Oman. We discussed how climatic events were traditionally used to provide relative dating, and how the occurrence of a climatic event is itself situated in time through reference to well-known social or political events, such as large-scale migration to East Africa, the rule of Imam Mohammed bin Abdullah Al-Khalili in parts of the Omani interior, the overthrow by Sultan Qaboos bin Said Al Said of his father, and the two World Wars. Climatic events are recognized in popular memory not only as individual catastrophic events, but also as part of climatic cycles: Ibra01 and M018 recall heavy storms following hard on the heels of long periods of drought. In communities for which storytelling is traditional, cultural narratives become engrained in popular memory and play a significant role in building resilient behaviour, particularly where repeated metaphors, stark images or people's names are woven into the story: they serve to warn against dangerous behaviour – for example, camping in wadi basins – and to promote versatility and resourcefulness – for example, conserving grain during periods of drought in order to sow once the rains arrive, building away from the wadi bed, purchasing goats in times when the pasture is insufficient for cattle, and trusting local advice.

The stories of the climatic events that we mention are invaluable, for while these stories may become popular legend, their like will not return. People in southern Oman may describe the recent cyclones Mekunu and Luban of 2018, for example, in terms of loss of life and damage to infrastructure, but the experience is less immediate: communities no longer form part of the natural environment in the way their forebears did; they can move upstairs rather than need to seek natural shelter; young people are, on the whole, unaware of the stars as a factor in weather patterns; few in urbanized settings can read the winds and the clouds; and, through current media, television and smartphones, the tradition of storytelling, once so deeply embedded in the culture of northern and southern Oman, is evaporating. As we concluded a draft of this chapter, the Anglo-Omani Society has announced a project, Tales of Ajdaduna, calling for Omanis to submit videos of their parents or grandparents narrating stories relating to Oman and migration to Zanzibar in the pre-Sultan Qaboos era. We sincerely hope that Omanis from north and south will rise to this call, and contribute to a digital archive of events and tales from an era that will not be seen again.

Notes

1 For the Mehri and Śḥerēt archives, see Watson and Morris (2016a, 2016b); for an overview of the MSAL, see Simeone-Senelle (1997, 2011); for details of our fieldwork, see Watson, Morris et al. (2019).
2 Sultan Faisal bin Turki ruled Oman (Muscat) from 4 June 1888 to 4 October 1913.
3 *Narinja*, a novel by Jōkha Al-Ḥarthi (published in Arabic), mentions that this took place at the end of the First World War.
4 The late 1930s: in Story 3, Ibra03 said that when his father arrived in Tanzania, the Second World War had started.
5 *zājirah* in the local Arabic dialect.
6 Known locally as *ḥaḍarīn*, mountain pastoralists. They would traditionally come to the mountain villages to help with the date harvest.
7 The speaker uses the phrase يتربعوا ويشلوا بيوتهم to describe the harvesting process.
8 *xiṣb*.
9 A village in the gravel desert constructed in the early 1980s.
10 No one died due to the storm; however, people did die in their attempts to repair the *falaj*.
11 Imam Mohammed bin Abdullah Al-Khalili, who ruled the Omani interior from 1919–54.
12 *Al-xarsah* refers to a year when severe rains ruined the date crops and destroyed several houses. The verb *xaras* in the dialect means 'to soak in water'.
13 The *falaj* water in this case comes from the wadi. In Oman, there are three types of *falaj*: *ġaylī*, where the water comes from the wadi; *'aynī*, where the water comes from springs; and *dā'ūdī*, where the water comes from underground.
14 The year was traditionally divided into 'star seasons', each lasting around thirteen days. Particular stars were associated with certain weather patterns, and others to certain activities, such as *al-ṣawwā*, which marks the beginning of the frankincense

harvesting season, and *al-ġufr*, which rises at the very end of April and marks the return of the trade boats from Sawāḥil (Miranda Morris, p.c.).
15 According to J004, many head of cattle, goats and camels also drowned during these floods.
16 For terms for different types of wind in the MSAL, see Morris, Watson et al. (2019).

References

Al-Ḥaṭrūshi, S. (2014), *Physical Geography of the Sultanate of Oman*, Sultan Qaboos University-Academic Publication Council, Oman. Published in Arabic. Available online: https://www.squ.edu.om/research-ar

Al-Manji, S. and J. C. E. Watson (2019), *Climatic Events and the Role of Narratives in Resilience*. Symbiotic Relationship between Language and Nature in Southern and Eastern Arabia Workshop, 24–26 April 2019, Leeds.

Al-Manji, S. S. Bashir (2018), *Planning for Resilience to Extreme Weather Events in Oman, 2000–2015*. PhD thesis, University of Leeds. Available online: http://etheses.whiterose.ac.uk/20810/

Almazroui, M., M. Nazrul Islam, P. D. Jones, H. Athar and M. Ashfaqur Rahman (2012), 'Recent Climate Change in the Arabian Peninsula: Seasonal Rainfall and Temperature Climatology of Saudi Arabia for 1979–2009', *Atmospheric Research*, 111: 29–45.

AlSarmi, S. H. and R. Washington (2013), 'Changes in Climate Extremes in the Arabian Peninsula: Analysis of Daily Data', *International Journal of Climatology*, 34: 1329–45.

Ball, L., D. MacMillan, J. Tzanopoulos, A. Spalton, H. Al Hikmani and M. Moritz (2020), 'Contemporary Pastoralism in the Dhofar Mountains of Oman', *Human Ecology* 2020. Available online: https://doi.org/10.1007/s10745-020-00153-5

Barlow, M., B. Zaitchik, S. Paz, E. Black, J. Evans and A. Hoell (2016), 'A Review of Drought in the Middle East and Southwest Asia', *Journal of Climate*, 29 (23): 8547–74.

Birks, J. S. and S. E. Letts (1977), 'Diqal and Muqayda: Dying Oases in Arabia', *Tijdschrift voor economische en sociale geografie*, 68 (3): 145–51.

Boom, A., J. Wilson, and J. C. E. Watson (23 March 2020), 'From Naming to Numbers', MSAL Online Workshops. Retrieved from: https://ahc.leeds.ac.uk/modern-south-arabian-languages/news/article/1525/professor-janet-watson-hosts-series-of-online-workshops

Evan, A. T., and S. J. Camargo (2011), 'A Climatology of Arabian Sea Cyclonic Storms', *Journal of Climate*, 24 (1): 140–58.

Hopper, M. S. (2016), 'Cyclones, Drought, and Slavery: Environment and Enslavement in the Western Indian Ocean, 1870s to 1920s', in G. Bankoff and J. Christensen (eds),

Natural Hazards and Peoples in the Indian Ocean World, 255–82, New York: Palgrave Macmillan.

Hughes, M. K. and H. F. Díaz (2008), 'Climate Variability and Change in the Drylands of Western North America', *Global and Planetary Change*, 64 (3–4): 111–18.

Membery, D. (2001), 'Monsoon Tropical Cyclones: Part 1', *Weather*, 56 (12): 431–8.

Middleton, N. J. and T. Sternberg (2013), 'Climate Hazards in Drylands: A Review', *Earth-Science Reviews*, 126: 48–57.

Morris, M. J., J. C. E. Watson et al. (2019), *A Comparative Cultural Glossary across the Modern South Arabian Language Family*, Oxford: Oxford University Press.

Ravi, S., D. D. Breshears, T. E. Huxman, and P. D'Odorico (2010), 'Land Degradation in Drylands: Interactions among Hydrologic–Aeolian Erosion and Vegetation Dynamics', *Geomorphology*, 116 (3): 236–45.

Simeone-Senelle, M-Cl. (1997), 'Modern South Arabian', in R. Hetzron (ed.), *The Semitic Languages*, 378–423, London: Routledge.

Simeone-Senelle, M-Cl. (2011), 'Modern South Arabian', in S. Weniger, G. Khan, M. Streck, and J. C. E. Watson (eds), *The Semitic Languages: An International Handbook*, 1073–113, Berlin: Walter de Gruyter.

Spalton, A. and H. Al Hikmani (2014), *The Arabian Leopards of Oman*, London: Stacey International.

Speece, M. (1981), *Draft Environmental Profile of the Sultanate of Oman*, US Man and the Biosphere Secretariat, Department of State, Washington, DC.

Spinoni, J., J. Vogt, P. Barbosa, N. McCormick, C. Cammalleri, D. Masante and G. Naumann (2019), 'A New Global Database of Meteorological Drought Events from 1951 to 2016', *Journal of Hydrology: Regional Studies*, 22: 100593. Available online: https://doi.org/10.1016/j.ejrh.2019.100593

UNISDR (2012), *How to Make Cities More Resilient: A Handbook for Local Government Leaders*, Geneva. Available online: http://www.unisdr.org

Watson, J. C. E. and A. M. al-Mahri (2017), 'Language and Nature in Dhofar', in S. Bettega and F. Gasparini (eds), *Linguistic Studies in the Arabian Gulf: Quaderni di RiCOGNIZIONI. Rivisti di Lingue e Letterature Straniere e Culture Modern*, 87–103, Turin: University of Turin.

Watson, J. C. E. and A. Boom (in press) 'Modern South Arabian: Appraising the Language–Nature Relationship in Dhofar', in L. Souag and M. Lafkioui (eds), *Proceedings of the 47th Annual Meeting of the North Atlantic Conference on Afroasiatic Linguistics (NACAL 47)*, Villejuif: LACITO Publications.

Watson, J. C. E. and M. J. Morris (2016a), *Documentation of the Modern South Arabian Languages: Mehri*. ID: Mehri (0307), London: SOAS. Endangered Languages Archive, ELAR. Available online: ELAR Collections (elararchive.org).

Watson, J. C. E. and M. J. Morris (2016b), *Documentation of the Modern South Arabian Languages: Shehret*. ID: Shehret (0308), London: SOAS. Endangered Languages Archive, ELAR. Available online: ELAR Collections (elararchive.org).

Watson, J. C. E., M. J. Morris, A. M. al-Mahri et al. (2019), 'Modern South Arabian: Conducting Fieldwork in Dhofar, Mahrah and Eastern Saudi Arabia', in W. Arnold and M. Klimiuk (eds), *Arabic Dialectology: Methodology and Field Research*, 83–99, Wiesbaden: Harrassowitz.

Wilhite, D. A. and M. H. Glantz (1985), 'Understanding the Drought Phenomenon: The Role of Definitions', *Water International*, 10 (3): 111–20.

Part Three

Arabia: Conservation and Revitalization

11

Peoples' (non-)participation in Conservation: A Case from Oman

Dawn Chatty

Introduction

Wildlife conservation schemes, which by design set out to protect endangered fauna and flora, have a relatively recent history in Arabia. Their philosophical underpinnings, though, stem from a long African colonial and post-independence tradition. By the early to mid-twentieth century in East Africa and elsewhere, mobile pastoral peoples were forced off their grazing lands in order to create parks and sanctuaries for wildlife and tourists (Howell 1987; Turton 1987; McCabe et al. 1992). The 'scientific' assumptions of those times were that local peoples overstocked and overgrazed the natural environment and were therefore obstacles to effective modern natural resource management. 'Scientific' management of these areas required the removal of the indigenous population for the long-term benefit of these wildlife preserves. Towards the end of the twentieth century, however, there appeared to have been a change of heart, and some conservationist circles began to hold conceptual discussions of 'conservation with a human face' (Bell 1987), and the need for community participation (Cernea 1991; IIED 1994). Studies based on a few promising examples of African conservation efforts began to emerge where indigenous human populations appeared to be effectively integrated into conservation and development projects (IIED 1994).

However, when transposed to the Middle East, Africa's new-found conservation wisdom lost something in the translation (see Map 11.1). As I will demonstrate, using a case study of an internationally supported, wildlife reintroduction project in Oman, conservation schemes in Arabia have continued to regard local populations as obstacles to be overcome – either with monetary compensation or with special terms of local employment – instead of active partners in sustainable conservation and development. Without partnership, these conservation efforts are doomed either to ultimate failure or, at the least, to costly programmes which 'guard' the wildlife from the human element.

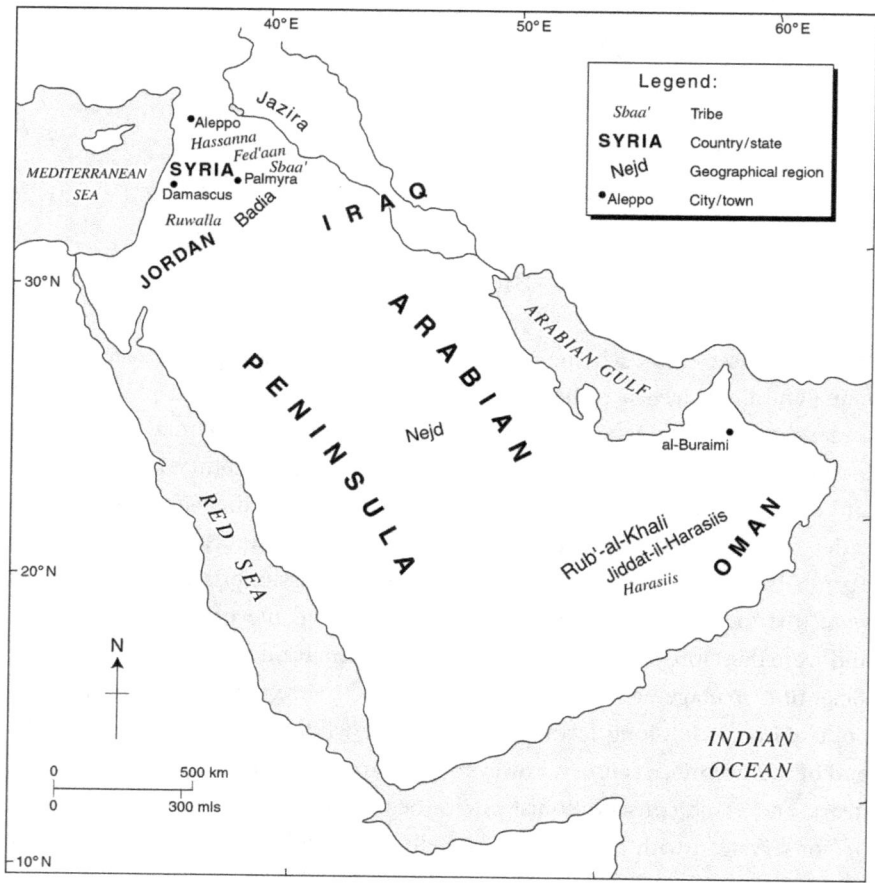

Map 11.1 The Arabian Peninsula. Author's credits.

Recent historical precursors to current conservation paradigms

Formal government-organized parks and protected areas first made their appearance in America and Europe during the nineteenth century. Significant areas of land were set aside as wilderness, to be preserved 'untouched by humans', for the good of man. In 1872, a tract of hot springs and geysers in north western Wyoming in the United States was set aside to establish Yellowstone National Park. The inhabitants of the area, mainly Crow and Shoshone native Americans, were driven out by the federal army, which took over the management of the newly created protected area (Morrison 1993). In the United Kingdom, conservationists were mainly foresters whose philosophy stressed that the public good was best served through the protection of forests and water resources, even if this meant the displacement of local communities (McCracken 1987: 190). This philosophy was transferred abroad to all of Great Britain's colonial holdings. Now, more than a century later, most national parks in the developing world have been, and, to an extent, continue to be, created on the model pioneered at Yellowstone and built upon by the early British colonial conservationists. Although challenges to this philosophy have emerged and found some successes (e.g. Forest Peoples Programme, The Dana Declaration on Mobile Peoples and Conservation), the fundamental principle of operation remains to protect the park or reserve from the damage which indigenous and local communities inflict.

Recent studies have clearly shown that models of intervention developed in the West, in its particular historical context, have been transferred to the developing world with no regard for the specific contexts of the actual receiving environment or peoples (e.g. Anderson and Grove 1987; Behnke and Scoones 1991; Brockington 2005, 2002; Holmes 2013; Igoe 2010; Manning 1989; Sanford 1983). Yet nearly every part of the world has been inhabited and modified by people in the past and apparent wildernesses have often supported high densities of people (Adams and McShane 1992; Pimbert and Pretty 1995). There is good evidence from many parts of the world that local people do value, utilize and efficiently manage their environments (Nabhan et al. 1991; Oldfield and Alcorn 1991; Scoones et al. 1992). These findings suggest, in complete reversal of recent conservation philosophy, that it is when local or indigenous people are excluded that degradation is more likely to occur. 'It suggests that the mythical pristine environment exists only in our imagination' (Pimbert and Pretty 1995: 3).

Colonial and post-colonial policy towards indigenous people

As was the case in the formation of Yellowstone National Park in 1872, the army or colonial police force in the developing world has been employed to expropriate and exclude local communities from areas designated as 'protected' often at great social and ecological costs. Accompanying this forced removal was the view that indigenous people who rely on wild resources were 'backward' and so needed help to become modern and developed. Occasionally the 'primitive' or 'backward' habits of the indigenous people were regarded as attractive for tourism and in carefully regulated circumstances, a limited number of groups were allowed to remain in or near traditional lands. The situation of the Maasai in Kenya and Tanzania is one such example (Jacobs 1975; Lindsay 1987). These reserves served the purpose of preserving primitive Africa where 'native and game alike have wandered happily and freely since the Flood' (Cranworth 1912: 310, cited in Lindsay 1987: 152).

By the 1940s and 1950s, late colonial policies and early independent government policies began to alter. The image of the harmless, pristine native was replaced by that of a dangerous and uncivilized local. Meanwhile indigenous populations, already highly constrained if not prohibited from pursuing their livelihoods as they had in the recent past, became more often regarded as backward people and as impediments not only to the state's conservation policy, but also to its general desire to modernize and develop the state. As Lindsay summarized (1987: 152–5), the government constructed dams and boreholes, and tapped watering holes. Livestock numbers appeared to increase rapidly over subsequent decades until by the 1960s; conservationists began to perceive that wildlife in the reserves was being threatened by the Maasai and their growing livestock numbers. With growing tourist revenues, the government declared a livestock-free area in the middle of the reserve to protect wildlife. Local Maasai elders began to demand formal ownership of all the land in the region. A confrontation between resident pastoralists and government and conservationists was inevitable. Maasai then took to killing wildlife such as rhinoceroses and elephants in protest against the threatened loss of more of their traditional grazing land.

Recent alternatives to the traditional conservation paradigm

Until quite recently, scientific investigation was dominated by the Cartesian positivist or rationalist paradigm. This assumed there existed only one reality, and that the aim of science was to discover, predict and control that reality. It was then assumed that knowledge could be summarized into universal laws or generalizations. Contemporary conservation science is firmly set within this paradigm.[1] This has produced a body of work based on a top-down, transfer of a Western model of conservation that has consistently missed the complexity of ecological and social relationships at the local level as well as local indigenous knowledge systems (Buege 1996: 76; Pimbert and Pretty 1995: 13).

For several decades, now, a minority opinion has grown that argues for a more pluralistic way of thinking about the world and how to change it (e.g. Checkland 1981; Kuhn 1962; Pretty 1994; Vickers 1981). It is becoming increasingly clear that ecological systems of plants and animals exist as a function of their unique pasts. Understanding a particular history of a community or ecosystem is critical for its current management. As ecosystems are now more clearly regarded as dynamic and continuously changing, the *importance of people* in their development is beginning to be acknowledged. Recent studies, for example, indicate that Amerindians played a far greater role in manipulating scrub savannas in the Americas than had previously been believed (Anderson and Posy 1989). In Africa, conservationists have come to realize that some biodiversity loss in protected areas actually stems from the Western conservationists' restrictions placed on the activities of local communities. For example, the Serengeti grassland ecosystem is now coming to be understood as having been maintained in the past by the presence of the Maasai and their cattle. With their expulsion, the Serengeti is increasingly being taken over by scrub and woodland, leaving less grazing for antelope (Adams and McShane 1992).

Currently in these early decades of the twenty-first century, the central concern of conservation science should be focused on finding ways to put people back into conservation, or as Bell has argued, to give conservation a human face (Bell 1987). This concern should be based upon the new, more sophisticated understanding of human populations as managers and nurturers rather than simply destroyers of their own environments.[2] Most indigenous pastoralists are acutely aware of their close cultural ties with nature, and of how necessary it is to conserve this resource for their continued well-being (Hobbs 1989).

'Participation' has by now become part of the normal language of development theory. It has become so fashionable that almost everyone claims participation to be part of their work. In the 1970s the term 'participation' was employed by Western conservationist to describe what was, in fact, nothing more than the submission of indigenous and traditional people to these protected area schemes. Often it was no more than a public relations exercise in which local people were passive actors. In the 1980s, it came to be defined as local interest in natural resource protection. Now, in the twenty-first century it is finally being seen, by some, as a means of involving people in protected area management.

In some parts of the world, there is a growing recognition that without local involvement there is little real chance of protecting wildlife.

Omani case study

Unlike Africa, the Arabian Peninsula does not have a long history of interest in conservation. Its neo-colonial period was very short, and only lasted a few decades in the middle of the last century. Its land mass is, in the main, arid, and not suitable as a wooded reserve. It has limited large mammal species, making it unattractive for wildlife or tourist reserves. The earliest expression of interest in conservation in Arabia came about a decade or so just after the Second World War as the alarming rate at which gazelle, oryx and other 'sporting' animals were being caught or killed by regional elites using motor vehicles and modern semi-automatic rifles became clear. In the south-east corner of Arabia, the Sultan of Oman, Said bin Taymur, issued a decree in 1964 banning the use of vehicles for hunting gazelles and oryx.[3] He also commanded the setting up of a 'gazelle patrol' – made up of local tribesmen granted the authority to stop, search, and report transgressions back to him – to protect these graceful mammals in the central Omani desert which bordered Saudi Arabia and the Trucial States. Hunting parties from outside Oman were most probably taking advantage of its wide open and indefensible borders along the Empty Quarter to enter the country for hunting outings of gazelle, oryx and bustard. Despite the Sultan's ban, the oryx continued to be hunted and in 1972 it was declared extinct from Oman and the rest of Arabia. The loss was lamented by the only human population to inhabit this region, the Ḥarāsīs camel and goat herding tribe. Nearly 200 years earlier the Ḥarāsīs tribe had been pushed into this remote and desolate region which came to be known early in the twentieth century as the Jiddat il-Ḥarāsīs. There, they found few large mammals other than the oryx and the gazelle which they occasionally hunted for food. Armed with ageing nineteenth-century Martini single shot rifles, they only hunted oryx for its meat. An adult male member of the Ḥarāsīs might shoot one or two a year – if he was a very good shot – and its meat was then air dried and served up judiciously to family and kin.

As Stanley Price makes clear, it was unlikely that sporadic Ḥarāsīs hunting pressure in open country with only ancient rifles and camels to hide behind could ever have eliminated the population of Arabian oryx (Stanley Price 1989: 42). It was the motorized hunting parties with automatic weapons from outside the Sultanate that succeeded in doing so, despite the indigenous tribe's wishes to preserve the animal in its vast shared arid environment. In 1976 the new Sultan, Qaboos bin Said, put into effect a ban on the hunting or capture of all large mammals – specifically oryx and gazelle. But cross-border hunting continued. The following year, a second decree was issued clarifying this ban.[4] It unequivocally stated that no permission would be given to foreign hunting parties to enter and operate in Oman.

For several decades before the extermination of the world's last herd of wild oryx in 1972, plans drawn up in collaboration with the International Union for the Conservation of Nature (IUCN) had been implemented to create a World Herd in captivity, at a number of zoos around the world, for eventual reintroduction into the wild of Oman. In 1974, Sultan Qaboos bin Said gave the green light to his expatriate advisor on the conservation of the environment to explore the potential for restoring the oryx to Oman as part of its natural heritage. In 1977 and 1978, a consultant attached to the IUCN toured extensively throughout the interior of Oman, with a Ḥarāsīs guide, searching for the best location to set up the reintroduction effort. Two unpublished reports were produced for the IUCN (Jungius 1985) both concluding that the ideal habitat for the oryx reintroduction project should be in the Jiddat il-Ḥarāsīs and concentrated in the north east in an area known as Yalooni, as it had 'the best vegetated pan on the Jiddat, with resources of grazing, shrub and tree browse' (Stanley Price 1989: 60). The reports also recommended that the whole of the Jiddat il-Ḥarāsīs should be proclaimed a wildlife reserve or sanctuary. It was as though this region of the country was *'terra nullius'*, a land empty of people. These recommendations were accepted by the advisor to the Sultan on conservation and environment, and in 1980, the first oryx from the World Herd were flown back into the country and released into the main oryx enclosure that had been built at Yalooni. Ten Ḥarāsīs tribesmen were hired to serve as oryx rangers, tracking these animals, watching their social behaviour and generally keeping accurate daily records of their movements.

The Ḥarāsīs tribe of the Jiddat il-Ḥarāsīs

The Ḥarāsīs along with the Wahiba, the Duru and the Jeneba are the four main nomadic pastoral tribes in the central desert of Oman. The Wahiba tribe of about 7,000 people occupy the southern coast of Oman and the desert interior known as the Wahiba Sands. To the West of the Wahiba Sands are the Duru camel-raising tribe, numbering about 9,000 (cf. Chatty 1996). Spread out along much of Oman's southern coast and adjacent interior are the Jeneba, a large and widely dispersed tribe; their numbers are more than 15,000. To the south of the Duru and Wahiba are the Ḥarāsīs tribe. Moving over what was – until the 1950s – a vast, waterless plain of more than 42,000 sq km, the Ḥarāsīs are a 'refuge' tribe. They are a people, largely of Dhofari origin who have been pushed into this inhospitable core area of the central desert of Oman. They are the most remote and isolated of already marginal peoples. The region they inhabit separates north Oman from Dhofar and is the backwater of both regions. As such, the region has attracted individuals and groups expelled from their own tribe as punishment for major infractions of traditional codes of conduct and honour in the past. The Ḥarāsīs tribe speaks Ḥarsūsi, a southern Arabian language related to Mehri, an indicator of their lack of contact and relative isolation certainly in the past few centuries (Johnstone 1977). The tribe's usufruct or rights to access graze and browse found in the Jiddat il-Ḥarāsīs were established in the 1930s when the Sultan and his political advisor, Bertram Thomas, decided to confer the name Jiddat il-Ḥarāsīs[5] upon the territory which had fallen to them as much by occupancy as by the lack of desire of any other tribe to be there (Thomas 1938). Only once in the 1930s was their right to this territory challenged by a neighbouring tribe, and this was probably an opportunistic move associated with the first oil exploration licenses granted by Sultan Said to the Anglo-Persian Oil Company.

The tribe is small, numbering about 5,000 people (cf. Chatty 1996). Although their claim to the Jiddat was once contested, no other tribe has actually attempted to move into this most desolate of landscapes with little if any seasonal grasses, no natural water sources and unfit for human habitation during the scorching summer months. It was only with the oil activity of the 1950s that the fortunes of the Ḥarāsīs and their grazing lands on the Jiddat were transformed. In 1958, an exploratory party came to a point called Haima in the middle of the Jiddat il-Ḥarāsīs and sank a water well there to support its oil activity. Another well was sunk at a point 70km towards the coast, called al-Ajaiz. These two wells were the first water sources on the Jiddat il-Ḥarāsīs, an area approximately the size of Scotland. Al-Ajaiz became something of a magnet attracting pastoral families to its well and its seasonal browse. The Haima well was also used, but not to the same extent as that at Al Ajaiz, as the area surrounding Haima was a salt flat with very little graze or browse for the herds of camels and goats.

The traditional economy of the Ḥarāsīs was based on the raising of camels and goats by natural graze to produce milk rather than meat. At the core of their way of life was migration determined by a combination of seasonal and

Peoples' (non-)participation in Conservation: A Case from Oman 249

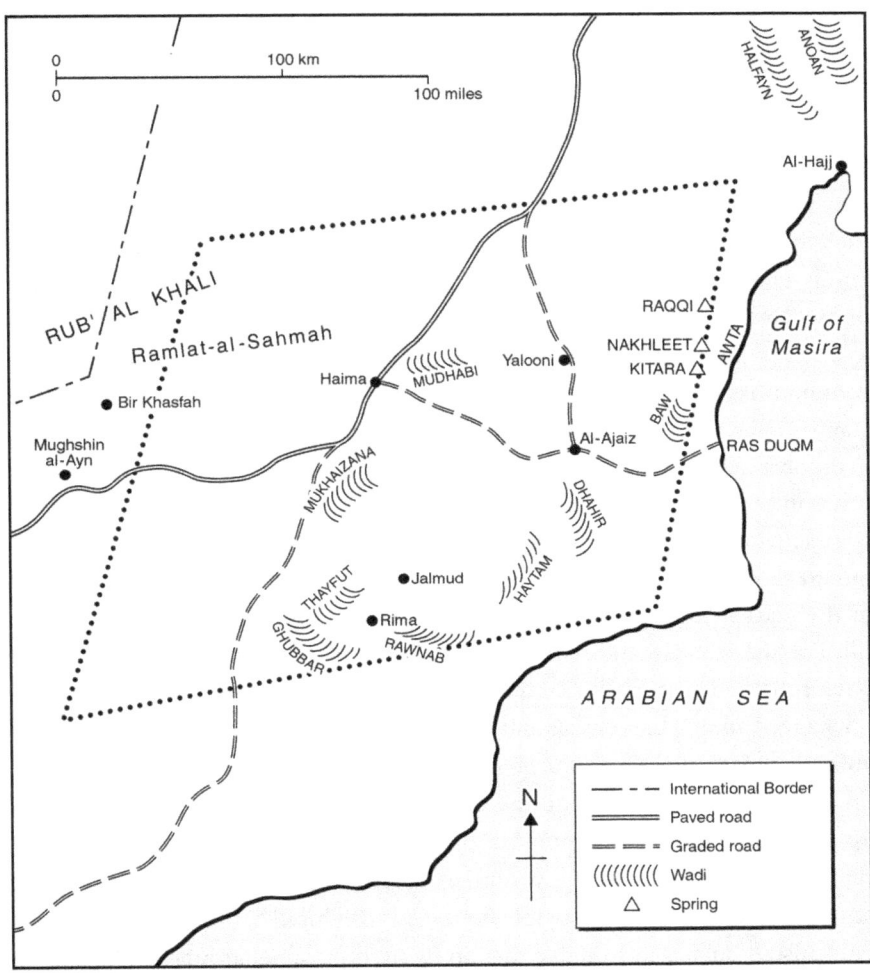

Jiddat-il-Harasiis

Map 11.2 Jiddat il-Ḥarāsīs. Author's credits.

ecological variables in the location of pasture and water. Survival of both herds and herders made movement from deficit to surplus areas vital. Households were, and are still, generally extended family units, the average family being composed of nine members.

The Ḥarāsīs household is composed of the nuclear family of husband, wife and children as well as two or three adults, of one degree of kinship or another, who make up the rest of the household. On average a household keeps 100 goats which are owned by, and the responsibility of, women and older girls.

The household also has twenty-five camels, of which five or six are generally kept near the homestead – these are the heavily pregnant or lactating ones. The remainder of the camels are left free to graze in the open desert. The whereabouts of these animals is very carefully monitored, and an elaborate camel information exchange system operates among all the tribesmen. When they meet, tribesmen first exchange news about the conditions of pastures, then the whereabouts of various loose camels, and finally news items of various family members. Homesteads are generally moved a significant distance three or four times a year.[6]

Basic to the organization of all pastoral people is the existence of sedentary communities in adjacent areas and access to their agricultural products. For the Ḥarāsīs tribe, their trading towns have been along the northern desert foothills of the Sharqiyyah, particularly Adam and Sināw. The cash economy of the village was reinforced by the continual influx of 'capital on the hoof'. Transactions were completed and money exchanged hands. Significantly though, when the final purchases were made, the bulk of the money had simply moved from one end of the market to another – from the animal buyer's pocket to the merchant's till. For the Ḥarāsīs, the relationship with the villages reinforced not a cash, but a subsistence economy. Until the late 1970s, this economic interaction was unchanged among the Ḥarāsīs and extended no further than these border desert villages and towns. Over the following few decades many households split up with women, children and the elderly (along with their goat herd) taking up residence in the social housing provided by the government at the tribal centre at Haima or in other government housing projects. The other part of the household remained on the desert floor, and with hired herders from India and Baluchistan, managed to move the family herd of camel around and camping temporarily in ʿazbah (pl. ʿazab) every couple of months.

Conservation, development and contestation

In 1981, I began a fourteen-year close association with this small camel- and goat-herding tribe. My role was to assist the government in extending social services to this remote community. A Royal Decree had been issued by Sultan Qaboos bin Said indicating that government services were to be extended into the interior desert in such a way as not to force its inhabitants to give up their traditional migratory way of life. Sultan Qaboos was encouraging the government ministries to push 'development' forward into the remote interior of the country to offer its people the same services which the government had extended to the settled folk in the rest of the country during the first ten years of his reign. His perception of the desert landscape as a 'created' physical, social and cultural environment inhabited by mobile or nomadic pastoral people as well as animals and plants was undoubtedly informed by his own mother's origins as a Qara tribeswoman in Dhofar.

Over a two-year period, as a 'Technical Assistance Expert' with the United Nations Development Programme (UNDP), and with the help of two Peace Corps volunteers, I was allowed by the Minister of Health and the Minister of Education to set up both mobile and sedentary health services as well as a weekly boarding school for boys with day-enrolment for girls (Dyer 2006). Other government services with relevance to these mobile pastoralists were more difficult to organize. Here the policy formulations of the Sultan were reinterpreted by the bureaucratic hierarchy to create a landscape in the desert which attempted to reproduce the settled, 'civilized' landscapes they were familiar with in the coastal and mountain valley settlement. For example, opening government offices in the remote tribal centre of Haima generally meant borrowing all the rules and regulations of a civil service developed around 'settled' peoples' needs. Thus, government welfare benefits became possible for unmarried, widowed, and divorced women, the handicapped and disabled. But elderly widowers or bachelors with no family to support them were excluded from government support. Ḥarāsīs concepts of welfare and aid extended to elderly men and women alike. There was recognition that in the extreme environment of the Jiddat il-Ḥarāsīs, generation was as important as gender in determining need.

Conservationists – both national and international – regarded the central desert of Oman as their own back yard, ignoring the presence and authenticity of its local human inhabitants, the Ḥarāsīs tribe. Conservationists viewed the desert as a landscape as well, but one shaped by plants and animals, not people. Their concern was to restore a balance to this landscape by returning to it animals that had been hunted to extinction in the 1970s. Thus, the international flagship conservation effort in the Jiddat, the Arabian Oryx Re-introduction Project, came into effect in the early 1980s. Between 1980 and 1996, 450 Arabian oryx were returned to 'the wild' in the Jiddat il-Ḥarāsīs or were born there. In 1994, Oman succeeded in getting this conservation project recognized formally as the UNESCO World Heritage Arabian Oryx Sanctuary. But ongoing and constant friction between the Western managers of the conservation project and the local Ḥarāsīs tribesmen regarding their 'rights' to graze their domestic herds in large parts of their territory – now officially a UNESCO nature reserve – eventually resulted in a physical and emotional distancing from the project by the Ḥarāsīs and severe diminution of any sense of ownership or use rights to this newly established government animal sanctuary.

The Yalooni project

The Arabian Oryx project experienced a prolonged 'honeymoon' period, and for the first three years there were no conflicts between the Ḥarāsīs tribe, the growing expatriate conservation management team at Yalooni, and other Omani employees. Gradually, however, difficulties began to appear. The first of these difficulties manifested themselves in terms of competition over grazing between the herds of domestic goat and camel and the reintroduced oryx during prolonged drought (Stanley Price 1989: 212-13). Just a couple of years after the sanctuary had been set up, lack of rainfall in other parts of the Jiddat, drove a number of families into the area designated as protected. The Yalooni management informed the Ḥarāsīs families that they could no longer camp nearby. The Ḥarāsīs were bemused at first, but then annoyed and angered. 'Grazing and browse is very limited; Why are our animals not as important as the oryx', they asked. This tension was never resolved. That was followed by conflicts between the lineages of the Ḥarāsīs tribe over access to the limited employment as oryx trackers and the special benefits that accrued – like occasional free petrol, and water to take back to their homesteads at the end of a work shift. That was then followed by arguments and threats between the Ḥarāsīs and the neighbouring Jeneba tribe which shared a fuzzy and fluid border with them. The Jeneba were outraged that they had been ignored in this conservation effort even though they had little experience of life in the core desert area and were not skilled at tracking. This tension was just the most recent example of their inter-tribal animosity going back decades.

Although the goodwill with which the project was initially accepted by the Ḥarāsīs remained evident among the older generation who had grown up with the oryx, the younger generation began to express their lack of commitment to the reintroduction scheme by a silence that bordered on complicity. Although the young Ḥarāsīs recognized the appearance of poaching (first reported for gazelle in 1986), and its yearly increasing level by their rival tribesmen, they rarely reported it. Unlike their elders who had manned the 'Gazelle patrols' in the 1960s and 1970s and brought suspicious individuals to the attention of the police, the younger generation just sat by and watched the live capture and poaching happen. This change of attitude and support among the local people pointed to the flaws in planning, design and implementation which top-down conservation projects all too often make.

The Ḥarāsīs had been greatly saddened by the extermination of the oryx. It had once graced the whole of the arid desert regions of southern Arabia, and had been pursued and hunted until, by the middle of the twentieth century, it was found only in the Jiddat (Stanley Price 1989: 37). The Ḥarāsīs had seen the progressive decline in numbers take place and had recognized the looming tragedy. Their stories and campfire tales spoke about this decline. But they had been unable to stop the motorized hunting parties that descended upon them in their search for oryx herd. The idea of setting up an oryx sanctuary in their traditional territory had never been discussed with them, nor had they been consulted on the most suitable area to place such a sanctuary.[7] The aims of the project, its goals, the implied restrictions on infrastructural development, and even the importance of their cooperation were never put forward to the tribal community. Once this internationally supported project had actually commenced, however, the Ḥarāsīs went along with the spirit of the enterprise; they could hardly stop it. They did feel a sense of pride in seeing the oryx returned to the Jiddat il-Ḥarāsīs. And for a limited number of men there was the opportunity of paid employment as 'oryx rangers' tracking and generally keeping an eye on the reintroduced animals.[8]

As long as the Ḥarāsīs were perceived to have no aspirations of their own, no desire to see an improvement in their access to water, no desire to have regular road grading, or infrastructural development in their traditional homeland, relations with the oryx reintroduction project remained untroubled. But the Ḥarāsīs, like people everywhere, were opportunistic. They wished to improve their lives and had no special desire to remain in some sort of pristine traditional state just for the sake of such 'protectionist conservation'. Slowly at first, and later with greater speed, the Ḥarāsīs came to realize what was being expected of them, and what constraints they were under. They came to understand that, in drought conditions, they were expected not to camp within the vicinity of an oryx herd, even when all other grazing areas were depleted.[9] At about the same time, the tribe's long-standing campaign to have a water well dug by the Ministry of Water and Electricity in a promising area north of Yalooni appeared to be blocked by the advisor responsible for the oryx reintroduction project. Furthermore, the Ḥarāsīs felt that efforts to get the national petroleum company to regularly grade roads in this north-eastern quadrangle of the Jiddat where the oryx project was located were also being thwarted. At the same time, the long-standing rivalry between the Ḥarāsīs tribe and their neighbours, the Jeneba, found new expression. An old blood feud between the two tribes had been settled by the Sultan's representative in 1968, and relations between the two tribes cooled down. More numerous and better educated, and having had longer exposure to schooling, Jeneba tribesmen managed to get most of the skilled jobs available in the tribal centre of Haima, the administrative capital of the Jiddat il-Ḥarāsīs. Some wanted the better paying jobs at the oryx project but discovered that the only positions at the project positions were restricted to Ḥarāsīs tribesmen. Although the relationship cannot be proved, the fact that there has been a tremendous rise in the rate of poaching (by 1998 only 130 animals remained of a herd estimated at around 400 in 1996) and that those caught have all been Jeneba tribesmen suggests that intertribal rivalry is on the rise.[10] Furthermore, to the disaffected, largely unemployed youths and rival tribesmen, the oryx sanctuary made no sense other than to put wild animals first before people and domesticated herds. They saw no benefit to themselves, their families, or their community. Among the rival tribesmen, the opportunity to make some money by illegal capture thus becomes a temptation difficult to resist, especially as they had no sense of ownership or participation in the animal sanctuary.

In 1986, a significant part of the Jiddat il-Ḥarāsīs was identified for a national nature reserve as a preliminary step in turning the entire Jiddat into a UNESCO World Heritage Site. In 1994, the Jiddat was established, by Royal Decree, as the Arabian Oryx Sanctuary. Few, if any, Ḥarāsīs understood that the decree was the first step towards dividing the Jiddat into three land-use zones: a core area with the strictest environmental protection; a buffer zone, with fairly strict protection, in which a limited number of activities would be permitted if they were compatible with conservation objectives; and a transition zone where most activities would be permitted unless clearly damaging to conservation objectives (IIED, 1994). Nor did they know that a Western land-use and management plan was being prepared for the entire area.[11] A cursory examination of the preliminary report clearly revealed that the Ḥarāsīs were still not being consulted or integrated into the conservation scheme in any way other than as passive participants (Oman 1995). This lack of consultation with this local, and traditional population was defended by the expatriate advisors with the claim that the tribe would not have understood the 'sophisticated' issues involved. Yet it was the Western experts and expatriate advisors who did not recognize the Ḥarāsīs' own stewardship of the Jiddat and the common understanding among them of areas – *hawta*(s) – set aside for use during drought, or crises in other parts of their traditional territory.[12]

Working quietly and consistently for the past twenty years, the Ḥarāsīs tribe have begun to challenge this conservation zoning system. They have succeeded in overcoming strong expatriate resistance to having a reverse osmosis water plant built by the government in an area that is considered a buffer zone of the sanctuary. This has created major difficulties for the oryx management team.

A similar situation is likely to occur in respect to local roads. The management plan intends that a careful network of local roads be established 'in consultation with the stakeholders in the area' (Environment 1995). These are, in the following order, wildlife conservation, tourist access, mobility of government staff and finally the *'legitimate movements* of the indigenous pastoralists' (emphasis mine). The Ḥarāsīs and Jeneba tribes are unlikely to allow themselves to be the last considered, as though only an afterthought. Quietly and persistently, as in the past, they will work to achieve what they feel is necessary for the needs of their communities.

Fortunately, the goodwill of the Ḥarāsīs tribe remains largely intact. Being a small, marginal tribe and for decades far removed from the seat of government, they are used to long-protracted battles until their points of view are recognized. However, for the long-term sustainability of conservation development it is in the interest of the state and the conservation authorities to try to bring the Ḥarāsīs population and neighbouring tribes into a truly participatory relationship with the project. Otherwise, the project has no long-term future. With ever-increasing numbers of Ḥarāsīs youths attending the high school at Haima (the first class graduated in 1993) there is still the possibility that the local population could be drawn gradually into the conservation project – through concerted education, curriculum development and skilled employment – in a more significant capacity than the 'passive participation' (Pretty et al. 1994) of the past. Truly interactive participation may prove to be the solution to the current malaise.

Two representations of the desert landscape came to a head in the Jiddat il-Ḥarāsīs: a Western conservation protectionist vision of a pristine landscape of plants and animals; and local tribal vision of a landscape where there were sets of cultural and historical concepts relating people and domestic animals to desert spaces and places. When, between 1996 and 1998, poaching and illegal capture of the oryx by rival tribes resulted in the loss of more than 350 animals, the Ḥarāsīs could do little to stop this downward spiral. Other tribes were actively acting out their disaffection; the Ḥarāsīs youth had become alienated; and the Ḥarāsīs elders were no longer interested in the landscape transformed by the oryx project from which they had been dislocated. In 2007, The Arabian Oryx Sanctuary became the first World Heritage site to ever be deleted from the UNESCO list of World Heritage Sites. The justification for this unprecedented step was the rapid decline in oryx number (from 450 to 65) and the supposed degradation of its grazing area.

Conclusion

Sustainable conservation requires, above all else, the good will of local, traditional and indigenous populations. In the case of the Ḥarasīs, that goodwill was squandered and the oryx project severely crippled. After 1998, the oryx were rounded up from the wild and placed in secure enclosures at Yalooni and protected by army patrols. However, Ḥarāsīs interest in the oryx has not been destroyed and could be encouraged with careful planning. As McCabe and others (1992: 353–66) have demonstrated, linking conservation with human development offers the most promising course of action for long-term sustainability of nature and human life. McCabe has argued that nature reserves and other protected areas must be placed into a regional context. If the economy of the human population is in a serious state of decline, the establishment of a wildlife reserve in their midst does not auger well for long-term sustainability. If, on the other hand, the problems of the human population are addressed and the community envisages benefit from a combined conservation/development scheme, then cooperation and long-term sustainability is possible. Measures which address the needs of wild and domesticated animals as well as the human group, such as land-use mediation workshops, veterinary care prophylactic health campaign for animals and humans, water wells and water distribution, seed distribution/extension of fodder crop growing, are part of an array of programmes that can draw wildlife conservation programmes closer to sustainable community development efforts. Such measures would have a positive outcome in the Jiddat il-Ḥarasīs.

Notes

1 Grande makes similar associations in the excellent article 'Beyond the Ecologically Noble Savage: Deconstructing the White Man's Indian', *Environmental Ethics*, vol. 21: 307–20.
2 Rutten and Mulder (1999) address the concept of the ecologically noble savage. They analyse pastoralists' grazing practices and demonstrate that resource use and 'conservation' may be the outcome of narrow self-interest as well as political considerations.

3   Three of the four species allocated to the genus Oryx in contemporary taxonomy are found in Africa: Oryx gazella (gemsbok); Oryx beisa; and Oryx dammah (the scimitar-horned Oryx). Only the Oryx leucoryx (Arabian or white oryx) is found in the Middle East.

4   The first decree was ambiguous in its intended audience and so a second decree was issued that identified foreign hunting parties. Reported in the local press and conveyed to me by key informants.

5   The Jeneba tribe protested that this territory was its own and simply allowed the Ḥarāsīs to live there because they had no land of their own. However, the Sultan decided that as the Ḥarāsīs were the sole occupiers of the Jiddat, it would carry their name (Thomas 1938).

6   In 1980 the Omani government cooperated with the United Nations to implement a two-year anthropological study and needs assessment of the Ḥarāsīs tribe. I led this project and continued with annual assessment of the project for the next decade.

7   One Ḥarāsīs tribesman was consulted. He was known to the expatriate advisor through his work for the national oil company. But he was not part of the political leadership of the tribe, who were not consulted, in fact, until the handover of Yalooni was a *fait accompli* (see Chatty 1996: 136).

8   Ten Ḥarāsīs men were given jobs as rangers in 1980 and the number grew to seventeen by 1986 (Stanley Price 1989: 203). These jobs were well paid by local standards. But more significantly they were meaningful and involved using skills already honed after a lifetime in the desert-tracking animals, cars and people.

9   A confrontation over grazing competition in the mid-1980s should have raised the alarm with conservationists. Several oryx calves had been frightened either by the Ḥarāsīs camps or the presence of their goats and the oryx reintroduction manager requested that the Ḥarāsīs move away. Some refused. They simply could not understand that the survival of their herds of goats was less important than a few wild oryx.

10 The estimated number of oryx poached in 1996 is drawn from several informants. In 1997 poaching of mainly female oryx increased dramatically and in 1998 only thirty female oryx were reported to remain in the wild. The project management team has since (1999) brought all the thirty female oryx back into the camp enclosure while it reconsiders how to keep the project alive. Poaching for live oryx has been spurred on by the large purses (sometimes in excess of £30,000) which the wealthy elite in neighbouring countries are offering for wild oryx to add to their private zoos. The pattern of poaching in the Jiddat is suggestive of traditional tribal raiding. The Jeneba obviously see the oryx as 'belonging' to the Ḥarāsīs. So, the act of poaching is an expression of economic and political rivalry.

11 See the report *Preliminary Land Use and Management Plan: The Arabian Oryx Sanctuary* commissioned by the Ministry of Regional Municipalities and

Environment (1995), Sultanate of Oman. It has since been superseded by further studies, none of which are available to the general public. Further information is available periodically on the UNESCO World Heritage Sites web pages.

12 The Ḥarāsīs had an intimate knowledge of the Jiddat and organized areas of higher resources – good graze and browse – for use during times of drought or other crises. The *hawta* was a herding sanctuary for the tribe's camels and goats identified by common agreement where, furthermore, no interpersonal conflict could be conducted.

References

Adams, J. and T. Mc Shane (1992), *The Myth of Wild Africa: Conservation without Illusion*, New York: W. W. Norton and Co.

Anderson, D. and D. Posey (1989), 'Management of a Tropical Scrub Savanna by the Gorotire Kayapò of Brazil', *Advances in Economic Botany*, 7: 159–73.

Bell, H. (1987), 'Conservation with a Human Face: Conflict and Reconciliation in African Land Use Planning', in D. Andrew and R. Grove (eds), *Conservation in Africa: People, Policies and Practice*, 79–101, Cambridge: Cambridge University Press.

Benkhe, R., I. Scoones, and C. Kerven (eds) (1991), *Redefining Range Ecology: Drylands Programmes*, London: IIED.

Botkin, D. (1990), *Discordant Harmonies: A New Ecology for the Twenty-First Century*, New York: Oxford University Press.

Brockington, D. (2005), 'The Contingency of Community Conservation', in K. Homewood (ed.), *Rural Resources and Local Livelihoods in Africa*, 100–120, Oxford: James Currey.

Brockington, D. (2002), *Fortress Conservation: The Preservation of the Mkomazi Game Reserve, Tanzania*, London: International Africa Institute.

Buege, D. (1996), 'The Ecologically Noble Savage Revisited', *Environmental Ethics*, 18: 71–88.

Cernea, M. (1991), *Putting People First: Sociological Variables in Rural Development*, New York: Oxford University Press.

Chatty, D. (1996), *Mobile Pastoralists: Development Planning and Social Change in Oman*, New York: Columbia University Press.

Checkland, P. (1981), *Systems Thinking, Systems Practice*, Chichester: John Wiley.

'Dana Declaration on Mobile Peoples and Conservation, Statement of Principles' (2002), *Nomadic Peoples*, 7 (1): 159–76. Also see www.danadeclaration.org

Forest Peoples Programme. See Statement of Principles at www.forestpeoples.org

Grande, S. (1999), 'Beyond the Ecologically Noble Savage: Deconstructing the White Man's Indian', *Environmental Ethics*, 21: 307–20.

Hobbs, J. (1989), *Bedouin Life in the Egyptian Wilderness*, Austin: University of Texas Press.

Holmes, G. (2013), 'Exploring the Relationship between Local Support and the Success of Protected Areas', *Conservation and Society*, 11 (1): 72–82.

Howell, P. (1987), 'Introduction', in D. Anderson and R. Grove (eds), *Conservation in Africa: People, Policies and Practice*, 105–9, Cambridge: Cambridge University Press.

Igoe, J. (2010), 'The Spectacle of Nature in the Global Economy of Appearances: Anthropological Engagement with the Spectacular Mediations of Transnational Conservation', *Critique of Anthropology*, 30 (4): 375–97.

International Institute for Environment and Development (IIED) (1994), *Whose Eden? An Overview of Community Approaches to Wildlife Management*, London: IIED.

International Union for the Conservation of Nature (IUCN) (1994), *Guidelines for Protected Area Management Categories*, Commission on National Parks and Protected Areas, Gland: IUCN.

Johnson, T. (1977), *Harsuusi Lexicon and English-Harsuusi Word List*, Oxford: Oxford University Press.

Jungius, H. (1985), 'The Arabian Oryx: Its Distribution and Former Habitat in Oman and Its Reintroduction', *Journal of Oman Studies*, 8: 49–64.

Kuhn, T. (1962), *The Structure of Scientific Revolution*, Chicago: Chicago University Press.

Lindsay, W. (1987), 'Integrating Parks and Pastoralists: Some Lessons from Amboseli', in D. Anderson and R. Grove (eds), *Conservation in Africa: People, Policies and Practice*, 150–67, Cambridge: Cambridge University Press.

Manning, R. (1989), 'The Nature of America: Visions and Revisions of Wilderness', *Natural Resources Journal*, 29: 25–40.

McCabe, T. et al. (1992), 'Can Conservation and Development Be Coupled among Pastoral People? An Examination of the Maasai of the Ngorongoro Conservation Area, Tanzania', *Human Organization*, 51 (4): 353–66.

McCraken, J. (1987), 'Conservation Priorities and Local Communities', in D. Anderson and R. Grove (eds), *Conservation in Africa: People, Policies and Practice*, 63–78, Cambridge: Cambridge University Press.

Morrison, J. (1993), *Protected Areas and Aboriginal Interests in Canada*, Toronto: WWF – Canada Discussion Paper.

Nabhan, G. et al. (1991), 'Conservation and Use of Rare Plants by Traditional Cultures of the US/Mexico Borderlands', in M. Oldfield and J. Alcorn (eds), *Biodiversity: Culture, Conservation and Ecodevelopment*, 127–46, Boulder: Westview.

Oman (1995), *Preliminary Land Use and Management Plan: The Arabian Oryx Sanctuary*, Muscat: Ministry of Regional Municipalities and Environment.

Pimbert, M. and J. Pretty (1995), *Parks, People and Professionals: Putting Participation into Protected Area Management*, Geneva: United nations Research Institute for Social Development (UNIRSD). Discussion Paper 57.

Pretty, J. et al. (1994), *A Trainer's Guide to Participatory Learning and Interaction*, IIED Training Series no. 2, London: IIED.

Ruttan, L. and M. Mulder (1996), 'Are East African Pastoralists Truly Conservationists', *Current Anthropology*, 40 (15): 621–52.

Sanford, S. (1983), *Management of Pastoral Development in the Third World*, London: John Wiley and Sons.

Scoones, I. et al. (1992), *The Hidden Harvest: Wild Foods and Agricultural Systems*, London: IIED and Geneva: WWF.

Stanley Price, M. (1989), *Animal Re-introductions: The Arabian Oryx in Oman*, Cambridge: Cambridge University Press.

Thomas, B. (1938), *Arabia Felix: Across the Empty Quarter of Arabia*, London: Reader's Union.

Turton, D. (1987), 'The Mursi and National Park Development in the Lower Omo Valley', in D. Anderson and R. Grove (eds), *Conservation in Africa: People, Policies and Practice*, 169–86, Cambridge: Cambridge University Press.

Conclusions

Jon C. Lovett, Janet C.E. Watson and Roberta Morano

Language and culture embody the way that humans interact with each other and with the natural world. But they are more than that, they are the way knowledge is transmitted across space and time, between places and through generations. The interaction is also reciprocal. At risk of being called out for being teleological and giving agency to the non-human natural world, the way humans manage nature determines the way nature manages humans. If water catchments, rangelands and seas are tended, grazed and fished at sustainable levels using methods that are in keeping with seasonal ecological dynamics and aperiodic climatic extremes, then the complex social-ecological system of biogeochemical cycles will be self-regulating (Lovelock 1979). This process creates a dialogue of action between humans and nature; and a dialogue of language between humans about how to govern, prepare, predict and manage the self-regulating interaction. The complex systems of governance needed to create 'long-enduring institutions' are now relatively well understood for the management of common pool resources where access is difficult to regulate but resources are subtractable (Ostrom 2009), but the way that language is created and used for the dialogue is not well researched, and our intention is to make a contribution to this under researched field in this book about language and ecology in southern and eastern Arabia.

Language contains the words that describe and symbolise nature; and culture determines how individuals, communities and societies perform the interactions. In his Nobel prize lecture 'Economic performance through time' the economist Douglass North (North 1993) describes how language creates 'mental models to explain and interpret the environment' and in so doing provides 'a common cultural heritage ... [that] constitutes the means for the intergenerational transfer of unifying perceptions'. This cultural heritage and environmental interpretation can be transmitted in many ways. For example, in Indonesia lullabies to small children are used to transmit information about the potential threat of tsunamis (Sutton et al. 2021), which are a catastrophic, relatively rare and unpredictable event that everyone needs to be prepared for, but which might not happen in an individual's lifetime and so there is no direct experience for reference.

Both language and culture can be unique to a particular natural environment and might have co-evolved over millennia to create a distinct sustainable symbiosis with traditions that are transmitted through generations. For example, there is evidence that relatedness of Transeurasian languages is associated with the spread of millet cultivation over thousands of years in northeast Asia (Robbeets et al. 2021). If the relationship between people and nature is not sustainable in all three dimensions of economy, society and environment – then the system collapses. This can be either abrupt with a catastrophe, or gradual with a decline and withering. History is replete with examples of what happens when human society culturally disconnects from its natural environment: Viking colonies in Greenland; Rapa Nui of Easter Island; the Maya of Mexico; Garamantes of the Sahara to name only a few from different types of environment around the world ranging from the arctic to arid regions. In each of these cases the cause of collapse is likely to have been complex and not only associated with environmental factors such as over-exploitation of natural resources and the result of changing climate, but also failures of social structures, diminished trade and warfare (Brooks et al. 2005; Lima et al. 2020; Orlove 2005).

Parallel to the way that we can learn about the effect of societal disconnection from a study of history, we can also explore how contemporary societies have achieved sustainability and co-evolved with their natural environment through an understanding of their language and culture. This indigenous knowledge and the way it is communicated has increasingly been the focus of research and applied to both mitigation and adaptation in a world in which globalization has caused dramatic economic and social disruptions, and where climate change threatens increasing frequency of weather extremes of heat, drought, floods and storms. Southern Arabia has been particularly affected by both globalization and climate change. The culture of traditional communities, who have lived in an often-hostile and unpredictable climate for many generations, is being swept aside by ways of living and consumerism in which individuals and society are no longer reliant on, and connected to, the land that surrounds them. At the same time, fundamental characteristics of the environment are changing, for example the frequency of heat extremes and storms has increased, threatening to make some parts of Southern Arabia uninhabitable and disrupting important events such as the Hajj (Almazroui 2020; Kang et al. 2019).

The chapters in this book cover a wide range of types of communication of the cultural heritage that forms the human interaction, understanding and interpretation of nature and the wider environment of landscape, water, sea and sky. Chapter 1 gives examples of gestures that 'often reveal the deep level of knowledge and understanding of the practice described' and demonstrates how these gestures can cross language boundaries and represent signatures of experience and expertise from the past, transcending current usage of existing spoken words.

Similarly, names carry much more information that simply a means of identification. Chapter 2 describes how the names of plants give facts about how useful they are for livestock nutrition, or the habitat where they came from. For example, the name might say that it is 'milk-less' or 'lacking in generosity', or from a 'stony plain'. Names also describe cultural uses; a sweetly scented plant is called 'the little plant of the bridal bed'.

The natural world provides metaphors for how to behave or what to do. Chapter 3 describes the Musandam Peninsula, a barren landscape set in rich fishing grounds. The sea pervades the language, for example the greeting exchange 'What wind is it?' to which the reply 'it's a north-west wind' refers to choppy seas and so not a good time to travel or go fishing.

In a mostly dry land, water inevitably plays a central role in the language of nature giving meaning to place names as described in Chapter 4, for example a place where water might be seeping. The search for water, the means of channelling it for irrigation, the ways of fetching and carrying it are all rich sources of language. But the region's aridity has a climatic paradox because monsoon rain and cyclones from the Indian Ocean can bring flash floods and destruction, providing a prolific seam of metaphor to be mined in poetry and a warning to those who might camp or build in a dry wadi before a storm breaks:

> I've known from before the thundering rain clouds / the one that brings great quantities of dust / sheets of rain from water-buckets | Its flood covers the earth / even up to the ancient highlands / with violence (the flood) rolls down | Its roiling surge encompasses the land / sending clouds over all of humankind / and snatches away everything that is valuable.

Plants, crops and language are discussed in Chapter 5 with a selection of fifteen culturally important species. Some of these are of global stature, playing a central role in history and culture, such as the fig in the Quranic surah 'I swear by the fig tree and the olive!' Others are not so well known outside their area of origin, such as the locally important legume *wars* with its many uses as a dye, food additive and medicine, which gives rise to multiple applications of the plant name in language.

Passage of the seasons and importance of rain in southern Arabia, and vastness of the desert sky filled with stars, is inevitably going to give rise to language and stories that will be transmitted across generations. Chapter 6 lists names of seasons and constellations; and tells folklore about what happens to a sheep when the cold wind comes, and legends about daughters mourning for their father with the tale mapped out by stars in the shape of a casket.

The monsoon winds brought trade to southern Arabia from the Indian Ocean and China; and the Red Sea corridor connected this trade to the Mediterranean. This made the coastal areas of Yemen and southern Oman important parts of these valuable trade routes, especially for frankincense and myrrh. Lying parallel to the coast is Wādī Ḥaḍramawt, which is the location of the many proverbs and songs about climate, crops and nature described in Chapter 7.

Folklore returns in Chapter 8 with stories in Kumzari about a beautiful princess as a dove and the boy who came to find her in a fabled city, won her heart and she laid her head on his arm. Elsewhere in the chapter another princess journeys across the sea in a boat covered in barnacles and algae; and in another a boy shouts to his mother telling her where to search for him when he's abducted by a sorcerer.

Ascending mountains and the monsoon are key features in poetry of the endangered Śḥerēt and Mehri languages described in Chapter 9. The monsoon provides a motif for social and political change, and the mountain provides drama and isolation for the poet climbing high to face the *mdīt* wind in the early morning and dusk. A fascinating part of the chapter explores the use of couplets in *nānā* poems by contemporary female poets, such as this one about the monsoon by ʾĪdāl al-ʿAmrīʾ:

Leave me the monsoon and let me bear it as I will
In payment for my age and all the years that have bled away

Cultural narratives of climatic disasters and resilience are analysed in Chapter 10, which shows how these events are intwined with social and political change both within Oman and the broader regional monsoonal trade links to eastern Africa and Zanzibar. These stories offer potent warnings of the power of nature when unleashed through floods and droughts, and also tell personal tales of how people survived these extremes of weather.

The final chapter – Chapter 11 – describes what happened when cultural perceptions of 'scientific' wildlife management using the concept of 'fortress conservation' were superimposed on Ḥarāsīs communities in the central desert of Oman. Modernization came to the desert in the form of oil extraction, road building, hunting from vehicles with automatic weapons, drilling boreholes for water wells, movement of people to government housing projects and alienation of land for wildlife conservation.

It is important not to be overly romantic about the quality of life in traditional communities living close to, and depending on, their local natural environment. There is a risk of creating a vision of a world of people in harmony with nature whilst sitting in the comfort of solid housing, good education, public services and health care. We know from our own experience that traditional life is hard work and that an illness, easily cured by modern medicine, can kill.

Equally, it is important not to diminish the depth of intergenerational knowledge and experience held in the language, stories, poetry and songs; nor the havoc, chaos and damage done by modernization and loss of connection between people and the environment that supports them. In the classic book *Pedagogy of the Oppressed* the Brazilian educator Paulo Freire describes how people are dehumanized by educational systems in which those being taught have no real-life connection to the curriculum imposed upon them. Instead of being liberated by education, the students become oppressed and induced into making choices that drive a wedge between themselves and the very essence of what sustains them.

The mental model and common cultural heritage embodied in language that co-developed and co-evolved through generations of interaction with nature, landscape, climate, sea and sky can be lost within a few decades to be replaced by a dependence on ideas and products created and imposed externally. Both worlds of modernity and tradition can co-exist, but the relationship needs to change to one where there is a better understanding, and traditional knowledge and language is an integral part of education. What we have tried to show, and provide evidence for, in this book is the way that language is used to create the human-to-human dialogue for the human-to-nature interaction in an environment that can be both giving of its natural resources, and extreme in its unpredictability. The hope is that we can contribute to the unfolding understanding of the many different ways language is used to convey across space and time the subtle nuances needed to manage our complex and dynamic natural environment.

References

Almazroui, M. (2020), 'Rainfall Trends and Extremes in Saudi Arabia in Recent Decades', *Atmosphere*, 11 (9): 964. Available online https://doi.org/10.3390/atmos11090964

Brooks et al. (2005), 'The Climate-Environment-Society Nexus in the Sahara from Prehistoric Times to the Present Day', *The Journal of North African Studies*, 10 (3-4): 253-92. Available online: https://doi.org/10.1080/13629380500336680

Freire, P. [Translated by Myra Ramos] (1972), *The Pedagogy of the Oppressed*, New York: Herder and Herder.

Kang, S. et al. (2019), 'Future Heat Stress during Muslim Pilgrimage (Hajj) Projected to Exceed "Extreme Danger" Levels', *Geophysical Research Letters*, 16: 10094-100. Available online: https://doi.org/10.1029/2019GL083686

Lima, M. et al. (2020), 'Ecology of the Collapse of Rapa Nui Society', *Proceedings of the Royal Society B (Biological Sciences)*. Available online: https://doi.org/10.1098/rspb.2020.0662

Lovelock, J. (1979), *Gaia: A New Look at Life on Earth*, Oxford: Oxford University Press.

North, C. D. (1993), 'Economic Performance through Time', *Nobel Prize Lecture*. Available online: https://www.nobelprize.org/prizes/economic-sciences/1993/north/lecture/

Orlove, B. (2005), 'Human Adaptation to Climate Change: A Review of Three Historical Cases and Some General Perspectives', *Environmental Science & Policy*, 8: 589-600. Available online: https://doi.org/10.1016/j.envsci.2005.06.009

Ostrom, E. (2009), 'Beyond Markets and States: Polycentric Governance of Complex Economic Systems', *Nobel Prize Lecture*. Available online: https://www.nobelprize.org/prizes/economic-sciences/2009/ostrom/lecture/

Robbeets, M. et al. (2021), 'Triangulation Supports Agricultural Spread of the Transeurasian Languages', *Nature*, 599: 616-21. Available online: https://www.nature.com/articles/s41586-021-04108-8

Sutton, A. S. et al. (2021), 'Nandong Smong and Tsunami Lullabies: Song and Music as an Effective Communication Tool in Disaster Risk Reduction', *International Journal of Disaster Risk Reduction*, 65 (2021): 102-527. Available online: https://www.sciencedirect.com/science/article/abs/pii/S221242092100488 X?via%3Dihub

List of Geographic Place Names

Place name	Page number
ʿAbd al-Kūri, Island	2
Abu Dhabi	84
Adam	250
Aġayṣ̌aṭ	109
Al-Ajaiz	250
Al-ʿĀmirāt	218
al-Ghaydhah	17, 18
Al-Ḥajar Mountains	131, 215–217, 219, 220, 222, 226, 228
Al-Jabal al-Akhḍar	215
Al-Jaḥlah	223
Al-Khubb	223
al-Mahrah	2, 3, 17, 18, 107, 109, 117, 205, 211, 212, 216
Andur	109
ʾAnkīd	203
Arabian Sea	2, 99, 203, 218, 220, 221
Ashwaymiyyah	115
Bahla	223
Bahrain	3, 122, 222, 224
Baiḥān	187
Bāṭinah	220
Bishʿīthān	18
čōō	89
Daba	82
Dākhiliyyah	216
Darbat	63
Darsah, Island	2
Dawʿan	187
dēqina	93
Dhahbūn	18, 230

Place name	Page number
Dhalkūt	218
Dhiddūr	231, 235
Dhofar	2, 3, 6, 13, 17, 18, 22, 26, 30, 47, 49, 50–55, 60–63, 66, 67, 69, 71–73, 76, 79, 84, 107–111, 117, 125–127, 131, 132, 141, 202, 206–208, 210–213, 215–220, 226, 228, 229, 250, 253
dīdamur	92
Dubai	97
ēr suqrō	93
Falaj Bū Manīn	227
Falaj al-Mišuq	226
Falaj al-Muštaq	227
Ftakhayt	231
furṭa	92
Gabgabat	228, 232
Gəzərēt	110
ġōban	92
ġubb	92
Gulf, Persian	122
Gulf, the	12, 15, 95, 99, 154, 163, 164, 203, 217
Habrut	109
Ḥadbīn	17
Ḥaḍramawt	2, 4, 5, 167–170, 182, 184–185
Haima	3, 250, 252, 253, 256, 257
Ḥallāniyyāt Islands	66
Ḥāsik	17, 63, 66, 68, 109, 218
Ḥayy as-Salām	72
Hormuz, Strait of	3, 82, 99, 215
Ibra	214, 220, 221
Indian Ocean	84, 95, 170, 220, 265, 266
Jabal Al-Qarā'	218
Jabal Qamar	66, 69, 218, 225, 226
Jabal Samḥān	111, 218
Jiddat il-Ḥarāsīs	248–251, 253, 254–260
Khaḍrafi	72

Place name	Page number
Khasab	82, 83, 92, 97
Khawr Muġsayl	66
Khor Shet'ane	191
kōkba	93
ku xāyg	93
Kumzar	81–84, 86, 88, 89, 91–93, 99
Kuwait	17, 84, 163, 195, 222
Lēmē	195
Madīnat al-Ḥaqq	73
manjal	93
Marmūl	18
Masirah Island	3, 221, 271
maysaġ	93
Mecca	195
Mirbāṭ	63, 66, 111, 208, 218
Mōmur	92, 194, 195
Musandam (Peninsula of)	3, 6, 81, 82, 84, 191, 195, 198, 217, 265
Muṣay	107
Muscat	84, 220, 237
Najd	17, 109, 111, 164, 187, 231, 234, 236
Nišṭawn	114
Nizwa	225
Nōged	67
Nūṭəf	109
Oman	18, 21, 22, 29, 34, 99, 107, 109, 122, 127, 130–132, 134–136, 141, 212, 215–222, 224–228, 236, 237, 243, 248–250, 253, 256, 260, 266, 267
Oman, Sea of	99, 220
Pānakō	92
Qafifah	222–224, 227
Qāṭan	233–235
Qishn	205
Quxayg	194, 195
Ra's al-Ḥadd	217
Rabkūt	17, 18, 222, 226, 230

Place name	Page number
Rakhyūt	218
Ra's Musandam	217
Raysūt	218, 220
Sadḥ	17, 18, 218
Ṣaḥalnōt	17
Salalah	17, 18, 109–111, 218, 220, 222
Samā'il	217, 220
Samḥa, Island	2, 59
šamšir ēlī	94
Sar Kardēō	198
Sar Mistō	195
šāratē	93
Šarbithāt	66, 110, 218
Saudi Arabia	2, 3, 5, 6, 15, 108, 114, 122, 125, 131, 134–136, 139, 142, 222, 248
Sharqiyyah	216, 252
Sināw	216, 222, 227, 228, 252
Sohar	84
Ṣolót	63
Soqoṭra	1–6, 47, 49, 50–62, 64, 67–69, 72–78, 125, 140
Tanūf	222, 225
Ṭāqah	66, 218
Ṭarbūt	112, 203
Tarīm	185
ṭaybuba	93
United Arab Emirates (UAE)	2, 127, 130
Uṭawm	229, 230
Wādi al-Ḥawāsina	219
Wādi Dhukūr	231
Wādi Dōʕan	187
Wādi Gēzaʕ	17
Wādi Ḥaḍramawt	169, 170, 266
Wādi Hanwōf	17, 18
Wādi Jirdān	186
Wādi Nṣawr	229

Place name	Page number
Wādi Ṣālaffan	230
Wādi Ṣālaffan	17, 18
Wahiba Sands	249
wījī murwānī	88
Xižól	73
xōr šumm	92
xōran	92
xōru ġuẓrō	92
Yalooni	249, 254, 255, 258, 259
Yemen	1–6, 8, 15, 18, 34, 79, 107, 109, 115, 117, 122, 125, 127, 128, 130, 133, 134, 136, 140, 143, 164, 170, 172, 177, 187, 212, 216–218, 220, 221, 266
ẓdēf	93

Index

abbreviations/appendix 198
acoustic paths 38–9
al-Bawāriḥ 160
al- Marbaʿāniya 159
al-Nuʿāyim (The Ostriches) 158–9
al-Sarāyāt ('the Night Travellers') 159
al-Ṯurayyā ('the Chandelier') 160–1
amusing names 53–4
animals 55, 57, 69, 75, 108, 110, 119–20, 137, 152, 156, 171, 175–6, 184–5
   counting 63–4
   domesticated/domestic 178–9
   ecological system 245, 247, 250–6
   group names 66
   personification 37
   in poems 205
   tales 193, 197–8
   wild 177–8
Arabic dialects
   consonants 11
   languages 4–5
   short vowels 9
   transcription 9
astronomy-related vocabulary 149–51

Bāqī, Ṭufūl bint Muḥammad (Bish Ḥaqf) 208–9
Baṭāḥira
   bat 53
   birds 66
   derogatory nicknames 74
   fauna 55
   netted fish 53
   place names 68
   water management 108
   wrasse 51
Baṭḥari
   consonants 10
   as endangered MSAL 3–5
   gesture documentation 17
   shark description 55
   spoken parts 6, 15
biodiversity 1, 168

boat 82, 94–6, 100, 120, 191–3, 196, 264
breeze 87, 112, 157, 200–4, 206, 208–9

consonants 9–13, 158, 169
culture
   folktales 198
   global 101
   indigenous 149–51
   Islamic 154
   naming 47
   regional history and 8
   sea 94–5, 196
   water 106
culture-specific practices 16–18, 34–5, 40

Dhofar
   female poets 200
   geography and climate 216–18, 224, 226–7, 248, 251
   MSAL speakers 2–3, 6, 13, 17–18, 105
   naming 49–73
   nānā genre 204–5
   plant names 123–5, 129–33
   pointing gesture 22
   speech and gesture 26, 30
   toponyms 106–9
Documentation and Ethnolinguistic Analysis of Modern South Arabian (DEAMSA) 17

ecology. *See also* Modern South Arabian Languages (MSAL)
   ecological system/knowledge 19, 149, 184, 244–5, 249
   language and 1, 3, 7–8, 199
elongation 38–9
evil actions 76–7

fauna 7, 55, 67, 168, 170, 241
flora 2, 7–8, 17, 19, 206, 241
   classification 67
   gestures 36–7

in Ḥaḍramawt 168
idioms and proverbs 170
naming 54
focal entity (the *figure*) 24
folklore 264
  abbreviations/appendix 198
  Kumzari language 7, 189–98
frame of reference (FOR) 24–5

geographic place names 267–71
gestural kinds 16
gesture 263
  animal personification 37
  community 15
  culture-specific practices 17
  diversity 16, 20
  manual action 34–6
  in Mayan culture 25
  region-specific 17
  semiotic community and 16
  speaker-specific expertise 36–7
  traversed path 38–9
  Yucatec 25
Gurindji Kriol 26

Ḥaḍrami/Ḥaḍramī 2, 10
  birds 181–2
  cereals 172–3
  clouds, lightening and rain 170–1
  date-fruit related terms 176–7
  domestic animals 179
  domesticated animals 178–9
  Ḥaḍramawt, trade route 167–9
  idioms and proverbs 170
  insects 183–4
  other animals 180
  palm tree pollination songs 173–5
  rodents 180
  snakes 180–1
  sorghum 171
  wild animals 177–8
  zodiac, use in agriculture 171
Ḥarāsīs tribe of the Jiddat il-Ḥarāsīs 247–50
Ḥarsūsi language
  consonants 10–11
  endangered MSAL 3–5
  gesture documentation 17, 214
  relationship with Mehri 248
  spoken parts 6, 15
  wars, use by women 125

Hobyōt language
  consonants 10
  counting livestock 63
  ditty or rhyme in 70
  as endangered MSAL 3–5
  gesture documentation 17
  insect name 52
  spoken parts 6, 15
  hooked points 22–3

ʾĪdāl bint Suhayl bin ʿAlī al-ʿAmrī 206–7
idioms and proverbs 170, 184–5
images 22, 25, 106, 111–12

Jibbali/Jibbāli language 5, 15, 121–2, 124, 128–9, 131, 133, 199
  breeze (*bōbet*) 204
Jiddat il-Ḥarāsīs 9, 246–9, 251, 253–6

Kumzari language 3
  Arabic dialects 4, 9
  boats, types 94–7
  changes of sea, impact on 97–100
  connection to nature 100–2
  consonants 9, 12–13
  dichotomy of space 189–91
  folklore references 189–98
  greetings 84–5
  intersection of natural and supernatural 194–8
  lexical interaction with livelihood 191–4
  oral traditions 6–7
  relationship with sea 82–91
  seascape 92–4
  seasons and cycles of the year 86
  species 91
  vowels 9
Kumzari people 8, 81–4, 95, 100–1, 102

language-ecology relationships 1, 3.
  See also names; naming
  and culture 261–2
  human interaction 263
  themes and genres 7–9
lifestyle 8, 17, 20, 48, 50–3, 107–8, 138, 184, 216
lip and tongue pointing 23–4
livestock 8, 23, 37, 40, 48–9, 53–4, 56–7, 61–5, 68, 71, 75, 77

loathed entities 75–6
Luban (cyclone) 234

Mahra/Mahrah
MSAL 6
  poetic tradition 106
  political topic 112–13
  toponymy 107
  water management 108–10
Mehri language
  consonants 10–11
  elongation 38
  as endangered MSAL 3–4
  expression of direction 27–9
  gesture documentation 17–18, 21
  hooked point 22–3
  lip and tongue pointing 23
  livestock description 37
  monsoonal wind 200–4
  plant names 49
  pointing type 21
  rainstorms and floods 111–13
  song on rodents 72
  spatial representations 26–7
  spoken parts 15
  time representation 32
  unwritten 5
  vowels 9
Mekunu (cyclone) 234
Mexico 25, 262
  Ngigua language 26
Modern South Arabian languages (MSAL). *See also* names; naming; *specific languages*
  Arabic speakers 6
  consonantal system and transcription 11–12
  critical importance 16
  five mainland 17
  gesture use 18–19
  lip and tongue pointing 23–4
  natural environment categories 48–9, 52, 59–60
  pointing gestures 19–21, 23
  spatial representation 26–31
  speech communities 15, 48, 67
  time representation 32–4
  wayfinding 21

Musandam Peninsula. *See also* Kumzari language
  Kumzar town 6, 8, 81–9, 91–3, 97, 99–100, 269

names
  amusing 53–4
  avoidance and suppression 73–4
  birds 52–3
  deliberate concealment 74–5
  diachronic change 72–3
  fauna 55
  feared or loathed entities 75–6
  flora 54–5
  foodstuffs and drinking 55–6
  importance 48
  insect world 50–2
  pasturage 56–7
  plant species and livestock 48–50
  rainfall 58
  rangeland 57–8
  spouse name avoidance 73–4
  use of derogatory nicknames 74
naming
  characters 59–60
  conveying appearance 58–9
  cultural significance 53
  diminutive form 60–1
  evil action 76–7
  group 66–7
  livestock 62–5
  memorable years 69
  people 65
  of places 67–9
  positive and negative 61–2
  rhymes 69–72
  ways 58–77
  years 69
nānā genre of poetry 200, 204–9, 264
nicknames 65, 74
northern Omani 10

Oman
  Arabic dialects 4–5
  climatic system 214–15, 220
  culture-specific artefacts 34
  cyclones and floods 218–19, 224–8
  Dhofar, southern province 216–17
  drought 217, 220–4

food conservation 222-3
geographical region 1-3, 215
hooked point gestures 22
livestock 223
Mehri speakers 18, 29, 49
MSAL 15, 21
northern 3, 5, 8, 10, 107, 125, 213-29
personal and historical narratives of climatic events 213-34
southern 5, 9, 128-9, 132-3, 216-18, 220, 223-35, 264
unwritten languages 5-6
water management 222
Year of Hail 226
orature and nature. See also Jibbali/Jibbāli language
Mehri and Śḥerēt (a.k.a. Jibbāli) languages 199-200

pasturage 56-7
plant names in Southern Arabia 2, 8, 47-77. See also names; naming
acacia (*Vachellia (Acacia) nilotica* – Family Fabaceae) 132-3
aloe (*Aloe dhufarensis, A. vera, A. praterissima* – Family Asphodelaceae) 123
bitter orange (*Citrus aurantium* – Rutaceae) 139
Christ's thorn, Lote tree (*Ziziphus spina-christi* – Family Rhamnaceae) 134-5
date palm (*Phoenix dactylifera* – Arecaceae) 136-8
dragon-blood tree (*Dracaena cinnabari* – Asparagaceae) 138
dwarf palm (*Nannorrhops ritchieana* – Family Arecaceae) 128
fifteen common names 121-2
fig (*Ficus carica* – Family Moraceae) 123-4
gesture 36
henna (*Lawsonia inermis* – Family Lythraceae) 126-8
Indian ginseng (*Withania somnifera* – Family Solanaceae) 133-4
olive (*Olea europaea* – Family Oleaceae) 128-9
reed (*Juncus socotranus; J. rigidus* – Family Juncaceae) 136

tamarisk (*Tamarix aphylla* – Family Tamaricaceae) 130-2
wars (*Flemingia grahamiana* – Family Fabaceae) 125-6
wild rue, African rue, Syrian rue (*Peganum harmala* – Family Nitrariaceae) 130
poems 111, 199, 204-6, 264. See also *nānā* genre of poetry
poets. See also ʾĪdāl bint Suhayl bin ʿAlī al-ʿAmrī; Ṭufūl bint Muḥammad Bāqī
female 200, 205, 264
folk 185
ḥarf 205-6
Śḥerēt and Mehri 199, 210
pointing
gestures 19-21
in MSAL 21-4

Qatar
Arabic dialects 4-5
geographical region 1, 3-4
Qatari
al-Bawāriḥ 160
al-Marbaʿāniya 159
al-Nuʿāyim (The Ostriches) 158-9
al-Sarāyāt ('the Night Travellers') 159
al-Ṯurayyā ('the Chandelier') 160-1
astronomy-related vocabulary 149-51
consonants 10
Ḍarbat al-ʿAjūz ('the Old Woman's Punch') 159
demography of users 3-4
language and storm patterns, seasons and winds 154-6
meteorologic phenomena, research on 151-4
time periods, determination 161-3
traditional knowledge 8
vocabulary of wind 158
wind names according to direction 157

rainfall 58, 108-9, 125, 217
rangeland 56-8
resilience 3, 9

sea
Arabian 2, 216, 218-19
breeze 202-3

Kumzari people's relationship with
  89–102, 190–4, 196
 local knowledge 156–7
 marine terms 59–60, 66, 69
 metaphors 263
 MSAL culture 108–9, 111–12, 120
 polysyllabic words 169
 Red 5, 264
 species 51
 transportation 161
semiotic community 15–19, 34, 40
 defining character 17
 practice 15
Sheret language
 breeze (bōbet) 204–6
 close contact regions 217
 code name 214
 consonants 10–11
 as endangered MSAL 3–4
 expression of direction 27–9
 gesture documentation 17–18, 21
 lifestyles 17
 lip and tongue pointing 23
 pointing type 21
 reduplicating 38
 research on 18
 spatial representations 26–7
 spoken parts 15
 time representation 32
 unwritten 5
 vowels 9
Soqoṭra
 geographical region 1–3
 names and naming 47, 49–77
 unwritten languages 5–6
Soqoṭri
 consonants 12
 demography, users 6
 derogatory nicknames 74
 flora 2
 herd or flock size 64
 semiotic family 15
 unwritten languages 5
 vowels 9
 vulgar terms 59

space representation 106
 gesture 24–6
 in MSAL 26–31
speech community 15
Sultan Qaboos bin Said 250
sustainable conservation 242, 256

Tales of Ajdaduna 235
time, representation
 concept 31–2
 in MSAL 32–4
Ṭufūl bint Muḥammad Bāqī 208–9

UNESCO 2, 149–50, 251, 254–5, 258

vegetation 48–50, 59, 67–8, 152
vowels 9, 38–9

water and space
 irrigation and distribution 107–8
 toponyms 106–7
 universal relationship with life 113–14
wayfinding 21
wildlife conservation
 American and European history 242–3
 Arabian history 241–2
 government welfare benefits 250–2
 indigenous people's role 243–4
 Omani case study 246–7
 traditional paradigm 244–6
wind 85, 111, 113, 137, 153–4, 156–9,
  190–3
 mdīt 111–12, 200–3, 210–11, 264
 monsoon 200–4
 nānā genre 204–6

Yalooni project 252–6
Yellowstone National Park 243
Yemen
 Arabic dialects 4
 culture-specific artefacts 34
 geographical region 1–3
 gesture documentation 17–18
 MSAL 15
 unwritten language 5–6

www.ingramcontent.com/pod-product-compliance
Lightning Source LLC
Chambersburg PA
CBHW052215300426
44115CB00011B/1691